D0165321

Archaeology as human ecology

Archaeology as human ecology:
Method and theory for a
contextual approach

KARL W. BUTZER

Henry Schultz Professor of Environmental Archeology
The University of Chicago

CAMBRIDGE
UNIVERSITY PRESS

Published by the Press Syndicate of the University of Cambridge
The Pitt Building, Trumpington Street, Cambridge CB2 1RP
40 West 20th Street, New York, NY 10011-4211, USA
10 Stamford Road, Oakleigh, Melbourne 3166, Australia

© Cambridge University Press 1982

First published 1982
Reprinted 1984, 1985, 1987, 1990, 1993, 1994

Printed in the United States of America

Library of Congress Cataloging-in-Publication Data is available

ISBN 0-521-24652-0 hardback
ISBN 0-521-28877-0 paperback

For ELISABETH

Beethoven Op. 138 ("Leonore")

Contents

Preface

I have chosen the title *Archaeology as Human Ecology* to emphasize the dynamic interactions between human groups or societies and their environments. This book is intended to provide an introduction to the methodology and theoretical framework for such a study. The central concept is the human ecosystem. This serves as an organizing principle to illuminate the interdependence of cultural and environmental variables, as well as an organizational framework within which to discuss the various scientific approaches critical to understanding the processes of such interaction. The *context* of the book's subtitle refers to both the locus of and the dynamic processes that define human ecology.

The first section, the introductory part of the book, explains and elaborates the ecosystem approach. A second section then develops the three subsidiary fields of study that contribute the substantive data critical to understanding prehistorical and historical human ecosystems: (a) geo-archaeology, the study and interpretation of sediments and physical landscapes; (b) archaeometry, the use of physical and chemical methods of measurement, including raw-material provenance, dating, and site prospecting; (c) bio-archaeology, the study of plant and animal remains that reflect subsistence activities as well as biotic environments.

The third and final section of the book integrates these components within a spatial framework as well as a temporal or diachronic framework. Spatial archaeology can be seen as a fourth field of study, although it is closely interwoven with the others. The spatial dimensions of component data, at different scales (micro, meso, macro), are developed in each chapter, and the spatial paradigm has been chosen to serve as one of the frameworks for synthesis in this final section. This is complemented, in the last two chapters, by theoretical and interpretative discussions within an adaptive paradigm. These deal with the major systemic transformations and modifications of the prehistorical and historical record: hominization, the taming of the environment, and the growth and decline of high civilizations.

The methodological emphasis is directed to geo-archaeology and a spatial paradigm. This reflects my own training and experience in geomorphology and geography. Bio-archaeology and paleoeconomy could have served equally well, but I would have been unqualified to write such a book. Furthermore, bio-archaeological concepts have already been incorporated into archaeological research with some measure of success, whereas geo-archaeology has tended to remain a field apart. I therefore believe that the systematic development of geo-archaeology, in six chapters, as a theme of central archaeological significance, serves a broad professional need. This same framework could, alternatively, be developed in similar detail for bio-archaeology. The two related chapters on archaeobotany and zoo-archaeology are designed to serve as a syllabus for such a development. I believe that more detailed treatment of these themes would be redundant, and classroom testing of this manuscript during two years has reinforced my opinion that the syllabus approach to bio-archaeology is particularly effective in stimulating term-paper formulation. The chapter on archaeometry is deliberately brief. I do appreciate the important long-term contributions of archaeometric research, particularly dating methods, to archaeology. But I also believe that these play a relatively subordinate role in an ecosystemic framework, and I have therefore limited discussion to the essential components and their integration within the whole.

Archaeology as Human Ecology proposes a new paradigm (complementary, rather than exclusive) for the study of archaeology. By focusing on human ecosystems and by integrating methodologies from the physical, biological, and social sciences, this theoretical approach complements that of the social archaeology championed by many New Archaeologists. The book was developed in courses directed to graduate and undergraduate students in archaeology, Near Eastern civilizations, and geography. Consequently, no special science training was or is required, and the themes are developed from first principles up, with as little jargon as the subject matter permits. The emphasis is not on techniques but on understanding interrelationships – which is the spirit of ecology. The goal is to educate the reader in terms of productive interdisciplinary thinking. I hope that students and professional archaeologists can share some of the contagious excitement to which I have been exposed during more than 20 years of collaborative work, an enthusiasm that has sustained me during the four years of writing this book.

First and foremost I owe a debt of gratitude to the archaeologists with whom I worked, discussed, and argued during the course of productive field projects that took me to Egypt, then Spain, sub-Saharan Africa, and eventually to my own turf in Illinois. It was a former student, Daniel Bowman, who on a Spanish hillside in 1969 wondered about my preoccupation with empirical objectivity, and so redirected my thinking toward theoretical issues. At about the same time, an exchange of letters with the late David Clarke, an unsurpassed theoretical archaeologist, drew my attention to the potential of explicit model building. During those critical years of reorientation, countless discussions with Elisabeth Butzer provided a major stimulus toward formulation of a more ecologically oriented, behavioral approach. A Guggenheim fellowship in 1977 gave me breathing space, after 18 years of uninterrupted teaching and fieldwork, to develop many of the intellectual threads that converged in the end.

Richard Klein was a constant source of encouragement, and he made many valuable suggestions for the manuscript. Individual chapters and sections were also read by Thomas Bell, Vaughn Bryant, David Helgren, and Richard Morrill, and Cambridge University Press's reviewer, Geoff Bailey, helped me sharpen my thinking during the final stages of revision. Dan Greenway drafted the illustrations with his usual professional care. The final drafts of the manuscript were cheerfully typed by Diana Valdivia on a very trying schedule. Preparation was supported by the University of Chicago and by the Swiss Federal Institute of Technology, Zurich. To all, my sincere thanks.

Flossmoor, Illinois   Karl W. Butzer
October
1981

PART I

Perspectives

CHAPTER 1

Context in archaeology

Introduction

Archaeology is at a crossroads. During the late 1960s and early 1970s, center stage in North American archaeology was reserved not for competing interpretations of historical processes but for discussion of the New Archaeology. This phenomenon can be interpreted as a public debate, generated in no small part by the exponential increase in empirical data during the 30 years prior to 1960. The gathering of facts had become increasingly additive, rather than contributing to a cumulative body of real information. Syntheses tended to be descriptive, simplistic, and speculative. The New Archaeology began as an American intergenerational conflict, as an introspective reassessment of means and purpose. But these painful beginnings, with the new castigating the old, were then followed by constructive debate among a new international generation of archaeologists in regard to goals and the optimal strategies to attain them. The net impact has been healthy, with refinement in the strategies of empirical research and far more sophisticated interpretation.

Nonetheless, the so-called great debate in archaeology also created its own simplifications. By polarizing old and new approaches, the impression was given that archaeologists were either empirical or theoretical. But on closer inspection the small group of active participants in the great debate are seen to be neither pure theorists nor pure deductivists. Archaeology is, by its nature, ultimately empirical. The great debate is far more than a matter of philosophical abstractions. It is a fundamental reevaluation of the conceptual framework of archaeological research, a quest for a paradigm that will rationalize both the laborious data gathering and the frustrating interpretative activities of the discipline.

Those in the swelling ranks of the emerging consensus are of one mind in only one essential matter – that fresh and more productive vistas

3

must be opened. The great diversity of possible innovative approaches is illustrated by the many articles and books, ranging from ethnoarchaeology to computer simulation, that appeared during the 1970s. They suggest that archaeologists have begun to opt for a pluralistic paradigm in their search for better insights and that a rapid radiation of new research directions is under way. The majority of these trends reflect an intellectual confrontation with several facets of cultural anthropology. There also is a considerable debt to the discipline of human geography, in particular to spatial theory. What remains poorly articulated is the equally fundamental environmental dimension.

Ironically, environmental archaeology is one of the oldest interdisciplinary bridges in the field. Archaeologists have always been conscious of environmental context, and from the earliest days diverse groups of scientists have participated directly or indirectly in excavation. Compared with some 5,000 individual members of the Society for American Archaeology, there are about 500 members in the new Society for Archaeological Sciences, with little overlap in affiliation. This surprising ratio suggests substantial empirical input from those involved in the applied sciences, who nevertheless have little impact on the dominant intellectual currents within archaeology.

Perhaps the environment is taken for granted. Certainly the environment is specified as a variable in most processual equations, but in all too many instances such an equation is then resolved by treating that variable as a constant. Also, archaeologists often take a static, classificatory approach to the environment, even when the human variables happen to be considered as part of a dynamic system.

It is my belief that the concept of *environment* should not be considered synonymous with a body of static, descriptive background data. The environment can indeed be considered as a dynamic factor in the analysis of archaeological context. The basic ingredients of archaeology are artifacts and their context, ranging from food residues to sediment and landscape matrix. The term *context* means many things to many people, but the word is derived from the Latin verb *contexere*, "to weave together" or "to connect." For archaeology, context implies a four-dimensional spatial-temporal matrix that comprises both a cultural environment and a noncultural environment and that can be applied to a single artifact or to a constellation of sites. Context, so defined, is a primary focus for several approaches within archaeology. For example, spatial archaeology is concerned with horizontal patterning of aggregates within a site as well as with interconnections between sites. Context also has long been the focus for archaeometry, which is concerned with temporal frameworks, materials analysis and technology, and raw-material sources. But most important, context has been the traditional focus for a poorly defined but wide-ranging enterprise sometimes described as environmental archaeology, including such specializations as archaeobotany, zoo-archaeology, and geo-archaeology.

In an excellent introductory text, Evans (1978:xiii) defined environmental archaeology as "the study of the past environment of man." He specifically emphasized techniques and indicators useful in reconstructing the environments of ancient human communities, as well as the applications of such techniques. This definition is not only narrow but also unacceptable.

To use an analogy, the distinction is between geological archaeology and archaeological geology. To me, archaeological geology is geology that is pursued with an archaeological bias or application. This is fundamentally distinct from geological archaeology, carried out by means of geological methods, techniques, and concepts, but constituting what is first and foremost an archaeological endeavor (Butzer, 1977c). At issue are the goals, rather than the techniques.

I have long held the view that our ultimate goal is to determine the interrelationship between culture and environment, emphasizing archaeological research "directed toward a fuller understanding of the human ecology of prehistoric communities" (Butzer, 1964:vii, 5). But in the early 1960s such relationships proved difficult to identify, both for archaeologists and for those in the applied environmental sciences. In part, the problem was a paucity of empirical data, but the problem was compounded by lack of an adequate conceptual framework within which to analyze complex relationships among multivariate phenomena.

In the interim, much has changed. The information base has been increased by an order of magnitude, and although it is still far from adequate, at least it now permits the formulation of coherent hypotheses. But, most important, systems theory has suggested a model with which to illustrate and even analyze complex interrelationships. Systems theory has had profound influences on conceptual formulations in several disciplines: in environmental science since a seminal paper by Chorley in 1962, in ecological anthropology since Geertz's *Agricultural Involution* in 1963, and in archaeology since an article by Flannery in 1968.

That a cybernetics model cannot be transferred in toto to another discipline requires little emphasis, and most of us will appreciate that systems jargon can obscure an issue as easily as illuminate it. Furthermore, it would be foolish simply to apply a biological systems approach in the social sciences. But the basic principles of systems theory are essential to integrate the environmental dimension within a contextual archaeology.

Context and ecology

Odum (1971:8) has defined an ecosystem as a community of organisms in a given area interacting with the physical environment, so that energy flow leads to clearly defined food chains, biotic diversity, and exchange of materials between the living and nonliving parts. Transforming this concept to human populations, the essential components of the noncultural environment become distance or space, topography or landforms, and resources – biotic, mineral, and atmospheric. Modern geography is particularly concerned with the interrelationships between human communities and their environments, and increasingly so with the spatial expression of the attendant socioeconomic phenomena. This focus differs only in its spatial emphasis from ecological anthropology (Hardesty, 1977; Moran, 1979), which is equally concerned with intersecting social and environmental systems.

Such broad systems concepts are, however, too complex for practical application. Yet the problem can be minimized by identifying primary research components, as distinct from ultimate systemic objectives. The primary or lower-level objectives relate to the techniques and immediate goals of each method, such as spatial archaeology, archaeometry, and environmental archaeology. The secondary or higher-level objective is the common goal of context, shared by all the contributing methods.[1]

Thus, the primary goal of environmental archaeology should be to define the characteristics and processes of the biophysical environment that provide a matrix for and interact with socioeconomic systems, as reflected, for example, in subsistence activities and settlement patterns. The secondary objective of this and of all the contributing methods is

---

[1]By identifying primary and secondary goals, it is possible first to explicate how each approach contributes individually to contextual archaeology. In this way, multidisciplinary inputs can be channeled toward a common goal, obviating the need for distinct ecological and geographical paradigms, as proposed by Clarke (1972:7). Second, explicitly hierarchical goals help to identify basic research components and facilitate intermediate analysis and resolution, as well as attainment of ultimate systemic objectives.

to understand the human ecosystem defined by that systemic intersection (Chorley and Kennedy, 1971:4). A practicable general goal for contextual archaeology is the study of archaeological sites or site networks as part of a human ecosystem. It is within this human ecosystem that earlier communities interacted spatially, economically, and socially with the environmental matrices into which they were adaptively interwoven.[2] The term ecosystem, here and elsewhere in this study, is used as a conceptual framework with which to draw attention to ecosystemic interrelationships. No formal systemic structures are proposed or employed.

Less concerned with artifacts than with sites, contextual archaeology focuses on the multidimensional expression of human decision making within the environment. And, without attempting to deal directly with ecological phenomena such as energy flows and food chains, it aims to stimulate holistic research by calling attention to the complex systemic interactions among cultural, biological, and physical factors and processes.

Five central themes are singled out for specific emphasis, namely, space, scale, complexity, interaction, and stability or equilibrium state (Butzer, 1978a). These concepts were originally geographical or biological, but they have direct anthropological and archaeological applications, and they incorporate spatial as well as temporal dimensions. Furthermore, each of these properties is measurable and therefore replicable, and so amenable to scientific study (Butzer, 1980f).

Space. Rarely are phenomena distributed evenly in space. Topographic features, climates, biological communities, and human groups exhibit spatial patterning and thus are amenable to spatial analysis.

Scale. Spatial analysis is used to distinguish small-, medium-, and large-scale objects, aggregates, or patterns. Similarly, the configurations of living communities or physical aggregates are established,

---

[2]So defined, contextual archaeology includes several scales and dimensions. To clarify, scale is a metrical concept, distinct from dimension, that has both magnitude and direction, with respect to two or more coordinates, and conveys a sense of scope or perspective. Contextual archaeology implies variable scales, because both socioeconomic and spatial systems can be examined at the detailed level or the general level. It also includes several dimensions, namely, spatial (the site subsystem), hierarchical (the environmental subsystem), and ecological (the interactive processes). So, for example, this approach can be applied to simple foraging societies, in which settlement and subsistence are organized primarily on a horizontal plane, as well as complex societies characterized by significant vertical structures.

maintained, or modified by processes that operate at several spatial and temporal scales and that may be periodic or aperiodic. Microscale and macroscale studies obviously are complementary, and both are necessary for comprehensive interpretation.

Complexity. Environments and communities are not homogeneous. This makes both their characterization and delimitation difficult, thus requiring flexible, multiscale spatial and temporal approaches.

Interaction. In a complex environment with an uneven distribution of resources, human and nonhuman communities interact internally, with each other, and with the nonliving environment; they do so at different scales, from varying degrees of proximity, and at changing or unequal rates.

Equilibrium state. The diverse communities of any environmental complex are all affected to some extent by negative feedback resulting from internal processes or external inputs. In consequence, readjustment, whether minor or major, short term or long term, is the rule rather than the exception.

These five perspectives can be explicated by a number of examples that will serve to illustrate the several scales and dimensions of a contextual approach.

Scales and dimensions of contextual archaeology

A false-color LANDSAT photograph of central Illinois or eastern Africa will provide an impressive illustration of differential biotic productivity that will show how inappropriate is the basic assumption of most geometric spatial analysis – the assumption that space is homogeneous. The reds and blues show concentrated and diffuse regional patterns, some sharply demarcated, others grading across broad transitions. A census of wildlife distributions at any given moment will show similar complex aggregations.

The importance of biotic patterning in human-resource evaluation is matched by the importance of the topographic and sedimentary matrix in designing an archaeological survey or in interpreting site locations. So, for example, in the Nile Valley of Middle Egypt the known late-prehistorical sites are in no way representative of Predynastic settlement patterns, but are largely a function of selective surface preservation of only those sites on the margins of the valley (Butzer, 1960*a*). Similarly, the sites of rock engravings in southern Africa are predicated on the locations of suitable rock outcrops, microscale topographic change, and environmental variability (Butzer et al., 1979). Spatial archaeology has contributed much of value in recent years (e.g., Clarke, 1977), but many of its practitioners still do not conceptualize real space as opposed to abstract space.

The mosaic distribution of biophysical phenomena also serves to illustrate the synchronic attributes of scale. Arborescent foods can be perceived at the microscale of the individual tree or cluster of trees, at the mesoscale of individual upland or floodplain forest components, or at the macroscale of the regional forest-prairie mosaic. As a consequence, the average pollen profile may serve to establish a paleoclimatic sequence of some stratigraphic value, specific to a regional habitat or biome, but it more often than not contributes little to elucidate the complexity of a potential resource catchment, unless the palynologist approaches the problem as an archaeologist (e.g., Bryant, 1982).

This spatial perspective of scale is complemented by the temporal or diachronic framework: seasonality and predictability of collected or produced foods; the significance of cyclic anomalies, major perturbations, and long-term shifts of equilibrium thresholds that define the environmental system. Temporal variability will affect, at various scales, the biomass of plant and animal foods, and even the quantitative and qualitative characters of biotic communities. As a consequence, ecosystemic variability, trends, and transformations probably will also affect demography, subsistence strategies, settlement patterns, and even the social fabric with different degrees of intensity, depending on the magnitude of change and on the information and decisions of the human communities.

The role of complexity is readily illustrated by the parallel problems of classification and demarcation of artifact types and climatic types. What are the most appropriate criteria? Better yet, what are the practicable criteria in view of the data base? Do these describe useful classes? Are these classes mutually exclusive? The computer helps to tidy up appearances, but it does not necessarily resolve the basic logical problems of defining assemblages of artifacts and sites or the defining of biophysical phenomena. The problem is vastly compounded when one attempts to identify process and response among a chain of interlocking subsystems. The roles of possible concatenations of negative inputs can be simulated by computer, but the result will be no more than a working hypothesis. It will require multiple lines of specialized contextual investigation to identify the key components and the low or intermediate-order processual interactions.

The matter of interaction can be illustrated by the example of Axum, an early civilization that flourished in northern Ethiopia during the first millennium A.D. (Butzer, 1981a). Axum owed its prosperity to international trade, but its market resources were found in several distinct environments occupied by alien peoples bound in various relationships to Axum. Gold came from the semiarid lowlands that Axum temporarily dominated but never fully controlled. Ivory and frankincense were initially abundant in local upland forests, but as both elephants and trees became increasingly scarce, ivory had to be obtained from distant parts of humid Ethiopia. In fact, the demographic base of Axum eventually exceeded the subsistence productivity of its local habitat. When international market demand faltered during the seventh century, Axum lost the means to control its critical trade resources. Because it lacked an adequate subsistence base in isolation, excessive demographic pressure led to severe landscape degradation and general impoverishment. Concomitantly, repeated failure of the spring rains meant one rather than two annual crops on unirrigated lands. Drastic depopulation ensued. Eventually there was a shift of power and population to new and more productive environments in central Ethiopia. Axum provides an example of how spatial and temporal availability of resources, and the interactions between a society and its resource base, can be of fundamental significance in the analysis of historical processes.

In the larger perspective, it is apparent that elaborate prehistorical and historical cultural systems have enjoyed centuries of adaptive equilibrium, with or without sustained growth, that have then been followed by discontinuities. The five millennia of Egyptian history (Butzer, 1981b) and Mesopotamian history (Adams, 1978) show cyclic alternations between centuries when population and productivity increased in apparent response to effective hierarchical control and other centuries marked by demographic decline and political fragmentation. Endogenic and exogenic inputs led to repeated readjustments. Whereas minor crises were overcome by temporary structural shifts, major crises required reorganization of the political and economic superstructure, with or without a transformation of identity. But the fundamental adaptive system continues to survive in Egypt and modern Iraq as a flexible but persistent social adjustment to a floodplain environment. In the long-range view, elaborate cultural systems are dynamic rather than stable or homeostatic, because structural changes are repeatedly required to ensure viability and even survival (Butzer, 1980c).

A unifying thread in these illustrations of the hierarchical components of a contextual paradigm is provided by *adaptation* (specifically as a strategy for survival) and *adaptability* (as the capacity of a cultural system to adjust) (see Chapter 15). These concepts, as defined in cultural terms rather than biological terms (Kirch, 1980a), are at the heart of the human ecosystem; they provide criteria for the analysis of historical process and culture change that I believe to be more suitable than those of the popular ontogenetic model that compares civilizations and cultures with organisms that first grow and then die. Archaeologists share with cultural anthropologists, historians, and students of human geography the ultimate objective of historical interpretation. Many conceptual methods and models are also shared. But the analytical techniques and scientific methods of the archaeologist have less in common with the techniques and methods in these other fields. This point can be demonstrated by drawing attention to the literature on natural extremes and social resilience: Central in all instances are the roles of the individual and of the community in decision making (Burton et al., 1978; Torry, 1979). In default of any historical records or a reasonable degree of ethnographic continuity, prehistorical archaeology can never hope to elucidate the nature of this decision-making process. We may or may not be able to identify the outcome of such a process, but we shall never know why, how, or when it was initiated.

Archaeology as archaeology

It has been said that archaeology is anthropology or it is nothing (Willey and Phillips, 1958:2). I beg to differ with this view. Archaeology and cultural anthropology do, or at least should, enjoy a close symbiotic relationship, and archaeology is indeed critically dependent on stimuli and models grounded in social, ecological, and evolutionary anthropology. But archaeology has been equally dependent on geology, biology, and geography at various times during its development. Archaeology is a complex social science in its own right – a view recently articulated by Gumerman and Phillips (1978) as well as Wiseman (1980). But, like geography, archaeology is heavily dependent on both the empirical methods and models of the natural sciences, qualifying as a social science mainly by virtue of its objectives. The specific methodologies of other disciplines, including cultural anthropology and biology, cannot simply be transferred; they must be transformed, according to a new paradigm rather than a secondary paradigm, if they are to have productive input. For this reason, I feel as uncomfortable with an unadapted cultural anthropological paradigm as with a biological one. Context represents a traditional concern of archaeology,[3] and, as more comprehensively defined here, it is developed with conceptual input from cultural anthropology, human geography, and biological ecology.

I am therefore arguing for a contextual archaeology rather than an anthropological archaeology. My plea is for deliberate exploration and development of an approach that will transcend the traditional preoccupation with artifacts and with sites in isolation, to arrive at a realistic appreciation of the environmental matrix and of its potential spatial, economic, and social interactions with the subsistence-settlement system. The human ecosystem so defined will open up truly ecological vistas that have been largely neglected. This contextual approach, heavily dependent on archaeobotany, zoo-archaeology, geo-archaeology, and spatial archaeology, is new not in terms of its components but by virtue of its integrated, general goal of understanding the human ecosystem. The key to this systemic approach is the set of perspectives described earlier: space, scale, complexity, interaction, and stability. Contextual archaeology complements the traditional concern for analysis and socioeconomic interpretation of artifacts and artifactual patterns by providing new spatial, hierarchical, and ecological dimensions. It is a matter of some urgency that this dynamic perspective be developed and implemented in both college education and field or salvage projects, because it is indispensable for our comprehension of human ecosystems.

It can be argued that traditional social and economic interests in the variability of technology and style are subsumed in an overarching contextual paradigm that seeks to explain multigenerational stability in various systemic interrelationships between peoples and their environments (Schoenwetter, 1981). Heuristically, however, it is preferable to concentrate on those approaches and themes singled out as central to contextual archaeology. No one paradigm deserves to be enshrined as superlative; alternative viewpoints are essential to good scientific practice. By systematically developing the methodology of an alternative (rather than exclusive) paradigm, and then applying it to the fundamental issues of adaptation, stability, and change, it will be possible for

[3]Differing concepts of context have been applied by Taylor (1948, 1972), Helm (1962), and Schiffer (1972).

students and professionals to appreciate the procedural potentials and to evaluate the merits of a contextual approach.

The subsequent chapters of this book develop these perspectives, beginning with an introduction to the spatial and temporal variability of environmental systems. Then the methodologies of the individual subfields (geo-archaeology, archaeometry, archaeobotany, and zoo-archaeology) are introduced, providing study components to examine the interaction spheres between prehistorical peoples and their bio-physical environments. This discussion goes beyond ecological inter-pretation of sites and their containing landscapes to consider the im-pact of settlement on site formation and the impact of subsistence activities on plants, animals, soils, and overall landscape modification. Finally, the integrated contributions of contextual archaeology are ap-plied to a spatial analysis of settlement patterning and to a temporal examination of cultural continuity and change.

CHAPTER 2

Environmental systems: spatial and temporal variability

Space and scale in ecology

The practical and theoretical issues of environment and context in archaeology require a familiarity with environmental systems. These provide both the spatial and temporal frameworks, physical and biotic, within which human communities interact and that, equally so, interact with human communities.

The *biosphere* encompasses all of the earth's living organisms, interacting with the physical environment in an infinite number of component systems. For practical reasons, biologists commonly select only a part of the biosphere for direct study, and they may focus on vertical (hierarchical) or horizontal (spatial) interactions.

Levels of vertical organization begin with genes and cells and then range upward successively to organisms, populations, and communities. The population comprises groups of individuals of any one kind of organism, whereas the community includes all of the populations occupying a given area (Odum, 1971:4–5). Finally, the community and the nonliving environment function together in an ecosystem. Study may concentrate on an individual organism or a single population (autecology), or on a community (synecology). Such communities may be large or small, with a corresponding difference in the degree of dependence on inputs from adjacent communities. The communities, and the ecosystems they imply, range in dimension from local to subcontinental in scale.

In terms of horizontal organization, the largest terrestrial communities define the earth's key biotic landscapes. These are *biomes*, described as "major regions in which distinctive plant and animal groups usually live in harmony with each other, so that one may make tentative, but meaningful, correlations between all three" (Watts, 1971:186).

A biome includes an unlimited number of partly overlapping *habitats*, representing the space in which different populations or communities

14

live. The spatial transition between two or more different communities represents the *ecotone,* a tension belt that is narrower than the habitats of adjoining communities but that may have considerable linear extent (Odum, 1971:157). A particular locale within a habitat, together with its immediate setting, is a *site.* Finally, biotic and abiotic spatial aggregates can be contrasted as biochores and physiochores (Schmidthüsen, 1968:78). The biochore is the area occupied by one or more communities, such as the range of a single population, a plant "formation" or animal "zone" that includes several communities, or an overarching biotic province. A physiochore is a particular area defined by a set of physical parameters along the intersection of atmosphere and lithosphere. Biomes or their multiple-component habitats all have spatial, biotic, and abiotic dimensions and therefore comprise both a biochore and a physiochore that are spatially coincident.

Ecology emphasizes functional relationships rather than phyletic or genetic relationships. This is effectively illustrated in the concept of *niche.* Odum compared habitat with the address of an organism and niche with the occupation of the organism. Explicitly, niche includes the physical space occupied by the organism, its functional role in the community, and how it is constrained by other species and abiotic factors (Odum, 1971:234). Central to the maintenance of an ecosystem is the regulation of trophic levels (i.e., vertical food chains) and patterns of energy flow (Figure 2-1). Consequently, biomes, as major world ecosystems, maintain a functional unity across space by virtue of communities that have similar functions, whether or not species composition remains the same. So, for example, the species and even the genera of dominant trees and animals within the circumpolar needle-leaved forest are different from region to region across the Northern Hemisphere's boreal zone. Thus species are, to a large extent, replaceable in space as well as in time (Odum, 1971:140).

Biomes as environmental systems

The ecological concepts discussed in the preceding section are central to environmental analysis, because a biome is equivalent to a macroenvironment. Such large-scale environments are normally delimited on the global maps found in textbooks on biology and geography. They also, on occasion, are linked to "culture areas" in which human communities are believed to have similar material cultures (Kroeber, 1939; Carter, 1975). Although these divisions generally are too coarse to

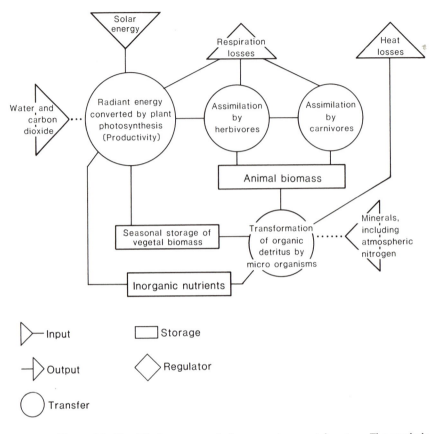

Input

Storage

Output

Regulator

Transfer

Figure 2-1. Simplified energy cycle for an environmental system. The symbols used in Figures 2-1, 2-2, and 2-6 follow those of Chorley and Kennedy (1971).

serve as a useful frame of reference for subsistence potentials, they are convenient for discussion of the key environmental variables and their modes of interaction.

The four basic components of an environmental system are atmosphere, hydrosphere, lithosphere, and biosphere (Figure 2-1). The critical variables within these major categories are outlined in Table 2-1 in the format of a checklist. Enumeration of these variables is primarily of heuristic value, because the raw data in any one subcategory are difficult to abstract into a form useful to explicate systemic interactions. For example, synthetic expression of climatic types can be achieved only by the use of costly computer programs. Even then the variables require simplification, both in terms of computer time and in terms of the

Table 2-1. *Key variables of an environmental system*

Atmosphere (Crowe, 1979)

Macroclimate, including radiation patterns and thermal distributions; evaporation, water vapor, and precipitation; atmospheric pressure and winds; seasonality and aperiodic variations of these elements

Microclimate, small-scale deviations from modal climate resulting from variable exposure to climatic elements (e.g., shade versus sun slopes) and topographic contrasts that affect low-level air currents; other local climates of the soil, of forests, of cities, etc.

Hydrosphere (Chorley, 1969)

Oceans and seas, with saltwater shores modified by wave activity and local river influx and partly influenced by tidal variation

Freshwater lakes, partly modified by wave action or stream input

Streams, permanent or temporary, dominated by channeled flow, as well as other land surfaces, directly modeled by diffuse runoff.

Soil water and groundwater, particularly capillary and gravitational moisture capable of vertical and lateral movement, ion transfer, and rock alteration

Ice, including freeze–thaw cycles in soil and rock, permanently frozen subsoil, temporary snow mantles, and glaciers

Lithosphere (Butzer, 1976a)

Rocks and structures, providing minerals that are eroded, transported, and deposited in materials cycles and that affect permeability and porosity and the nature of potential mineral nutrients, as well as local transformations such as vulcanism, earthquakes, and landslides

Terrain, including elevation, roughness, spacings of valleys and mountains, and inclinations and lengths of slopes; controls dominant geomorphic processes, potential energy, rates of change, and local probability of flooding or soil waterlogging

Soils, differing from intact bedrock in texture, nutrient types, organic content, and microorganic activity.

Biosphere (Odum, 1971)

Organic compounds, including proteins, carbohydrates, and humus.

Plants, mainly photosynthetic organisms that incorporate inorganic substances and water

Animals, including primary consumers of organic matter (herbivores) and secondary consumers of other organisms (carnivores)

Microorganisms, such as earthworms, soil insects, bacteria, and fungi that transform organic detritus, providing energy and stimulating or inhibiting other biotic components

Biomass and primary productivity, determining community energetics in relation to species diversity, population levels, food chains, community respiration, and storage

Nutrient cycling, including mineral cycles, nutrient exchange rates between organisms and environment, and nutrient regeneration from organic detritus by microorganisms

---

limited amount of empirical data for elements such as evaporation or wind speed and direction. This problem has bedeviled climatology for almost a century, as exemplified by the countless simplified classifications devised to illustrate the organization and distribution of climates on the continents. Even when climatic regions are identified as fitting specific biochores, the emphasis on delimitation is unfortunate, if for no other reason than that biotic and physiographic boundaries are arbitrary abstractions that cut across complex transition belts.

The terrestrial segment of the hydrosphere is somewhat elusive to deal with, because horizontal boundaries often are ephemeral, and parts of the hydrosphere either are in constant interchange with the atmosphere or are internetworked with the lithosphere. Similarly, the soil mantle, as the most important single element of the lithosphere, is commonly interdigitated with the biosphere in terms of microorganism activity and nutrient cycling. Classification is further impeded by innate taxonomic problems and by the fact that land surfaces differ greatly in terms of age and environmental history.

Finally, biotic distributions are difficult to characterize, because genetic, historical, and ecological criteria all require attention. Vegetation, for example, can be described in terms of floristics (genera and species), physiognomy (based on leaf shape and seasonality, as well as height and spacing of the largest plants), or formations (which link dominant species and physiognomic properties). But even a physiognomic or formational approach aimed at ecological synthesis is complicated by the historical trajectory (e.g., plant migration and local isolation or extermination). In the case of animal zonation, species ranges are largely determined by physical barriers, dispersal patterns, and paleoclimatic history, whereas the animals themselves often have become adapted, in the form of local ecotypes, through physiological acclimatization or minor genetic divergence (see Chapter 11). Even in isolating biotic communities with a degree of functional unity, the mobility, seasonality, and limited specialization of many larger mammals and birds make boundary definition highly arbitrary.

Thus there is no ready procedure to define and apply the ecosystemic variables that characterize world biomes. The problem is compounded in attempting to describe, let alone operationalize, the interactions. Three examples of interaction can be profitably discussed here.

The interrelationships among vegetation, soil, and lithosphere are most obvious in patchy (i.e., *mosaic*) distributions. Areas with poor topographic drainage, low-nutrient parent material, or bedrock with unusual permeability or mineralogy favor deviations in soil and vegetation types from the regional norm. Such *edaphic* factors (see Chapter 4) are responsible for tundra islands within the subarctic boreal forests, grassland patches amid tropical woodlands, and riverbank gallery forests in desert or grassy environments.

The systemic role of biotic communities interacting with the physical environment is best exemplified by energy flows and energy balances (i.e., energetics). Useful components for reference are *biomass,* the living weight of all plants and animals, and *primary productivity,* the rate at which plant matter is produced by photosynthesis (Figure 2-1). However, in detail, the relevant equations are complex and can be resolved only for simplified biotic or cultural subsystems (e.g., Rappaport, 1971*a*; Nietschmann, 1972). Population dynamics and interpopulation relationships are critical to a broader appreciation of energetics within the complex hierarchy of communities in the food chain. Furthermore, a single time slice cannot accommodate the normal and anomalous variabilities in energy flows effected by cyclic oscillations among several components within each trophic level. Despite such practical limitations, the usefulness of the energetics approach in ecological anthropology has been demonstrated by Hardesty (1977).

The interactions among all four major environmental realms are most dramatically illustrated by the geomorphic activities of running water, waves, ice, gravity, and wind. For example, radiation energy evaporates water from the ocean; it is carried as water vapor by winds onto land, where it is dropped as rain, to become diffuse surface runoff and river discharge; after eroding an increment of the soil cover and performing local channel modification, the water returns to a lake or sea, where it may first play a role in delta extension and subsequently in wave action. In the meantime, moisture added to rock interstices permits chemical weathering, and free soil water transfers mineral nutrients within the soil profile or flushes them out into the rivers, where, together with inert mineral sediment, they sweep downstream as solutes and suspended clay or silt, with sand and gravel jumping or rolling along the channel as bed load. The broadly defined roles of geomorphic processes on the land surface, within the soil, and along the interface of land and water are expressed in the concept of mineral cycles. These processes determine the stability of the soil mantle and the physical transformation of the lithosphere, and therefore they are the most tangible of the various materials cycles in an ecosystem (Figure 2-2).

The complexities of even the rudimentary and partial systems sketched here serve to show that modern functional ecosystems are essentially impractical for empirical study. Not surprisingly, past systems remain beyond reconstruction. However, for most ecologists the ecosystem serves primarily as a paradigm, a broad conceptual

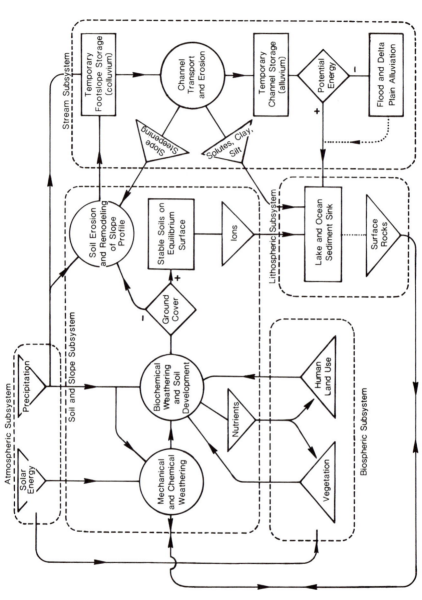

Figure 2-2. A simplified mineral cycle involving weathering, soils, and running water. Vegetation type, human interference, and climatic change can affect the critical ground-cover "regulator." Changes in climate, sea level, and tectonic input can affect the potential energy (available relief).

approach within which to organize and interpret data. The environmental system has a similar focal and heuristic value in contextual archaeology. Specifically, energy and mineral flows highlight two of the most significant spheres of interaction among the components of the environmental system in general and of the human ecosystem in particular.

Equilibrium properties

Like other interactive networks, environmental systems comprise integrated feedback subsystems that operate in a self-regulatory manner and enrich the system by providing it with greater flexibility (Chorley and Kennedy, 1971). *Feedback* is a systemic property whereby change, as introduced by one of the variables, is transmitted through the whole structure, back to the initial variable. Negative feedback sets up a closed loop of change that dampens or stabilizes the effect of the original change, maintaining a *stable equilibirum* or a *dynamic equilibrium* (Figure 2-3). Positive feedback reinforces the effect of the externally induced changes, accelerating changes in the direction of the initial action. Eventually, limits are provided by individual variables that cannot operate indefinitely in one direction.

The atmosphere provides good examples of both types of feedback. Despite repeated anomalies, such as cold winters, wet summers, and severe storms, the basic atmospheric controls set constraints to each aberration until this negative feedback induces a return to a "normal" mode of behavior. Long-term climatic changes involve a concatenation of events. For example, a decrease in temperature increases the amount of snowfall, prolonging the snow-cover season and increasing the reflectivity of the earth's surface (albedo), thus reinforcing the cold. If these positive-feedback mechanisms prevail long enough, the atmospheric circulation may settle into a new, adjusted modal behavior that will once again be maintained by negative feedback.

Natural systems are characterized mainly by negative-feedback propensities, so that changes in the energy environment will favor readjustment of the system variables into an oscillating pattern, called *steady state* (Figure 2-3). Such self-regulatory change is called *dynamic homeostasis* (Chorley and Kennedy, 1971:15). Self-regulation is complicated by two factors: (a) *secondary responses,* which occur when one or more changes continue to operate after the initial energy change has been reversed (e.g., valleyside gullying may begin in response to a temporary environmental condition, but headward channel erosion,

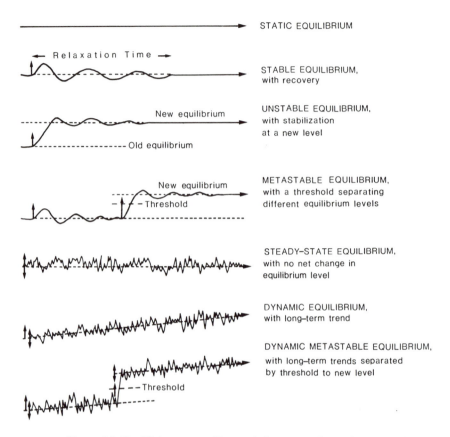

Figure 2-3. Equilibrium types. The vertical arrows indicate changes in the controlling variables. Modified from Chorley and Kennedy (1971:Figure 6.1).

once started, will commonly continue); (b) *thresholds,* which are reached when a small change in one critical variable forces the system into a radically different dynamic equilibrium, often irreversibly so (Chorley and Kennedy, 1971:237). Systems prone to such drastic transformations are *metastable* (Figure 2-3).

The time that elapses between the onset of a perturbation and the reestablishment of the steady state is the *relaxation time* (Chorley and Kennedy, 1971:15), which provides a measure of the elasticity of the system (Orians, 1975). The ability of the system to resist external perturbations and to respond to inputs without crossing a threshold is called inertia or *resilience* (Holling, 1973; Orians, 1975).

Much of the cyclical stability of environmental systems is related to seasonality, so that it is useful to distinguish constancy, in which the state is the same for all seasons in all years, from contingency, in which the state is different for each season but the pattern is the same for all years (Colwell, 1974). For example, landforms, the oceans, and many deep-seated thermal springs exhibit complete constancy, whereas most biota are noted for various degrees of contingency. Together, constancy and contingency define *predictability* (Colwell, 1974), a concept useful for measuring variations in periodic phenomena. For example, rainfall is most predictable in equatorial rain forests because of its high constancy. It is also relatively predictable in the Mediterranean Basin woodlands, with their marked summer drought, because the winter rainfall patterns provide a high level of contingency.

When perturbations are primarily random or *stochastic* in character, predictions regarding system behavior can be made in probability terms. *Probabilistic* patterning contrasts with *deterministic* occurrences, where behavior is mathematically predictable. Random departures from predictable regularity represent *noise*. Finally, there may be *statistical* regularity when random events become predictable as a group, evaluated in the context of longer time series. Examples are provided by the statistical frequencies of peak floods that spill over a river's banks or that inundate an entire floodplain.

Scales of environmental variability

Variability is a central aspect of context. The scales or orders of environmental fluctuations or change can best be gauged from the empirical record, as outlined in Table 2-2.

The wavelengths of environmental variations range from a few years to several million years. There is a proportional relationship whereby longer-term changes tend to have greater amplitudes and more universal effects. But closer inspection shows many exceptions. Some of these dimensions can be illustrated by the western coast of North America (Wolfe, 1978). Here the early Tertiary period had an annual temperature range, between the warmest and coldest months, of 5°C. During the late Tertiary the annual range increased to 17°C to 27°C. Tertiary climatic fluctuations had a wavelength of 9 to 10 million years, with an amplitude of 7°C during the early Tertiary and 2°C to 4°C during the late Tertiary. During the Pleistocene ice age, the last 2 million years, wavelengths were drastically shortened, averaging just under 100,000 years, with an amplitude of 10°C to 20°C. On a planetary scale, the

Table 2-2. *Scales of climatic variation*

First order (less than 10 years): year-to-year oscillations, including the 26-month atmospheric "pulse," the Great Plains dust bowl of 1934–9, and the Sahel drought of 1971–4

Second order (several decades):[a] short-term anomalies, such as well-defined trends in the instrumental record, including the Arctic warmup of A.D. 1900–40 and the dry spell in East Africa A.D. 1900–60

Third order (several centuries):[b] long-term anomalies, such as the worldwide "little ice age" of about A.D. 1400–1900 or the warm European "little optimum" of A.D. 1000–1200, of sufficient amplitude to show up in geological records; third-order climatic variations include repeated oscillations during the 10,000 years of the Holocene

Fourth order (several millennia):[c] major perturbations, such as severe interruptions within the last interglacial, the stadial-interstadial oscillations of the last glacial, and the warm and often drier millennia between 8,000 and 5,000 years ago (Altithermal, Climatic Optimum)

Fifth order (several tens of millennia):[d] major climatic cycles of the order of magnitude of glacials and interglacials, spanning 20,000 to 70,000 years, with eight glacials verified during the last 700,000 years

Sixth order (several million years):[e] geological eras, including the durations of ice ages such as the Permocarboniferous (ca. 10–20 million years long, about 290 million years ago) and Pleistocene (formally began 1.8 million years ago, with major cooling evident for 3.5 million years)

---

[a]Fritts et al. (1979); Lamb (1977); Butzer (1971b).
[b]Ladurie (1971); Grove (1979).
[c]Kukla (1975); Woillard (1978); Flohn (1979).
[d]Kukla (1975); Butzer (1974b).
[e]Wolfe (1978); Crowell and Frakes (1970).

contrasting environmental zonations between early Tertiary, Pleistocene glacial, and modern patterns are shown in Figure 2-4.

The fifth- and sixth-order changes of geological time are of obvious interest to mammalian and primate evolution, but adaptive responses are more likely to take place in relation to lower-order variability. The wavelengths of some empirically determined third- to fifth-order changes are compiled in Table 2-3. Perturbations are identified with the smallest units of resolution in the geological record, regardless of amplitude. Biome shifts can be identified on the basis of pollen records, soil-forming trends, and lake cycles. Typical perturbations last 1 to 3 millennia, whereas the identified biome shifts suggest two modal classes with 5 to 7 millennia and 12 to 50 millennia persistence. Repeated long-term periodicities may exist, but they have not yet been demonstrated for regions of continental magnitude.

Of particular interest are the long, detailed records of pollen, sediment, and oxygen isotopic changes (Johnsen et al., 1972; Kukla, 1975; Woillard, 1978). These exhibit several distinct patterns during the

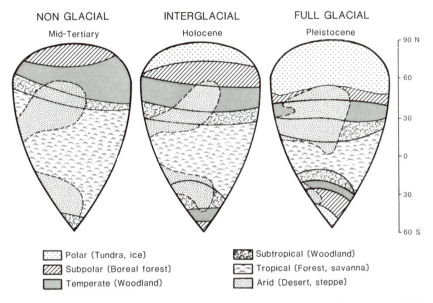

NON GLACIAL — Mid-Tertiary
INTERGLACIAL — Holocene
FULL GLACIAL — Pleistocene

Polar (Tundra, ice)
Subpolar (Boreal forest)
Temperate (Woodland)
Subtropical (Woodland)
Tropical (Forest, savanna)
Arid (Desert, steppe)

Figure 2-4. Models for planetary biotic zonation during mid-Tertiary nonglacial conditions, during the present interglacial, and during a Pleistocene full glacial. The idealized continent represents the composite land mass in each latitudinal belt. Modified from Butzer (1976*b*: Figure 16-2).

course of interglacials and glacials. The warmest episodes of the last interglacial period and Holocene period were marked by steady-state or dynamic equilibria, interrupted by several perturbations, each with a recovery time of 1 to 3 millennia (Figure 2-5). The switches from interglacial to glacial and back again are examples of a dynamic, metastable equilibrium, with critical thresholds crossed 70,000 years ago at the beginning of the last glacial period and again 10,500 years ago at the end of the last glacial. Particularly striking are the severe perturbations during the transition from last interglacial to last glacial, suggesting a complex interplay of negative feedback and positive feedback. The last glacial-to-Holocene transition, on the other hand, was remarkably abrupt in some kinds of records, but marked by a single violent oscillation in others. Also of interest is the high amplitude of cyclic changes throughout the last glacial, with repeated perturbations at several scales. This suggests that glacials represent inherently less stable circulation modes of the atmosphere, repeatedly counteracted by potent negative-feedback mechanisms.

The process-and response system of the earth's atmosphere remains

Table 2-3. *Wavelengths of perturbations and biome shifts in the recent geological record (in millennia)*

Region and perturbation	Range	Modal value	Biome shift	Control period
France (pollen)[a]	0.3–2.0	0.7–2	5–50	140
Central Europe (rivers)[b]	0.2–3.0	2		10
Czechoslovakia (loess)[c]	1.0–10	2–5	5–25	125
Illinois (loess)[d]	0.5–2.5	0.7–2	5–12	30
Mediterranean (vegetation)[e]	1.25–12.5	2–10	5–50	125
Mediterranean (streams)[b]	1.25–7.5	2–5		10
Egyptian desert (streams)[f]	0.1–4.0	1.5–3		30
Tibesti, central Sahara (streams)[g]	0.15–3.0	0.4–2.5	8	30
Chad Basin (lake levels)[h]	0.1–12	0.15–2	8–12	30
Upper Nile Basin (discharge)[f]	0.25–3.5	0.8–2	7–12	30
Rudolf Basin (lake levels)[i]	0.2–2.0	0.5–1	7.5–20	40
Vaal-Orange Basin (streams, springs)[j]	0.4–4.5	0.6–4	4–12	30
Southern Cape, S. Africa (soils, vegetation)[k]	1.0–10	1–3	5–20	40
Antarctica, Greenland (ice cores)[l]	0.18–6.0	0.4–3	3–50[m]	125
Median	0.5–5.9	1.1–3.3	5–24	

[a]Woillard (1978). [b]Butzer (1980a). [c]Kukla (1975).
[d]Butzer (1977a). [e]Florschütz et al. (1971). [f]Butzer (1979).
[g]Jäkel (1979). [h]Maley (1977); Servant (1973). [i]Butzer (1980b).
[j]Butzer (1978b); Butzer, Stuckenrath, et al. (1978).
[k]Butzer and Helgren (1972); Schalke (1973).
[l]Johnsen et al. (1972).
[m]Duration of major oxygen isotope deviations in solid precipitation.

poorly understood. It is evident that plate tectonics have influenced sixth-order trends by shifting continental locations and creating mountain ranges in critical areas. It is also apparent that variations in the earth's orbital parameters (speed of spin, inclination and wobble of axis, asymmetry of orbit) have influenced the spacing of fifth-order climatic changes. But inputs from solar variability (small- and larger-scale emissions), volcanic dust in the atmosphere, reversals and changes in the geomagnetic field, as well other factors, are also very probable. The brief and remarkably severe fourth-order variations

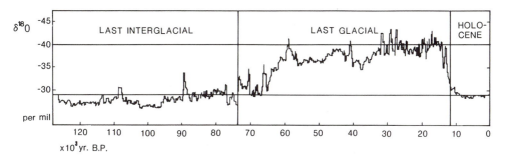

Figure 2-5. Climatic changes during the last 125,000 years as indicated by changes in the oxygen isotope composition of the Greenland ice sheet. The temporal scale is slightly distorted. Modified from Johnsen et al. (1972).

remain unaccounted for; yet they were evidently critical in triggering or modifying fifth-order changes. In sum, climatic change is a response to multivariate factors that are part of a system for which we barely know the variables, let alone their quantitative potentials.

Of significance to contextual archaeology is that climatic changes of several wavelengths and amplitudes have repeatedly punctuated the prehistorical past. Statistical stability of sorts have prevailed for some spans of up to several millennia, but the superimposed first-, second-, and third-order variations, for example, have had significant impact on biomass in many environments. The repeated perturbations in many instances resulted from a primary input of only a few centuries, perhaps as little as 50 years (Flohn, 1979), whereas the subsequent recovery time extended over a few millennia. Many fourth-order and most fifth-order variations were associated with wholesale transformations of biomes. Altogether, this is a fascinating field for further exploration.

Models for ecosystemic change

The empirical evidence assembled in the preceding section illustrates several possible equilibrium patterns inherent to major natural ecosystems: (a) steady-state equilibrium, (b) dynamic equilibrium, (c) dynamic equilibrium punctuated by major perturbations, followed by recovery, and (d) dynamic metastable equilibrium, with long-term crossing of a threshold. These patterns can be linked to different scales of variability. They also display a generalized interrelationship between wavelength and amplitude, and they affect physical and biological components dif-

Table 2-4. *Models for scale changes in ecosystems*

Small-scale variability (first and second order)	Medium-scale variability (third and fourth order)	Large-scale variability (fourth and fifth order)
Year-to-year anomalies, or cyclic variations, up to several decades	Dynamic equilibrium, with major perturbations or low-threshold equilibrium shifts lasting a few centuries or millennia	High-threshold, metastable equilibrium changes, with biome shifts during course of several centuries but persisting for millennia, even tens of millennia
Steady-state or dynamic equilibrium	Fundamental changes in hydrology, productivity, and all categories of biomass	Hydrological and geomorphic systems include new components, creating different soil and sediment assemblages
Fluctuations in seasonal availability or aperiodic availability of water, primary productivity, and biomass of plant foods	Shifts in soil-slope balance favor readjustments of stream behavior, with downcutting or alluviation, tangible in geological record	New ranking of dominants and subdominants in biotic communities, with transformation in biome physiognomy and biochore definition
Affects resource levels for macro-consumers and animal biomass; impact greatest in biomes with low predictability	Qualitative composition of biotic communities persists, but mosaic structures in general and ecotones in particular (e.g., species number and selected population densities); minor changes in biochore definition	Geological and biotic discontinuities provide stratigraphic markers tangible over continental areas
No change in stream behavior or biochore definition		

ferently. The nature of three orders of variability is outlined in the models presented in Table 2-4.

The variable wavelengths of environmental variation that are documented in Table 2-3 provide examples that suggest general patterns at several scales. However, a simplified data scheme of this type glosses over fundamental differences among the physical and biotic components of ecosystems.

This point can be illustrated by the central European geomorphic record, which shows that relatively brief climatic anomalies of a few centuries duration had significant hydrological impact (Butzer, 1980a). Hydrology is a complex subject that must take account of the ratios of precipitation runoff to (a) soil infiltration, (b) periodic concentrations of stream discharge, and (c) the amplitudes and recurrence intervals of peak floods. Such changes affect the balance of soil development and soil erosion on slopes everywhere by modifying soil microclimates, the completeness of soil binding and rainsplash-retarding ground cover, and the amount and speed of surface runoff, as well as topsoil stripping, slumping, or gullying. In turn, the stream network responds both to runoff concentration (brief accentuated flood crests or protracted but less violent high-water surges) and to slope sediment supply (great or small). The net result is that streams may begin either to straighten and deepen their channels (downcutting), or to increase their sinuosity or branching tendencies, favoring net sediment accumulation (alluviation) (Figure 2-2).

Cycles of downcutting, followed by renewed alluviation, can be verified in the central European record at intervals of several centuries to several millennia. Some younger gullying cycles can be linked to human interference, but most were in response to climatic impulses. The responsible third-order anomalies are only partly visible in the pollen record (possibly as a result of coarse sampling increments), although such changes are more apparent in tree-ring records (Becker and Frenzel, 1977). This argues that the slope-soil-stream subsystems had lower critical thresholds than did the vegetative subsystems in humid central Europe. Striking changes in the pollen record are evident only at the fourth-, fifth-, and sixth-order levels, that is, shifts between the standard "postglacial" pollen zones (Butzer, 1971a:530–3), or internal transformation of biomes during the course of the last interglacial (Kukla, 1975), or even total replacement of woodland and parkland by tundra-steppe at the beginning of the last glacial (Frenzel, 1968). The fifth- and sixth-order changes not only helped trigger downcutting-and-alluviation cycles but also introduced new slope processes, such as frost-assisted gravity movements and windborne dust (loess), while fundamentally changing stream sediments from predominantly suspended clay and silt to predominantly sand or even gravelly bed loads (Butzer, 1971a:Chapter 18; Kukla, 1975).

Thus ecosystems are characterized by different subsystems that have distinct thresholds, and individual subsystems have several potential thresholds in response to changes of different orders. From the data sources of Table 2-3 it appears that the hydrology and fluvial subsystems, in general, tend to be most sensitive to environmental inputs, whereas physiognomic plant formations and mammalian communities (as presently sampled) appear to be least sensitive; the soil-slope subsystem and the biotic components of complex communities or biomes appear to have intermediate responses. It seems ironic that landform constellations, the more durable of environmental phenomena, are in the long term governed by processual subsystems that provide some of the most discriminating records of detailed, small-scale changes. This explains the almost unlimited potential of geo-archaeological research in contextual analysis.

Another basic inference can be drawn from Table 2-3. Inertia varies from one biome to another. Woodland environments of high predictability, such as those of western Europe and the Mediterranean Basin, have experienced the greatest biome resilience. Middle-latitude parklands along the humid-semiarid ecotones of the American Midwest and east-central Europe are prone to greater variability, both seasonal and annual, and exhibit lower inertia in the geological record. Hyperarid deserts, such as the Sahara, are highly predictable, and biome shifts in the recent geological past have affected only the mountains (e.g., the Tibesti) and the desert margins. The semiarid tropical and subtropical environments of Africa have had low predictability and limited inertia. Finally, the greatest stability of all is evident in the ocean-atmospheric subsystem that feeds the ice sheets of Greenland and Antarctica, glaciers that have persisted for at least 3 million years.

The dynamics of environmental systems can be understood only in light of historical investigation, that is, from a *diachronic* perspective that focuses on temporal process and effect and so transcends the limitations of a contemporary approach. Like all perspectives, the *synchronic* is a simplified model of reality, because processual change is "frozen" in order to explicate the components, form, and interactions of a system. These approaches are complementary, a point unfortu-

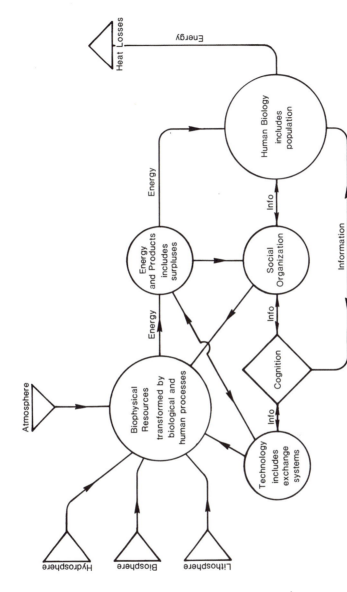

Figure 2-6. Simplified energy cycle for a human ecosystem (does not include storage function). Based in part on Bennett (1976).

nately overlooked by many environmental scientists and ecological anthropologists. The diachronic approach to ecosystems is indeed productive, and it is applied in Chapter 15 to consider cultural adaptation.

Unique character of human ecosystems

In concluding this chapter on environmental systems, it is appropriate to introduce the human ecosystems that are the primary focus of this study. Human ecosystems differ from modal biological ecosystems in kind as well as in degree. For one thing, information, technology, and social organization play inordinately greater roles. More critically, human individuals and groups have unique capacities for purposive behavior, involving (a) the matching of resources with objectives, (b) the transforming of natural phenomena in order to meet these objectives, and (c) the capacity to think about these processes objectively without actually implementing them (Bennett, 1976:35–6).

The pivotal role of human cognition is illustrated in the greatly simplified energy cycle shown in Figure 2-6, which omits the storage functions for "human biology" (population), "technology" (skills and capital), and "energy and material products" (surplus). This role is illustrated both by value systems and goal orientation that are not characteristic of simple ecosystems (Bennett, 1976:Chapter 3) and by the significance of group attitudes and decision-making bodies in the complex societies of the historical record. Similar differences will characterize any food-chain model devised, at least for complex societies, where the trophic levels will comprise a hierarchy of socioeconomic sectors.

The importance of the cognitive role will be discussed further in Chapter 13, but it is important to appreciate at this time that goals, values, and perceived needs are critical in understanding human actions and that culture, perception, and behavior condition the way in which individuals and societies interact with their environments. In particular, geo-archaeological and bio-archaeological research are directed not only at elucidating environmental resources and constraints but also at understanding resource utilization and human intervention within a given environment.

PART II

Foundations

CHAPTER 3

Geo-archaeology I: basic principles

Objectives

Geo-archaeology implies archaeological research using the methods and concepts of the earth sciences. The term is not synonymous with archaeological geology, and it is not necessarily linked to geology:

1. A fundamental distinction must be drawn between technique and goal. Earth-science methodologies contribute critical empirical information and conceptual approaches to an understanding of prehistorical context. Such contributions complement those provided by archaeobotany, zoo-archaeology, archaeometry, and spatial archaeology.

2. The distinction between geology and earth science is equally fundamental, because the geosciences comprise geography and pedology, as well as geology. Each provides component data essential to the study of environmental systems. The full array of these components includes a formidable list of subfields and composite approaches. Geophysics, geochemistry, stratigraphy, sedimentology, geomorphology, soils, hydrology, climatology, and spatial analysis are all relevant to geo-archaeology in varying degrees.

Inevitably, no one individual can master more than a few of the more useful techniques. But a competent geo-archaeologist should be able to evaluate diverse sources of empirical data, as generated within the archaeological project and as available from external sources, in order to apply the information to construct an integrated model of a geo-environmental system. Ideally, this model eventually will be linked with information on biota, demography, and material culture to generate a higher-order model of prehistorical settlement and subsistence patterning.

As a formal label, geo-archaeology is a relatively recent designation for an enterprise that has a long and distinguished tradition. Many early excavations were undertaken by earth scientists. During the 1920s, 1930s, and 1940s, a number of geologists and geographers participated in multidisciplinary projects or implemented interdisciplinary endeavors. All of these contributed procedural or conceptual building stones that profoundly influenced prehistorical archaeology. Included in this group are Elinor Gardner, Kenneth Sandford, Robert Lais, Siegfried Passarge, Kirk Bryan, Ernst Antevs, Sherburne Cook, and Frederick Zeuner. Simultaneously, at least three archaeologists with a true interdisciplinary bent deserve mention: Gertrude Caton-Thompson, Louis Leakey, and Alfred Rust.

During the 1950s and 1960s, empirical work increased dramatically (Burgess, 1980), whereas methodological statements remained few. Ian Cornwall (1958) broke new ground with a procedural text directed to the potentials of sediments and soils in archaeological analysis and interpretation. Despite its modest title, *Soils for the Archaeologist,* this book provided the first systematic treatment of what has come to be designated as geo-archaeology. Using the example of the Nile Valley, Butzer (1960*a*) subsequently illustrated how a geo-environmental approach could help explain regional settlement patterning while facilitating the archaeological survey. Butzer (1964:Chapter 15) provided a geological classification of archaeological sites as part of a more comprehensive approach to regional and site-specific environmental archaeology. Neologisms commonly appear post facto and reflect intellectual currents under active discussion by a wide constituency. At least three independent formulations of geo-archaeology can be identified: Colin Renfrew (1976, in appraisal of a December 1973 conference); Rapp et al. (1974), Rapp (1975); Butzer (1973*a*, 1974*a*, 1975*a*, 1977*c*).

More important than the history of an idea or a subdiscipline is the direction that future research will take in critical areas. For geo-archaeology, the primary concern remains a clear appreciation that goals and techniques are not identical. Rather than a repertoire of techniques or a processual counterpart to the traditional subfield of geochronology, geo-archaeology is first and foremost a conceptual approach. Consequently, this discussion of basic objectives will be elaborated in terms of the study components, the procedures, and the ultimate collaborative goals.

Study components

The standard impression of geo-archeological study is one of soil or sediment analyses from various site levels, providing paleoenvironmental information as well as relative dating with respect to external paleoclimatic sequences. This is unfortunately true of most "geological" site examinations, in part because of limited geo-archaeological materials (real or perceived), in part because of the specialist's traditional approach [90% of its practitioners consider geo-archaeology a secondary interest (Burgess, 1978)], in part because the excavator may preempt creative input by a qualified specialist (Butzer, 1975a). As Gladfelter (1981:347) has argued:

> At least five major interests have emerged within geo-archaeological field studies: (a) survey techniques that use geochemical, electromagnetic and other remote sensing procedures to locate sites or features within a known site; (b) documentation of site-forming processes and the spatial context of a site in the larger habitat setting; (c) elaboration of techniques and approaches for differentiating cultural and natural features, including post-occupational disturbances by biological, pedological, and geological processes; and (d) development of intra- and extrasite temporal contexts by relative and/or absolute dating; (e) integration of paleogeomorphic and biological information for the environmental reconstruction of the paleo-landscape. Geo-archaeological involvement must occur at all stages of these investigations: design, excavation and analysis.

Geo-archaeology is still in the process of developing a sophisticated approach to archaeological research, so that it is imperative to identify the full range of study components. This has been attempted in Table 3-1, which can serve as an agenda for the next five chapters. A basic premise of this programmatic outline is that a site is part of a landscape that once was integral to a human ecosystem (Fedele, 1976). The physical record is much more than a spatial and temporal backdrop. Site formation and destruction are culturally controlled or predicated, and the reciprocal relationships between people and their environment are reflected both within the site and in its containing landscape (Butzer, 1977c; Davidson, n.d.).

Most geo-archaeological reports, some of my own included, have failed to focus on cultural factors in site formation, on physical disturbance and modification of cultural residues, and on the unique potential of this research mode in archaeological survey. There has been no proper discussion of the processes of human intervention in the soil landscape and the hydrological cycle. Sometimes, when the direct or indirect impacts of land use are implicated, authors continue to insist on the primacy of climatic impulses. For example, when Vita-Finzi (1978:122, 155) confronted the differential timing of recent alluvial cycles within an area, he invoked proximity to potsherd concentrations or latitudinally shifting cyclonic belts, rather than different settlement

Table 3-1. *Primary study components in geo-archaeology*

Landscape context

1. Site microenvironment, defined in terms of the local environmental elements that influenced original site selection, the period of its use, and its immediate burial or subsequent preservation. Sediment analyses of site strata represent an obvious study procedure in a sealed site.
2. Site mesoenvironment, primarily the topographic setting and landforms of the area utilized directly for subsistence. This geomorphic information, combined with bio-archaeological inputs, helps define the adjacent environmental mosaic.
3. Site macroenvironment, essentially the regional environment provided by a particular biome or ecotone. The constellation of effective geomorphic processes, together with biotic information (Chapters 10 and 11), is indispensable in constructing a model of the regional ecosystem.

Stratigraphic context

1. Reconstruction of sequential natural events such as soil development, erosion, and sedimentation, recorded by detailed sediment units (microstratigraphy) in the site and its environs.
2. Evaluation of the local physical sequence in terms of regional landscape history and potential matches with dated subcontinental or even global stratigraphies. External correlation can serve as a chronometric aid, can assist in paleoenvironmental interpretation, can facilitate cross-checks between different categories of data, and can be used to test the temporal validity of archaeological horizons.
3. Direct paleontological correlation (Chapter 10 and 11) and radiometric dating (Chapter 9).

Site formation

1. People and animals, as geomorphic agents, produce archaeological sediments, with physical, biogenic, and cultural components that require identification and interpretation.
2. Distinction of materials: (a) materials that were introduced to the site by people or animals, in their original form or as finished products; (b) materials that represent alteration products from on-site processing or biochemical decomposition; (c) materials that were transformed from primary on-site refuse and debris into new sediment through human and other physical agencies.
3. Evaluation of archaeosedimentary processes to help elucidate settlement and subsistence activities in space and time.

Site modification

1. Preburial dispersal of archaeological residues through the actions of running water, gravity, frost, deflation, animal trampling, and deliberate human removal.
2. Postdepositional site disturbance through various agencies: burrowing animals and lower organisms, soil frost, expansion and contraction of clays, gravity and microfaulting, and biochemical alteration.
3. Site destruction and artifact dispersal caused by various forces: weathering, running water, deflation, slumping, and human intervention.
4. Interpretation of sealed or exposed cultural residues in terms of primary, semiprimary, or secondary context (as defined in Chapter 7).

Landscape modification

1. Identification of human intervention in the soil landscape, in the form of disturbed or truncated soil profiles and redeposited soils.
2. Human intervention in the hydrological cycle, as reflected in erosional gullies, alluvial fills, and lake sediment records.
3. Human constructs in the landscape: filled-in ditches, pits, and postholes; earthworks and spoil heaps; roadways, terraced fields, and irrigation networks; middens and burials adjacent to focal settlements.
4. Assessment of the cumulative direct and indirect impacts of human land use in spatial terms and in the temporal perspective of sustained landscape productivity or degradation (Chapters 10 and 11).

histories. This tendency to favor physical explanations at all costs is unfortunate. The reciprocal relationships between people and their potential resources are as real as the degraded landscapes so commonly created during the course of intensive land use.

People are geomorphic agents. They carry inorganic and organic materials to a site, deliberately or inadvertently, including matter for constructing shelter and housing, making and using tools, and processing and consuming food, as well as matter for fuel, clothing, and ornamentation. These mineral and organic materials, as well as their products, by-products, and residues, are prone to repeated mechanical and biochemical comminution and degradation, during and after occupancy of the site. Repeated minor and major sedimentary breaks are caused by removal of rubbish and by the processes of destroying and rebuilding. Afterward, gravity gradually levels settlement debris, with autocompaction, rainsplash and runoff, sporadic disturbances by floodwaters and windstorms, and possible addition of external mineral sediment.

The cultural components of a site can vary from a scatter of bones, artifacts, and human residues on a Paleolithic butchery floor to thick accumulations of mudbrick and refuse within a Near Eastern agricultural village. Thus the human input can range from less than 1% to more than 99% and the archaeological sediment may record a span of as little as a few hours or as much as several millennia. Physical and biological processes may be paramount at all times, or perhaps only sporadically during a catastrophic event or after site abandonment. Such "natural" biophysical processes may also be accelerated or inhibited by cultural activities. Whether the object of interest is a level containing scattered hand axes in a cave stratum or the total expanse of a great settlement mound, the controlling geomorphic system includes cultural components that modify its steering dynamism, its dominant processes, and its tangible results.

This site-specific archaeosedimentary system calls for special expertise, procedures, and interpretative models. The scope of investigation involves not only the initial site formation and the repeated potential metamorphoses during occupation but also the subsequent burial or partial erosion and the eventual dispersal or mixing of artifacts and other cultural residues on or away from the site.

The impact of human activities is not limited to restricted settlement sites. Prehistorical foragers dug pits to serve as game traps, wells, and graves, and often they left sizable refuse middens in or adjacent to their encampments. Whereas foraging activities were likely to be incidental and ephemeral in affecting the hydrological cycle, prehistorical farmers commonly had an impact on the soil-slope-stream system (see Figure 2-2) that was both extensive and intensive and often was of considerable duration. British agricultural landscapes of the Neolithic and Bronze Age were crisscrossed by drainage ditches, partly leveled by low terraces, bounded by earthen or stone walls, and dimpled by burial mounds. Indians in southwestern North America dug irrigation ditches, built dams, and reinforced river banks. In countless situations, prehistorical planters and herders were able to disturb vegetation and ground cover until a threshold was reached at which the amount and speed of runoff were enhanced after rainstorms, filling in ditches and the like by sheetwash and gravity, and truncating or burying soil profiles. In the end, soil formation, slope processes, and stream behavior may have been modified sufficiently to leave a clear record of disturbance, possibly culminating in an episode of landscape degradation, with attendant accelerated soil erosion.

Techniques and procedures

The range of techniques that have the potential to be applied to geo-archaeological goals is derived from several subdisciplines and is therefore almost unlimited. Yet the purpose of geo-archaeology is not to implement an impressive battery of sophisticated tests but to select those procedures that within the constraints of available financial and human resources will yield the results most critical to proper evaluation of a particular context.

Some examples of basic field and laboratory techniques applicable to several stages of analysis (Rapp, 1975; Farrand, 1975a; Shackley, 1975; Gladfelter, 1977; Hassan, 1978) are outlined in Table 3-2. They imply that geo-archaeological fieldwork must be carried out inside and outside of the site. They call for repeated revision of research strategies, both during the course of the fieldwork and between seasons. And they mandate multidisciplinary data integration, aimed ultimately toward functional interpretation of sites or site components. Published results should reflect the full range of geo-archaeological and other inputs.

Ultimate collaborative goals

To reiterate, geo-archaeology implies archaeology done primarily by means of earth-science methods, techniques, and concepts. The goal is to elucidate the environmental matrix intersecting with past socioeconomic systems and thus to provide special expertise for understanding the human ecosystems so defined. This task is not an easy one, nor

Table 3-2. *Basic analytical procedures in geo-archaeology*

In the field

The site

1. Recording vertical profiles within the excavation as well as in other adjacent pits or trenches cut in order to clarify the nature of the site sediment sequence and its external contacts.

2. Sampling representative archaeosedimentary materials, as well as nearby natural soil profiles and potential microdepositional analogs, for laboratory study.

3. Relating the site to its landscape by local topographic survey or geomorphic transects.

The landscape

1. Terrain mapping of the mesoenvironment, in conjunction with available aerial photography, detailed topographic maps, and relevant satellite images.

2. Location of other sites and cultural features, preferably in conjunction with systematic archaeological survey, by using geomorphic inference and available aerial photos, possibly aided by geophysical site prospecting.

3. Examination of natural exposures, in terms of stratigraphic subdivisions, sediment properties, and soil profiles, to reconstruct regional landscape history, to provide a wider context for the central site, and to assess possible impacts of the prehistorical community on the environment.

In the laboratory

1. Systematic interpretation of maps, aerial photos, and satellite images to complement field mapping.

2. Sediment analysis for particle size and composition to identify potential geomorphic processes affecting the archaeosedimentary system in time and space and to establish a microstratigraphic sequence both within the site and in the adjacent mesoenvironment; complementary work in mineralogy and micromorphology, as warranted.

3. Sediment analysis for geochemical and biochemical properties such as pH, calcium carbonate content, organic matter, phosphates, etc., in order to assess cultural inputs to the archaeosedimentary system.

4. Provisional modeling of the sequence of site formation, abandonment, and postdepositional change, as well as of spatial and temporal activities during the course of human occupance.

Revision of research strategies

The component and aggregate results obtained in the field and laboratory must be used to reassess the project's research strategies (during the course of a particular field season, if possible, and certainly between seasons).

Multidisciplinary data integration

1. Identification (and, possibly, modeling) of pertinent microenvironments, mesoenvironments, and macroenvironments to establish spatial and ecological parameters for the socioeconomic and settlement patterns suggested by excavation and survey results.

2. Interpretation of the archaeosedimentary system in terms of micropatterning, burial, and preservation of the indicators of human activities on the one hand and biophysical processes on the other.

3. General evaluation of the site or site complex as primary, semiprimary, or secondary.

one likely to provide firm answers in the near future. But we are indeed obligated to continue to develop better interdisciplinary procedures in order to achieve more objective interpretation.

In explicit theoretical terms, geo-archaeology can and should contribute substantially to the definition and resolution of the five basic contextual issues (scale, space, complexity, interaction, and stability) described in Chapter 1.

Not only is geo-archaeology essential for identification of microenvironments, mesoenvironments, and macroenvironments, for analysis of topographic patterning, and, more indirectly, for analysis of climates, biota, and human groups; it also has considerable potential for delineation of those periodic processes and aperiodic events that affect physical, biological and cultural aggregates on different spatial and temporal scales. It may well aid in the characterization and delimitation of environments and communities that are inhomogeneous, by virtue of its flexible, multiscale spatial and temporal perspectives. It is critical in any attempt to model the interactions between communities and the nonliving environment. Finally, an appreciation of geo-environmental dynamics is indispensable for investigation of potential readjustments, major and minor, long term and short term, among the human and nonhuman communities of the environmental system in response to internal processes or external inputs.

Geo-archaeologists dedicated to elucidating such contextual issues must be more than casual practitioners of applied science. They should be committed archaeologists. Unfortunately, there are at this time only a few qualified practitioners, primarily because most university training programs remain as inadequate as the research designs typical of most archaeological field projects (Butzer, 1975a). Achievement of an integrated scientific approach is possible only as a collective achievement that bridges narrow specialties. Regardless of the number of earth-science techniques we apply, we cannot hope to remedy the current situation without fundamental changes in concepts within the archaeological mainstream.

At the same time, geo-archaeologists themselves must contribute actively toward implementing a contextual approach in training and research. In this way, archaeologists from different specialties can develop a fuller appreciation of context. Archaeology cannot rely on an unlimited supply of outside technicians and services; in fact, the interests of archaeology are inadequately served by part-time practitioners of the applied sciences. Instead, geo-archaeology must extend its roots deep within archaeology, the better to serve the discipline.

CHAPTER 4

Geo-archaeology II: landscape context

Sedimentary matrix

Landscape context can be defined at small, medium, and large scales. The most detailed is the site microenvironment, defined in terms of the local physical and biotic parameters that influenced the original site selection, that were effective during the period of site use, and that were responsible for its burial and subsequent preservation. The record most immediately available for study and interpretation is the sediment that embeds the site components. This sediment may be penecontemporaneous with site occupance, or it may be younger, often substantially so. The first objective in site analysis is to examine the sedimentary matrix of the site and so to identify the related depositional environment. Such study requires considerable geomorphological expertise.

The basic effect of the geomorphic processes is to model the earth's surface. Of this wide range of potential forces, some are internal or endogenic, deriving directly from the lithosphere. These include the faulting and folding linked to ongoing earthquake activity and the lava flows and ash falls associated with volcanic eruptions. The other group of forces is external or exogenic, reflecting the impact of atmospheric or hydrospheric agents on the lithosphere (see Table 2-1). These processes include the effects of running water (both channeled and diffuse surface runoff), gravity (both slow and rapid effects, and in wet and dry media), wind, ice, and waves.

The external geomorphic agents are central to materials cycles (see Figure 2-2), and all involve erosion, transport, and deposition of physically comminuted or chemically decomposed materials derived from the earth's crust. An outline of weathering processes and products can be consulted elsewhere (Butzer, 1976a:Chapter 3; Brunsden, 1979). Erosion and deposition always go hand in hand, but not necessarily in the same place. Deposition is dominant in some areas, leaving a sedimentary record. In other areas, erosion is characteristic, commonly with a record of small and large erosional forms, some specific, others generalized.

It is important in identifying sedimentary modes to remember that deposition is not an indiscriminate process that can happen anywhere. Whether or not deposition occurs, and where, is determined by several factors: the sediment supply, the nature of the ground cover (if any), the topographic setting, and the constellation of effective geomorphic processes. Thus, deposition is part of a systemic structure with discernible regularities, a structure potentially amenable to relatively specific interpretation. Sediments may accumulate (a) at discrete points, such as around springs or in caves, (b) in linear arrangements, such as along stream valleys or coastlines, and (c) over extensive surface areas, such as slopes, dune fields, or sheets of windborne dust or volcanic ash.

The presence of a tangible deposit, thick or thin, extensive or localized, means that net sedimentation has prevailed during countless short-term episodes of small-scale erosion, transfer, and deposition. The preserved deposit may be thin or thick; it may be unique, or it may be part of a complex package, such as the variable strata exposed in the average archaeological excavation. For example, there may be a suite of thin lenticles, extensive lenses, and massive beds that all reflect a single process, such as running water; the breaks may represent intervals of nondeposition or of erosion, and the different bed forms probably are due primarily to temporal variations in the available energy, such as the suddenness, the violence, and the duration of a flood episode. Commonly, however, a variable sediment package reflects several different processes, probably in interplay and responding to different energy levels. For example, gravity and diffuse runoff may first build up a sheet of eroded soil on a valley margin, subsequently to be remodeled by stream action and terminated by increasingly important wind components.

The end effect is that a single location may acquire a succession of sediment units that record repeated landscape events, however small or brief. The event-specific or process-specific lenticular records are called *facies*. Such facies define *depositional microenvironments*. A major component of geo-archaeological research is elucidation of those facies sequences that constitute the archaeological matrix.

The subsequent sections will outline the major types of point, linear, and areal sedimentary contexts that are particularly common as archaeological matrices. A selection of informative examples will be cited

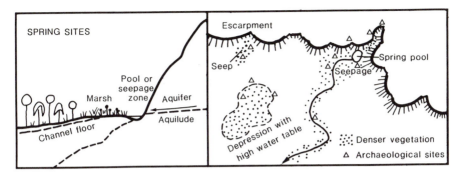

Figure 4-1. Schematic cross section and plan view of spring sites.

after each category. For background reading on the geomorphologic processes themselves, see the texts of Butzer (1971:Chapters 10–15; 1976a) and Evans (1978:Chapter 5). Aspects of the related sedimentology problems have been addressed by Shackley (1975), Davidson and Shackley (1976), Gladfelter (1977), and Hassan (1978). The selective reader can advance directly to Table 4-1 and discussion of the topographic matrix.

Point depositional environments

Springs. Soil waters and rock waters can emerge at discrete points in space to give rise to seepage zones, marsh, open pools, and streams (Figure 4-1). Most such springs represent the end of a brief underground trajectory of atmospheric water, passing through soil and rock during the course of the hydrological cycle. Most such waters enter existing streams imperceptibly, but conspicuous springs may form when an aquifer of porous and permeable sand, gravel, or indurated rock is intersected by erosion at a level just above an impermeable aquilude. Shallow aquifers flow in proportion to percolating rainfall and tend to be variable in their spring discharges. Deep-seated bedrock springs are more commonly noted for perennial flow, with little or no variation. Particular cases are provided by artesian springs, which emerge from extensive, even subcontinental, aquifers under high pressure, and thermal springs, which derive from deep volcanic sources within the earth's crust.

Many springs introduce primary sediment or modify local soils and rock waste. The resulting range of spring deposits can include organic mucks or sands, lime precipitates such as laminated travertines and

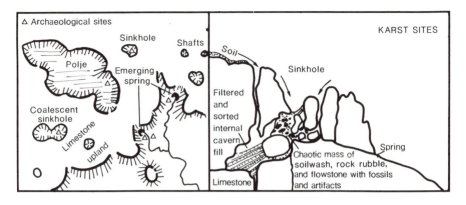

Figure 4-2. Schematic plan view and detail section of karst sites.

organic tufas with plant impressions, and sediments of various textures impregnated with lime, salts, or iron.

Archaeological examples include Tule Springs, Nevada (Shutler, 1967), Clovis, New Mexico (Haynes and Agogino, 1966), Phillips Spring, Missouri (Kay, 1978), and Amanzi Springs, South Africa (Butzer, 1973b).

Karst. When limestone and dolomitic bedrocks become pitted by the process of solution, the result is a karst topography, characterized by jagged and cavitated rock surfaces, deep fissures and shafts, simple or coalescent sinkholes, and large valleylike depressions (poljes) (Figure 4-2) (Sweeting, 1972). These peculiar landscapes resulting from long-term corrosion and solution by mildly acidic waters commonly are punctuated by springs and caves. At whatever scale, karst provides special edaphic settings for vegetation communities, favoring mosaic environments in which spring activity, running water, and even wind can contribute to a complex sedimentary record.

The fossiliferous cavern and fissure fills at Swartkrans, Sterkfontein, and Taung, South Africa (Butzer, 1975c, 1976c; Brain, 1976; Partridge, 1978) are typical examples.

Caves. Limestone solution is the most common explanation for caves, which develop where valley margins wear back to intersect former

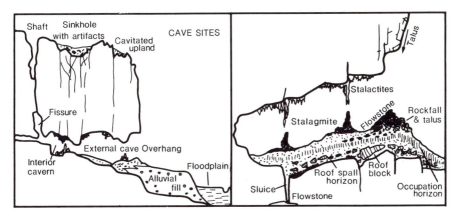

Figure 4-3. Schematic general and detailed sections of cave sites.

underground caverns, or where karstic springs and subterranean streams emerge. Caves can form in almost all rock types along coasts, where wave erosion creates cavities near the watermark. Some unusual caves have also been formed on cliff faces, where rocks of different hardness are interbedded, or where erosion selectively attacks weak bedding planes. Whatever their origin, caves range in size and exposure from simple rock overhangs or abris to open exterior caves and deep interior fissures or caverns (Figure 4-3).

Cave deposits generally fall into two categories: externally derived material that enters via the entrance or roof and wall fissures; internally produced sediments. The former include soil wash, stream beds, windborne dust and sand, and cultural residues. The latter include roof and wall rubble (talus, spall, rockfalls) and, with limestone bedrock, a variety of precipitates, both dripstone (stalactities, stalagmites, columns) and flowstone (travertine).

Archaeological examples are numerous. A selection might include Rodgers Shelter, Missouri, and Meadowcroft Shelter, Pennsylvania, in sandstone (Wood and McMillan, 1976; Adovasio et al., 1977), Abri Pataud and Lazaret, France, and Cueva Morín, Spain, in limestone (De Lumley, 1969; Farrand, 1975a, 1975b; Butzer, 1981c), and the Klasies River mouth, South Africa, in quartzite (Butzer, 1978c). A basic methodology for cave-sediment analysis is available elsewhere (Laville, 1976; Laville et al., 1980).

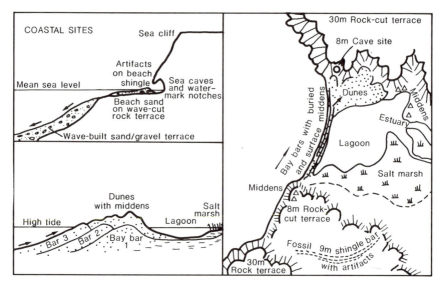

Figure 4-4. Schematic sections of rocky and sandy coasts and plan view.

Linear depositional environments

Seashores. The world's coastlines provide a highly variable but continuous environmental complex that is narrow and to some degree linear (Figure 4-4). Cliffed coasts include a specific range of microenvironments, such as wave-built and wave-cut beaches and adjacent notches or sea caves. Low-relief coasts, on the other hand, may include sandy beach ridges, barrier bars, and spits, together with foreshore dunes and lagoons, salt marshes, and tidal mudflats. Landforms and deposits reflect rock type, gradients, and, above all, wave energy. The related environmental mosaic favors distinct biotic communities and corresponding resource opportunities.

Archaeological examples include innumerable instances in which handfuls of lithic artifacts are embedded in beach sand or gravel. But more informative are sea caves such as Cape Ashakar, Morocco (Stearns, 1967), and coastal middens such as those of South Africa, Brazil, and Alaska (Giddings, 1966; Fairbridge, 1976; Volman, 1978). Archaeological implications of shoreline changes have been illustrated in Italy by Delano Smith (1978) and in Greece and Turkey by Kraft et al. (1977, 1980a, 1980b) and Van Andel et al. (1980). On a larger scale, shoreline changes are also pertinent in evaluating Pleistocene land-sea bridges, such as those of Beringia, Southeast Asia, and in the Mediterranean Basin. Equally relevant here are the increasing numbers of underwater surveys and excavations involving submerged caves and drowned harbors in the Mediterranean and along the coasts of northwest Europe, Japan, California, and Florida.

Lakeshores and marshes. The margins of freshwater lakes and marshes are analogous to seashores, but the energy levels are substantially lower, the relief is less, the habitat mosaic is narrower, and the organic component is far more prominent. Low-wave-energy shores are sometimes arranged in parallel zones of subaquatic, nearshore, and backshore biotic communities. Facies vary accordingly from finer and more homogeneous sediments in the acquatic realm to coarser and more mixed types inshore. There also are distinct geochemical environments (Figure 4-5):

1. In eutrophic (i.e., neutral or mildly alkaline) lakes in the humid middle latitudes there is a gradation from lacustrine chalk or marl (lime mud) to mixed organic-calcareous oozes in the semiterrestrial (shore) zone and humic, waterlogged, anaerobic soils (gleys) above the watermark.

2. In oligotrophic (i.e., acidic) settings in the humid middle latitudes the sequence ranges from subaquatic peat (dy) and organic oozes (gyttja) to reed and sedge peats (fen), to wood peat (carr), to blanket bogs of highly acid sphagnum moss, and finally to peaty eluviated soils (podsols) as drainage improves on increasing slopes.

3. In saline or alkaline basins in semiarid environments the facies sequence might range from a clayey soda marl under water to extensive salty, cracking mudflats around the rapidly fluctuating lake margins and then to organic cracking clays that interfinger with dune sands or stream beds inland. Diatom blooms, which are found on the surface of stagnant but clear waters in a variety of chemical environments, contribute microscopic silica skeletons that modify or dominate an alternative form of organic sediment.

Archaeological associations are varied and plentiful. The Neolithic "lake dwellings" of Switzerland were built along the shore and later were submerged and preserved by sedimentation as the water level rose (Olive, 1972; Bocquet, 1979). Wooden houses and causeways of similar age are preserved within the acidic blanket bogs of Britain (Sim-

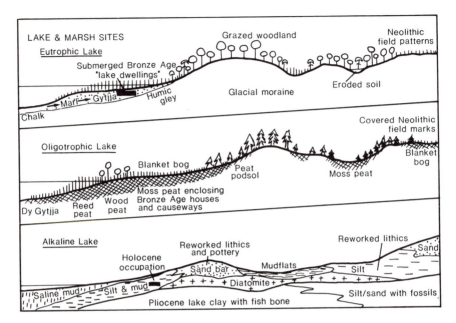

Figure 4-5. Hypothetical topographic sections adjacent to eutrophic and oligo-trophic high-latitude lakes and alkaline low-latitude lake.

mons and Proudfoot, 1969). Older sites such as the Pleistocene occupations near Ahrensburg, Germany, have provided well-preserved organic materials and undisturbed archaeological associations (Rust, 1962). The Olduvai Basin, Tanzania, and Lubbock Lake, Texas, illustrate the range of semiarid basin settings (Hay, 1976; Johnson and Holliday, 1980; Stafford, 1981).

Delta fringe. The mouths of a delta are linked by a linear mosaic of low-energy and low-relief shore features, including bars, spits, and lagoons (Figure 4-6). The distributary channels, followed by low banks of higher ground, wind their way between marshes and mudflats. The complex of riverbank, shore, marsh, and lake settings of a delta fringe provides one of the most diversified environments available (Butzer, 1971b).

Archaeological examples are provided by archaeological survey of the western Mississippi delta (Gagliano, 1963), by hominid and artifactual occurrences in the former Omo delta of eastern Africa (Leakey et al., 1969; Butzer, 1980b), and by the 150- to 200-km progradation of the Tigris-Euphrates delta in historical times (Larsen and Evans, 1978).

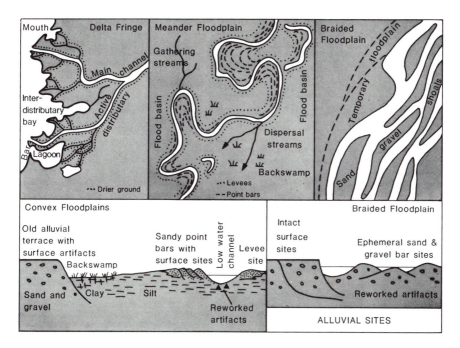

Figure 4-6. Schematic plans and sections of delta and floodplain sites.

Floodplain. The depositional plains of streams and rivers can be grouped into four main classes:

1. Large silty to clayey convex floodplains such as those of the Mississippi, Nile, and Mekong are characterized by meandering channels, raised berms or levees, parallel ridges (point bars) on convex channel margins, cutoff channel segments, periodically submerged flood basins, and perennially wet backswamps (Figure 4-6). Convex floodplains develop in response to rapid sand accumulation in channels and levees and slower silt and clay accretion across the flood basins during repeated overbank discharges.

2. Silty to sandy flat floodplains accompany the sinuous channels of most smaller and intermediate streams. They develop through progressive channel shifts, with more sporadic overbank discharges.

3. Sandy to gravelly braided channels anastomose their way across valley bottoms in semiarid environments (Figure 4-6), particularly in areas of high relief and areas of strong flood surges.

4. Sandy to gravelly alluvial fans, crisscrossed by diverging braided channels, tend to develop as gently concave features along breaks of

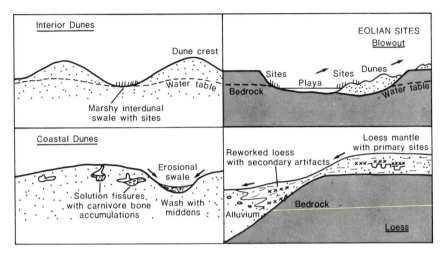

Figure 4-7. Generalized eolian-site settings.

gradients, such as at the foot of a mountain range or where seasonal tributaries join perennial rivers.

Archaeological examples of sandy to gravelly alluvial "terraces" include the Thames, Somme, and Vaal river valleys (Wymer, 1968; Verron, 1976; Helgren, 1978), where most sites are secondary. The Nile provides multiple examples of ancient convex floodplains that include some primary sites along former levees and channels (Butzer and Hansen, 1968:Chapter 4; Phillips and Butzer, 1973; Butzer, 1976b). Complex geo-archaeological details of flat floodplains can be illustrated in the northwestern Great Plains (Agenbroad, 1978; Albanese, 1978), at Isimila and Olorgesaillie, East Africa (Hansen and Keller, 1971; Isaac, 1977), and at Salzgitter-Lebenstedt, Germany (Butzer, 1971a:468–71). Specific problems in the interpretation of alluvial sites have been discussed by Gladfelter (1977), and postdepositional disturbances in high-energy environments have been illustrated by Turnbaugh (1978).

Areal depositional environments

Eolian sites. Wind-sculptured surfaces are created wherever the vegetation cover is incomplete and there are loose dry fine particles available for removal. Narrow eolian environments may run parallel to shorelines or braided floodplains, but an abundance of sand, transferred as bed load, can lead to the development of extensive dune fields capable of migrating great distances across level surfaces. Interior dune fields, undulating sand sheets, and irregular sand seas are most prominent in arid environments where ancient sandstones are comminuted by erosion and the resulting sands are concentrated by periodic stream action. Some dune types reflect the presence of vegetation, namely U-shaped parabolic dunes (open to the prevailing wind) and smaller blowout dunes common to foreshore or valley-margin settings. Longitudinal barchan (horns open downwind) and complex transverse dunes generally are formed in barren areas.

Wind is also responsible for erosional features, including (a) general surface deflation that removes fine materials and helps concentrate coarse sand and stone at the surface as lag or desert pavement, (b) blowouts that scar unconsolidated deposits, and (c) hairline ridges or yardangs, sculptured from silty or clayey beds by wind blast.

A different type of eolian deposit is loess, a windborne suspended dust that settles over wide areas to form a mantle or veneer downwind of seasonal rivers transporting abundant silt. Loess often is washed out of the atmosphere by rain, and even on the ground it is repeatedly reworked by running water. It therefore allows for rapid burial under low-energy conditions, and it retards leaching because of an intermediate to high pH.

The relevance of eolian features for site location, preservation, and exposure is considerable (Figure 4-8). Although the majority of archaeological sites amid coastal dunes and floodplain-margin dunes are secondary, rapid burial has preserved large lithic concentrations and shell middens in many areas. Amid interior dune fields and sand sheets, interdunal swales or blowouts, often of great age, have been modified in the wake of repeated environmental changes (e.g., higher water tables create ponds or marshes that attract settlement, as in the Sahara) (Rognon, 1980). Deflation has exposed countless sites, eventually reducing them to a lag in which multiple levels can coalesce into one (Butzer and Hansen, 1968:Chapter 4). Finally, loess, whether primary or secondary, has preserved countless sites, ranging from Koster, Illinois (Butzer, 1977a), to various Mousterian and Upper Paleolithic encampments of the Ukraine (Klein, 1973), although problems of derivation often are serious (Brunnacker, 1978).

Slopes. Hillsides consist of crest slopes, midslopes, and footslopes (Figure 4-10). Mainly shallow deposits can build up on the midslope and

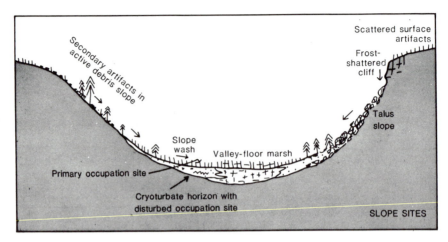

Figure 4-8. Schematic section of slope-site disposition.

particularly on the footslope. Such deposits include slow accumulations of rock rubble or talus below cliff faces, as well as rapid rockfalls, landslides of rock and soil on unstable hillsides and mountainsides, and mainly slow accretion of soil products or rock waste along footslopes by gradual gravity movement of particles (soil creep), by sliding and upturning (slumping), by rainwash erosion (colluvium), or by plastic flow of water-saturated soil, commonly frost-aided (solifluction).

Whereas such soil accumulations along footslopes or in upland swales (Figure 4-9) help preserve archaeological sites, there is serious risk that upslope sites or even upland sites can be eroded and then redeposited on footslopes. Stream flow selectively picks up lighter materials, but gravity moves heavier objects faster and farther than light ones on slopes of 23° to 25° and more (Rick, 1976). In this way, objects of different materials and sizes are fundamentally rearranged. Frost dynamics within the soil favor differential heaving of soil and rock, reorienting or moving artifacts upward (Wood and Johnson, 1978). Such cryoturbation is not unique to slope settings, but it is particularly effective on inclined surfaces. An example of a footslope site within interfingering colluvium and marsh beds, partly undisturbed, partly modified by cryoturbation, is Torralba in central Spain (Butzer, 1965, 1971a:456–61).

Volcanic sites. Although vulcanism is endogenic in origin, the rapid and massive extrusions of lavas, mudflows (lahars), and airborne debris

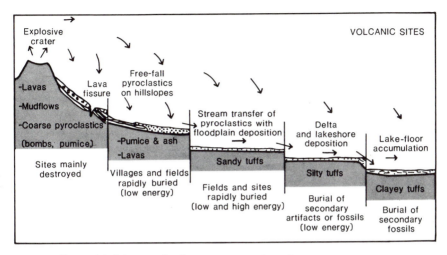

Figure 4-9. Schematic landscape segments for volcanic sites.

provide important archaeological contexts. The airborne pyroclastics include large blocks or "bombs," pebble-sized pumice, sand-sized ash, and dust-sized tuff (Figure 4-9). Tuffs are carried over many hundreds of kilometers by wind, washed together in streams, and then often transported even greater distances, to be deposited rapidly on flood-plains and delta plains or in lakes. They provide an excellent burial medium, with reasonably good preservation, as evidenced by the best known archaeological and fossil sites in the East African rift valleys. The role of ash falls in preserving Pompeii is well known, and Thera on the slope of Santorini in the Aegean Sea (Davidson, 1978) is another example. Some particularly illuminating examples of the geo-archaeology of volcanic deposits have been documented for North America and Central America (Sheets and Grayson, 1979).

Geo-archaeological synthesis of microenvironments

The depositional microenvironments previously outlined are synthesized in the geo-archaeological classification presented in Table 4-1. The general summations concerning erosion, transfer, and sediment properties are more detailed than those in the text in order to allow greater precision. The reader unfamiliar with geomorphology can focus on the archaeological-prospects column and use this in conjunction with Figures 4-1 to 4-9 to sample the procedural strategy.

Table 4-1. *Geo-archaeological classification of microdepositional environments*

	Erosion	Transfer	Bedding, texture	Sorting	Archaeological prospects
Spring	Local vent erosion, with deep-seated bedrock erosion or corrosion	Hydrodynamic low- to high-energy mobilization of detritus and solutes	Lenticular heterogeneous sedimentary packages, sometimes contorted, including organic mucks, sands, and precipitates (Ca, Na, Fe)	Poor to good	Favored loci for settlement or kill-butchering sites; conditions for burial preservation above average; variable soil environments, including saline and thermal
Karst	Denudation of soils on land surface; deep-seated bedrock corrosion (e.g., fissures, cavities, caverns)	Low-energy spring mobilization, surface runoff, gravity; also possible eolian components	Primarily massive, often heterogenous, units, dominated by humic loams or gravelly wash, interdigitated with chemical precipitates	Mainly poor	Good traps for artifacts and bone, but rarely used for occupation sites; alkaline soil environment with abundant mineralizing solutions
Cave	Bedrock erosion/corrosion along joints, bedding planes, lithologic contacts; roof or wall collapse (gradual or rapid)	Hydrodynamic but low-energy mobilization of solutes or detrital sediment; gravity transfer of rubble from roof or rock faces	Lenticular heterogeneous sedimentary sequences ranging from chemical precipitates (dripstone, flowstone) to internal or external detritus (spall, rock falls, talus, soil wash, alluvium)	Generally poor	Excellent low-energy medium, suitable for repeated use by people and/or animals, with incremental sedimentation and limited later erosion; alkaline
Seacoast	Wave and current erosion at, above, and below mean sea level, often aided by tides; local eolian erosion; other sediments introduced from river catchments	Hydrodynamic processes of highly variable energy, both wave- and non-wave-generated (latter including lagoonal, marsh, estuarine, and eolian agencies)	Thin to massive beds, often with complex facies interdigitation, ranging from clays to cobble gravels, with some precipitates in backshore sediment traps	Generally good at and below watermark, variable above	Includes excellent microenvironments for short- or long-term human use, but wave reworking introduces a problem, and sea-level fluctuations may drown countless sites; salt not favorable for bone and plant preservation
Lakeshore & marsh	Local wave erosion; most sediment introduced from river catchments	Fluvial introduction of suspended and solute loads; some coastal transfer by waves and currents	Thin to massive beds, ranging from clayey to sandy, with some chemical precipitates and abundant organic components	Poor to good	Provides some excellent settlement or exploitation settings, with low-energy sedimentation favoring burial; acid marsh/peat excellent for organic preservation

	Erosion	Transfer	Deposits	Preservation	Comments
Delta fringe	Little local erosion, with sediment carried in from watershed	Hydrodynamic mobilization of suspended and solute sediment; some coastal subaquatic transfer by wave propagation and currents	Characteristically extensive, massive beds, dominantly clayey/silty, with some sands and precipitates	Mainly moderate to good	Despite favorable sedimentary environments, settlements very localized on distributary banks or shorelines; include prominent middens
Flood plain	Channel cutting; surface denudation; localized but pervasive small-scale scour	Hydrodynamic mobilization of suspended and bed-load sediments at variable energy thresholds	Complex vertical and lateral facies sequences, commonly lenticular, partly cross-bedded, ranging from clays to cobble gravels	Moderate to good	Suitability for settlement or exploitation varies according to season and microenvironment; preservation of intact sites threatened by periodic erosion and repeated geomorphic instability
Eolian	General deflation favors pavements, localized scour of yardangs, excavation of blowouts	Aerodynamic mobilization of suspended and bed-load materials	Well-stratified, partly cross-bedded sands in dunes and sandfields; massive, partly laminated, loess in mantles of suspended silt-sized particles	Usually excellent	Primary swales or erosional hollows can provide foci for exploitation if water tables rise or rainfall increases, sometimes forming ponds, lakes, or marshes, in part spring-fed; deflation telescopes sites; soil dynamics expel objects
Slope	Slow or rapid stripping of upland, crest slope, or midslope (soil or rock waste)	Complex range of dry, plastic, and hydrodynamic transfers, often in combination with frost	Thin to massive bedding, poorly stratified, with mixed facies common; sometimes contorted or festooned; loamy to rubbly textures	Generally poor	Sedimentation in swales or on footslopes may preserve parts of surface sites, but secondary palimpsests are more common, due to multiple reworking; cryoturbation may mix levels
Volcanic	Mainly endogenic, partly explosive sediment derivation	Aerodynamic, in part viscous, transfer (lava, lahars), commonly reworked by streams and lakes	Massive extensive beds, including both uniform and mixed-caliber pyroclastics in fine silt to boulder or bomb grade	Moderate to excellent, improving with distance from source	Free-fall fine-grade pyroclastics are excellent for direct or secondary site burial and preservation

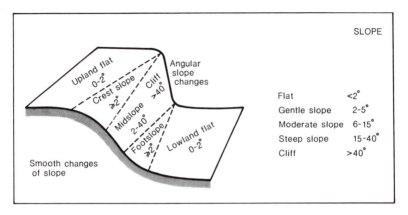

Figure 4-10. Slope forms and classes.

Topographic matrix

Many relatively intensive prehistorical activities are carried out beyond the site microenvironment. Food, fuel, and other materials are derived from a sustaining area: a coast and its adjacent coastal plain; a floodplain and its surrounding low hills; a series of springs and small streams below a mountainside; a series of blowouts and widely spaced valley bottoms, within an undulating sand field; a cluster of lakes dispersed across an old, rolling glacial plain; a range of habitats horizontally and vertically arranged between the floor of a rift valley and its surrounding high volcanoes and fault escarpments.

This medium-scale environment is of immediate importance to both foragers and farmers, because the slope, relief, and forms of the topographic matrix or terrain determine the detailed patterns of soil and biotic distributions. For an introduction to medium-scale landscape analysis, see the manual of Marsh (1978).

Terrain can readily be classified as illustrated in Figures 4-10 to 4-12: (a) Slope refers to inclination and can arbitrarily be labeled from gentle to steep. Some useful slope classes and their positions with respect to the typical elements of a hillside are shown in Figure 4-10. (b) Relief refers to the maximum difference in elevations in a defined area. Relief can be combined with average slope to describe distinctive relief types (Figure 4-11): plains, tablelands, hills, and mountains. (c) Forms are usefully described according to valley cross section as rectilinear, convex, concave, or concavo-convex (Figure 4-12). Such valley forms often are associated with distinctive landscapes: rectilinear valleys with arid

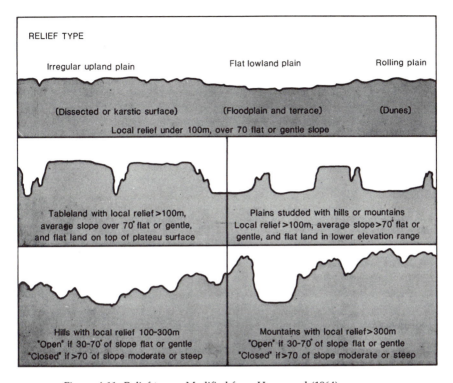

RELIEF TYPE

Irregular upland plain   Flat lowland plain   Rolling plain

(Dissected or karstic surface)   (Floodplain and terrace)   (Dunes)

Local relief under 100m, over 70 flat or gentle slope

Tableland with local relief >100m, average slope over 70° flat or gentle, and flat land on top of plateau surface

Plains studded with hills or mountains Local relief >100m, average slope >70° flat or gentle, and flat land in lower elevation range

Hills with local relief 100-300m "Open" if 30-70° of slope flat or gentle "Closed" if >70 of slope moderate or steep

Mountains with local relief >300m "Open" if 30-70° of slope flat or gentle "Closed" if >70 of slope moderate or steep

Figure 4-11. Relief types. Modified from Hammond (1964).

lands; concave valleys with prior glaciation; concavo-convex valleys with erosional topography in humid high and middle latitudes; wide convex valleys with some humid tropical plains (Butzer, 1976a: Chapters 17–20).

These concepts of slope, relief type, and valley form can be rapidly applied to yield precise morphometric description of a topographic matrix, marking a first step in the mapping of site context. They permit the field observer or map reader to perceive the variability of space. Finally, by contributing to the definition of a spatial framework for a site or a site network, the terrain parameters aid in the reconstruction of prehistorical soil and biotic landscapes. These interrelationships can now be explicated.

Terrain, soils, and biota

The topographic matrix is much more than a topological framework into which the site is placed. It is, instead, critical in determining con-

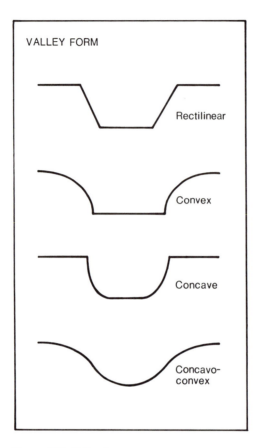

Figure 4-12. Valley forms.

figurations of different substrates, groundwater level, soil drainage and flood hazards, shade versus sunny slopes, surface runoff versus subsurface percolation, potential energy, and localization of deep and shallow soil profiles.

For soil landscapes, terrain is important because it influences the natural moisture regime and the balance of soil formation and erosion. Steep and sunny slopes not only are free-draining but also tend to be dry, whereas depressions and extensive flat surfaces are wet, even in uplands, and shade slopes are on the damp side. Consequently, it is possible to distinguish several moisture regimes: Automorphic soils are free-draining; planomorphic soils are seasonally wet, mainly on upland flats; hydromorphic soils are permanently wet on lowland flats; xeromorphic soils are excessively dry on steep sun slopes; ombromorphic

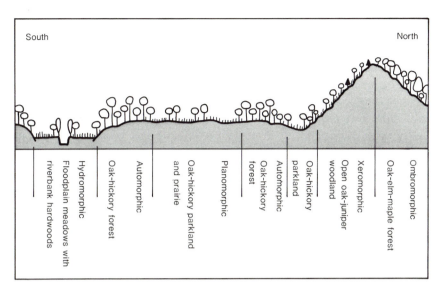

Figure 4-13. Relationships between soil moisture regimes and vegetation patterning in Illinois. Floodplain patterns are simplified.

soils on lower shade slopes are free-draining but damp (Bunting, 1965:Chapter 6). As in the case of the soil-erosion balance (see Figure 2-2), the specific parameters for moisture regimes vary according to substrate and climatic environment. The role of topography in creating complex soil landscapes has been developed from several perspectives by Hugget (1975) and Hole (1978b).

The details of the soil mosaic both reflect and contribute to the edaphic controls of the vegetation cover. In effect, substrate, slope, relief, and soils determine the medium-scale patterns of vegetation in any one area.

This interplay can be illustrated using the forest-grassland mosaic of central Illinois in the vicinity of the Koster site. For background data, see the work of Zawacki and Hausfater, (1969) and Butzer (1977a:39–41). Level upland plains of loess and glacial deposits are dominated by prairie (bluestem sodgrass), with oak-hickory woodlands on the rises of the rolling glacial topography and along the margins of stream valleys, and irregular terrain in general. Grassland was prominent throughout Holocene time (King, 1981) and commonly is ascribed to climate (particularly midsummer droughts) or periodic burning (Indian fires or natural fires) or both. In fact, traditional prairie tracts frequently coincided with seasonally wet (spring and late summer) planomorphic soils, and forest was well established on the free-draining upland margins. The upland forest-grassland mosaic consequently reflects a combination of climate, burning, and soil moisture regime. On intermediate to steep slopes, regardless of substrate, broken xeromorphic woodlands of oak, hickory, and juniper are found interspersed with grassy patches on southwestern exposures, whereas ombromorphic forests of oak, elm, and maple are typical of shade slopes facing east or north. Lastly, the floodplains exhibit a different mosaic: riverbank forest of willow, poplar, and oak; grass and sedge along periodically inundated basin floors; a variable woodland with oak, pecan, and elm on intermediate ground; grass on higher gravelly terraces and loamy valleyside fans. Oak-grass parkland once fingered up the drier margins of the tributary valleys. The resulting patterns are shown schematically for a composite landscape in Figure 4-13; with some variations in detail, they express soil-vegetation relationships throughout much of the upper Midwest.

A similar strategy of interrelationships can be inferred in the savanna mosaics of Africa. Here the level plains tend to grassland, with scattered trees or patches of bush, in response to a long season of low-sun drought, an excess of rainy-season soil water, and periodic burning. Slight rises or veneers of coarse-textured sediment support open tree stands, and some form of bush or woodland is the rule on all hillsides that have even a thin soil mantle. Woodland follows stream banks and, on large floodplains, interfingers with thickets and seasonally flooded grassland. African and Illinoian soils are, of course, different, but there are striking morphological parallels in profile development.

These examples serve to argue that soils and biota that appear homogeneous over wide areas on general maps are, in fact, complex in their detailed patterning, even in areas with identical lithology. By defining the diversity of soil moisture regimes, terrain is the primary variable in edaphic patterning and consequently provides an operational model for potential soil and biotic distributions. In most field situations, the soil record of a particular period can be reconstructed from surface, relict, buried, or redeposited soil vestiges. Because any paleobotanical record generally is limited to one or two sites or profiles, it can provide no more than a general impression of local vegetation diversity. It is therefore the reconstructed terrain and soil map that provides the best clue to predicting these local biotic details.

In sum, medium-scale integration of earth-science data is fundamental to definition of the regional environmental mosaic. This, in turn, is fundamental not only for evaluating site selection and spatial subsistence patterning (Butzer, 1977*b*) but also for purposes of archaeological survey (Chapter 14).

Regional matrix

The site macroenvironment is the biome or ecotone of which the medium-scale mosaic is a part. These are the great landscapes that represent the broadest units of study, whether for definition of the regional resource matrix or for definition of the general ecosystem. This regional matrix comprises biotic configurations as well as the assemblage of physical features and processes that, altogether, describe the several interfaces between atmosphere and lithosphere. The geo-archaeologist is initially interested in the physical components – the landforms and soils and the processes that form and modify them. Corresponding to the biomes, the physical landscape assemblages form *morphogenetic regions*, as outlined in Table 4-2. Useful comparative maps of physiognomic vegetation by A.W. Kuchler can be found in *Goode's World Atlas* (Espenshade, 1975), and excellent faunal data are available in the *Atlas of World Wildlife* (Bramwell, 1973). Biota are discussed more explicitly in Chapters 10 and 11.

Environmental shifts

The preceding discussions of sedimentary, topographic, and regional matrices were based on the assumption that research was focused on conditions contemporary with a particular phase or span of human occupance. It should be borne in mind that the environmental and endogenic changes of the last 2 million years have significantly modified the details of topographic patterns, soil distribution, and dominant geomorphic processes. At the scale of several tens of thousands of years, topographic changes have involved primarily elevations and drainage; going back hundreds of thousands of years, things have been more radically transformed, with former upland plains perhaps reduced to residual hills, with local relief perhaps doubled or trebled.

Changes at higher latitudes have been particularly far-reaching in the wake of glacial-interglacial alternations. Glacial and periglacial environments were substantially different from those effective today. Glaciers ground to a halt abreast of gigantic melt-water spillways and across from loessic plains, and frost-assisted gravity movements remodeled

Table 4-2. *Morphogenetic regions and related biomes*

Morphogenetic region[a]	Related biome[b]
Glacial	No biota on ice sheets and large ice caps
Periglacial: active soil-frost environments with vigorous slope and fluvial processes; eolian activity commonplace on drier upland plains, and widespread waterlogged soils on lowland plains; active rubble production and slope instability in montane zones	*Tundra, forest-tundra mosaics, and alpine meadows:* low productivity, with limited seasonal human plant foods; limited number of dominant large gregarious herbivores, providing moderate to high animal biomass
Humid-temperate: effective but mainly subdued slope and fluvial processes, favoring stable soils; extensive waterlogging of flat plains in winter-cold regions sculptured by Pleistocene glaciation	*Deciduous, coniferous, and mixed forests with cold-season dormancy:* moderate productivity and moderate seasonal availability of human plant foods; many dominant and subdominant herbivorous species, mainly solitary or in small groups; moderate animal biomass in open woodlands, and low biomass in closed forest, where smaller mammals are most prominent
Semiarid/subhumid temperate: effective fluvial processes, with moderately stable soils and subordinate eolian activity; Pleistocene loess mantles widespread	*Grassland, with cold-season dormancy:* moderate productivity and seasonal availability of plant foods; large gregarious herbivores of several species, providing high biomass
Arid: sporadic fluvial processes; slow slope change, with minimal soils; prominent eolian activity or inherited forms	*Desert and shrub/grass subdesert:* low to very low productivity; few plant foods; low biomass of solitary small mammals
Semiarid/subhumid-tropical: effective fluvial processes, with moderately stable soils; seasonally wet, flat plains	*Savanna parkland and scrub, with dry-season dormancy:* moderate to high productivity, with seasonal or perennial plant foods; many species of large gregarious herbivores, providing high biomass
Humid-tropical: effective but relatively subdued fluvial processes, but vigorous with heavy monsoon rainfall; mainly deep soils, with considerable slope dynamism	*Rainforest and mixed deciduous/evergreen woodland:* high to very high productivity, with abundant and perennial human plant foods; moderate biomass of large gregarious herbivores in broken environments, but low biomass of solitary and mainly smaller mammals in closed forest

[a]Butzer (1976a). [b]Odum (1971).

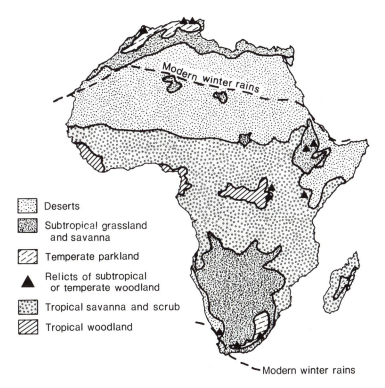

Figure 4-14. Probable African vegetation ca. 18,000–15,000 B.P. Note that the tropical rainforest has almost been eliminated, with expansion of the Sahara toward the equator and extensive nontropical semiarid environments in northwest and south-central Africa. Reconstruction based partly on pollen and biogeographical data (e.g., enclaves of plants and nonmigratory birds on isolated mountains), but primary evidence continues to be provided by well-dated sedimentary sequences of a qualitative nature.

slopes everywhere. The paleoenvironmental patterns of the last glacial in the Midwest and on the northern European plain are, in fact, jarringly unfamiliar (Butzer, 1971a:Chapters 18 and 21; 1976a:Sections 10-9, 18-6, and 18-7 and Chapter 17).

At lower latitudes, shifts in vegetation belts were substantial, as apparent from the last glacial reconstruction for Africa 18,000 B.P. (Figure 4-14). Yet morphogenetic shifts were far less revolutionary than those at higher latitudes, generally involving little more than quantitative adjustments in the seasonal regime of modern process assemblages. Only locally was the rank order of the dominant medium-size processes changed (e.g., from soil formation to slope erosion to swamp development to soil, or from soil formation to stream alluviation to dune accumulation to soil development). The basic reason that major biome shifts at lower latitudes are difficult to detect in the sediment record is that geomorphic changes involved little more than the rates and relative importance of agents still in operation today. This implies changes in degree rather than in kind.

These examples of the variable impacts of Pleistocene environmental shifts are sufficiently obvious to require little further comment. However, similar but more subtle changes also characterized Holocene times, a point seldom fully appreciated. Paleoenvironmental evaluations are, in fact, more difficult and problematic than is implied in much of the literature. Like the study of sedimentary and topographic matrices, regional landscape context requires the expertise of a specialist. All too often the assumption of a landscape context that is stable and comparable to that of today is based on faulty diagnosis. The repercussions for high-level archaeological interpretation frequently are serious.

CHAPTER 5

Geo-archaeology III: stratigraphic context

Stratigraphic nomenclature

Stratigraphy involves the study of geological or archaeological levels, their internal sequences of superpositioning, and external correlation of the units of one profile with those of another (Harris, 1979). Geological and paleontological usage recognizes five main types of stratigraphic procedures: (a) lithological comparison of rock sequences, (b) correlation of equivalent fossil horizons, (c) correlation of strata with similar paleomagnetic patterns, (d) linkage by absolute dating of profiles, and (e) matching with an established, preferably dated, external paleoclimatic sequence. Each of these procedures uses different units to designate vertical components for rock, faunal, paleomagnetic time, and environmental sequences and, whenever appropriate, to provide hierarchical terms for further internal subdivisions (Bishop and Clark, 1967:397–407; Hedberg, 1976; Salvador and Opdyke, 1979):

lithostratigraphy	(bed, member, formation, group)
biostratigraphy	(zone)
magnetostratigraphy	(zone)
chronostratigraphy	(substage, stage, series)
climatostratigraphy	(e.g., stadial/interstadial, glacial/interglacial)

In practice, the various hierarchical terms are applied differently in various countries, and unless a uniform procedure happens to be enforced by key journals or national committees on nomenclature, usage may even vary from one individual to another.

A rock stratigraphic unit must be clearly defined and must be mappable. Formal nomenclature should be applied only when (a) a suitable type site, providing good internal resolution and boundary contacts, is properly described with pertinent laboratory data and (b) a measure of basic mapping has been carried out. Unless and until these criteria are met, informal names, such as beds (uncapitalized), should continue to be used. Names should be judiciously selected from local toponyms, with preference given to cultural features as opposed to physical features. Stratigraphic terms should not be taken from personal names, a sporadic practice in contradiction of the rules.

The basic lithostratigraphic unit is chosen for convenient field mapping and should not require laboratory data for field resolution. This is the Formation (always capitalized). Subdivisions that are regionally persistent and practicable, but that commonly require laboratory tests for secure identification (e.g., textural data, clay mineralogy, heavy minerals), or that are too complex for mapping at an intermediate scale (e.g., 1:50,000 to 1:250,000), are best designated as Members. The presence of striking marker horizons of locally persistent facies may warrant further identification of formal Beds (capitalized). At the other end of the scale, larger aggregates of several formations that represent convenient landscape units, or logical large-scale sedimentary packages, may be designated as Groups.

Biostratigraphic terminology is less complex, with formal Zones commonly defined by one or more characteristic genera or species, or by means of particular assemblages. The faunal "span" has been used as an informal counterpart to Zone. For further discussion of paleontological dating, see Chapter 11.

Formal magnetostratigraphic criteria have only recently been added to the more traditional modes of stratigraphic classification. Long- and short-term reversals of earth polarity are documented in the paleomagnetic traces of many long sediment cores (see Chapter 9). They provide distinctive temporal patterns that may allow global correlation of diverse lithostratigraphic sequences, according to paleomagnetic Zones defined by normal or reversed polarity. Once the related paleomagnetic markers have been reliably dated by use of potassium-argon, they can serve as an independent time guide or chronozone, particularly applicable to fifth- and sixth-order climatic changes (see Table 2-2).

Chronostratigraphic units are calibrated by the use of radiocarbon, potassium-argon, and other "absolute" dating methods (see Chapter 9) and commonly are applied to the relative time spans represented by rock, biostratigraphic, and magnetostratigraphic units. This approach tends to be controversial in formal (as opposed to informal) application. In the United States, the Stage level is applied to time units equivalent to individual glacials or interglacials (i.e., fifth-order units) (see Table 2-2). Substages, correspondingly, pertain to stadials or interstadials (i.e., fourth-order units), and Series pertain to sixth-order units.

Climatostratigraphic models underlie most stratigraphic work dealing with the Pleistocene. Formal names such as Wisconsinan Glaciation can be used in some areas where glacial-interglacial stages have been reasonably well resolved as part of glacial, loess, or deep-sea stratigraphies. More generally, however, there is sufficient uncertainty, if not persistent error, be it in the use of pre-Illinoian nomenclature in the United States, pre-Würmian terms in Europe, or the now fully discredited "pluvial sequence" of Africa (Butzer and Isaac, 1975). On the other hand, informal climatostratigraphic notions, as well as correlations to middle latitude continental sequences or marine isotopic zones, remain indispensable as working procedures.

Lithostratigraphy: site and setting

The microstratigraphy (i.e., the detailed archaeosedimentary column) of a particular site is a temporal record of events, such as erosion, sedimentation, and soil formation. Some of these events may have affected no more than a part of the site, others much of the local topographic matrix, and some the entire region. The degree to which such events are strictly local or cultural or both can normally be determined only by establishing additional lithostratigraphic sections adjacent to but outside of the site. Temporally overlapping columns of this sort can filter out excessive detail of what may be no more than stochastic cultural processes within a single occupation phase. The screened record may then provide a broader spatiotemporal framework for climatic oscillations or cultural impacts on the landscape (Figure 5-1).

Frequently a site-specific microstratigraphic column, or one developed from adjacent artificial cuts or natural exposures, can serve as the type site for a formal lithostratigraphic unit that is relevant to the sequence of occupation. Mapping of such a formation may, for example, have value for both landscape reconstruction and archaeological survey.

A site-specific lithostratigraphy can therefore be screened to isolate the sequence of real environmental changes, which can then be matched with dated regional or even global climatostratigraphic models to provide relative dating. It may also be amenable to direct chronometric dating. Beyond the effective 40,000-year dating range of radiocarbon, biostratigraphic or magnetostratigraphic calibration may be

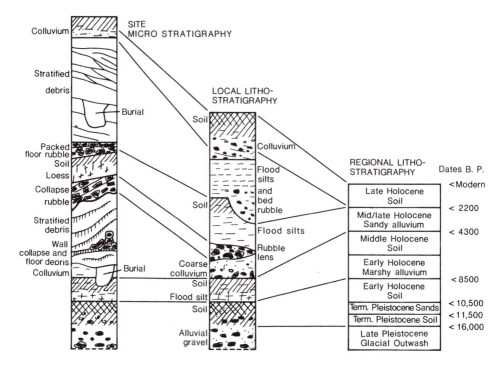

Figure 5-1. Site-specific, local, and regional stratigraphies illustrated by a hypothetical Bronze Age village site in south-central Europe.

useful, particularly because relatively little detail is preserved in the long time intervals represented by older sedimentary units. By interpolation or extrapolation, dating can allow approximate temporal calibration of the occupation sequence. Or, if sufficient dates are available, differential sedimentation rates can be estimated. This not only will help clarify the nature of environmental processes but also may permit time estimates for landscape events or cycles with a resolution level of millennia, centuries, or even decades. With such a degree of data control it also becomes feasible to examine the question whether these events indicate the normal oscillations of a dynamic equilibrium, whether they reflect unusual perturbations, followed by recovery, or whether they represent thresholds crossed to new equilibrium levels. In any event, microstratigraphic interpretation can help determine what types of events dominate the preserved sediment column: single events (e.g., a catastrophic flood), recurrent high-magnitude events over a few decades, or gradual processes and changes.

Whether or not all these goals can, in fact, be realized, sensitive interpretation of the local lithostratigraphy allows much more than relative dating. It provides a contextual appreciation, however imprecise, of the wavelengths and amplitudes of environmental variability and of the relative roles of frequent low-magnitude oscillations versus the less common high-magnitude events. Such a "sense" for the dynamics of the local ecosystem is invaluable for good geo-archaeological work. It provides the experience necessary to evaluate the archaeosedimentology of the immediate site and, beyond that, to assess the impact of cultural activities on the surrounding landscape.

External correlations

Stratigraphy is not the primary objective of geo-archaeology, but it is a fundamental part of the empirical infrastructure that geo-archaeologists must have at their disposal. As explained earlier, construction of detailed, site-specific, and local stratigraphies is the essential first step in establishing stratigraphic context. When good radiometric controls are available, such as a large suite of reasonably consistent radiocarbon dates, external stratigraphic links and correlations may appear to be unimportant. Such self-sufficiency is seldom possible, however, except during the last 5,000 years or so, and even there an exploration of external frameworks is generally profitable.

External cross-referencing serves four main purposes:

1. A chronometric aid. When local radiometric or other absolute dates are few or inconsistent, and particularly when none are available, external correlations are indispensable for chronometric calibration. This is generally the case beyond 20 or 30 millennia, when radiocarbon dating becomes problematical. Various lithostratigraphic, biostratigraphic, and climatostratigraphic techniques to be discussed later may be appropriate.

2. An aid in paleoenvironmental interpretation. Oscillations or changes in hydrological and sedimentation patterns, vegetation, faunal composition, and so forth that are locally documented can rarely be evaluated in isolation. This should not be read as a call for unfettered speculation on a continental or hemispheric scale, but as a call for cautious examination of those external records that are reasonably interlinked, either within a single morphogenetic region or biome or by virtue of direct systemic interplay.

3. A cross-check on the several types of information available. Different categories of contextual data, such as a local lithostratigraphy, can

profit from internal and external comparisons. Many apparent inconsistencies prove to be the results of faulty assumptions, single-hypothesis explanations, or sheer error. Cross-checks can help isolate such potential problems and draw attention to alternative explanations.

4. A test of the temporal validity of archaeological horizons. Geo-archaeological and bio-archaeological precisions or radiometric dating frequently imply that particular cultural features or processes are not contemporaneous, either within a region or between different regions. This may reflect dating errors, a spatially consistent time lag, or more complex temporal differentials. Recognition and objective exploration of such disjunctions are vital to prehistorical research.

Altogether, it can be argued that external correlation is a logical second step in the study of stratigraphic context. But this second step is warranted only when the local stratigraphic ensemble has been carefully constructed and analyzed. Many archaeologists indulge in external comparisons before the proper groundwork has been laid. Equally undesirable, however, is the mole's view of a site as a closed system.

The problems and potentials of external correlation differ substantially for Holocene and Pleistocene time ranges. During the last 10,000 years, climatic fluctuations have been relatively subdued in most humid environments. Here pollen records show few sharp breaks and little obvious relation to glacier fluctuations at high elevations or at high latitudes (Hafsten, 1977), whereas Holocene geomorphic cycles are by no means synchronous (Butzer, 1980a). In semiarid settings, variations have been more dramatic, as shown by fluctuations in lake volumes and levels (Butzer, 1980b) and by tree-ring-documented changes in growing-season climate (Fritts, 1976). It is common to find tangible local changes in one or another environmental subsystem, although external yardsticks are inconsistent or ambiguous. For example, Grove (1979) has convincingly shown that Holocene glacier behavior was not truly synchronous on a continental scale, let alone a worldwide scale. As a result, intraregional comparisons of different categories of information tend to be more productive than extraregional exploration. Much the same can be said for chronometric dating. Greater temporal precision (centuries or even decades) is required than for Pleistocene events, so that only detailed chronostratigraphies, and in reasonable proximity, are of specific interest.

For Pleistocene time spans, both coarser temporal units (measured in millennia or exponentials thereof) and incisive landscape changes favor different yardsticks in external correlation.

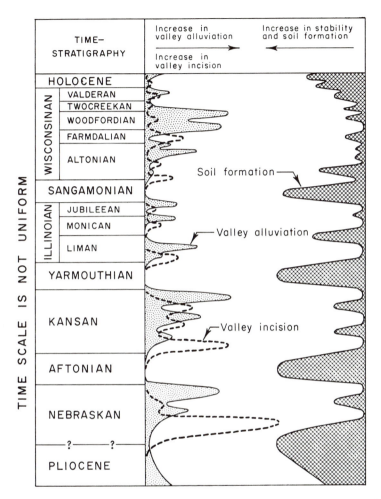

Figure 5-2. A generalized time stratigraphy for the central United States based on glacial lithostratigraphies. Time is semilogarithmic, with detail also increasing upward. From Frye (1973:Figure 2) (copyright University of Washington, with permission).

Ideally, external correlation in Pleistocene time ranges involves a combination of lithostratigraphic, biostratigraphic, and chronostratigraphic methods. Biostratigraphic zonation (see Chapter 11) includes (a) the temporal spans of single organisms or assemblages of several species or genera and (b) repetitive alternations of distinct assemblages through a vertical profile. Both approaches incorporate assumptions and sources of error. Chronostratigraphic methods include both "abso-

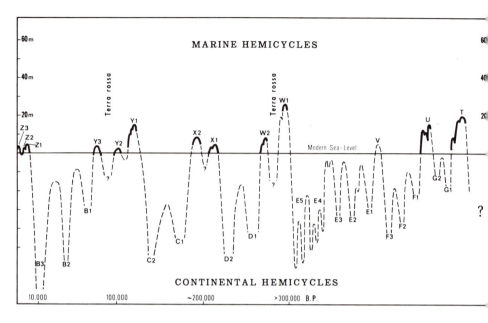

Figure 5-3. Relative sea-level fluctuations recorded by beaches, coastal sands, and soils on the coast of Mallorca, Spain. The record prior to about 300,000 B.P. is incomplete and chronologically distorted. Low sea levels reflect high-latitude glacial advances, but the overall downward trend of interglacial sea levels is influenced by gradual uplift of the island.

lute" dates and dated reference schemes, such as geomagnetic patterns (reversals, events, and defined secular variations, see Chapter 9), all subject to possible errors of judgment or empirical detail. Even so, an investigation of a particular Pleistocene site and its setting will, as often as not, need to rely primarily or exclusively on lithostratigraphic correlation. Two basic approaches are available.

Middle-latitude site stratigraphies can commonly be tied in directly to well-defined regional lithostratigraphies, such as sequences of glacial and interglacial beds, sequences of high-energy (periglacial) and low-energy (temperate) deposits, and sequences of loess units and soils (Figure 5-2). Biostratigraphic sequences of alternating forest and steppe floras or faunas may also be available. In coastal regions, a suite of appropriate beaches, coastal dunes, soils, or erosional forms may also serve to record sea-level fluctuations that responded primarily to worldwide changes in the ratio of glacier ice to ocean water (Figure 5-3). Stratigraphic frameworks of these kinds have been illustrated elsewhere (Butzer and Isaac, 1975). In each case the principle is direct

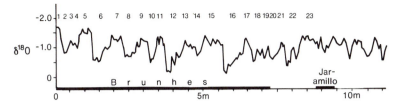

Figure 5-4. Oxygen isotope zonation of deep-sea core V28-239 from the equatorial Pacific Ocean. The column is calibrated by depth and in paleomagnetic stages with the Brunhes-Matuyama geomagnetic reversal dated 730,000 B.P. by potassium-argon dating. The units marked 1 to 23 designate warm and cold horizons (odd and even numbers, respectively). The curve reflects surface-water salinities and densities, related to high-latitude glaciation, as well as local temperatures. Small deviations from the $\delta^{18}O$ standard record glacials, and large deviations, interglacials. Modified from Shackleton and Opdyke (1976: Figure 2).

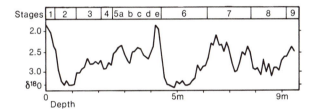

Figure 5-5. Detailed isotope zonation of stages 1 to 9 in deep-sea core RC11-120 from the southern Indian Ocean. Stage 5 represents the last interglacial with its three warm peaks (5a, 5c, 5e), and stages 2 to 4 represent the last glacial (see also Figure 2-5). The stage 5/6 boundary is elsewhere dated about 125,000 to 130,000 B.P. by interpolation from the Brunhes-Matuyama reversal, as well as by direct radiometric dating. This curve records a little more than 300,000 years. From Hays et al. (1976).

regional linkage (e.g., corrosion or cutting of a cave by a specific sea level or during a weathering interval, and intrusion of sand or gravel into that cave by an advancing dune or an aggrading stream).

Extraregional correlation is generally more difficult, because climato-stratigraphic assumptions are involved. Pleistocene moisture trends were not universal and cannot be used (Butzer, Stuckenrath, et al. 1978). Major Pleistocene temperature trends were indeed global, and they are reflected in the microfaunal and oxygen isotope zonation of deep-sea cores (Figures 5-4 and 5-5) (Ruddiman and McIntyre, 1976; Shackleton and Opdyke, 1976; Berggren, 1980) in the oxygen isotope record of long ice cores (Johnsen et al., 1972) (see Figure 2-13) and cave travertines (Harmon et al., 1978), in long pollen sequences (Van der

Hammen et al., 1971; Woillard, 1978), and in complex loess, soil, and molluscan suites (Kukla, 1975). Given sufficient detail, a local lithostratigraphy with partial radiometric control may replicate part of this global record of Pleistocene thermal oscillations (Butzer, Beaumont, and Vogel, 1978). Even better is the situation in which a site stratigraphy can be both directly and indirectly linked to a global climatostratigraphy, as, for example, in a coastal cave, where beach and dune sands can document sea-level fluctuations, and beach mollusca may record the oxygen isotope deviation of ocean waters (Butzer, 1978c). Nonetheless, correlations are no more than working hypotheses, because each individual approach has its own assumptions and sources of error, and all correlations are themselves inherently subjective.

In overview, external correlation is a standard procedure for the study of stratigraphic context, once a detailed local stratigraphy has been established. Such correlations vary according to the kinds of opportunities available in a particular setting and time range. The distinction between intraregional correlation and interregional correlation is important, as is the difference between direct linkage and inferred matching. External correlations are useful, if not invaluable, as chronometric aids, as a framework for paleoenvironmental interpretation, and for internal and external cross-checking. They are best attempted with convergent lithostratigraphic, biostratigraphic, and chronostratigraphic controls. But even in the ideal case they are explicitly part of the normal specific procedure of hypothesis formulation and testing. Consequently, they are neither firm nor immutable, and they are not intended to be so.

CHAPTER 6

Geo-archaeology IV: site formation

Archaeological sediments

The sedimentary record of an archaeological site provides critical environmental and stratigraphic information. Less well appreciated is that sediments are also of assistance in interpreting settlement patterns and subsistence activities. The reason is that archaeological sediments typically include a mix of physical, biogenic, and cultural components:

1. Physiogenic components reflect the fundamental physical processes modal to the site, with or without the activity of humans or animals. They result from erosion, transfer, and deposition normal to the general site locale or to specific microdepositional environments within the site. Eolian dust, water-laid silt and sand, slope movements, and cave spall and flowstone can be cited as examples.

2. Biogenic components result mainly from the activity of animals visiting or resident in a site, such as domesticated stock, household animals, rodents, earthworms, snails, and insects in a village-mound settlement, or wasps, owls, bats, porcupines, hyenas, felids, and bears in a cave. The cave denizens introduce a range of external material to the cavern, and the mound dwellers may introduce matter or may mix and process organic-mineral sediment. Biogenic activity in caves is most important during breaks in occupation or after site abandonment. In village mounds, biogenic input is reduced after abandonment, but the various subsurface organisms then aid decomposition of surface rubble, favoring biochemical soil formation.

3. Anthropogenic components include (a) various mineral and biological materials, deliberately or incidentally brought to the site, (b) residuals and features derived from alteration of human imports or from human activity, and (c) mineral sediments due to human acceleration of normal geomorphic processes (e.g., roof-spall production by repeated fires in a shallow cave) or interference in the normal geomor-

phic system (e.g., soil instability reflected in slope erosion and stream alluviation around and downstream of a village settlement).

The underlying principle of archaeosedimentology is that people and animals are geomorphic agents that produce a specific range of archaeological sediments that require special attention and interpretation. The different forms of genesis of archaeological sediments facilitate subdivision into the three categories of primary, secondary, and tertiary forms:

1. Primary materials are introduced to the site by people, either in their original forms or as finished products. Included here are artifacts, ornaments, raw materials for manufacture or building, fuel, and a wide range of foodstuffs. On a smaller scale, dirt is also accidentally brought in on the feet, on clothing, and on other objects. Animals further introduce materials (e.g., porcupines bring bones, and large carnivores drag their prey into caves).

2. Secondary materials are the alteration products deriving from on-site processing or biochemical decomposition. At a Paleolithic habitation site, such secondary materials potentially could include the following: broken and worked animal bones and shells; the remnants of fibers, charcoal, and charred organic matter; mineral ash; human feces and urinary phosphates; structural remains, such as post-molds, pits, and laid stones; lithic debitage and manufactured stone artifacts; ornamental and ritual objects, such as shell necklaces, body ochre, and parietal and mobile art. The residues of a Neolithic village probably would include a range of additional items such as potsherds; a greater variety and mass of food by-products and animal dung, and masses of structural debris, such as rough or cut rock, kiln-fired brick and mud-brick, adobe, wood, and fiber. Deliberate human burials and accidental animal burials also belong in this secondary category. Animals contribute actively to these alteration products, not only in the animal pens of the Neolithic village but also in the Paleolithic cave: owl "pellets" with intact rodent bone, bat guano rich in nitrates, hyena feces heavy with calcium and phosphates, and bear dung with abundant nitrate, phosphate, calcium, and potassium. Another form of animal contribution results from subsurface mixing or ingestion by burrowing rodents and soil organisms, such as earthworms, eventually aiding postdepositional soil formation on a settlement site.

3. Tertiary materials include the primary and secondary debris that is removed, transported, and deposited through human and other physical agencies in the form of secondary trash heaps, structural fills, and water-laid beds. Much of the material in and around a long-

term-occupation site is not in the context in which it was discarded or abandoned. In a demographically expansive village, primary refuse next to a habitation area will eventually need to be artificially leveled or removed, and collapsed houses will be at least partly cleared away prior to rebuilding. Settlement mounds consist largely of secondary refuse and rubble that have been carried or pushed to the periphery of the site or used to fill out new foundations, artificial terraces, or voids in walls. Such debris is the mechanical equivalent of archaeological "backdirt." Further reworking of such rubble will result from rainwash, aided along the site periphery by gravity movements (see Chapter 7). Even some Paleolithic caves display veneers or cones of tertiary refuse outside their entrances, reflecting housekeeping efforts long before archaeological excavation. The distinction between secondary and tertiary archaeosediments may be difficult to make in some field situations, but the difference is important to both the excavator and the geo-archaeologist.

Evidently the cultural component varies dramatically between an ephemeral Paleolithic camp and a long-term settlement mound. The processes and components can best be outlined by using two hypothetical examples, a Paleolithic cave site and a Neolithic village mound.

A Pleistocene prototype: cave sediments

Standard geo-archaeological procedure in cave analysis has long been to regard the sediments as physical rather than cultural residues. Authoritative studies such as those of Farrand (1975a, 1975b), Laville et al. (1976, 1980), and Le Tensorer (1977) continue to underplay the prominent roles of anthropogenic and biogenic agencies. A first step in rectifying this imbalance has been taken by Butzer (1978f, 1981c) and Goldberg (1979a), who have discussed these problems. The following presentation is based on my experiences with sediments from suites of Spanish and South African caves; the results of some of these studies are still being prepared for publication.

The various cultural components of cave sediments can be enumerated as follows:

1. *Lithic debris.* Appreciable amounts of primary rock were brought into caves by Paleolithic occupants in the form of slabs, pebbles, and natural or artificial fragments, sometimes from an adjacent cliff base, sometimes from alluvial gravels a few hundred meters away, sometimes from special quarry sources many kilometers distant. Inside the cave, such rocks were converted into artifacts, debitage, and fine chip-

ping debris or were otherwise used as hammerstones or anvils. In some cave levels, the sum total of artifactual rock may account for all sediment coarser than 2 mm and much or most of that in the size range from 200 to 2,000 microns. For a discussion of microdebitage, see the work of Fladmark (1982). For example, in the limestone cave of El Pendo, Cantabria, all of the chert and quartzite and most of the ochre, feldspar crystals, and micas were introduced, and plagioclase and micas in the 50- to 100-micron range derive from decomposition of diabase debitage (Butzer, 1980c). In Nelson Bay cave in South Africa, the majority of the artifacts were made from the same quartzite as the roof spall, posing serious problems in distinguishing debitage from frost splices (Butzer, 1973b). Although such artifactual components must be filtered out of statistics aimed at elucidating background environmental data, published statistics on sand and grit components of cave sediments have generally ignored such possible problems. Furthermore, in terminal Pleistocene and Holocene cave strata there tends to be an increase in rock rubble, either from inside or from outside of the cave, deliberately brought in or moved about, and sometimes built into fireplaces or other structures; such "manuports" must also be distinguished from debris of physical origin and emplacement. Finally, it seems probable that strong fires set in caves favored roof-spall detachment, by alternately heating and cooling the adjacent roof rock; whether or not this agency is indeed effective remains uncertain, because I have never been able to establish a positive correlation between spall frequency and thickness or abundance of hearth horizons.

2. *Mineral soil.* In wet weather and in certain damp environments, such as near the seashore, soil and sand are easily introduced to caves and middens by human feet, as well as by the hide and fur of slain game or cave-dwelling mammals, and by mollusca brought in as food. Even with a good cover of vegetation around a cave entrance, small groups of humans using a cave repeatedly over millennia can introduce substantial quantities of inorganic "soil." Mineral components are also introduced through fecal matter and even through the agency of mudwasps and nest-building birds. Although it may be difficult or impossible to quantify, this anthropogenic and animal soil component is not only real but also probably important.

3. *Plant matter.* Fibers and plant foods were inevitably introduced as primary foodstuffs, as secondary food products (in the digestive tracts of humans and animals), and as raw materials for fuel, dress, bedding, and construction. In the long run, the resulting feces, carbon, and

wood ash added organic colloids, amino acids, cellulose, resins, phosphates, nitrates, potash, and manganese to the sediment.

4. *Animal products.* Animal protein, bone and shell were also introduced in quantity and ultimately added to the accumulating residues: bone, shell, horn, feathers, tissue, and feces, in part more or less intact (bone fragments, mother-of-pearl), in part as decomposition products (bone phosphate, calcium, nitrogen, or potassium compounds, organic acids, carbonates, silica colloids). Microfaunal bone from owl pellets, bone rubble from hyena coprolites, gnawed bone from porcupine dens, and relatively intact, partly disarticulated bone from felid kills also deserve mention.

In different ways, prehistorical cave occupants directly or indirectly contributed substantial inputs of rock, mineral soil, and organic colloids or ions. During the course of repeated and protracted occupation they helped build up a share of the sand and grit. They also supplemented the clay and silt fraction, favoring development of a special clay-humus component by adding soluble mineral compounds (calcium, phosphate, potassium, nitrogen, sulfur, magnesium), acids (including human and animal urine), and organic carbon.

The chemical evolution of these organic products is complex and depends on the subsoil environment. For example, bone is dissolved by weak acid solutions of organic origin (uric acid, bat guano, plant-derived carbonic acid), and the resulting phosphatic solutions will combine with calcium (at pH > 7) to form nearly insoluble compounds, some of which may replace calcite in adjacent flowstone or limestone (Goldberg and Nathan, 1975). If the pH is less than 5 or 6, phosphorus ions, as well as those of potassium, sodium, or calcium, may combine with iron and aluminum compounds and be adsorbed into the colloidal micellae of clay-mineral structures (Cook and Heizer, 1965). Depending on their form, phosphorus compounds may be difficult to quantify accurately or even consistently, whether by measures of available P or measures of total P (Proudfoot, 1976).

Measures of organic carbon, phosphorus, potassium, and pH, evaluated in the context of sediment color, bone, artifactual debris, and hearths, provide partial documentation of human occupation in cave strata. But curves for C, P, and K, even when enhanced by X-ray diffractograms, thin-section micrographs, or scanning electron microscopy, can contribute only tentatively or indirectly to explanations for organic compounds. In fact, geochemical measures of key ions and anions cannot even identify organic residues according to gross categories such as meat or plant products. Experimental work at the Smithsonian Institution and Tübingen University has suggested that gas chromatographic analysis of amino acids may identify animal residues from bone, fat, blood, etc. More sophisticated modes of organic chemistry, as well as trace-element analysis have the potential to pinpoint the diagnostic components of specific food materials. But, unfortunately, such results on derivative organic compounds will not be available in the near future. Thus, microscopic identification of preserved botanical structures or bone fragments remains critically important.

Another problem in assessing the intensity and nature of human occupation or animal occupation concerns the roles of contemporary and postdepositional oxidation and/or mobilization. For example, a black lens with abundant charcoal powder and high carbon values probably can be identified as a hearth. However, the fact that it is conspicuous is due to low-temperature fires with only incomplete oxidation; high-temperature fires produce reddish or whitish laminae that are much thinner and therefore less likely to be recorded, even though they probably indicate larger or more prolonged fires and, by inference, more intensive activity.

The fixing of P in the presence of Ca (e.g., as collophanite) and the adsorption of P, K, Na, and Ca in clay-mineral structures in mildly acidic soil environments have already been mentioned. Phosphorus can also be mobilized downward in a cave profile (i.e., leached), and phosphorus peaks in the Paleolithic strata of Cueva Morín may be a meter or so below major occupation horizons (Figure 6-1) (Butzer, 1981b). Similarly, I have found that potassium in most cave sequences decreases steadily with depth, reflecting its instability in mildly alkaline environments. In Cueva Morín, a number of dug pits (Azilian or Terminal Paleolithic) have practically no artifacts and moderate P values, but high C and K values, probably as a result of wood ash. Similar features would, after 75,000 years of frost-heave disturbance, leaching, and oxidation, show up as a downshifted moderate P peak, which might well be attributed to cave bear dung in the absence of artifact or preserved bone. These points serve to explain why organic compounds do not provide a foolproof index of activity patterning, particularly not in older contexts. But caution must be exercised even in much younger strata, depending on soil microenvironments.

Biogenic and anthropogenic aggregates of several kinds pose special problems, particularly for textural analyses:

1. *Coprolites.* Fecal material eventually breaks down in the average

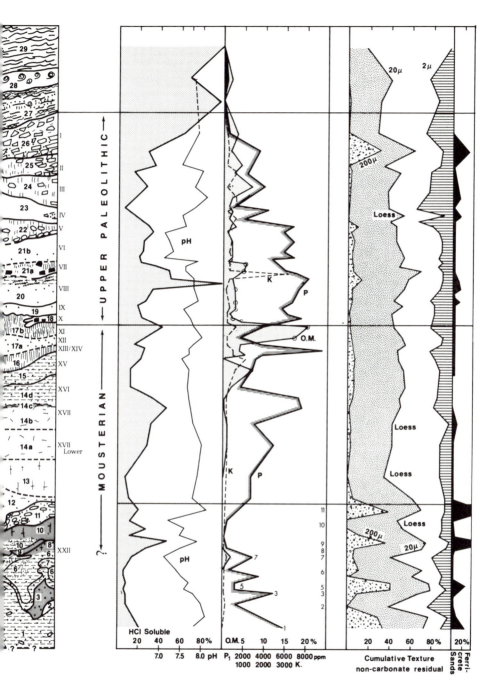

Figure 6-1. Composite archaeosedimentary profile for Cueva Morín, Cantabria, Spain. The sedimentary units are identified by Arabic numbers (from below), the archaeological levels (at side of column) by Roman numerals (from above). Modified from Butzer (1981b).

cave situation, but it may represent a high proportion of some strata in terms of bulk. Dry feces are variable in their proportions of soluble plasma and mineral residue, and the latter varies in terms of size grade. For beds rich in hyena coprolites, primary aggregates are resistant because of high proportions of structured mineral matter (calcium phosphate) and fragmentary bone inclusions, whereas cave bear dung is unusually rich in solubles and clay-humus aggregates, with bone residues providing sand-sized or larger particles.

2. *Wood ash.* The burning of various kinds of fibers releases opal phytoliths (silica skeletons of fine to medium silt size, see Chapter 10) and calcite crystals (fine silt size), creating a new class of minerals. These may contribute substantially to the powdery white or pale yellowish fine-sand-sized aggregates typical of the light-colored lenses that interfinger with dark hearth lenses in countless cave deposits. Under ×30 magnification these ash particles are seen to be porous and inhomogeneous, with granular structure. Only certain varieties react to acid, but all break down in strong alkalies such as the sodium hydroxide used to dissolve siliceous and organic compounds.

3. *Fired clay.* Cave fires commonly produce temperatures of 600°C and higher in contact sediments, baking them to oxidize reddish brown or brick red aggregates at intermediate temperatures, to reduce pale gray or yellowish aggregates at higher temperatures, and to organic dark brown aggregates at lower temperatures involving incomplete combustion. Ranging in shape from amorphous to laminate structures, these fired aggregates range in size from 100 to 500 microns or more. There may also be intergrades between wood-ash particles, yellowish to reddish burnt "clay," and dark carbonaceous aggregates (e.g., in the lenticular interdigitation around erstwhile hearths).

All in all, these different aggregates simulate sand, silt, and clay-sized mineral grains. Together with the possibility of lithic debitage in the sand and grit grade, and the possibility of geochemical recombination of organic ions as clay-humus molecules, cultural factors can significantly and often totally skew the textural spectrum derived by mechanical laboratory processing. The import is that archaeological cave sediments must be carefully pretreated if they are to convey any useful information. Goldberg (1979a) proposed micromorphological examination, whereby anthropogenic and biogenic particles or aggregates can be directly identified. An alternative procedure is to carry out the normal grain-sized techniques, then examine all silt and sands coarser than 37 microns (the smallest available sieve grade) under the microscope: Debitage can be removed at this time, biogenic aggregates can be dissolved in alkali, and a cleansed sample can be run a second time to provide a "filtered" textural spectrum of material coarser than 37 microns. The quantitative difference, together with geochemical tests for available and total phosphorus, potassium, and organic matter, will suggest the degree to which the initial statistics on fine silts and clay are meaningful, as well as whether or not clay-mineral X-ray diffractograms will be informative.

This analytical discussion is intended to draw attention to some of the procedural problems posed by cave sedimentology and suggest some ways in which physical and nonphysical inputs can be separated to provide information on each. It follows that a new sedimentary system must be modeled for almost every cave. This can be illustrated by a specific example.

An example of cave geo-archaeology: Cueva Morín

Cueva Morín is a limestone cave located 11 kilometers southwest of Santander, near the Cantabrian coast of northern Spain (Butzer, 1981*b*). The bulk of the sediment in this cave (Figure 6-1) was derived from soil and stony debris from the surface above, washing down the rock face and into the entrance. Sediment caught at the drip line was then progressively moved into the cave interior by runoff during heavy rains. These external sediments include clay (from soil horizons), silt (partly windborne dust or loess), quartz sand (partly from veneers of ancient alluvium), and, more rarely pebbles or sand grains of concretionary iron (a lag from the erosional surface above). Another fill component was generated inside the cave. This includes splices and spall of roof origin detached by frost weathering; dripstone and flowstone are uncommon. Finally, repeated occupations by Mousterian and Upper Paleolithic groups over a span of some 75,000 years prior to 10,000 B.P. was responsible for (a) importation of mineral and organic materials from outside the cave, (b) disturbance of existing stratification and mixing of older sediments and contemporary sediments, and (c) geochemical modification as a result of decomposition of biological residues.

Periods of intensive occupation easily doubled the "background" sedimentation rates by adding a grit and coarse-sand component not present in the limestone residue, supplementing the sandy-clay silt derived from limestone solution, augmenting the clay-humus colloidal fraction, adding soluble mineral compounds, and generally increasing the organic component. Organic matter accounts for 5% to 20% of most occupation levels, phosphate compounds 1% to 2%, and artifactual debris and bone 2% to 50%.

Intensive occupation affected the rates of sediment accumulation. The cutting of pits by the Azilian occupants (archaeological level I) is another example of such disturbance, and several contacts between levels V, VI, and VII also suggest digging activities by Gravettian and Aurignacian occupants. Several early Aurignacian structures provide another example.

More insidious was the impact of repeated occupations that mixed fresh cultural components into older mineral sediments that had been accumulating slowly for centuries or millennia. In other instances, renewed occupation disturbed as much as 10 cm of older occupation residues (e.g., through human trampling after periods of rain, when water puddled on the cave floor). In this way, substantial proportions of older cultural sediment were reworked into a significantly younger matrix. Derived, evolved Aurignacian artifacts found in the lower part of the Gravettian level V provide a case to point.

The implications of repeated but sporadic occupation are considerable, not only for paleoenvironmental interpretation of the sediment column but also for evaluation of primary archaeological contexts:

1. Periods without occupance will be poorly represented, particularly during times of reduced external soil erosion, so that the temporal record is distorted or incomplete.

2. Periods of repeated intensive occupation will lead to "smudging" of the environmental trace and, in some cases, to overrepresentation of sedimentary thickness and complexity, with beds being composed primarily of cultural components and simulating sedimentation details that may be no more than background "noise."

3. Disturbance can produce mixed artifactual assemblages in the lower parts of individual strata, and the significance of modern mud trampling suggests that associations will be primary only if they are preserved in discrete and three-dimensionally intact lenses.

Examination of the archaeological levels in Cueva Morín indicates that contacts tend to be sharpest in the front of the cave, where occupation was most intense, with indistinct but often highly irregular contacts toward the back. In fact, the contacts suggest that the upper sedimentary units in the cave are as much consequences of the occupation history as of environmental processes. This is borne out by the sedimentology data, which sometimes show as much variability within a unit as between units. Furthermore, many of the archaeological levels contain few primary associations, such as pits or hearths, but are dominated by amorphous cultural accumulations, with little or no lenticular differentiation.

This example not only cautions against the widespread assumption that caves are ideal for the preservation of primary associations but also serves to illustrate that archaeological sequences within caves represent a special kind of archaeosedimentary system that must be studied by an appropriate set of geo-archaeological procedures and excavated with sophisticated strategies.

A Holocene prototype: village mounds

Applied geomorphologists have in recent years contributed actively to what has been labeled urban geomorphology, but most of this work has been directed to the impacts of highway construction and suburban developments or problems of foundation stability (Gray, 1972; Coates, 1976; Leveson, 1981). There is no systematic body of data or even a list of procedures for dealing with cultural sedimentation in towns or cities. The basic archaeological principles can be gleaned from the work of Lloyd (1963) and Adams (1975), and some information on the historical development of urban foundations has been collated by Legget (1973: Chapter 5–7). Insight into geochemical considerations can be obtained from the work of Cook and Heizer (1965), Davidson (1973), Hassan and Lubell (1975), and Sjöberg (1982), and sedimentary examples have been developed by Davidson (1973), Gunnerson (1973), Folk (1975), and McIntosh (1977). The outline that follows is based on my examination of urban sites in Ethiopia, Spain, and Egypt and presents a model that is not necessarily for univeral application.

As in the case of caves, sedimentation processes and configurations vary from one village mound to the next, and often from one level to another. Nonetheless, there do appear to be some modal patterns among sites located in semiarid and arid environments. The problem can be approached in two steps: first, a discussion of the specific sediment types; second, an analysis of the general sedimentation cycle.

The anthropogenic sediments specific to major settlement sites, mounds, and the like can be characterized as follows:

1. Organocultural refuse generally takes the from of fine-grained, often clayey and highly organic sediment with relatively little crude rubble other than potsherds. The structure commonly is platy or lami-

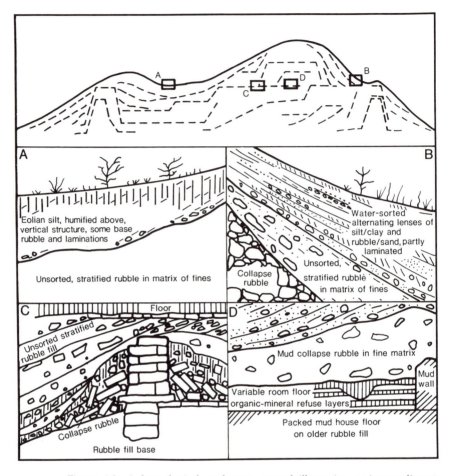

Figure 6-2. A hypothetical settlement mound illustrating various sediment facies: eolian silt (A), gravity-induced collapse rubbles and water-reworked debris (B), collapse rubble and artificial fill (C), and primary refuse, followed by collapse rubble and artificial fill (D).

nated, arranged in extensive, thin lenticular packages of variable color and composition (Figure 6-2D). This category includes hearths, ash, sherds, food products and waste, animal dung, other organic residues, inorganic processing remains, and so on, generally rich in phosphates and with a pH lower than average. The problems of identifying the exact origins of the organic residues are similar to those encountered with Paleolithic cave deposits. Methods for general, rather than specific, microarchaeological analysis of such residues have been described by Hassan (1978).

2. Collapse rubbles are heterogeneous chaotic masses of crude rubble derived from mudbrick, burnt brick, adobe, wood, fibers, and secondary sherds. The large interstitial voids are only partly filled with fines, particularly when adobe and mudbrick (Bullard, 1976; Goldberg, 1979*b*) soften, decay, and then become compact, or when finer sediments or soluble carbonates, gypsum, or sodium salts filter down into the voids from above. True collapse rubbles are sometimes interbedded with and are more commonly covered by poorly sorted, stratified beds of mixed rubble and fines, with inclinations of up to 25° due to gravity sliding or water-assisted gravitational transfer (Figure 6-2B,C). Overall, phosphate levels are low, and both pH and calcium carbonate content are high, but variable. The processes of wall collapse as a result of abandonment and weathering have been outlined by McIntosh (1977), Carter and Pagliero (1966), and Gullini (1969).

3. Water-laid sediments result from sheetwash or channeled flow in small surface runnels or original drainage pipes or ditches. These are highly variable lenticular beds adjusted to topographic irregularities, being thicker in hollows, pockets, and other depressions. Basal sediments tend to include a mixture of sizes, because crude rubble is only minimally arranged when running water moves swiftly for short intervals before percolating rapidly into interstitial voids. Eventually, flow lines become better developed, and a higher proportion of runoff travels along them for greater distances. At such times, laminated or "graded" fills may develop, with thin increments of clayey silts following upon sorted sands or fine gravel, in repetitive packages. Beds tend to be discontinuous and 2 to 20 cm thick, with rare crossbeds of small scale (i.e., structures smaller than 30 cm) and low angle (< 20°). Ultimately, defined erosional runnels may develop, but as sheetwash and rainsplash smoothen projecting surfaces and remove softer materials, slopes begin to stabilize, and sediment supply decreases (Figure 6-2B). Such water-laid sediments are of highly variable biochemical composition, but adequate sustained flow can flush solubles out of the site, so that related deposits have low pH values and low carbonate contents. For a discussion of mound erosion, see the work of Kirkby and Kirkby (1976).

4. Biogenic and geochemical alterations ensue as surfaces stabilize and rainwash abates. In more humid environments, vegetation begins to fix the surface while roots and microfauna once more increase sediment aeration and permeability. Rotting out of wood and fiber in the matrix creates new voids, which are then filled with new sediment or

stabilized by the precipitation of solubles. A modest soil may develop near the surface as structure and organic content improve. Together with the vegetation and rooting network, however incomplete, this soil continues to favor slope stabilization and inhibits the impact of rain-splash and runoff. Soil pH tends to be lower than in the cultural sub-strate. In more arid environments, biotic activity is limited, but incom-plete sediment wetting may begin to concentrate solubles near the surface, by capillary attraction, favoring partial cementation and thus reducing erodibility (Liebowitz and Folk, 1980); in such instances, pH values increase.

5. Eolian sediments are common only in arid environments or where there is a good source of distant windblown dust or local ash and charcoal (Wilkinson, 1976; McIntosh, 1977). Net eolian accumulation is possible only where sheetwash is minimal. Eolian silts of such origin resemble loess and lack conspicuous stratification (Figure 6-2A) (Folk, 1975; Liebowitz and Folk, 1980). Eolian silt is generally of low density and permeated with biogenic hollows, and its high infiltration capacity serves to reduce surface runoff. Organic and phosphate contents are variable, depending on the source; pH and carbonate levels tend to be high.

The basic sediment types described earlier belong to larger process assemblages, among which two patterns can be identified. During times of demographic expansion, construction in a village mound out-weighs decay, and garbage or collapse rubbles due to accident or selec-tive razing show little net accumulation because they are cleared away or dumped elsewhere. During times of slow demographic decline or catastrophic destruction by natural or human disasters, garbage and collapse rubbles build up and are then affected by running water, biogenic modification, and wind. A basic classification of sedimenta-tion patterns is constructed according to these principles in Table 6-1.

Processes common to particular foci of human activity (Nissen, 1968; David, 1971; McIntosh, 1977) can be discussed more fully in the follow-ing categories:

1. Habitation floors during active occupation may be composed of stamped mud, fiber matting, hide coverings, and rugs or laid stone. Despite intermittent sweeping, mixed refuse often is allowed to accu-mulate on such floors at a slow rate, perhaps matching the gradual buildup on the roadway in front of the dwelling, where accretion is partly balanced by rainwash erosion.

2. Abandoned living floors rapidly accumulate refuse and rubble,

Table 6-1. *Hypothetical sedimentation patterns in a mound settlement*

Settlement units	Positive demographic phase	Negative demographic phase		
		Initial	Short term	Long term
Habitation floor	Slow accretion of mixed organocultural refuse, mainly fine-grained and lenticular	Rapid accretion of cultural refuse and rubble by human agency, gravity, or rainwash	Incremental or total wall collapse, creating chaotic masses of heterogeneous structural rubble	Filling of interstitial voids with water-transported sediment (clayey silt or solubles), followed by biogenic activity, with possible addition of eolian dust
Streets and alleys	Slow accretion of mixed organocultural refuse, but repeated removal of coarser rubble and larger obstacles; roadways kept open, but gradually rise in level	Large-scale collapse rubbles block roadways; they begin to fill with secondary interstitial sediment introduced by water	Rainsplash and sheetwash erosion, with accumulation of complex, lenticular water-laid sediments in pockets and depressions	Vegetation and biogenic activity fix soil and impede runoff, favoring infiltration in moist environments (soil formation); subsurface enrichment of solubles, or eolian dust accumulation (in dry environments), also stabilizes surface
Community structures (walls, civic buildings, terraces, drainage systems)	Locally, structural rubble deliberately aggraded as foundations or fresh surfaces; wells, aqueducts, drainage pipes and ditches, moats, etc., periodically cleaned of part or all of accumulating garbage and debris	Massive collapse rubbles and gravity infillings of drainage systems, etc.	Redeposition by water-aided gravity movements, sheetwash, and channeled flow, with water-laid lenticular sediments in hollows and depressions, filling interstitial voids and possibly lining new drainage tunnels	As above, biogenic alteration or eolian accumulation or both

even prior to collapse, through human agency, animal activities, gravity, and rainwash. Eventually, gradual or sudden roof and wall collapse will create large masses of structural rubble, such as stone, fired brick, mudbrick, mud, wood, and other fibers (Figure 6-2C).

3. Roadways tend to be foci for garbage accretion at times of active settlement, although large obstacles, such as the products of accidental structural collapse, usually are removed to refuse dumps. Streets and alleys are regularly swept clean in some cultural contexts but not in others, but in any event they tend to build up with time.

4. Roadways of decaying or abandoned village quarters are rapidly blocked by wall collapse, and this material is then reworked by running water and possibly mantled with eolian dust.

5. Unroofed enclosures attached to habitation areas and used for special activities, such as animal stalls and gardens, are subject to processes similar to those that affect living floors during occupation, but after abandonment, the sedimentation is similar to that in roadways, being open to the elements.

6. Larger structures involving community effort, such as artificial terraces and the foundations for walls or monumental buildings, frequently are built of cultural rubble, and garbage and debris are prone to accumulate in deep wells, aqueducts, drainpipes and shafts, sewers, and moats (Wilkinson, 1976), rearranged or redistributed by gravity and running water.

7. Abandonment or destruction leads to massive accumulation around civic structures, with infilling of wells and drainage systems. Subsequently, water-aided gravity movements, sheetwash, and channeled water flow will rearrange part or much of this rubble, with accretion in hollows and depressions and perhaps creation of fresh drainage lines marked by alternating stream erosion and deposition.

All in all, a good case can be made that the archaeosedimentary facies peculiar to village mounds and other urban agglomerations are amenable to systematic study, both in terms of the spatial distribution of activity types and in terms of the vertical record of demographic processes. During the phases of site formation, architectural form and layout, as well as construction materials, control the form of a mound, whereas human activity patterns control the rates of sedimentation. During and after abandonment stage, changes in form and materials composition are affected by a different range of processes, mainly (but by no means only) physical in origin (see Chapter 7). Sediment analysis must be carried out in the field and the laboratory

(McIntosh, 1977), because samples processed on consignment can convey only a small fraction of the information that on-site examination can give the geo-archaeologist.

The whole complex of processes synthesized by the model of Table 6-1 is involved in producing the kinds of net accumulation rates proposed by Gunnerson (1973): 10 to 400 cm/century, as calculated for 13 cities and towns, including Bronze Age Troy and twentieth-century Manhattan. Short-term catastrophes may produce accumulations on the order of 25 cm/year over wide areas, as during the saturation bombings of European and Japanese cities during World War II. But most aggradation in a long-term settlement site takes place under less dramatic conditions. Because of the great range of cultural processes involved, rates are also far more variable than Gunnerson (1973) anticipated.

Examples of urban geo-archaeology: Giza and Axum

The potential of geo-archaeology in town sites can best be gauged from specific examples, one drawn from Old Kingdom Egypt, the other from Axum, Ethiopia.

Excavations by Kromer (1978) on the desert plateau near the great pyramids of Giza showed that what first appeared to be a settlement site was nothing but a huge dump site on a hillside. Construction of the third great pyramid, of Mykerinos (ca. 2548–2530 B.C.), required the razing of a settlement used by special craftsmen who had produced mortuary goods for Cheops and Chephren. The removed material was transported as much as 1 km and then spilled out along an 8° slope, where it accumulated to a thickness of at least 6.5 m across an area of more than five hectares (12.5 acres).

Kromer (1978) identified repeated episodes of dumping along the slope that had created an extensive ledge of secondary habitation residues. But his published sections can be used to reconstruct a more informative stratigraphic sequence (Figure 6-3): (1) A basal 2-m unit of thick-bedded mud residues includes inclined lines of potsherds, with local concentrations of sherd and mudbrick rubble. (2) The next unit averages 1.5 m in thickness and follows conformably, but it is thin-bedded, with mud residues interdigitated with sand lenses (generally less than 5 cm thick). (3) On top of a major erosional break, more than 1 m of thick-bedded sand and mud, mixed with sherds and brick rubble, fills a depression that cuts diagonally down the slope. (4) Then there is a discontinuous bed of up to 50 cm of variable rubble. (5) There finally

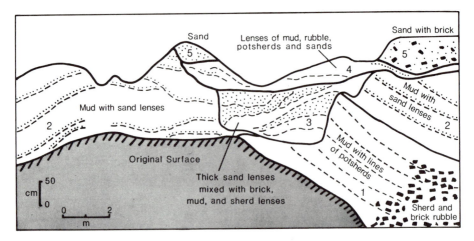

Figure 6-3. Tertiary settlement rubble near Giza, representing the razed debris of a craftmen's town. Vertical exaggeration 2:1. Modified from Kromer (1978:Figure 5).

follow sands, mixed with fine brick debris, up to 70 cm thick in some spots. Kromer (1978) believed that the sandy lenses were eolian and that the capping sands were dunes; the presence of minute rootlet horizons in the sandy lenses was believed to record annual rhythmites, and he argued accordingly that some lenses marked breaks of four to six years in local dumping. Nonetheless, the sandy lenses thin out, rather than thicken, downslope, where they sometimes grade into sherd horizons; it is also unusual for dune sands to be admixed with debris.

Lacking proper analysis, these strata remain ambiguous. Kromer (1978) claimed a single original settlement that during the Fourth Dynasty included segregated workmen's quarters and that later was razed and then dumped at the excavation site. My impression is that several settlements may well have been incorporated in the dump, as well as drift sand removed from the projected pyramid platform. The break between the second (b) and third (c) units described earlier may record a debris slide following heavy rains, with the mechanics of subsequent dumping being substantially different. It is technically possible to determine if mud residues come from simple sun-dried mud, from deteriorated mudbricks, or from intact bricks (Butzer, 1978b). By inference, it would have been feasible to distinguish deposits from the base of a long-term site (or from a long-abandoned settlement, as opposed to an active one) and to isolate true eolian sand, local sandy slope wash, and dumped sands. As it stands, Kromer's interpretation of a single antecedent town and its evolution is inferred more from historical context than from in situ evidence. These excavations stand as an example of what can be lost by inadequate procedures.

A different type of urban record is provided by the strata under the "obelisks" of Axum's Stele Park. This sequence, synthesized in Figure 6-4, documents most of the key social and environmental changes in that town during the last two millennia (Butzer, 1981*a*).

The original surface was deeply rotted bedrock, mantled with an unknown thickness of soil (unit 1). The B horizon, probably a noncalcareous brown clay loam, was stripped off to form part of a complex of artificial terraces during Early Axumite times (A.D. 100–350). Variable concentrations of local rubble, much of it partly decomposed, were first mixed into artificial fills (unit 2), and then a number of short, rough-hewn stelae were set on top of the resulting low, 1.5-m terraces. In several cases, the same terraces were the scenes of protracted and intensive fires that left thick horizons of ash and that oxidized up to 30 cm of the underlying soil, suggesting large pyres, possibly set around the new stelae. Eventually, a level, built-up surface as much as 2 m thick had been created in the western part of Stele Park. Tall, plain but dressed stelae, associated with baseplates hollowed out for offerings, were set on this surface. Later still, large masses of rocky fill, derived from fresh, angular quarry rock, were piled up behind walls over 3 m high. The largest decorated stelae were prominently mounted on top of these. Subsequently, thick masses of brown alluvial clay were trapped in front of or behind these foundation structures, where they are mixed with dispersed rock rubble. This clay closely resembles contemporaneous floodplain deposits of the adjacent stream, but is unlike any high-lying local soils. Either floodplain soils were being dug and brought up to Stele Park, or sporadic, exceptionally high floods were depositing the clay in local sediment traps up to 4 m above the functional floodplain. A general enrichment of unit-2 soils as well as of these clays with 1% to 3% carbonates favors a "natural" interpretation.

The Early Axumite ceremonial and burial area, still lacking evidence of habitation residues, was then abandoned and either eroded by rain-wash or deliberately disturbed. A second episode of intensive use and reuse (Middle to Late Axumite) began during the late fourth century and continued until the early eighth century. Few elaborate structures were built, but much of Stele Park was covered with houses, although some stelae were still erected in sectors used primarily for mortuary

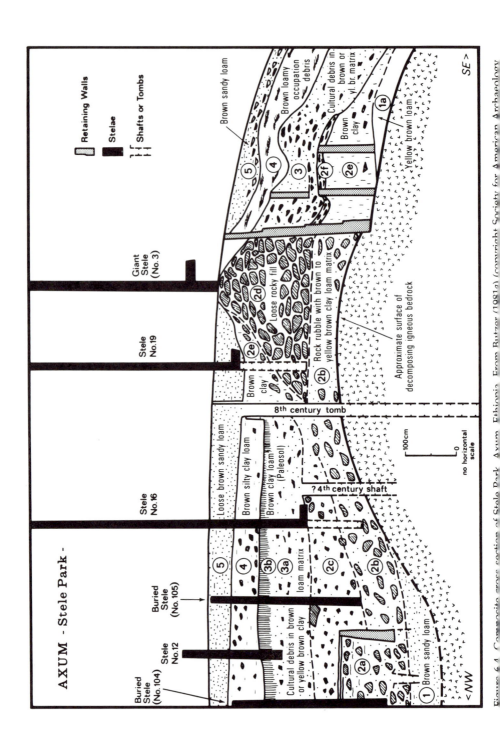

AXUM - Stele Park -

Buried Stele (No.104)
Stele No.12
Buried Stele (No.105)
Stele No.16
Stele No.19
Giant Stele (No. 3)

Retaining Walls
Stelae
Shafts or Tombs

Brown sandy loam
Brown loamy occupation debris
Cultural debris in brown or yl. br. matrix
Brown clay

1a

2e
2f
3
4
5

Loose rocky fill
2d

Brown clay
2e

Rock rubble with brown to yellow brown clay loam matrix
2b

Approximate surface of decomposing igneous bedrock

Yellow brown loam

SE

8th century tomb

Loose brown sandy loam
Brown silty clay loam
Brown clay loam (Paleosol)
Cultural debris in brown or yellow brown clay loam matrix

5
4
3b
3a

2c
2b

? 4th century shaft

100cm
0
no horizontal scale

Brown sandy loam
1

2a

NW

Figure 6.4. Composite cross-section of Stele Park, Axum, Ethiopia. From Butzer (1981a) (copyright Society for American Archaeology

purposes (e.g., the multiple "shaft tombs"). In most instances, these strata (unit 3) represent water-worked colluvia more than they do artificial fills, occupation levels, or collapse rubbles. By the late eighth century the site had been more or less abandoned. Rainwash activity climaxed at about that time, but eventually the surface stabilized, and a dark, prismatically structured soil began to form. Many centuries would be necessary to oxidize the organic matter of the Axumite strata and to develop such a prominent profile.

The site remained undisturbed until the fifteenth century, when the local quarter is first verified in traditional records. The small shrunken village sketched by a traveler in 1805 covered part of Stele Park, as did the much larger town mapped during excavations in 1906. Again, much of the archaeological sediment (unit 4), particularly to the back of Stele Park, represents an extensive rainwash accumulation, locally over 1.5 m thick. Many of the robbers' pits and shafts that intrude the sequence predate this wash. The fact that all the pit and tomb fills examined are highly organic (like unit 4) and occasionally show flood laminations further suggests that a major episode of vandalism dates from the time of fifteenth-century settlement.

Subsequent modifications (reflected in unit 5) include archaeological activities in 1954–7, removal of local houses, and concomitant landscaping of Stele Park.

Whereas the Giza study illustrated a suite of tertiary archaeological sediments, the Axum section includes primary, secondary, and tertiary components. Both examples illustrate the range of potential contributions by geo-archaeological techniques.

In conclusion, archaeological assessments of sedimentation and site formation constitute a complex research enterprise that is as yet almost undeveloped. But the obvious potential insights on settlement patterns and processes, as well as the indirect record of subsistence activities, indicate as many possibilities for creative geo-archaeological interpretation as do the methods of excavation and the macrobiological residues. The agencies and impacts of postdepositional site modification and destruction will be considered more explicitly in Chapter 7.

Geo-archaeology V: site modification and destruction

Cultural transformation of archaeological residues

Archaeological sites, of whatever size and complexity, are functions of human activities and of noncultural agencies, during occupation as well as after occupation. The regional and local geomorphic subsystem provides a landscape setting and contributes to the blend of cultural and noncultural processes that affect a site during its use and subsequently dictate its preservation or destruction. The degree to which such cultural residues provide a representative time slice of human activities (instantaneously fossilized, as it were) is only in part controlled by sedimentation, preservation on a stable surface, or dispersal by erosion. A multiplicity of cultural variables is another part of the same equation, before, during, and after the final phases of human activity related to a particular surface.

A framework for cultural transformations has been outlined by Schiffer (1976:Chapter 3) in terms of systemic versus archaeological context. Such a sophisticated approach is commendable for sociocultural interpretation, but for the purposes of excavation strategy the factors involved can more profitably be considered from three perspectives:

1. *Primary cultural deposition.* During the original utilization of an activity locus, the various archaeological materials are progressively discarded (partly in refuse areas), lost, or deliberately aggregated in burials, shrines, and caches. During abandonment, higher proportions of functional materials are left behind in areas of manufacture, use, and storage. Just how representative the aggregate of abandoned materials is of day-to-day activities will depend on whether abandonment was sudden or anticipated, whether or not the objects were easy to replace, and whether or not they were conveniently portable in terms of available facilities and projected travel distance. Structures, burials, etc., are less problematical, because they are fixed.

2. *Secondary cultural deposition.* Discarded or abandoned archaeologi-

cal materials can be reutilized by their original owners, by other members of the same social unit, or by another group of people occupying the same site. The time interval here can range from minutes to millennia. For example, a stone tool can be sharpened or modified by retouch or renewed flaking – during the course of a single animal-butchering event, during repeated use of an ephemeral site, during a switch from one activity to another on a multiple-activity surface, or during reutilization of that surface years or centuries later. Activity shifts and site reutilization, even by the same sociocultural group, serve to smudge the record of specific human activities; they may instead create atypical spatial distributions of various aggregates that incorrectly suggest real functional associations.

Reutilization of a site, such as a damp cave, can lead to trampling and serious disturbance of the top 10 cm or so of an earlier occupation level, with partial or even complete incorporation into a new depositional matrix (see Chapter 6); if diagnostic artifacts are absent from the reworked product, the mixture probably will go undetected, and the resulting artifactual statistics will be skewed and meaningless. Even in open-air sites, penecontemporaneous trampling can help disperse the artifactual material from a single occupation through as much as 50 cm of uncompacted sediment, possibly simulating multiple levels, when, in fact, "refitting" of lithic artifacts and debitage will indicate only one level (Cahen et al., 1979). In town sites, on the other hand, large-scale public construction commonly involves the razing and clearing of older structures, infilling of new level surfaces with old rubble or refuse, and so forth (Wilk and Schiffer, 1979) (see Chapter 6), possibly introducing diagnostic objects into much younger contexts that may lack contemporary artifacts. These examples illustrate the hazards of site reutilization and caution against the simplistic assumption that archaeological residues unaffected by nonhuman disturbance represent discrete and primary activity patterning.

3. *Cultural disturbance.* Human activities that rearrange or remove archaeological materials in a nonfunctional site include grave robbing, "pot hunting" and "picking over" for select artifacts, excavation, plowing, and various latter-day construction activities. Particularly insidious are the processes of picking over and plowing of surface sites, as well as selective excavation strategies that skew retrieval in favor of larger, diagnostic, or finished artifacts.

These three categories of cultural transformation suggest formidable, often insurmountable, problems in the interpretation of sociocultural

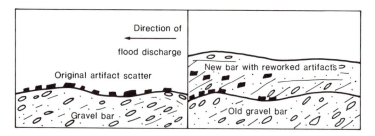

Figure 7-1. Dispersal and secondary bedding of gravel-bar workshop site.

context. But they represent only one side of the coin in the matter of what exactly is primary. These processes are complemented by a host of noncultural transformations that include preburial dispersal, post-depositional disturbance, and geobiochemical modification, as well as site destruction and related artifact dispersal. A conceptual framework for ancient sites has been provided by Fedele (1976), and a methodology for examination of such sites in their landscape is also available (Butzer 1981a).

Preburial dispersal

Dispersal can be defined as a primarily horizontal movement of surface aggregates that affects particles of different mass and shape at different rates and leads to distortion or elimination of original microspatial relationships. In the case of distortion, we can speak of partial dispersal; in the case of destruction of such interrelationships, we speak of effective dispersal.

Prior to their burial in and under sediment, portable archaeological materials are prone to mobilization in response to geomorphic processes. For residues buried immediately or soon after abandonment, moving water is the primary potential agency of dispersal. For residues that have never been sealed in sediment, the forces of gravity, frost, and wind can also contribute to dispersal over longer periods of time.

The greatest dispersal hazard generally coincides in time with site burial and tends to be a function of the net energy crossing the site surface. Moving water can exert its force in the form of turbulent channel discharge, which might scatter lithic artifacts that had been abandoned on a gravel bar or sandbar during the low-water season (Figure 7-1). Or its energy might be expended as a surge of water breaking through a low point on a channel levee to form a sand splay on the interior margin of a floodplain, or the gentle spreading of muddy

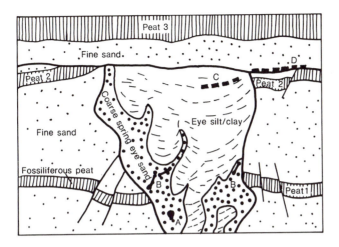

Figure 7-2. Disruption and dispersal of fossils and bones by eruption of artesian spring vent. A: Human fossil brought up from unexposed basal bed. B: Fossils reworked from peat 1 by eruption. C: Surface artifacts from top of peat 2 redeposited in spring-eye silts. D: Surface artifacts on peat 2 dispersed by flushing.

waters over a wide floodplain, leaving an increment of silt or clay. Particularly ideal are the low-energy conditions in floodplain backswamps and lakes. Springs usually provide low-energy sedimentation opportunities, but some deep-seated aquifers are prone to periodic explosions of energy as spring vents erupt and create havoc in related beds, leading to redeposition and dispersal (Figure 7-2) (Butzer, 1973a). Running water on slopes can also effect dispersal or burial or both. Surface runoff can range from a thin film of water moving through a grassy turf to a surge of water racing across a surface or being channeled into multiple rills. Very intensive rains, particularly in semiarid environments, can also lead to entrainment of large masses of silty material in mudflows that contain more sediment than water and that can mobilize even large rocks. Finally, seashores and lakeshores witness another potent form of aqueous energy.

The dispersal of artifacts can be illustrated by a test plot at Alexandersfontein, near Kimberley, South Africa, where Middle Stone Age lithics have been repeatedly moved by running water and incorporated into successive generations of colluvial sediments. Modern erosion, primarily by sheetwash, is undermining such surficial sediments, which form flat grassy surfaces that terminate abruptly 15 to 50 cm above bare spots with inclines of 1° to 5° that in turn run 5 m and more toward other flat grassy surfaces. Each rainstorm uncovers and redistributes more artifacts, which are eventually reburied farther downslope. After one such rainstorm, I plotted two natural clusters of artifacts, together with orientation of major axis (length) and angle of dip. Artifacts tended to cluster weakly in relation to minute lateral and longitudinal changes of inclination, toward the lower part of a 2° to 3° slope; "rose" diagrams of compass strike, complemented by statistical tests (Johansson, 1976), indicated a fairly strong preferred orientation within such clusters (Figure 7-3). However, the mean vector orientation deviated 14° to 20° from the mean slope direction, largely because of surface microvariations. Dips were mainly downslope, but were almost unpredictably affected by slope microvariations, becoming random where artifacts were perched on small stones (from which the fine matrix had been undermined) or had been trampled by animals (clear hoofprints, and impaled into sediment at 5°–47° angles). The major quadrant of dip diverged 90° from the slope direction, and the preferred orientation (Figure 7-3) with angle of dip increased in proportion to slope angle.

The overall implication of this Alexandersfontein study is that rainwash can be expected to create some clusters with apparently random orientation, particularly when the surface is irregular and the net dip is small, as could be expected on local surfaces of deposition inclined at less than 1°. Appropriate orientation parameters are essential to test such visual impressions. Other helpful characteristics at Alexandersfontein were edge abrasion of artifacts and an absence of items shorter than 1.5 cm among a total of 110 pieces; these had long been sorted out through differential mobilization. This suggests that local "levels" of sealed artifacts, even when clustered and demonstrably nonoriented, may be secondary unless the artifacts are edge-fresh, display a wide range of sizes, and include fine debitage; even so, partial dispersal is probable, in view of the mobility of surface aggregates in the region. These various conclusions from the Alexandersfontein experiment argue that nondispersal must be demonstrated; it cannot be assumed among sealed artifacts that lack intact features such as hearths and pits.

Archaeological materials can also be dispersed through the agencies of gravity, frost, and wind-assisted movements, complementing the agency of running water on both gentle and steep slopes. Below one Peruvian cave, on partly vegetated slopes of 10° to 44°, Rick (1976) found that lithics, bones, and potsherds had been moved 20 to 300 m during some 4,000 years, with gravity transporting the heavier items somewhat farther than the lighter ones.

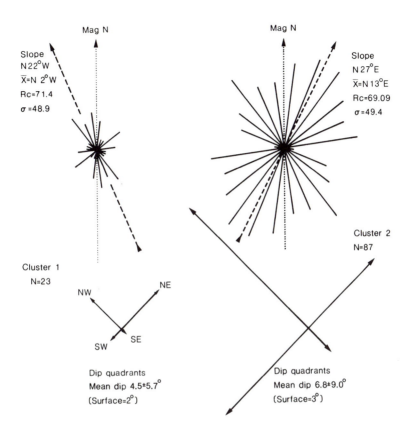

Figure 7-3. Direction of strike (15° quadrants), modal orientation of slope, direction of dip (90° quadrants), and mean dip (with standard deviation) for two surface artifact clusters at Alexandersfontein. Lengths of vectors proportional to numbers. Orientation parameters after Johansson (1976): $\bar{X}$ = vector mean; Rc = consistency ratio; σ = standard deviation.

Frost performs a similar function in colder environments as ice develops beneath stones (because of higher conductivity than through soil). The ice crystals can push a lithic artifact upward; it then shifts slightly downslope as the ice melts and the object settles back. This process has been replicated under laboratory conditions (Wood and Johnson, 1978). Patterned ground phenomena are a reflection of significant seasonal soil-frost intervention that sorts out fine sediment from stones into circular patterns on level surfaces and elongated ones on slopes.

At Torralba, a montane site in central Spain occupied during a cold Pleistocene glacial, I was able to show that ringlike arrangements of larger stones in the oldest archaeological levels were not of cultural origin but were the result of soil-frost sorting: On slopes of 2° to 5°, such rings were circular, with internal diameters increasing with the size of the stones; at inclinations of 5° to 10°, the rings were stretched into ellipsoidal garlands of rock caused by downslope movement; on gradients steeper than 10°, the garlands were torn apart by solifluction into stone stripes (perpendicular to the contours) or scatters in which individual pebbles either pointed downhill or were parallel to the contours (Figure 7-4). As a result of soil frost, the archaeological materials of this particular level were rearranged, although still in basic association (partial dispersal), on 2° to 5° grades, but they were effectively dispersed on slopes steeper than 8°.

Eolian influences on dispersal are particularly noticeable in blowouts (i.e., saucer-shaped depressions deflated in older sands). Artifacts exposed by removal of underlying sand are commonly perched on the slopes of such blowouts, at 5° to 15°, where they are highly susceptible to rainwash. Eventually, a once-dispersed scatter of artifacts can become concentrated on the floor of the blowout, simulating a primary cluster (Figure 7-5).

The geomorphic agents most relevant for dispersal have been described in Chapter 4 and elsewhere (Butzer, 1976a).

Postdepositional disturbance

Sealed sites can be described as archaeological materials within a sediment matrix (i.e., geologically in situ). Such occurrences contrast with surface sites, in which cultural residues are exposed on the surface (because of lack of sediment) due to matrix erosion from sealed materials or to exposure of sealed materials by disturbance processes. Many sites within the A horizon of a soil should be regarded as surface sites (Lewarch and O'Brien, 1981) when they have been downmixed into the soil by plowing or earthworm activity.

Disturbance is a concept useful to describe the rearrangement of sealed sites in place. Disturbance is here defined as a primarily vertical movement of buried aggregates, variably affecting particles of different mass, shape, and material, leading to changes in inclination, orientation, and vertical or horizontal position that distort or eliminate the original three-dimensional relationships. Such disturbance can be partial or complete, and it can be physiogenic, due to mechanical processes, or biogenic, due to biological processes.

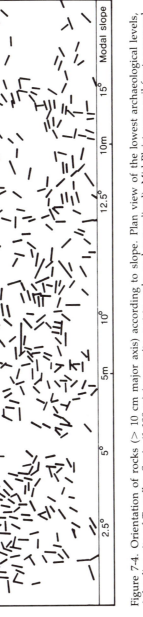

Figure 7-4. Orientation of rocks (> 10 cm major axis) according to slope. Plan view of the lowest archaeological levels, Acheulian site of Torralba, Spain (1,100 m) (composite, not to scale, and generalized). Mid-Pleistocene soil frosts arranged stones into rings on level ground and garlands on intermediate slopes, with diffuse downslope orientation on steeper gradients.

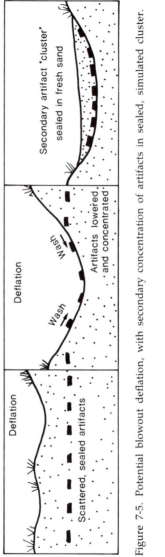

Figure 7-5. Potential blowout deflation, with secondary concentration of artifacts in sealed, simulated cluster.

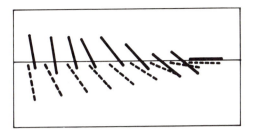

Figure 7-6. Experimental lift and angular rotation of wooden pegs by three freeze–thaw cycles. Note that wood has a much lower conductivity than stone and potsherds, so that rates and types of disturbances vary. Modified from Wood and Johnson (1978:Figure 9.11).

Soil frost. Frost penetrates more rapidly through stones than through soil, leading to selective ice crystallization under rocks. This leads to frost heave, and when the ice eventually melts, soil particles fill part of the space underneath, so that the rock does not fall back completely into its old position. As a result, the rock is slightly tilted or upraised or both. Repeated freeze-and-thaw cycles favor a slow upward migration of rocks, with progressive changes in inclination and even orientation (Figure 7-6). This jeopardizes vertical (and, to a lesser degree, horizontal) artifact associations within the seasonal freeze-thaw zone (base at 10 cm to 3 m depth, depending on the climate) in temperate environments. Under such conditions, partial disturbance, beginning at the time of initial abandonment, should be the rule rather than the exception. In cold or subpolar environments, such disturbance is intensified, during the course of differential downward freezing each autumn, toward an impermeable, waterlogged, or perennially frozen substrate. Intense cryostatic (frost) and hydrostatic pressures can be created, leading to wholesale distortions of the still-fluid subsoil. Such cryoturbation is recorded by contorted, festooned, or "flame" structures of materials, sorted according to texture or organic content, generally visible in color patterning. The geo-archaeological implications are important, because archaeological materials will be churned about, thus mixing distinct levels and creating multiple horizons out of one initial level (Figure 7-7) or regrouping one or more subsoil levels as telescoped surface lags, as, for example, in the Hungry Whistler site in Colorado (Benedict and Olson, 1978). Such disturbance commonly is "complete."

Mass movements. Soil frost can also assist in horizontal dislocation of subsoil aggregates through slow, frost-accelerated soil creep on gentle

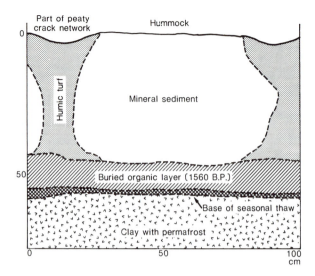

Figure 7-7. Substrate at the Engigstciak site, Yukon Territory, Canada. Artifacts and bones are found in the buried soil and in the peaty crack networks. They are probably derived from convectional movements related to seasonal freezing and thawing, as well as a rolling-under movement whereby slow solifluction on gentle slopes allowed segments of surface soil to slip between and then under blocks of frost-segregated mineral sediment. Modified from Mackay et al. (1961:Figure 5).

slopes or through frost-favored viscous soil sludging (solifluction). Creep and solifluction in temperate environments integrade with colluvial processes to produce slope wash, with "dry" downslope shifting of cliff-base rubble and with "wet" viscous mass movements such as mudflows, earthflows, and landslips (see Chapter 4). The sum total of such processes can lead to partial or complete disturbance in the horizontal dimension and, near the bases of hillsides, can produce multiple colluvial horizons that may even superpose archaeological materials in reversed vertical sequence (Figure 7-8).

Clay and salt dynamics. In warm environments with alternating wet and dry seasons, abundant expandable clays (montmorillonite or smectite) can produce effects as dramatic as those of frost. Such clays swell when wet and contract when dry, with the result that rocks and artifacts are mixed laterally and pushed upward by selective swelling adjacent to solid objects. Eventually, one or more subsurface archaeological horizons can be rearranged and ultimately transported up to the surface, where they will simulate a surface site. During the dry season, deep

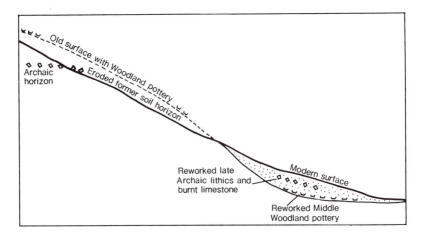

Figure 7-8. Hypothetical erosion of Archaic site, leading to downslope superpositioning of older Archaic occupation materials over younger Woodland pottery.

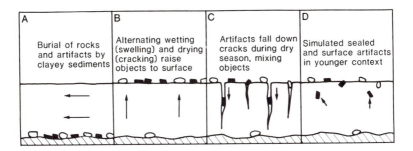

Figure 7-9. Artifact mobility in expandable clays.

dehydration cracks commonly form in such soils, and artifacts at the surface can tumble 10 cm to 1.5 m down such fissures, providing a potent mixing mechanism (Figure 7-9). In very arid environments, the top 20 to 50 cm of relatively fine soil also respond to occasional wetting by expelling air from voids as they fill with water; this tends, together with swelling of any expandable clays, to push up larger aggregates, which gradually accumulate at the surface. Two horizons can be created out of what was originally one subsoil horizon (Figure 7-10) (Butzer and Hansen, 1968:179). The wetting and drying of soil salts can produce similar effects in deserts, because the salts crystallize and expand while drying out. Wetting of clayey soils also facilitates human trampling, and Stockton (1973) has shown that under such conditions in a cave, small objects can move upward while larger ones move

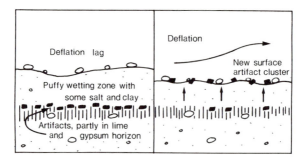

Figure 7-10. Artifact mobility in desert soils in response to air expulsion and salt or clay expansion during wetting.

down. Finally, disturbance of artifactual associations in spring contexts prone to occasional vent eruption or flush flow constitutes another water-related subsoil disturbance (Figure 7-2).

Deflation. Wind erosion in loose dry materials can expose sealed archaeological materials from one or more original levels and so transform them into partially or completely disturbed lag or pavement accumulations that may later be sealed again by fresh sediment (Figure 7-5). Deflation commonly attacks older eolian sands and silts, and even the desiccated floors of lakes.

Deformation. Differential compaction (e.g., of adjacent sandy and clayey substrates or of structural fillings such as storage pits) can lead to relative downward displacement of residues in clay-rich beds and organic beds, possibly disrupting a once-horizontal level. Such differential compaction, or the lateral slumping of surficial sediment units over wet clays or frost-disturbed substrates, can also lead to small-scale horizontal or vertical tension faults. Such microfaulting, with typical displacements of 10 to 75 cm, is particularly common in very cold environments, whether in recent or Pleistocene times (Figure 7-4). As a result, downthrusting or upthrusting can bring unrelated archaeological horizons onto a single level, whereas lateral movements can disrupt activity areas (Figures 7-11 and 7-12). True earthquake disturbance is also possible, as illustrated by Folk (1975) for the classical city of Stobi in Macedonia.

Bioturbation. A great deal of disturbance is due to the burrowing of animals, mainly rodents, particularly in dry external environments and

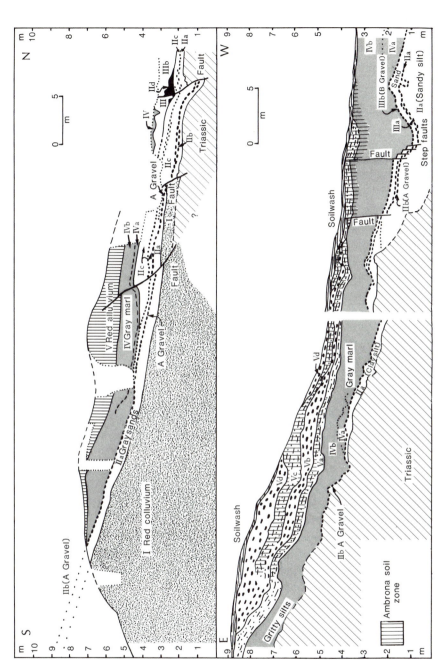

Figure 7-11. Deformation of mid-Pleistocene strata at the Acheulian sites Torralba and Ambrona, central Spain. Lubrication of underlying clays led to settling and lateral slumping, probably frost-assisted, after adjacent valleys had been cut by stream action. Modified from Butzer (1965).

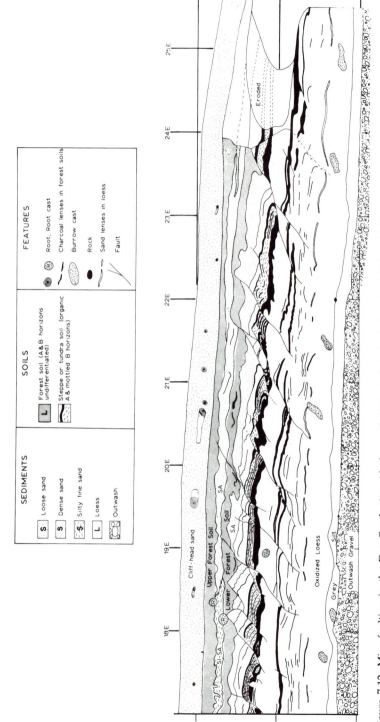

Figure 7-12. Microfaulting in the Dry Creek site, Alaska, with disturbed units dating from before 11,000 to 3500 B.P. Stakes are 1 m apart, and permanently frozen subsoil is normally found 1.2 to 1.5 m below the surface. Individual beds show frost distortion (cryoturbation), and multiple microfaults, mainly with 5-cm to 25-cm vertical displacements, reflect frost heave and frost-assisted slumping toward the lower terrace edge (right). From Thorson and Hamilton (1977:Figure 5) (copyright University of Washington, with permission).

cave environments. Artifacts can move down such burrows (known as *krotovinas*, when subsequently filled in with younger sediment), and so can charcoal fragments that may lead to faulty radiocarbon dates. Krotovinas may be so densely spaced in sandy soils that surface sites will be displaced into the subsurface on a large scale. For example, Archaic and Woodland artifacts are found dispersed through 50 cm of laminated sand filling an ancient blowout at the Sarah West site (Watseka, Illinois); however, all the artifacts are localized in relatively organic zones that lack laminations (i.e., in krotovinas). It has also been observed that millipedes have burrowed vertically through 4 m of dry cave sediment (Rose Cottage Cave, South Africa), transporting fresh straw through a honeycomb of small passages; the potential consequences for later radiocarbon dating of amorphous organic matter can well be imagined. On the other hand, earthworm castings are brought up to the surface, where they can rapidly cover objects. Over extended periods, earthworm activity in a highly humic soil can lead to gradual burial of a surface, with slow downward transfer of original surface materials until they are stratified as much as 25 to 30 cm within this biogenic sediment (Figure 7-13).

In drier soils in warm climates, termites achieve an almost incredible degree of soil mixing, and termite mounds are known to include diagnostic minerals from as much as 8 m below the surface (D. M. Helgren, personal communication); as a result of such large-scale ant activity, surface artifacts are not uncommonly displaced 30 cm and more down into the soil (Figure 7-13B). Although many subsoil rock horizons ("stone lines") found in Africa are old colluvial lenses, others are results of termite activity. Cahen and Moeyersons (1977) have described cases from Zaire in which artifacts and their related debitage have been vertically separated by a meter or more in sandy sediments, with the heavier objects evidently moving downward; combinations of termite activity and gravity-related processes linked to periodic wetting and drying probably were involved.

Vegetation contributes its share to bioturbation, in part through oxidation of organic matter from fills, leading to the opening of voids and favoring differential compaction. More widespread, perhaps, are the effects of roots of trees and woody shrubs that penetrate deep into even compact sediment; when the roots subsequently rot, younger soil washes in from above, and adjacent artifacts can fall in, changing both their vertical positions and orientations. Finally, the fine networks of roots of various plants can actually dislodge and distort archaeological

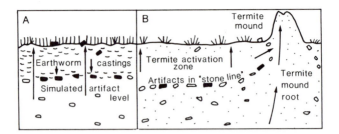

Figure 7-13. Downward movement and subsoil alignment of surface artifacts and rocks as a result of upward transfer of earthworm castings in a humic North American soil (a) and through termite activity in a semiarid African soil (B).

distributions in unconsolidated matrices if they reach beyond a particular horizon.

Viewed as an ensemble, these physiogenic and biogenic factors indicate an urgent need for proper field examination to identify potential disturbances of archaeological residues. Perhaps the most confidence-inspiring situation is that in which artifacts are found within intact, three-dimensionally defined hearth lenses or on organic floors linked to distinct features such as boiling and storage pits. Such requirements are best met in sediments with a strong cultural component, whether in a town mound, a house floor, or a cave. Major problems arise primarily where materials are found in predominantly mineral matrices lacking such nonportable features. In the case of inhomogeneous matrices with distinct stratification, a complex color patterning or distortion of sediments may directly document disturbance, whereas tedious assessment of horizontal patterning, orientation, and dip may well be essential for homogeneous matrices. A geo-archaeologist is indispensable in determing whether or not the original context is preserved, and orientation and dip studies normally are called for.

A more comprehensive survey of soil-disturbance factors has been provided by Wood and Johnson (1978). The related processes have been discussed further elsewhere (Butzer, 1976a).

Geobiochemical modification

The preservation, alteration, mobilization, and transformation of cultural and organic residues by inorganic and organic processes can be described as geobiochemical modification. Affected is the whole range of plant and animal food products and their primary and secondary

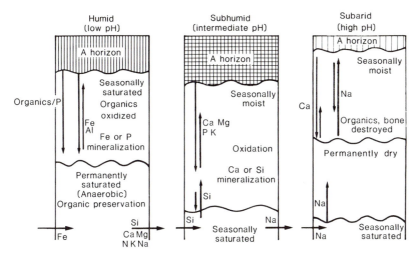

Figure 7-14. Some geochemical processes in the subsoils of different environments.

wastes, as well as organic raw materials and finished products used in manufacture and construction. The basic components are plant remains, bone, and biochemical residues and compounds (see Chapter 6). The principal active variables are water, mineral solutions, microfauna, bacteria, and fungi. The controlling microenvironmental factors are the moisture regime and the presence or absence of mineralizing solutions and sodium salts (Figure 7-14).

Moisture regime. With total and permanent dehydration, the processes of solution, oxidation, and destruction by organisms are inhibited, and organic materials and compounds tend to remain stable and oxidize very slowly. Botanicals and bone are readily preserved by total desiccation, although bone shrinks as it dries, and a lack of mineralizing solutions tends to leave it in a brittle subfossil state.

With permanent water saturation, anaerobic conditions inhibit or at least retard decomposition. However, biochemical compounds may be mobilized if there is lateral water movement, thus leading to partial loss of original components and their replacement by others.

Given a pattern of alternate wetting and drying, either seasonally or sporadically, organic materials tend to oxidize and decompose, whereas organic compounds may be vertically mobilized, rearranged, or even displaced. As a result, pH, calcium carbonate, organic matter, and phosphate values will eventually be changed, distorted, or otherwise rendered meaningless. For example, organic matter, potassium, and nitrogen are gradually destroyed or flushed out of the horizon, whereas phosphates may switch from soluble to fixed forms or may migrate down into lower subsoil horizons. Consequently, the preservation of such key indicators in a warm and wet, but aerated, microenvironment is time-dependent, and their values may be reduced to the level of background readings after several millennia. Similarly, anomalously high phosphate values at 50 to 100 cm in the subsoil may record a surface occupation (Eidt, 1973, 1977), possibly destroyed by plowing, rather than occupation levels at depth, because phosphorus is readily leached into lower horizons. Alternating cycles of solution, mobilization, and precipitation of soil compounds also allow for possible mineral replacement or accretion, a critical factor in fossilization of bone and botanical remains (see Chapters 10 and 11).

Mineralizing solutions. The presence of lime, soluble iron, mobile (colloidal) silica, and available phosphates favors concentration of such compounds, or combinations thereof, in soil waters. This is particularly true in subsoil environments prone to alternate wetting and drying or alternate oxidizing and anaerobic conditions. Calcareous, ferruginous, siliceous, and apatite cements may form in the process, either in preexisting voids or as replacements for dissolved minerals. Such mineralization leads to compact mineral products of high density and great durability.

Sodium salts. Sodium chloride (halite) as well as various other salts and alkalies (pH of about 9 or more) are inimical to the preservation of organic components in oxidizing environments. Bone and botanical remains are corroded, broken apart, and eventually decomposed, whereas organomineral compounds are destroyed or broken up and regrouped as new minerals.

The actual course of events in organic preservation is difficult to predict, and presence or absence of organic materials generally is interpreted with the benefit of hindsight. However, such considerations are useful in devising excavation strategies and are particularly important in evaluating the possibilities of selective preservation. An appreciation of the chemical processes that affect organic residues is equally important during the course of excavation, because horizons often are identified ad hoc according to organic coloration, and decisions regarding fine-mesh sieving and flotation for organic matter are made on the basis of the macroscopic residues encountered. Apparent deformations within a stratified sequence may be the result of oxidation and disappearance of organic materials, which can constitute almost 100% of some original bulk residues, generally characterized by limited compaction and exceptionally low densities. White mineral ash must be distinguished from partly combusted carbonized material, and from oxidized and partly vitrified reddish fire-contact laminae, in the process of distinguishing true hearth complexes from amorphous organic residues (see Chapter 6). Finally, chemical alteration, oxidation or humification, and related structural changes may be linked to soil or other weathering horizons that terminate or interrupt an occupation sequence (Dimbleby and Bradley, 1975; Liebowitz and Folk, 1980). These points serve to draw attention to no more than a selection of possible avenues for interpretation of the geobiochemical features of abandoned sites.

Particularly informative examples of chemical and other analyses of organic residues have been provided by Cook and Treganza (1950), Cook and Heizer (1965), Davidson (1973), Hassan and Lubell (1975), and Hall and Kenward (1980). A broader systematic framework within which to use chemical data as indicators of microspatial patterning activities has been outlined by Sjöberg (1982).

Site destruction and artifact dispersal

The history of an abandoned site is a function of human, biogenic, and physiogenic agencies acting directly on or within the site, as well as peripheral geomorphic processes that condition or accelerate its attrition. For example, suppose a lithic workshop on a riverine gravel bar is partly dispersed by a surge of torrential discharge, and its remnants are buried under thick gravels and sands; the abandoned irrigation canal is clogged with silt and obscured by drifting sands; the pillaged villa is burned to the ground and gradually covered with a spread of hillwash.

More complex is the metamorphosis of a prominent village mound not submerged under the sprawling foundations of one or more later cities. The interactions of the potential forces that work to level abandoned occupation mounds (see Chapter 6) can be outlined as follows (Figure 7-15):

1. *Compaction and weathering.* Gravity compaction and filling of the remaining voids, by microcollapse and small-scale subsoil water transport, will increase bulk density at the price of reduction in relief.

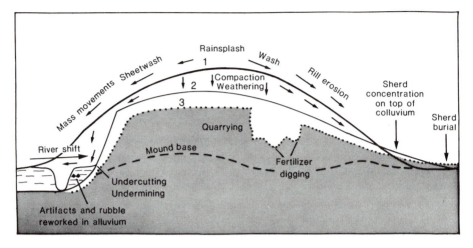

Figure 7-15. Morphological evolution phases (1, 2, and 3) of a mound, and typical processes responsible.

Chemical weathering, leaching, and biogenic activity are likely to further modify surface morphology.

2. *Mass movements, surface water, and wind.* Soil creep and slumping, together with sheetwash and rillwash, continue to erode the mound surface. Beyond the process of general denudation, promontories are reduced, concavities are infilled, and surficial sediment is swept from the mound center out onto the peripheries, where it accumulates as a broad apron of colluvial sediment, locally extending into shallow alluvial fans. In the course of time, original slopes of as much as 15° to 25° can be reduced to 2° and less. An impressive case of mass movements destroying parts of a site has been described by Folk (1975) at Stobi, where a landslide from an adjacent cliff face plowed 100 m or so across the town, later partly destroyed by earthquake. Deflation may also be active in removing fine dry material, although eolian accretion is perhaps equally common, as with silt-sized materials possibly derived from the seasonally dry riverbed at Stobi (Folk, 1975), or the various volcanic ash falls such as those burying Pompeii, Herculaneum, Akrotiri on Thera (Davidson, 1978), and several Central American sites (Sheets and Grayson, 1979:Chapter 17).

3. *Human intervention.* Abandoned settlement sites have commonly been used as quarries for rock, wood, adobe (including raw materials for brick making), pottery temper, and fertilizing compounds. In Egypt, entire town sites have been eliminated by fertilizer diggers (*se-*

bakhin) searching for phosphates as well as nitrates, potassium, and lime. Another secondary use of settlement sites in the Nile Valley has been as cemeteries, by virtue of the improved drainage on mounds that rise above the annual inundation level.

4. *Stream activity.* Beyond the standard hazards of on-site compaction, denudation, and human intervention, adjacent gullies and streams may attack a mound directly or indirectly. Gullies passing near a mound will stimulate development of tributary branches that cut back into the mound base, accelerating denudation and favoring rill formation on the steepening slopes of the gully catchment. Nearby streams and rivers may shift their courses close enough to a mound to lead to undercutting and repeated gravity collapse. Instructive examples of site destruction by running water have been provided by Davidson (1976), Davidson et al. (1976*b*), and Turnbaugh (1978).

Settlement mounds undergo an almost predictable geo-archaeological evolution (Kirkby and Kirkby, 1976). The topographic form is gradually flattened, following initial collapse and erosion of the walls, to become a circular or elliptical mound. As relief is progressively reduced, the declining angle of the mound profile approximates a normal (sine) curve. In fact, given identical conditions of climate, building materials, and initial mass and elevation, mound reduction is a function of time and can be used to estimate age (Kirkby and Kirkby, 1976). Mound evolution may also be cyclic, because such sites often are reused.

There are further important implications in the Kirkby and Kirkby (1976) study for preservation and interpretation of surface potsherds and lithics. Surficial denudation of finer materials will concentrate sherds on the surface, particularly as they move downslope and concentrate around the foot of the mound core. At the site periphery, sherd concentration again decreases as a result of burial within water-laid sediments or as bioturbation and plowing transport sherds down into the soil (Figure 7-15). On top of the remnants of the mound, quarrying and pit digging also help concentrate sherds, as well as redistribute them within the surface sediment. Over time, surface sherds are subject to (a) accumulation, as a lag, through progressive site erosion, (b) size comminution, through trampling, and (c) downslope transfer, as a result of running water and gravity (Kirkby and Kirkby, 1976). The net effect over the first 50 to 100 years after site abandonment is to increase surface sherd concentrations; thereafter, sherds decrease exponentially, according to a climate-related curve that is also influenced by mound relief and by the type and effectiveness of vertical mixing agents. These findings, both deductive and inductive, have profound implications for surface prospecting and archaeological testing on mounds. They also suggest a need for caution in predicting subsurface distributions from surface occurrences (Redman and Watson, 1970; Binford, 1972).

Environmental modification of archaeological residues

"The archaeological record at a site is a static, three-dimensional structure of materials existing in the present. The remains in this site have undergone successive transformations from the time they once participated in a behavioral system to the time they are observed by the archaeologist" (Schiffer 1975:838). As argued by Schiffer and as explicated here, two different sets of processes are involved in these transformations: (a) cultural activities that remove the residual materials from their original behavioral context into archaeological context and (b) environmental factors that modify these cultural residues through erosion or burial, destruction or selective preservation, and vertical or horizontal disturbance. Schiffer considered the latter "n-transforms" (i.e., noncultural tranformations) to be a set of experimental "laws" that explain and predict the interactions between culturally deposited materials and environmental variables. These n-transforms derive their systematic content from the natural sciences, but Schiffer argued that they should be studied and formulated by archaeologists.

Although I am sympathetic with this implicit plea that archaeologists begin to pay attention to such n-transforms, the issues of dispersal, disturbance, and chemical modification are evidently too complex to be diagnosed or appreciated by untrained excavators. This is the purview of the geo-archaeologist, and it can be argued that site formation and modification are the why and wherefore of archaeosedimentology.

Building on the content of this chapter, it is now possible to systematize the environmental transformation of archaeological residues by means of two graphic subsystems, one devoted to dispersal, burial, and disturbance (Figure 7-16, top), the second devoted to preservation of organic residues (Figure 7-16, bottom).

In the case of the mobilization flow diagram, various conditions of dispersal, burial, and/or disturbance produce surface or sealed sites that can be primary, semiprimary, or secondary. These terms require specific definition from an environmental perspective: A *primary site*

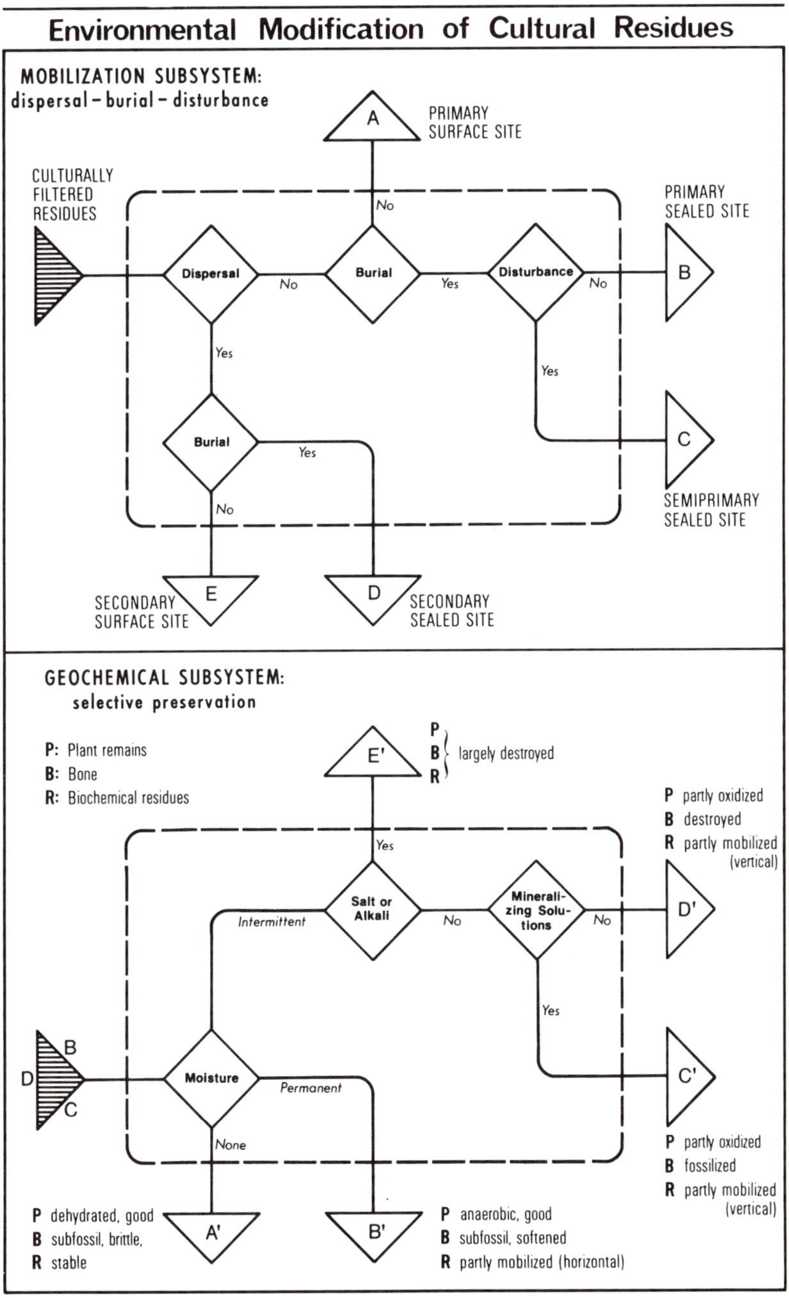

Environmental Modification of Cultural Residues

Figure 7-16. Systemic representation for environmental modification of archaeological residues. For key to symbols, see Figure 2-1.

comprises culturally filtered residues, either surface or sealed, that have been subjected to minimal dispersal and disturbance. A *semiprimary site* consists of such surface or sealed materials that have been subjected to partial dispersal and/or disturbance, but for which relative associations remain essentially intact over at least part of the site. A *secondary site* is composed of archaeological materials that have been subjected to effective dispersal and/or complete disturbance, retaining few informative associations or none. These definitions serve to describe aspects of environmental, not cultural, context. The distinction is essential to avoid a fairly pervasive conceptual confusion. Another qualification to Figure 7-16 is that it does not include all permutations of sealed, surface, primary, semiprimary, and secondary sites. Finally, Figure 7-16 does not consider potential secondary cycles that expose and possibly rebury archaeological residues.

The geochemical flow diagram (Figure 7-16, bottom) deals with the essential preservation processes and products relevant to plant remains, bone, and biochemical residues, particularly as generated in outputs B, C, and D (Figure 7-16, top) (i.e., affecting sealed sites). Organic residues are rarely preserved (or at least discernible) in the case of a surface site.

In combination, the two diagrams of Figure 7-16 provide a geoarchaeological classification for archaeological sites that is predicated on three environmental criteria: (a) surface versus sealed; (b) primary, semiprimary, or secondary; (c) the presence or absence of (and selective preservation of) organic residues. For example, the content of an Egyptian tomb might be BA' (primary, sealed, with complete organic preservation), that of a Danish bog CB' (semiprimary, sealed, fairly complete organic preservation), that of a French river gravel DC' (secondary, sealed, with some organic preservation), and that of an Archaic field scatter EE' (secondary, surface, essentially no organic preservation).

In conclusion, it may be argued that a proper understanding of the environmental modification of archaeological residues is or should be a critical goal in geo-archaeological study. Unless these processes are first elucidated, the cultural transformations may remain unnecessarily ambiguous or even undecipherable. Only when both the environmental and cultural contexts of a site are understood can sociocultural interpretation of the systemic context of a prehistorical community be attempted.

CHAPTER 8

Geo-archaeology VI: human impact on the landscape

Human activity and the soil-sediment system

The impacts of preindustrial human activities are concentrated in and around living areas, but these represent only a small part of a region. By focusing on sites, many archaeologists fail to appreciate the more diffuse but equally real impacts of people on the landscape at large. In the case of prehistorical foragers, these impacts may indeed be subtle and almost intangible, through the use of fire to facilitate hunting, local disturbance of vegetation, inadvertent dispersal of economic plants, and faunal changes as a result of selective hunting pressures (Butzer, 1971a). But farmers and herders normally have significant and even dramatic influences on the environment.

Central to this argument is that the vegetation cover and soil mantle provide a critical resource as well as a protective buffer between the atmosphere and the earth's crust. Under normal circumstances, in a humid landscape, rainfall is intercepted by taller plants, which break raindrop impact and prevent direct rainsplash on mineral soil. Organic leaf litter in various stages of decomposition covers the ground and creates a topsoil layer that cushions water impact, while also acting as a sponge to soak it up. The microfauna of the organic topsoil also maintain a spongy soil structure by converting organic residues into beneficial by-products, enhancing the aeration essential for good plant growth, and allowing water to infiltrate the soil. This diverts surface water from rapid runoff to slow lateral "throughflow" or to recharge the deeper-seated groundwater. Meanwhile, the rooting network helps bind the soil. The net result is that surface runoff is reduced in amount and velocity, soil moisture is enhanced, and groundwater seepage is maintained, even during drier times of the year (Figure 8-1). Stream discharge immediately after heavy storms is reduced or delayed, and dry-season flow is sustained. In this way, vegetation and soil not only condition productivity but also regulate the hydrological cycle. Human activi-

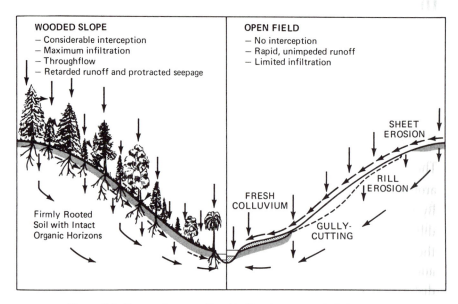

Figure 8-1. Contrasting runoff and infiltration on wooded slopes and cultivated slopes. From Butzer (1976*a*:Figure 6-2) (copyright © 1976 by Karl W. Butzer. Reprinted by permission of Harper & Row, Publishers, Inc.).

ties, however, are consciously or inadvertently focused on the biosphere. Consequently, depending on their intensities, these activities can modify or eliminate both vegetation and soil and thus interfere in the hydrological cycle. The resulting impact can be as dramatic as a climatic change in triggering readjustments by the environmental subsystem that regulates water, soil, and geomorphic processes (see Figure 2-2).

The components of such disturbances can be detailed as follows:

1. *Devegetation.* The native plant cover can be partially or completely removed, initially from local areas, eventually from much of the land surface, by a variety of processes: deforestation, field clearance, grassland burning, animal grazing, substitution of monoculture of an exotic crop, favoring a simplified secondary vegetation intensively grazed or browsed by domesticated animals (Figure 8-2). Leaf interception of raindrops is reduced by the cutting, burning, and browsing of trees and woody shrubs, and vegetative ground cover is reduced or removed by digging, hoeing, plowing, close grazing, and animal trampling. Even after human abandonment, forest regeneration is impeded by fire, grazing, and competition with light-loving plants, favoring an

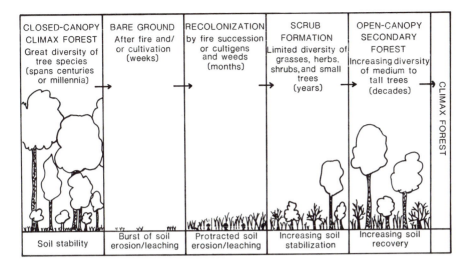

Figure 8-2. Vegetation succession in woodland. Protracted grazing by livestock can lead to an indefinite subclimax vegetation of degraded scrub.

open scrub vegetation or even a "cultural steppe." Such simplified plagioclimax vegetation (Figure 8-2) may be poorer in plant foods (fewer arboreal fruits and legumes, but more tubers and berries), and on low-nutrient soils it may lead to expansion of less nutritious grasses that are higher in cellulose content.

2. *Soil loosening.* Cultivation is designed to break the sod by cutting and tearing up the cohesive rooting network and by loosening the soil and exposing the now more friable soil aggregates to the elements. The hooves of domesticated stock also damage the sod and, together with close grazing by animals such as sheep, impair the regenerative qualities of the vegetative mat, helping to compact the soil and reduce its ability to absorb water (Figure 8-3). Loosened exposed soil is highly erodible, and its organic matter is rapidly oxidized in the sun; when abandoned, such soil tends to compact. Soil that has been compacted allows less water to percolate during rainstorms, accelerating surface runoff and favoring soil erosion.

3. *Soil-water and groundwater changes.* Devegetation and soil deterioration have important secondary effects on soil moisture. In cool wet environments with low-nutrient soils, removal of forest reduces plant evapotranspiration and raises the already high water table; furthermore, deforestation reduces soil biota, increases soil acidity, and thus favors leaching of soil nutrients. As a consequence, acid-tolerant plants

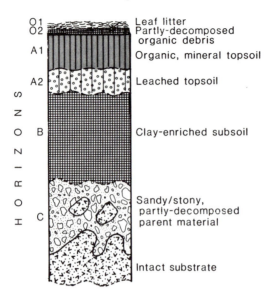

Figure 8-3. A standard soil profile. Plowing destroys the 01 and 02 horizons and degrades the A1 horizon. Once the A2 or B horizon is exposed, the soil is highly erodible. Modified from Butzer (1976*a*: Figure 4-6).

such as spruce, heather, and mosses expand, reinforcing the trend toward acid soils in which "raw" humus accumulates (Figure 8-4A). Seasonal dehydration of exposed soil leads to irreversible dehydration of iron and aluminum oxides, favoring subsoil hardpan formation and further impeding proper internal soil drainage (Figure 8-4B). Eventually, infertile and waterlogged cultural podsols, peats, and heath soils are generated, creating soils that are marginal or unsuitable for agriculture, while favoring an acidic vegetation of little grazing value. In this way, extensive cultural wastelands (moors and heaths) were formed in northwestern and northern Europe, particularly in montane environments and on sandy substrates (Simmons and Proudfoot, 1969; Evans, 1975:Chapter 5; Moore, 1975). In drier environments, the effect is reversed, but almost equally deleterious. Devegetation, dehumification, and reduced soil aeration and infiltration capacity, as well as accelerated surface runoff, all favor reduced percolation of rainwater into the subsoil and down to the groundwater. Water retention in the soil decreases, and the groundwater table drops, reducing spring discharge and cutting off much of the water supply to streams that otherwise would maintain a base flow during the drier spells between rains. Stream flow is less dependable, and sources of drinking water may be

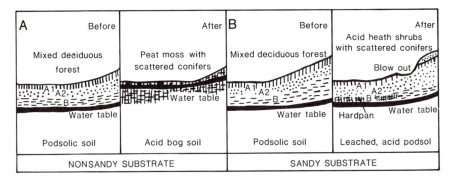

Figure 8-4. Changes in acid soils of cool wet environments resulting from fire clearance or cultivation. The secondary peat moss of A grows upslope as a blanket bog, and the secondary heath mat rests on highly erodible A2 horizons prone to deflation if disturbed.

curtailed; agricultural productivity is reduced on drier soil substrates poorer in beneficial soil biota (Figure 8-5). More aridic soil types expand as part of the cultural steppe (Ložek, 1975, 1976).

4. *Construction.* Human interference in the ecological balance is progressively intensified by building activities and the like. Rainfall deflected from roofs is concentrated on the disturbed ground around buildings. In the case of built-up towns, the increased and concentrated runoff is most erosive along the town perimeter (Figure 8-6). Areas around rural waterholes and wells are other foci of erosion. Unpaved roadways and trails are swept by runoff and often are converted into water-rilled surfaces and even gullies, whereas paved roads concentrate runoff along their margins, and road "cuts" are prone to mass movements and undercutting or rilling. Field terraces on hillsides and sloping valley bottoms are designed to be protective, but when they are no longer maintained, the loose surface soils as well as the rock walls and retainers can be rapidly swept away, with great destructive effect. Irrigation ditches trap sediment on low gradients; when abandoned, they channel and accelerate erosive forces on steeper inclines, much as do artificial drains. Dams lead to premature deposition of fine organic and mineral residues, depriving downvalley floodplains of sediment and natural fertilizers; when dams eventually collapse, the escaping waters can exert unusual erosive force and can pose safety hazards for crops, livestock, and humans. In effect, modification of landscape geometry (Moss and Walker, 1978), even in nonindustrial societies, implies interference in the harmonious adjustment of the innumerable components of a three-dimensional surface. Water attack

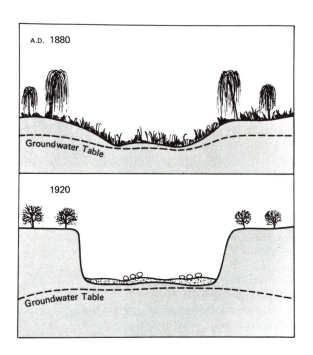

Figure 8-5. Consequences of soil erosion, gullying, and falling water tables in New Mexico A.D. 1880–1920. From Butzer (1976a:Figure 7-11) (copyright © 1976 by Karl W. Butzer. Reprinted by permission of Harper & Row, Publishers, Inc.)

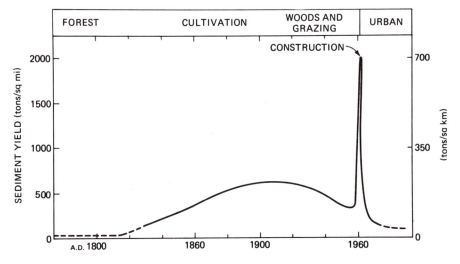

Figure 8-6. Effects of cultivation and urban construction on sediment removal from a Maryland watershed A.D. 1800–1965. Modified from Wolman (1967).

becomes focused on many weak points, leading to various degrees of hydraulic maladjustment.

5. *Accelerated soil erosion.* Devegetation exposes the soil to rainsplash and sheet erosion, effects intensified by cultivation, especially plowing, which destroys the sod and rooting system. On inclined surfaces, initial cultivation can lead to a burst of soil erosion, during which fine-grained suspended material is not only flushed off the slope but often swept away into distant streams. If more compact or stony substrates are intersected by erosion, or if fields are abandoned, a degree of stabilization is restored after a few years. But repeated plowing continues to bring up highly erodible fine soil to the surface, inevitably causing soil impoverishment as clay and organic matter are selectively removed (Moss and Walker, 1978). Sheetwash will affect the whole surface, but more concentrated and more potent rill erosion can develop on lower or steeper slopes, often aided by plow furrows. As rills grow, they may excavate deep gashes that then develop a momentum all their own: As water pours over the rim, it accelerates, plunging into the depression with enough energy to excavate and remove even heavy particles; the gash deepens and begins to eat back, forming a self-perpetuating gully; eventually gullies form intricate networks that continue to deepen and cut headward at a rate of up to several meters during every storm, eventually destroying whole landscapes that become unusable for agriculture (Figure 8-7). Mass movements, including soil creep and slumping, are already set in train or are speeded up by animal trampling on slopes of 5° or more; once gullying is under way, slumping and massive soil collapse continue to aid and even accelerate gully development. Mudflows can also sweep along heavily disturbed silty slopes, transporting even cobbles and blocks, as whole hillsides are set in motion. A last agency is deflation, which attacks dry incohesive soils during long summer droughts (Figure 8-1B), particularly in semiarid environments.

The sum total of processes that remove a soil faster than it can regenerate is called accelerated soil erosion. It is preeminently a cultural phenomenon linked to devegetation and destruction of the sod and organic topsoil by cultivation or overly intensive grazing (Butzer, 1976a:114–19). Within a few generations, or even a few years, such accelerated soil erosion can change surface forms and move more soil than can millennia of environmental change (Trimble, 1974; Butzer, 1977a). The consequences for productivity are correspondingly enormous, as whole landscapes lose much or all of their topsoil, often

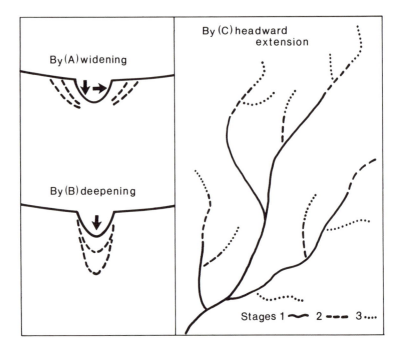

Figure 8-7. Gully enlargement and headward extension.

forcing their conversion to extensive grazing or secondary vegetation. Most, but by no means all, of the catastrophic soil erosion on record is associated with industrial societies. However, cultivation on intermediate slopes over relatively incohesive sediments had already produced equally devastated landscapes in some parts of the Mediterranean world during classical times. Even where the visible impact of soil erosion is less glaring, removal of 20% or 30% of the most fertile topsoil has a drastic impact on crop yields. Such conditions were not uncommon in selected areas of prime soil even three to five millennia ago.

6. *Hydrology.* Accelerated soil erosion goes hand in hand with equally fundamental changes in hydrological processes that reduce lowland productivity. A much higher proportion of rainfall runs directly downslope instead of filtering into the subsoil, eroding the surface and eventually depositing masses of increasingly mineral material and often stony material on footslopes and in shallow alluvial fans that bury more fertile lowland soils (Figure 8–8). Floodwaters rise rapidly and destructively, inundating prime lowlands regularly (Gentry and

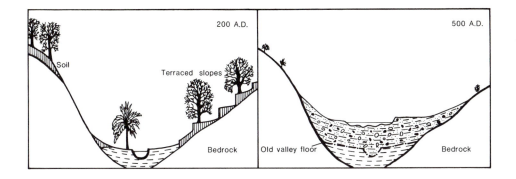

Figure 8-8. An Italian valley before and after stream alluviation as a result of soil erosion in late Roman times. Modified from Butzer (1976a:Figure 7-20).

Lopez-Parodi, 1980). Channels fill in with silt and sand, creating unstable "raised" rivers that frequently burst their banks or change their courses, and water tables rise and favor increasingly waterlogged bottomlands (Figure 8-9). Eventually, large parts of the cultivated lowlands may have to be turned over to grazing as agriculture becomes too precarious and less productive and epidemic disease festers amid expanding tracts of marshy ground.

The malarial coastal lowlands of the Mediterranean Basin were created in this way as much as 2,000 years ago, contributing their share to the economic decline of Greece and Roman Italy.

Another type of hydrological impact can be discerned in the irrigated lowlands of semiarid and desert environments, where seasonal field flooding and incremental irrigation lead to deposition of minute quantities of salt (White, 1973; Worthington, 1978) (Figure 8-10). Because this salt is seldom flushed out of the soil, particularly where the groundwater is high, salinization becomes a widespread process that gradually destroys the agricultural value of lands around the peripheries of irrigation networks, sometimes leading to progressive abandonment (Jacobsen and Adams, 1958; Hardan, 1971; Gibson, 1974; Lisitsina, 1976; Lawton and Wilke, 1979), partly in response to declining river discharge (Kay and Johnson, 1981). Modern salinization of ancient irrigated landscapes further endangers archaeological sites, because salt moves up from the ground water to evaporate at the surface, causing rock to flake off monuments.

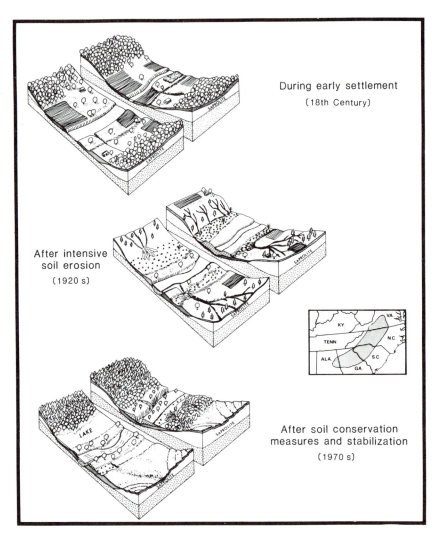

Figure 8-9. Evolution of Southern Piedmont landscapes A.D. 1700–1970. From Trimble (1974:Figure 29) (copyright Soil Conservation Society of America, with permission).

Geo-archaeological indicators of soil erosion

The scenario just described explains a constellation of processes that are symptomatic of an ecosystemic pathology, triggered or exacerbated by human land use. Such landscape changes can be documented in soil

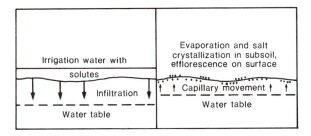

Figure 8-10. Irrigation and salinization.

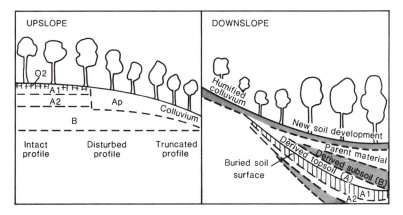

Figure 8-11. Upslope soil disturbance or truncation, and downslope colluvial deposition of soil derivatives in reversed order (strong vertical exaggeration).

profiles and geomorphic forms and sediments, as well as in diverse biological records.

Soil criteria. (a) Disturbed soil profiles. Plowing eliminates the distinctive subdivisions (leaf litter, fermentation, and humic-mineral zones) of the topsoil, creating a distinctive homogeneous plow (Ap) horizon sharply set off from the lighter B horizon below. Often such disturbed profiles can be recognized millennia later, particularly in permanently abandoned farmlands (Figure 8-11). (b) Truncated soil profiles. Erosion of the A horizon, or even part of the B horizon, can similarly be recognized (Figure 8-11), as, for example, in marginal areas of northwestern Europe, abandoned A.D. 1350–1700, where they take the form of fresh, thin A horizons over unusually shallow B horizons (Machann and Semmel, 1970). The remains of deserted farmsteads and villages serve to date such futile attempts at colonization. (c) Redeposited soils.

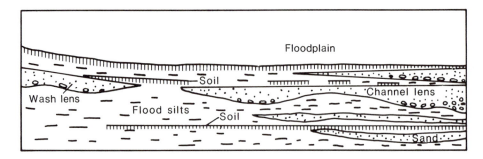

Figure 8-12. Interbedded flood silts, sand lenses reflecting peak floods, and wash lenses may result from sporadic influx of eroded soils and parent material, reflecting cultural disturbance of watershed.

Upslope erosion can bury footslopes, leading to abnormally thick A horizons, or even a reversed sequence of stony parent material over clayey subsoil and organic topsoil, in turn resting on top of a buried but intact profile (Figure 8-11). In some instances, several superpositions can be recognized and archaeologically dated by potsherds (Ložek, 1976). Such field evidence has been discussed further by Limbrey (1975:236–9); see also the work of Cook (1963), Proudfoot (1970), Dimbleby and Bradley (1975), Evans (1975:Chapter 5), Dimbleby (1976), Taylor (1979), and Simmons and Tooley (1981).

Geomorphic criteria. Geomorphic systems respond to soil erosion on various scales, depending on how sustained and widespread the pathologic condition. With the exception of redeposited soils on footslopes, the best traces are preserved in and under floodplains. There temporary stream aggradation may be recorded by lenses of coarse and poorly sorted soilwash interbedded with flood silts or by anomalously thick and extensive increments of such silts, reflecting periods of unusual lateral sediment influx or peak flood recurrence in combination with abnormal quantities of suspended sediments. Periods of renewed stability may be indicated by incipient capping A horizons (Figure 8-12). General stream aggradation typically will favor the development of a higher floodplain along great stretches of river, often documenting shifts in hydrological processes that include higher proportions of sand and gravel, with the result of rapid channel filling. River courses may shift repeatedly, possibly switching from a meandering pattern to an unstable braided system. Such braided channels, linked to prominent sandy alluvial fans at tributary confluences, suggest advanced sheetwash and gullying on more distant slopes, where coarser parent materials or wholly unweathered substrates are being exposed.

Eventually, as much of the watershed reverts to secondary vegetation, slopes stabilize, and the sediment supply is drastically reduced. This normally favors new readjustments in hydrological processes and floodplain geometry, with stream entrenchment that leaves the floodplain as a nonfunctional "terrace" several meters above a new and narrower floodplain, more closely approximating the initial hydrological parameters (Figure 8-13). Several such cut-and-fill cycles can create multiple terraces, each of which may coincide with an episode of catastrophic settlement expansion. Soil erosion may also be recorded by coastal siltation in relatively shallow embayments, leading to shoreline progradation out to sea, as more and more sediment is deposited from streams draining disturbed catchments well inland. Shoreline changes of this type, modified in detail by minor sea-level changes and tectonic displacements, are particularly striking in the Mediterranean Basin (Eisma, 1962; Kraft et al., 1977, 1980a, 1980b).

Geochemical criteria. Lake sedimentation patterns are equally sensitive to land use within a catchment, responding to disturbances by exponential increases in accretions of suspended sediment, charcoal, organic carbon, calcium carbonate, phosphates, and several other ions whose proportions vary according to the regional environment. For example, mid-Holocene deforestation and heath development in the northern uplands of Britain led to increases in potassium, manganese, sodium, and chloride concentrations at the same time that forests were declining, soil acidity was increasing, and suspended sediment was increasing in response to Mesolithic and Neolithic disturbances (Mackereth, 1965; Pennington, 1970). In northern Guatemala, deposition of carbonates and phosphates was accelerated in response to soil erosion and human settlement (Deevey et al., 1979).

Other cations and anions whose deposition may increase under similar conditions are those of ammonia, nitrates, iron, and sulfates. The exact sources of these minerals are difficult to determine with precision, because they may reflect accelerated leaching of disturbed soils, mechanical flushing of soil particulates rich in ions from slopes into a lake, increased human and animal waste effluents, or production by riparian vegetation in polluted waters. In Guatemala, Deevey et al. (1979) noted that silts produced by construction disturbance were unusually low in phosphorus. Another problem is that concentrations

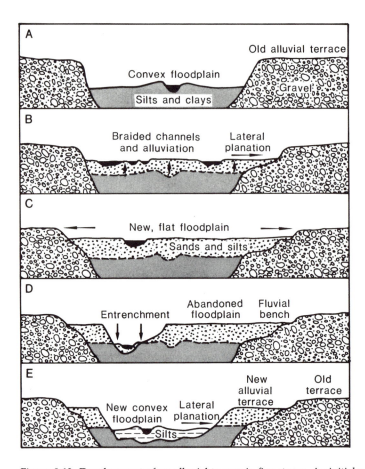

Figure 8-13. Development of an alluvial terrace in five stages. An initial convex floodplain (A) is buried by coarser sediments as a result of rapid alluviation by braiding channels (B). Eventually, a more stable flat floodplain (C) is created by alluviation. Another hydrological change leads to downcutting in alluvium (D) and abandonment of the flat floodplain. A new convex floodplain (E) is established by alluviation of fine sediments and lateral planation, approaching the conditions of stage A. Modified from Butzer (1976a:Figure 8-13).

vary with the rate of discharge: Ammonia, chlorides, and sulfates decrease with dilution, whereas turbidity, suspended solids, iron, manganese, and phosphates increase in direct proportion to the volume of water (Ruhe et al., 1980). Despite these difficulties of detailed interpretation, the geochemical records of many lakes preserve a reasonably continuous record that is quite sensitive to land-use processes.

Biological criteria. The biological record of land use may be equally tangible, given good conditions of organic preservation. Palynology has shown the impact of clearance and cultivation in Britain, Denmark, and the Netherlands through replicated "fire successions," with a temporary decline in arboreal pollen, followed by ephemeral peaks in the pollens of pioneer light-demanding plants, cereals, and weeds (Smith, 1970; Evans, 1975:Chapter 6; Groenman-van Waateringe, 1978) (Figure 8-14). Palynological work has also exonerated prehistorical peoples of culpability in some forms of biotic change. For example, a detailed 1,000-year record of vegetation and charcoal horizons in the forests of northeastern Minnesota has shown that fires there had natural origins, that their frequency increased during times of warmer climate, and that artificial fire protection in recent decades has led to changes in forest composition (Swain, 1973). The implications are that not all fire successions can be attributed to human action and that fire is an integral part of most natural ecosystems. Long-term human transformations of biota have been documented in Czechoslovakia, where deforestation, soil erosion, and progressive "steppification" of the landscape favored replacement of a mixed woodland open-country molluscan fauna by an increasingly xeric one during the course of 5,000 years of human occupance (Evans, 1972, 1975:116–21; Smolíkova and Ložek, 1973, 1978). For further discussion of biotic criteria, see Chapters 10 and 11.

Soil erosion in the geo-archaeological record

Soil profiles and alluvial fills can provide sensitive records of the indirect effects of severe human impact on the landscape. Their systematic examination is imperative in dealing with the archaeology of agricultural and pastoral groups. Good case studies of relatively early human disturbance in the geo-archaeological record are available for Europe. Several of these clearly predate the advent of agricultural settlement.

At Lepenski Vir, above the Iron Gates of the Danube in northeastern Yugoslavia, Brunnacker (1971) has documented how, in the Mesolithic village at this location (ca. 7500–6800 B.P.), house-floor leveling cut into existing soils, thus leading to colluvial reworking of sands, with eventual slumping of exposed sediment faces and formation of meter-thick lenses of humic cultural debris. The Neolithic village (ca. 6800–6300 B.P.) at Lepenski Vir intensified these processes until sheets of humic sand, slope rubble, and cultural debris as much as 1.8 m thick

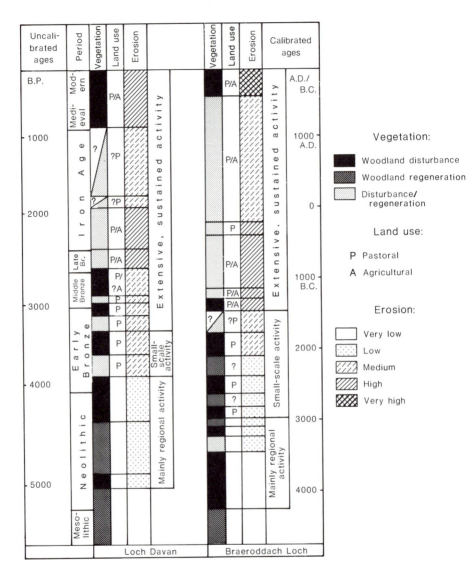

Figure 8-14. Records of vegetation, land use, and soil erosion in two lake cores from northeastern Scotland. Modified from Edwards (1979:Figure 1).

spread extensively around the site. Similar Mesolithic impacts have been documented in Britain, where repeated occupations at Oakhanger (Hampshire) led to burning of the deciduous woodland (abundant charcoal) and then site burial by eroded sand, ca. 6300 B.P. (Rankine and Dimbleby, 1960). At about this time, another Mesolithic occupation

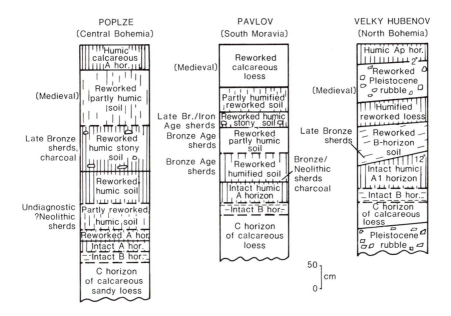

Figure 8-15. Soil and colluvial profiles from Czechoslovakia reflecting Neolithic, Late Bronze Age to Iron Age, and medieval disturbances and soil erosion. Modified from Ložek (1975) and Smolíkova and Ložek (1973).

at Iping Common (Sussex) led to deforestation, heath formation, and, indirectly, soil deterioration that eventually favored eolian activity (Evans, 1975:97–9). It appears that Mesolithic disturbance was highly localized and probably was due to the use of fire for the clearing of undergrowth (to spot game more easily) or in game drives (Simmons, 1969). The effects were temporary, except in marginal environments such as on wet uplands or nutrient-poor sands, where acidity increased and heath displaced forest, intensifying soil deterioration: Peaty bog soils developed on wet ground, and badly leached podsols, prone to erosion, developed on sand substrates.

Early Neolithic to Early Bronze farming activities are being increasingly detected in pollen diagrams and soil profiles of temperate Europe (Simmons and Proudfoot, 1969; Pennington, 1970; Smith, 1970; Evans and Valentine, 1974; Ložek, 1976; Slager and Van Wetering, 1977) (Figure 8-15). Such disturbance was invariably local, resulting in some sheet erosion, with sporadic colluvial deposition in low-lying areas and occasional mobilization of slope rubble in hilly terrain. The widespread diffusion of the plow, accompanied by rapid demographic expansion during the Middle and Late Bronze Age, had more general repercussions on the landscape after 3500 B.P.: extensive deforestation, cultivation, and floodplain aggradation (Ložek, 1976; Brunnacker, 1971, 1978*b*; Butzer, 1980*a*; Richter, 1980). There is evidence of stabilization and renewed soil formation by 2500 B.P., followed by another wave of slope soil erosion and valley alluviation after A.D. 100 in areas of concentrated Roman settlement (after A.D. 750 in landscapes east of the Rhine and Danube affected by medieval settlement expansion).

In the Mediterranean Basin the picture is similar, with local evidence of vegetation disturbance (oak woodlands degraded to Mediterranean scrub) beginning in Late Neolithic or Early Bronze times, but becoming commonplace between 3800 and 3100 B.P. in different areas, as soils were destroyed and valley fills aggraded (Eisma, 1962; Judson, 1963; Van Zuidam, 1975; Faugères, 1979; Davidson, 1980*b*; Van Andel et al., 1980). A second wave of soil erosion that was almost universal and sometimes catastrophic began in response to abandonment of terraced hillsides between A.D. 200 and 500; this occurred again later as a result of medieval colonization of more marginal environments (Vita-Finzi, 1969; Butzer, 1980*a*) (Figure 8-8).

A systematic picture of prehistorical human impact on the landscape has not yet emerged for other continents. However, some examples can be cited. At the Koster site in west-central Illinois, rates of colluviation were 50% higher than background levels during the phase of most intensive Archaic occupation (Horizon 6), ca. 5500 B.P.; disturbance of slope vegetation and soils by food-procurement activities as well as on-site habitation activities may well have been responsible (Butzer, 1977*a*) (Figure 8-16). Around Tepic, in western Mexico, three episodes of soil erosion have been identified and linked to phases of successively expanded agricultural land use, the most recent of which was historical (Cook, 1963) (Figure 8-17). The Tepic record is based on truncated soil horizons, relative degrees of soil reconstitution, and multiple cut-and-fill cycles that permit determination of local settlement concentrations. In northern Guatemala, lakes Sacnab, Yaxha, and Quexil record intensifying agricultural land use through exponential increases in their contents of grass pollen, clay, organic matter, carbonates, and phosphates since about 3500 B.P., correlated with demographic expansion until about a millennium ago (Deevey et al., 1979; Harrison and Turner, 1978). These New World examples serve to show that intensive land use and landscape degradation were not limited to European areas affected by plow agriculture.

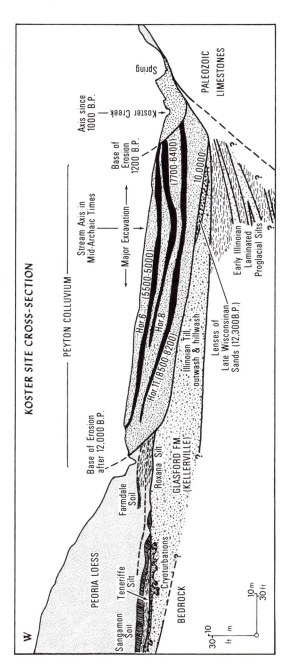

Figure 8-16. The major Archaic occupations (black horizons) in the loessic Peyton colluvium at the Koster site, west-central Illinois. Soil erosion on slopes was due to environmental conditions, but cultural acceleration is probable for at least horizon 6. From Butzer (1977a:Figure 2) (copyright Illinois State Museum, with permission).

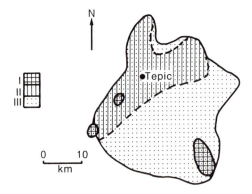

Figure 8-17. Settlement phases at Tepic, west-central Mexico, defined by soil-erosion criteria and pottery dating. Modified from Cook (1963:Figure 11).

A case study of accelerated soil erosion: Axum, Ethiopia

The preceding discussion illustrates the geo-archaeological impact of human land use at the general level, and it can be complemented by more detailed examination of a specific site from another continent, Africa. Axum, in northern Ethiopia, provides a good model. The urban geo-archaeology of that city in the first millennium A.D. was outlined in Chapter 6. Landscape changes affecting the surrounding drainage basin will be considered here (Figure 8-18) (Butzer, 1981a).

Axum is located on the piedmont of a group of volcanic hills, in the valley of a small drainage system (4 km²) that descends steeply from 22° to 45° hillsides onto 2° to 5° footslopes. Profiles were studied in a range of excavated sections and natural exposures: within the former city center (Stele Park, Debterá), along the length of the local stream (Enda Kaleb in headwaters, Mai Shum about midway, Enda Iyasus just upstream of Stele Park), and, on a transverse axis, on the piedmonts west and east of Axum.

The constructional debris indicated in Figure 8-18 includes artificial terraces and their fills, architectural remains, collapse rubbles, and mixed and partially reworked cultural debris (see Chapter 6). The gradation to the category of soil wash is a continuous one at Axum. The preeminently colluvial deposits singled out in Figure 8-18 include redeposited soils, water-laid soil mixed with cultural debris, and reworked collapse rubbles. The alluvial categories represent fine and coarse-grade stream-laid deposits, including silts and clays once carried in

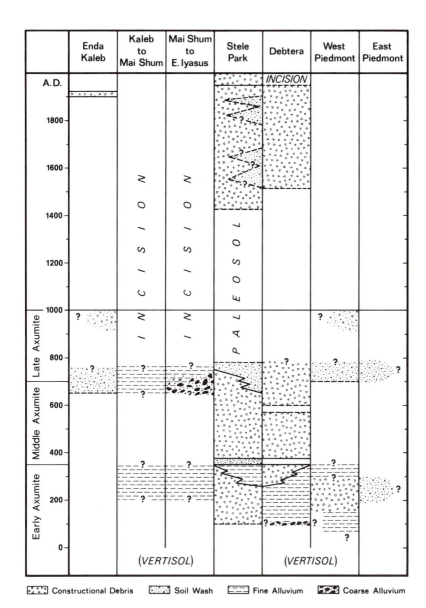

Figure 8-18. Geo-archaeological synopsis for Axum, Ethiopia. Modified from Butzer (1981a:Figure 4).

suspension, sands and gravels carried by bed traction, and intermediate deposits of mixed grade, such as sand-silt and sand-clay combinations with pockets, lenses, and isolated pebbles.

The oldest valley-floor surfaces around Axum comprise basal dark alluvial clays and the related heavy soils found over bedrock along the western piedmont. These cracking montmorillonitic clays delimit seasonally wet surfaces that predate Axumite settlement.

The first aggradation (phase I) coeval with Axumite settlement began about A.D. 100 and terminated A.D. 350 or so. This accumulation includes the reworked gray brown clays trapped in unit 2e of Stele Park (see Figure 6-4), prismatic brown clay under the Debterá, brown soilwash and rubble of the western piedmont, and reddish slope loams along the eastern piedmont (Figure 8-18).

This array of early Axumite deposits suggests strong periodic floods, wet slope soils, and seasonally abundant moisture. Deposition of one to two meters of relatively fine sediment across the local floodplain and over much of the adjacent piedmonts implies vigorous mobilization of material through a large part of the watershed. This much accumulation within one to three centuries implies culturally accelerated soil erosion in response to partial devegetation, deterioration of ground cover, an increased ratio of immediate surface runoff after rains, and higher peak discharge. But the sediments of the floodplain and the eastern piedmont also suggest a dramatic shift in slope equilibrium controls related to heavier rains or greater seasonal periodicity of runoff. In the context of intensifying land use in Early Axum, I would argue for a coincidence of cultural and acultural inputs into the environmental system. The composite result was a rapid change in the soil landscape that, by overall evaluation, did not significantly change potential soil productivity.

The second aggradation (phase II) began about A.D. 650 and lasted 150 years or so. Included are water-laid soil and cultural debris of the upper watershed (Enda Kaleb), crude gravels and brown sand loams of the Mai Shum valley sector, reworked cultural debris in Stele Park (see Figure 6-4), stony colluvial soil on the western piedmont, and redeposited slope soil along the eastern piedmont (Figure 8-18).

These Middle Axumite to Late Axumite deposits also have a modal thickness of one or two meters, but the sediment character differs from that of aggradation I. There is little trace of dark clay derivatives, but there is abundant slope rubble and architectural debris. Some material was reworked by water in very localized settings, but much of it implies vigorous denudation of the slopes above Axum, as, for example, a tongue of cobble and block rubble in a mudflow deposit. This argues for soil and slope instability in response to overintensive land use, particularly on marginal surfaces, combined with widespread field and settlement abandonment. But soil moisture was significantly less than during aggradation I.

The net impact of aggradation II was negative: Many slopes were denuded down to stony substrates that allowed no more than marginal browsing or charcoaling activities; extensive agricultural surfaces atop and just below the volcanic hills were either destroyed or reduced to a small fraction of their agricultural potential; even on the gentler low-land slopes, the more organic and better aerated A horizons were selectively stripped or were mantled with sandy to stony soil deriva-tives from the base of former soil profiles. The geomorphic evidence for culturally induced environmental degradation is direct; the case for vegetation and agriculture is indirect, but no less convincing.

The third phase of aggradation (phase III) may record little more than a short-term geomorphic readjustment following a late episode of abandonment or deliberate destruction (Figure 8-18).

The final phase of aggradation (phase IV) includes soilwash and debris in Stele Park (see Figure 6-4), reworked collapse rubbles in the Debterá, and twentieth-century excavations and land grading.

Land use and soil fertility

All forms of cultivation have a modifying and, to some degree, destruc-tive impact on soils. Even where soil erosion is minimal or is pre-cluded, soil fertility is prone to rapid and sometimes irreversible change. Fertility is a complex matter related to a variety of factors, each of which can be modified by cultivation or soil erosion (Pitty, 1979):

1. *Mineral nutrients.* The microorganisms of a healthy soil generate nitrogen in the form of ammonia, but cultivation, oxidation, and leach-ing deplete this supply. Phosphorus, potassium, calcium, and magne-sium are produced by slow rock weathering, and the resulting avail-able minerals are recycled back and forth between the vegetation and soil. As a result, devegetation can critically impair the mineral supply, whereas excessive leaching of exposed loosened soil flushes much of what is left into the runoff or groundwater (Likens et al., 1970). Unlike nitrogen, which is naturally replaced when the organic cycle is allowed to recover, phosphorus and potassium are particularly difficult to re-

plenish, so that long-term deficits affect all kinds of vegetative growth, even dominant woodland forms.

2. *Organic matter and microorganisms.* Properly decomposed nonacidic humus is essential to soil productivity, because it combines with clay particles to form molecular aggregates with high valences that link up with and stabilize ammonia, potassium, phosphorus, calcium, and magnesium. This beneficial "mild" humus is produced by the teeming soil microorganisms, of which the better types are very sensitive to dehydration, waterlogging, and acidification. Cultivation reduces microorganic activity, so that crude organic matter is not properly ingested, remaining in raw or acidic form. The reduced pH inhibits the microorganisms even further, and the base nutrients become mobile. As they are progressively lost from the molecular aggregates and replaced by hydrogen ions, acidity increases, and nutrients are washed out or leached. The organic cycle can be restored by allowing natural vegetation to regenerate over 20 years or more, but if the pH has dropped below 5 or so, the damage may be irreversible without application of artificial fertilizer (e.g., lime to raise pH, and mineral bases to allow the growth of plant types that generate nonacidic organic debris). This organic cycle is fundamental not only to retard leaching but also to ensure good permeability, water retention, and aeration–properties implied in the concept of soil structure. These properties again affect the organic cycle by ensuring a beneficial microclimate in the soil: not too dry and not too wet, with adequate aeration, thus allowing the microorganisms to thrive and respire carbon dioxide freely.

3. *Texture.* The basic mineral matrix of the soil is also important, particularly the quantity of clay minerals and the types of clays represented. Clays play two different roles. First, their presence is essential for water retention and for an inherent dynamism whereby soil aggregates expand when wet (retarding excessive percolation and mechanical leaching) and shrink when dry (providing aeration and access for subsequent infiltration by rainwater). Depending on how expandable the clay type is (montmorillonite high, illite intermediate, kaolinite very low), less than 5% to 10% clay is inadequate for proper moisture retention, whereas more than 25% to 50% is excessive, leading to temporary' or permanent waterlogging and poor aeration. Organic matter enhances the beneficial properties of clays by an order of magnitude, so that excessive cultivation of clayey soils favors compaction, poor aeration, and temporary waterlogging, reducing vegetative growth and inhibiting microorganic activity. Clays have different valences with

which to hold nutrient bases (kaolinite low, illite high, montmorillonite an order of magnitude higher than kaolinite), a capacity that is also greatly enhanced in clay-humus molecular aggregates. This number of available electrical links for mineral bases is called the exchange capacity; together with the pH, which gives an index of the proportion of available electrical charges that actually hold on to bases, the exchange capacity provides an objective measure of potential fertility. Altogether, selective erosion of clays by sheetwash, let alone destruction of the clayey segments or the soil profile by rill erosion of gullying, will have a catastrophic impact on soil fertility. Because clays form slowly over many millennia, severe soil erosion imposes essentially permanent restrictions on potential productivity.

Altogether, soil fertility is a fragile commodity, and many advanced forms of deterioration are almost irreversible, except with the application of special technology, at great cost of labor and capital investment, seldom available to subsistence economies. Several types of land use in prehistorical times can be expected to have had different effects on sustained fertility and productivity; discussions of these effects have been provided by Clarke (1976), Kirch (1978), and especially Denevan (1978).

The small, scattered, low-density populations of Neolithic Europe appear to have employed the long fallow system, cultivating small dispersed plots for a year or two, then allowing forest regeneration over 20 years or more. This method is generally not precarious: Erosive losses are negligible, soil nutrients and moisture are preserved, and regeneration is rapid. Larger populations can be supported by interposing short fallow periods of 4 to 20 years, generally sufficient to improve soil aeration and restore organic matter and nitrogen, thereby maintaining a reasonable degree of fertility and productivity (Greenland and Nye, 1959). But the simple probabilities of dehydration and sheet erosion are increased, and the typically denser spacing of fields tends to favor more disturbance and overall deterioration.

Bush or grass fallow periods of only one or three years require increased labor input, because weeds and pests become endemic, and maintenance of aeration and soil structure necessitates elaborate hoeing or plowing to loosen and mix the soil. Fertilization techniques probably were not understood by most prehistorical farmers, as suggested by a lack of any documentation from pharaonic Egypt (Butzer, 1976c:89–90). Consequently, declining crop yields were inevitable and progressive soil loss probable. When such plots were eventually abandoned, the leached and often more acidic soils were inadequate for nutrient-demanding trees, favoring a secondary vegetation dominated by different species; in cool wet environments this led to the expansion of acidic heaths or peat bogs. Forest recovery may have been permanently impeded by livestock grazing and deliberate burning, with animal trampling and continuing rainsplash erosion inhibiting soil recovery and accelerating soil erosion. Such increasingly degraded vegetation provides fewer plant types suitable for human consumption and, in competition with domesticated stock, can sustain fewer species of large game animals.

Soil erosion and depletion vary greatly according to the type of soil preparation. Hoe cultivation of small seeding areas breaks up only a fraction of the sod, and modern experiments have shown that such a no-tillage technique can reduce soil erosion to 1% or 2% of that typical for plowed fields, under otherwise identical conditions, with runoff cut to perhaps half (Phillips et al., 1980). Spot hoeing provides lower short-term yields but allows more sustained productivity, not only as a consequence of little or no soil loss but also because soil moisture is retained, seasonal dehydration is less probable, and soil temperatures are lower, with correspondingly less oxidation of organic matter, while soil structure and microorganic activity are maintained.

By contrast, plow agriculture produces higher yields per unit area in the short term and makes subsoil layers accessible to plants by deep plowing. But plowing can readily become an ecological disaster, and even under optimal circumstances erosion and soil depletion are almost unavoidable. Long-term yields can be sustained only by large-scale application of fertilizer – an almost impossible task for subsistence farmers. A third type of agricultural preparation is exemplified in high-productivity gardens adjacent to settlements. Such horticulture is normally predicated on liberal applications of animal and human manure. Good microorganic activity is maintained, and high yields are guaranteed indefinitely. Provided the climate is warm enough and irrigation is applied as necessary, two or three harvests per plot per year may be possible.

Agricultural strategies evidently have involved some degree of awareness of short-term and long-term maximization alternatives. Clearing and preparing the ground on a new plot may involve less work than combating secondary vegetation and pests while maintaining the soil productivity of old plots. The availabilities and effective costs of technology, labor, and new land were and remain major considerations in such decisions. Accordingly, pervasive if subtle modifications are imposed on the landscape.

Careful dating of British lake cores has provided a first approximation for the durations of periods of woodland clearance, cultivation, and regeneration. Small-scale local disturbances of the sort implied by long fallow or short fallow appear to have been too brief to be identified by current methods. Episodes of farming that lasted between 100 and 1,000 years have been documented from various British sites (Edwards, 1979; Turner, 1979). These represent the cumulative record of innumerable local clearances in a pollen source area with extensive and often sustained human activity – probably documenting situations with grass or bush fallow.

Geo-archaeological landscape features

The preceding sections have focused on the significance of human activities for soils, a factor generally underappreciated by archaeologists. It is now appropriate to consider the record of creative human intervention in the landscape (see Chapter 3). Major features of this type can be outlined as follows:

1. Plow (Ap) horizons in areas formerly cultivated but not currently cultivated (Limbrey, 1975:331–2) or buried under the spoil of old ditches, earthworks, or mounds.

2. Spoils from ditches, pits, and earthworks, as well as primary mounds, that bury older surfaces to create paleosols (Dimbleby and Speight, 1969). Loose erodible soil is only partly washed back into artificial depressions, leaving irregularities plainly visible in surface morphology.

3. Infillings of ditches, pits, palisades (postholes), and wells often are visible at the surface or from the air because of their greater moisture retention and richer vegetation, even where compaction has not created a negative imprint. The sediment infillings usually include complex stratified lenses due to textural sorting, mixing, reversal of soil profiles, and multiple humic horizons (Limbrey, 1975:292–9, 304–9; Evans, 1978:112–21; Vermeersch and Walter, 1978) (Figure 8-19). Such surface and subsurface patterns are critical for identification of archaeological configurations, and at the same time they provide testimony of land-use activities. Gabriel (1979) described a variety of archaeological features from the Sahara that are easily confused with "natural" geomorphic features: subterranean storage pits, smooth rock concavities ground out by milling stones, multiple grooves in rock faces used to sharpen tools, and various geometric stone arrangements representing the remains of occupation structures.

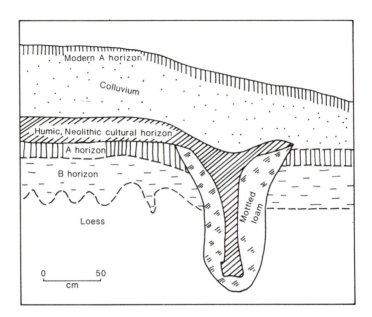

Figure 8-19. Palisade pseudomorph fill, ca. 5250 B.P., at Thieusies, near Mons, Belgium. Modified from Vermeersch and Walter (1978:Figure 3).

4. Prehistorical roadways and trails, even when not traveled by wheeled vehicles and animals, tend to form conspicuous negative imprints on the landscape as a result of accelerated runoff, rilling, and soil erosion. Such depressed linear features, as well as convex, rock-paved forms and rock-cut stairways, also affect vegetation patterns through moisture retention different from that of adjacent fields. Numerous examples can be cited from Italy, the borderlands of the Roman Empire, the Inca highlands of Peru, and the San Juan Basin of the American Southwest.

5. Terraced fields are conspicuous in many irregular and mountainous landscapes of most continents, ranging from Britain (Bowen, 1961; Fowler and Evans, 1967) to Southeast Asia (Spencer and Hale, 1961; Wheatley, 1965) and Latin America (Donkin, 1979). The idea of terracing is to build low rock walls along selected contours or across the lower slope of a field. Material is then excavated from below each such wall to be filled in above the next lower one, creating a stepped surface in which each field floor has perhaps half the original slope gradient. These terraces (called lynchets in Britain) retard runoff and soil erosion (Figure 8-20). Even when partly washed out by severe storms or after

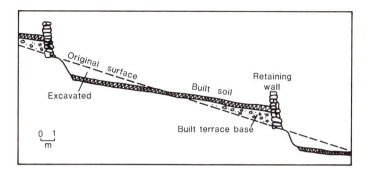

Figure 8-20. Hillside field terrace construction in Mediterranean Basin.

abandonment, such terraces remain conspicuous landscape features over many millennia.

6. Irrigation furrows, ditches, canals, and control gates are prominent parts of the archaeological record in many semiarid and desert settings. Their gross configurations have often been mapped (e.g., from aerial photos) during the course of ground surveys (Adams and Nissen, 1972), but detailed study and reconstruction (Achenbach, 1976; Farrington and Park, 1978) are still the exception rather than the rule. In fact, I was able to identify a small irrigation network during the first day of a visit to a major archaeological project (unnamed here) that had operated for a decade without even recognizing the sand-filled canals.

7. Middens are heaps of archaeological debris, commonly including organic wastes, shell, bone, or ash. They range in size from a few square meters to prominent landscape features 50 to 100 m long and 15 m or so high. Many large middens also served as occupation sites, but the majority of smaller middens were special-processing loci or the refuse dumps of larger settlements. Particularly striking are the coastal middens of some areas, composed largely of molluscan shells or shell residues (Evans, 1978:126–9), with interstitial eolian sand, soilwash, and ash. Another case in point is provided by the so-called snail mounds (*escargotières*) of Algeria and Tunisia, composed of ash, bone, and countless land snails (Hassan and Lubell, 1975).

8. Burials and burial mounds of prehistorical cemeteries also contribute to archaeological topographies, although simple graves tend to be refilled in much the same order as they were opened and can easily be overlooked. Rock piles (tumuli or cairns), megalithic blocks, and earth mounds are far more conspicuous, such as the Bronze Age "barrows" of England, consisting of earth-covered stone-lined burial tunnels

(Evans, 1975:116–17, 132–3). Even more complex is the stratigraphy of the multiple Indian burial mounds built in the central and eastern United States (Schroedl, 1978) (Figure 8-21). Burials may be identified (even when bone has been decomposed) through detailed phosphate analyses (Proudfoot, 1976) or by stain silhouettes identified in plan section (Biek, 1970).

9. Prehistorical flint mines were important in Britain and Belgium (De Laet, 1972; Evans, 1975:124–8; Bosch, 1979; Shepherd, 1980) and elsewhere. Most striking are large pits cut through soft overburden down to flint-bearing limestones, sometimes involving deep shafts that honeycomb the bedrock as much as 20 m below the surface. Such mines and their associated spoil heaps remain visible even after partial refilling (Figure 8-22). Bronze Age and Iron Age mines for critical ores tend to be even more elaborate, and the related slag from furnaces can be prominent in the geo-archaeological record.

10. Artificial soils are not unusual in some marginal agricultural environments in Europe, particularly in reclaimed fens, bogs, and tidal marshes along shorelines and poorly drained floodplains. Complex examples include drainage ditches, protective dikes, wood-plank roadways and revetments, and raised agricultural plots, first reinforced by ditch spoil and then veneered with imported mineral soil and organic fertilizers (Slicher van Bath, 1963; Limbrey, 1975:335–41). Underlying peat moss may first be cut away for use as fuel. This technique, in its more elaborate forms, continued in use through medieval and modern times as more and more marshland was settled. Artificially raised fields, intended to allow cultivation of poorly drained areas, are also widespread in tropical environments (Denevan and Turner, 1974; Turner and Harrison, 1981).

The various features outlined here provide an overview of the many geo-archaeological indicators that record human activities in the landscape, thus documenting the spatial patterns of settlement. Such features are relatively obvious, both morphologically and analytically, and they should serve to direct attention to the less visible but more universal records of general landscape modification and degradation documented in soil profiles and floodplain geomorphology. One major obstacle in regard to recognition of prehistorical three-dimensional land-use patterns is the increasingly heavy hand of industrial societies exerted on almost every facet of the landscape. A second obstacle is more easily remedied but no less urgent: the widespread disregard of land-use criteria in archaeological research design and methodological discussion.

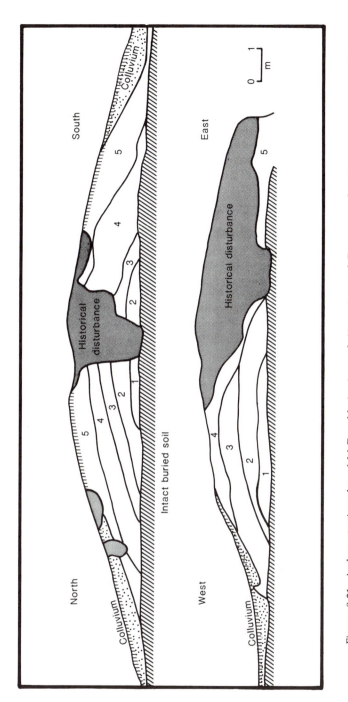

Figure 8-21. Archaeostratigraphy of McDonald site (mound A), east-central Tennessee, showing successive construction phases (1 to 5), tenth to fourteenth centuries A.D. Modified from Schroedl (1978:Figure 35).

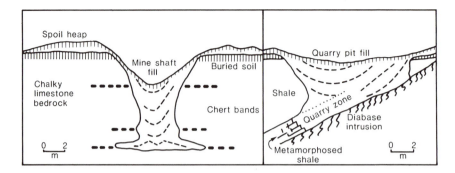

Figure 8-22. Prehistorical chert and indurated shale quarries in Britain. Modified from Evans (1975:Figures 54 and 56).

Landscape productivity and degradation

The human capability to modify the environment implies that the relationship between people and their environment is a reciprocal one. Consequently, in order to keep the subsistence-settlement system in a stable relationship with the environment, resources must not be overexploited. Land use denotes more than an adaptive strategy, because it implies the impact of people on a landscape. The geo-archaeological strategy developed here allows comprehensive assessment of the cumulative direct and indirect impacts of human activities on soils and sedimentation in particular and on ecosystems in general. Such an approach is critical to proper spatial and temporal perspectives on agricultural societies and pastoral groups.

The spatial perspective focuses on understanding the distribution and patterning of activities within a complex mesoenvironment. Such activities must, insofar as is possible, be defined in real inductive terms, such as by implementation of site catchment analysis (Vita-Finzi and Higgs, 1970; Higgs and Vita-Finzi, 1972; Higgs, 1975:223–4). Catchments can be profitably examined and reconstructed by teams of qualified researchers willing and able to employ new recovery strategies beyond the immediate confines of an excavation. The geo-archaeologist, like the modern land-use planner (Davidson, 1980a; Morgan, 1979), can devise terrain maps representative of the period of occupation that incorporate data on relief and surface roughness, texture of surficial sediments, and any indicators of intervention in the contemporaneous soil mantle and hydrological processes. Such criteria have significance both for predicting vegetation mosaics, in conjunction with biological evidence, and for assessing soil moisture, productivity, and erodibility (see Chapter 13). Along such lines, a group of researchers can then generate local models for primary productivity, biomass, and carrying capacity of macroconsumers, as well as the potential yields of cultivated versus gathered vegetable foods and domesticated versus wild animal resources. When these are complemented by appropriate archaeological surveys, a realistic spatial evaluation of prehistorical human activities is at least theoretically possible. Given the realities of research funding and the limited number of qualified experts available, it seems unlikely that such spatial resolution can be achieved in the near future. Perhaps the best we can hope for at the moment are compromise efforts, such as the empirical resource distribution and procurement analyses of Kirkby (1973), Flannery (1976:Chapter 4), and Harrison and Turner (1978).

In regard to temporal perspectives, the geo-archaeological record complements excavation and settlement surveys through its inherent sensitivity to stress in the ecological system. Intact natural ecosystems support complex food chains in which population sizes are regulated so as to maintain similar patterns of energy distribution from one year to the next. In degraded ecosystems, on the other hand, annual productivity fluctuates more strongly, because larger numbers of individuals and fewer different species allow little internal regulation, permitting strong fluctuations in consumer populations (Woodwell, 1970; Odum, 1971). This biological appreciation carries insights for soil landscapes, on the one hand, and human adaptive systems, on the other. Deforestation, grazing, and cultivation create fragile soilscapes that are susceptible to rainsplash, accelerated runoff, reduced infiltration and aeration, periodic dehydration, erosion, and declining fertility. High human population densities are possible, far exceeding those in foraging societies in which people are but a small segment of the consumer community. But agricultural and livestock productivity will fluctuate far more dramatically than that for game and vegetable foods in an intact ecosystem and will eventually decline without massive inputs of technology, labor, and capital. Agricultural ecosystems consequently represent short-term maximization strategies, unless carefully tailored through generations of trial and error to approximate a homeostatic equilibrium. The geo-archaeological record of soil erosion and related cut-and-fill cycles demonstrates that homeostatic equilibrium has rarely been maintained over the long run.

In the Dartmoor region of southwestern England, palynological studies and soil-stratigraphic work have documented progressive, but initially localized, disturbance. Late Bronze Age deforestation and farming then led to widespread soil leaching, acidification, and peat bog expansion that were completed during the Iron Age and thus destroyed most of Dartmoor's productivity (Simmons and Proudfoot, 1969).

In Middle Axumite times, the environment of northern Ethiopia probably had been stripped of most of its export resources, such as ivory, incense, and civet musk. When the disruption of international trade during the seventh century A.D. reduced revenues, Axum lost the wherewithal to control the resources of its border provinces; as a result, intensified land pressure at home led to rapid environmental degradation and essentially permanent destruction of much of Axum's agricultural potential (Butzer, 1981a). Similar examples can be cited from contemporary industrial societies, such as the United States, where estimated soil losses over half of the country are double the amount considered compatible with permanent agriculture (Pimentel et al., 1976; Brink et al., 1977). Such modern disturbance has corollary implications for the conservation of archaeological sites: Mechanized agriculture destroys sites, and, indirectly, the high peak discharges of degraded ecosystems favor site erosion or deep burial in the wake of rapid floodplain aggradation.

Geo-archaeological investigation of landscape context can, in conjunction with archaeological survey, elucidate the subtle reciprocal responses of settlement systems and ecosystems through time; it can also identify the drastic and sometimes irreversible modifications of regional ecosystems. The interrelated vegetational successions, the shifts in hydrological regimes, and the modifications in the delicate balance between soil formation and soil erosion are of more than esoteric landscape interest. They reflect significant changes in automorphic productivity, with direct consequences for both animals and people. Long-term adaptive success evidently is predicated on such dynamic environmental variables.

CHAPTER 9

Archaeometry: prospecting, provenance, dating

Scope and purpose of archaeometry

The term *archaeometry* has been in common use since 1958, when the first volume of the journal *Archaeometry* was published by the Research Laboratory for Archaeology at Oxford. The contents of this journal were and have remained technical expositions of physical and chemical methods applicable to dating and materials identification in archaeology. Other periodicals publishing substantial contributions to archaeometry include the *Journal of Archaeological Science* (since 1974) and *Revue d'Archéometrie* (since 1977) (Beck, 1980). A broader array of relevant techniques and applications has been presented in the Brothwell and Higgs compendium *Science in Archaeology* (1970, first edition 1963) and by Brill (1971). Despite some overlap with geo-archaeological and bio-archaeological research, the input of physical and chemical methodologies to archaeology continues to be distinctive. These efforts are here labeled as archaeometry, and three major applications are recognized: (a) subsoil prospecting, (b) materials identification and provenance, and (c) "absolute" or chronometric dating.

The great majority of archaeometric techniques require expensive equipment ranging in price from several thousand dollars to over a million dollars. The work tends to involve time-consuming procedures or highly repetitive manipulations that follow a well-defined routine and can be readily replicated. Many of the techniques can be learned and then applied, with reproducible results, in a comparatively short time.

In these several ways archaeometry tends to differ from geo-archaeology and bio-archaeology, in which equipment needs are modest, but competent application requires long years of experience and innovative adaptation of basic procedures to specific projects. Heavily dependent on observational methods and the comparative approach, geo-archaeological data and interpretations often are disturbingly difficult to replicate. It therefore comes as no surprise that geo-archaeologists still are overwhelmingly trained in the earth sciences, whereas large and rapidly growing numbers of North American archaeometrists are derived from archaeology-anthropology programs (Burgess, 1980). This new disciplinary interface is exemplified by C. W. Beck's "Archaeometric Clearinghouse," appearing periodically in the *Journal of Field Archaeology* since 1975, and by the international group effort that produces *Art and Archaeology Technical Abstracts,* published by the Conservation Center, Institute of Fine Arts, New York University, since 1955. The tangible impact of this trend can already be discerned in a shift away from scientific hardware and data manipulation to specific archaeological subfields (e.g., as focused on prehistorical exchange networks and materials technology). This direction of modern concerns is exemplified by the Center for Materials Research in Archaeology and Ethnology at the Massachusetts Institute of Technology.

This chapter is intended to be a brief and nontechnical introduction to the archaeological significance of prospecting, provenance, and dating techniques. The most comprehensive technical manual is that of Tite (1972).

Subsoil prospecting

There is wide variety among the techniques that are employed in archaeological exploration and survey. Apart from field investigation focused on lithic artifacts, potsherds, and topographic features, site location can be achieved by interpretation of aerial photos and other remote-sensing data (Gumerman and Lyons, 1971), optimally in association with geomorphic and soils mapping.

Once a site is located, the decisions whether or not to excavate and, if so, where to excavate can be made on the basis of visual considerations or quantitative criteria. Surface artifacts can be sampled from a selected grid system, or if there is any topographic expression, a micro-topographic map (with 20- to 100-cm contour intervals) can be constructed. But more often than not the critical configurations in regard to intrasite patterning and activity identification remain buried in the subsoil. Geophysical and geochemical exploration techniques acquire importance at this stage. Although they are expensive in terms of both equipment and man-hours, they may be more economical and informative than random excavation of multiple test pits or trenches.

The most common method for site exploration is the magnetic

survey. A portable proton magnetometer is applied to a grid layout to measure relatively small changes in magnetic-field intensity. The principle is that of a refined mine- or metal-detector sensitive to subsoil objects and features that differ in their absolute or relative concentrations of iron oxides and magnetic iron (Fe_3O_4), reflecting, in part, complex oxidation-reduction processes. Apart from iron objects, this technique can also be used to trace configurations due to fired materials and structures (bricks, sherd caches, pottery kilns), pits and ditches filled with organic soil and rubbish, and any solid walls, foundations, tombs, and roads that create sharp differences in magnetic intensities. An exploratory grid may have spaces of 1.5 or 3 m, for example, but more interesting magnetic gradients can subsequently be tested at closer intervals.

A complementary technique is resistivity surveying. This method measures differential electrical conductivities related to water content, carbon concentration, and object density (Klasner and Calengas, 1981). The two electrodes are spaced at a distance similar to that of the depth of expected subsoil features.

Singly or in combination, these geophysical survey techniques allow identification of subsoil gradients and patterned discontinuities that reflect walls and wall foundations, house floors, pits, tombs, embankments and ditches, and roadways (McDonald and Rapp, 1972:Chapter 15; Tite, 1972:Chapter 2; Graham, 1976). Other sophisticated techniques such as ground-penetrating radar and sonar (acoustic sounding) are prohibitively expensive, but radar imagery has been highly successfully applied to reconstruct lowland Maya drainage networks (Adams et al., 1981). Infrared vertical and oblique photography (Gumerman and Neely, 1972), if practicable, can also help to identify density configurations, because differential water contents influence the surface temperatures of the ground. Such differences may even be detectable in normal black-and-white photographs, in part through gray shadings of surface soil, in part through the patterning of ground vegetation.

Each of these geophysical prospecting techniques is predicated on subsoil sites with some measure of architectural expression. Exploration of nonarchitectural sites is more profitably carried out by geochemical testing, namely, phosphorus determination at fixed grid points (Proudfoot, 1976; Sjöberg, 1976, 1982; Eidt, 1977). In this way, a map plan of phosphate concentrations can be drawn up in order to identify occupation loci. By additionally measuring phosphorus at several depths, a three-dimensional image can be reconstructed, possibly

Table 9-1. *Methods and goals of subsoil prospecting in archaeology*

Method	Features	Application
Photography and remote sensing	Topographic irregularities	Site location
Microtopographic mapping	Subsoil irregularities, reflecting differential density, water content, and organic and iron concentrations (e.g., walls, house floors, kilns, pits, embankments, ditches, roadways)	Intrasite patterning
Geophysical prospecting		Site activity identification
		Settlement patterning reconstruction
Geochemical prospecting		

adequate to identify an activity area (Konrad et al., 1981). Such geochemical prospecting must be evaluated with respect to off-site control samples and is best complemented by other elements (e.g., magnesium and calcium). The technique can be used to distinguish pastoral and agricultural sites.

The basic strategy of subsoil prospecting is outlined in Table 9-1. Both the complexity and the importance of geophysical prospecting technology can be gauged from the publication of a specialized journal, *Prospezioni Archeologiche*, in Rome, by the Fondazione Lerici, since 1966.

Materials identification, provenance, and technology

The identification of raw materials used in various artifactual transformations involves physical as well as chemical techniques. For outlines of the many methodologies and selected examples, one can consult the work of Tite (1972), Beck (1974), and Carter (1978).

One of the basic approaches is petrological, to identify lithic varieties used for stone artifacts (e.g., flint, obsidian, other igneous rocks), as well as the clays and tempers employed in pottery manufacture. The traditional tool here once was optical identification of crystal structures in thin sections. Such work has been increasingly amplified by scanning electron microscopy, X-ray diffraction, and electron-probe microanalysis (Shotton and Hendry, 1979; Luedtke, 1979; Dickinson and Shutler, 1979; Shepherd, 1980), not to mention other geochemical tests (Sieveking et al., 1972). At issue may be basic mineral identifications, such as quartz, feldspars, micas, pyroxenes, hornblendes, and the like found in rocks and tempers. The analysis of pottery clays requires information on clay minerals and textural composition (Matson, 1960; Shepard, 1965; Butzer, 1974c; Peacock, 1977). However, precise comparisons of flints, obsidians, semiprecious stones, roof tiles, and pottery with specific potential raw-material sources are dependent on even more sophisticated geochemical testing (Wilson, 1978). In fact, determination of trace elements by the neutron-activation technique may be required.

Most metallurgical studies are focused on primary metals such as copper, iron, gold, and silver or alloy ingredients such as lead, zinc, and tin and employ several of a battery of geochemical tests (Tite, 1972:Chapters 7–9; Gilmore and Ottaway, 1980; Rapp et al., 1980). Various types of spectroscopy (mass, optical emission, atomic absorption, X-ray fluorescence) are most commonly used. Other techniques include neutron activation, lead isotope ratio determination, and specific gravity tests. The major and minor elements in glass, glazes, faience, and inorganic pigments are also determined by variations on this same array of techniques. Finally, organic materials such as wood, fibers, bone, skins, shell, amber, and adhesives can be identified by microscopy, spectroscopy, gas chromatography, and isotope ratios ($^{18}O/^{16}O$ or $^{13}C/^{12}C$) (Stross and O'Donnell, 1972).

The basic significance of most of these specialized studies is in providing an understanding of the technology involved and the source areas that suggest prehistorical exchange networks. Materials research as applied to technology and source identification has a long and distinguished history in archaeology, including the first (1926) edition of Alfred Lucas's *Ancient Egyptian Materials* (Lucas and Harris, 1962). An important link between materials research, technology, and ethnoarchaeology has been detailed in recent years (Merrill, 1968; Lechtman and Merrill, 1977; Gould, 1978; Hudson, 1979; Rice, 1982). Equally important alternative links are now being sought in experimental replication (e.g., stone tool use and manufacture) (Ingersoll et al., 1977; Hayden, 1979; Keeley, 1980). Last, but by no means least, "fingerprinting" of trace elements and isotopes in exotic raw materials has provided substantive information to reconstruct spatial frameworks for prehistorical exchange systems: late Paleolithic flint in eastern Europe (Kozlowski, 1973), late and post-Paleolithic obsidian in western Asia (Renfrew and Dixon, 1976), Neolithic *Spondylus* shells of Aegean versus Black Sea origin (Shackleton, 1970), early European and North American metallurgy (Sherratt, 1976; Farquhar and Fletcher, 1980), and inter-island pottery trade in the Pacific Ocean (Dickinson and Shutler, 1979).

A new dimension to such exchange inferences has been provided by a California study that estimated rates of prehistorical obsidian output (Singer and Ericson, 1977).

These examples suggest a contextual paradigm to integrate the highly technical, physical, and chemical studies, on the one hand, and the concerns of ethnoarchaeology, experimental archaeology, and theoretical archaeology, on the other (Table 9-2). Central here is a broad definition of manufacturing technology as the extraction, manipulation, transformation, and exchange of matter. At lower levels of analysis, this subfield is critically dependent on laboratory identification of materials and technological attributes, in combination with field identification of sources. At intermediate levels of interpretation, experimental data and replicability may allow identification of technological patterns and their temporal and spatial variabilities. Finally, at higher levels of systematic integration, these intermediate-level constructs may allow description or explication of technological subsystems responsible for aggregation and transformation of matter. In this connection, it can be argued (a) that raw-material origin or extrasite provenance is no less important than artifactual intrasite provenience and (b) that manufacturing techniques are as fundamental for evaluation of technology as are stylistic components.

Chronometric dating

The concept of time (see Chapter 5), although of singular importance in archaeology, is relative, because the emphasis is on intrasite and intersite comparisons. Most fieldwork is devoted to establishing synchronous horizons, microstratigraphic provenience, and local archaeological stratigraphies. "Absolute" (i.e., nonrelative or chronometric) dating is primarily sought to facilitate interpretation of temporal variability or of synchronic intersite patterning. For example, radiocarbon dates may approximate the actual time spanned by a site sequence, or they may indicate whether or not similar archaeological horizons in adjacent sites are contemporaneous, or they may interrelate the temporal dimensions of composite archaeological sequences from different regions. Unlike historians, to whom a few years generally make a great deal of difference, archaeologists are primarily concerned with obtaining reasonable approximations, for which internal and external consistency is of primary importance.

Chronometric dating tends to be a high-technology enterprise, domi-

Table 9-2. *Methods and goals of materials identification in archaeology*

Object	Method	Basic goal	General application
Unmodified or partly modified raw materials	Physical structures	Identification of raw materials	Patterning of exchange systems
Reconstituted products	Chemical elements (major, minor, trace)	Geographical source of raw materials	Manufacturing technology (e.g., pottery, mining and metallurgy, glassmaking, production of various textiles)
	Organic components	Production techniques	

Table 9-3. *Capabilities and limitations of major chronometric techniques*

Technique	Most suitable materials	Effective dating range	Major limitations
Radiocarbon (^{14}C)	Organic materials, inorganic carbonates	To 20,000–40,000 years, depending on material	Poor sampling; contamination by younger materials
Potassium-Argon (^{40}K/^{40}Ar)	Volcanic rock or minerals	Unlimited, but coarse calibration	Availability of unweathered volcanic rock; sample preparation; contamination
Uranium series (^{234}U, ^{230}Th, ^{231}Pa)	Coral, mollusca, travertine	30,000–300,000 years	Few facilities; technical controversies; contamination
Geomagnetism	Undisturbed sediments or volcanic rocks	Unlimited, but coarse calibration	Limited facilities available
Archaeomagnetism	Intact kilns or hearths	2,000 years	Calibration; limited applicability
Thermoluminescence (TL)	Pottery	10,000 years or more	Range of error; few facilities
Obsidian hydration	Obsidian artifacts	35,000 years	Requires calibrated regional framework
Amino acid racemization	Bone, marine shell	Several 100,000 years	Experimental stage only; few facilities
Geochemical dating	Bone	Relative	Site-specific applicability only
Varves, ice cores	Sediment, ice laminae	15,000 years or more	Limited applicability
Dendrochronology	Tree rings	7,500 years	Region-specific

nated by, but by no means restricted to, geophysicists and geochemists. Archaeological research funds have set up and maintained many of the available laboratories, and some of these are operated by trained archaeologists. Similarly, archaeological dating has provided excellent research opportunities for geophysicists since about 1950, and the professional ties are close. Although a wide range of dating methods is available, they vary greatly in terms of suitability, accuracy, and cost (Table 9-3). The subsequent discussion will emphasize these aspects, rather than the technical aspects, for which the reader is referred to the work of Tite (1972:Chapters 3–5), Michels (1973:Chapters 7–13), and Fleming (1976).

Radiocarbon. The basic standby in chronometry that is most applicable in archaeology is radiocarbon dating, which is available from almost 100 facilities. Cosmic-ray bombardment of carbon atoms in the atmosphere produces a proportion of radioactive ^{14}C isotopes. These are incorporated into all systems maintaining an equilibrium with atmospheric carbon dioxide (e.g., living organisms, the oceans, lakes and rivers, and cave and soil carbonates). ^{14}C, once it is incorporated into organic materials or inorganic calcium carbonate, decays at a predictable rate, with a half-life originally calculated at 5,568 years, but now known to be closer to 5,730 years. The remnant ^{14}C, as a ratio to the standard ^{12}C isotope, provides a measure of age. For a recent analysis of the range of problems and possibilities, see the review of Browman (1981).

Three basic problems are involved in this technique:

1. It has been demonstrated that changes in cosmic-ray input over time have led to changes in ^{14}C production. Conversion tables that incorporate the half-life corrections allow for rough calendric approximations for the last 6,500 radiocarbon "years" (Damon et al., 1974).

2. Sample quality, which can be affected by inherent subsoil contamination or poor sampling techniques, is only partially assured by sophisticated laboratory pretreatment. Except in certain cases (e.g., animal or human reworking, fossil adhesives such as bitumen, and inorganic carbonates from chemically and thermally stratified water bodies), ^{14}C dates tend to be too young.

3. Because of the short half-life, most radiocarbon counters have a practical capacity of 35,000 to 50,000 years, depending on their sensitivity. Various forms of isotope "enrichment" theoretically allow this range to be extended to 65,000 or even 75,000 years (Grootes, 1978). However, only 1% modern contaminant in an organic residue of a million years will simulate an age of 37,000 years, and 1% modern contaminant in a sample 23,000 years old will simulate an age of 21,700 years (Stuckenrath, 1977). It is, in effect, impossible to know whether or not such low concentrations of contaminants survive even the most stringent pretreatment. Comparisons of fossil soils dated by enriched ^{14}C with other independently dated stratigraphic sequences (Grootes, 1978:Figure 2) show that even the best finite ^{14}C dates beyond 40,000 years are no more than minimum estimates. The new method of accelerator dating is technically valid to 100,000 years (provided that background radioactivity can be fully eliminated from the cyclotron), but its application probably will be limited to minute samples of particularly precious materials that require great accuracy (Berger, 1979).

Potassium-argon. Vulcanism creates fresh potassium (^{40}K) that very slowly decays to argon (^{40}Ar) after a lava or volcanic ash has cooled. The half-life of 1,330 million years implies an unlimited dating range, although the technical precision is, at best, of the order of plus or minus a few tens of millennia. Whereas ^{14}C is useful for the last 20,000 to 40,000 years, ^{40}K/^{40}Ar is primarily applied in the time range of several hundred thousand years to several million years. Weathering, which is the rule rather than the exception, introduces atmospheric ^{40}Ar that gives excessively young dates, whereas older solidified volcanic debris frequently is incorporated in later volcanics to simulate dates far too ancient (Curtis, 1975). As a consequence, ^{40}K/^{40}Ar dating is prone to considerable error, not to mention the problem that suitable dating material is only rarely associated with archaeological sequences.

Uranium series. A number of uranium isotopes are fixed in cave, coralline, and lacustrine limestones, mollusca, bone, and peat during consolidation or fossilization. These subsequently decay, producing independent daughter elements with variable half-lives: ^{234}U 244,000 years, ^{230}Th 75,200 years, ^{231}Pa 32,500 years. Several alternative ratios can be calculated, such as ^{230}Th/^{234}U ("ionium-deficiency" or thorium-uranium method), with an effective dating range of 300,000 years, and ^{231}Pa/^{230}Th (protactinium-ionium/thorium method), with a 125,000-year range. Complications arise because the original ^{234}U concentration in water is variable and because episodes of solution and recrystallization can reset the radiometric clock to zero. Uranium dating has provided useful (but not uncontroversial) results for coastal and cave sites, primarily in the critical 30,000- to 300,000-year time range (Harmon et al., 1975; Peng et al., 1978; Schwarcz et al., 1980). Experimental dating of peat deposits also appears to be promising (Vogel and Kronfeld, 1981). Facilities are few, unfortunately, and commercial outlets are nonexistent.

Paleomagnetism. The dynamics of the earth's molten core lead to continual changes in the positions of the magnetic poles, as well as changes in the intensity and polarity of the magnetic field. Measurements of the magnetic records of volcanics and stable sedimentary rocks with some proportion of Fe_3O_4 have provided detailed geomagnetic sequences that frequently can be dated by ^{40}K/^{40}Ar (macroscale), ^{14}C (mesoscale), or historical controls (microscale).

1. The gross record includes long-term "reversals" and medium-term "events" during which the polarity of the earth's magnetic field

has been switched. For the last 730,000 years we have had "normal" polarity (Brunhes polarity epoch), possibly marked by brief events about 20,000 and 100,000 years ago. The preceding Matuyama polarity epoch, 2.48 to 0.73 million years ago, featured reversed polarity, interrupted by several major normal events at 2.16 to 2.12 and 2.04 to 2.01 million years ago (two Réunion events), 1.87 to 1.67 million years ago (Olduvai event), and 0.97 to 0.90 million years ago (Jaramillo event) (Mankinen and Dalrymple, 1979). Now that it is reasonably accurately calibrated, this time scale can be used for coarse dating of both marine and continental sequences – transcending even the regional dating accuracy of the $^{40}K/^{40}Ar$ method that provided the original calibration. Unfortunately, the geomagnetic record of unstable sediments can be destroyed and then reset (e.g., when limestones are partly dissolved and recrystallized, or when the fine matrix of coarse detrital sediments is mobilized).

2. Medium-scale paleomagnetic changes can be detected by detailed measurements of declination, inclination, and, particularly, intensity. Thus far, meticulous profiles developed from British and Swedish lake beds indicate unpredictable variations in sedimentation rates or repeated depositional breaks or both (e.g., Thompson, 1973; Thompson and Berglund, 1976). But a tentative yardstick is emerging for the last 15,000 years or so. This may be useful for cross-dating purposes, particularly if an uninterrupted sediment column spanning at least 3,000 years is available.

3. Small-scale paleomagnetic changes within the last two millennia or so are relatively well understood and can be detected in undisturbed kilns, fireplaces, and burnt clay (Tarling, 1975). Such archaeomagnetic work can provide dating cross-checks where archeomagnetic chronologies have been established, if samples are removed by a qualified person. In the American Southwest, where the small-scale changes of A.D. 1000 to 1500 are best documented, accuracy can be as good as ± 20 years (Eighmy et al., 1980).

Thermoluminescence. The heating of materials such as pottery to high temperatures sets a clock, as it were, after which radiation builds up as a product of radioisotope impurities. To measure this effect, ground-up pottery is twice heated rapidly to 500°C; the differential weak glow during the first heating quantifies this radiation and is called thermoluminescence (TL). Technically, TL can be used to date any pottery, but the α, β, and γ rays that contribute to TL vary according to soil matrix, pottery texture, and mineralogy, as well as other tricky variables (Aitken, 1976; Fleming, 1980). Even the very best TL dates have an error range of ±5% to 10%, after analysis of the soil matrix and similar refinements. Generally, TL is still useful primarily in authenticating the ages of ceramic works of art. Applications to burnt flint are fraught with assumptions and problems. More satisfactory results have been obtained for ocean sediments, which acquire a weak TL by exposure to sunlight prior to deposition (Wintle and Huntley, 1980). This technique also has the potential for application to terrestrial sediments such as loess (Wintle, 1980).

Obsidian hydration. Obsidian artifacts adsorb water to form a hydration layer, the thickness of which can be measured by thin-section microscopy. The rate of hydration on the surfaces of flaking scars is time-dependent, but it varies according to obsidian type and environment. Radiocarbon calibration is most commonly applied to make this relative technique usable in a particular region. When carefully implemented, using sufficiently large samples of limited variability and unquestioned provenience, obsidian hydration dating can provide dates with ± 50-year accuracy in the historical time range. With radiocarbon cross-checks, the maximum dating potential is of the order of 35,000 years (Friedman and Obradovich, 1981).

Amino acid racemization. The various amino acids present in the proteins of living organisms consist exclusively of l enantiomers; over time, racemization produces the corresponding d amino acids. The resulting d/l ratio of the amino acid is time-dependent, but the process varies according to the type of amino acid studied and the temperature and moisture conditions of the sediment matrix through time (Hare, 1980). Most commonly used is the aspartic acid from bone, which at 20°C has a half-life of about 15,000 years (Masters and Bada, 1978). Dating depends on radiocarbon calibration for one or more control samples from the same microenvironment. Most racemization dates beyond 40,000 years are extrapolations that may or may not do justice to the microclimatic history of the sample matrix and that therefore are unpredictable as to accuracy. Furthermore, racemization rates vary from one fossil genus to another. A more realistic model of Pleistocene temperature change, with uranium series cross-checks, suggests that fairly accurate dating can be derived from leucine racemization in specific marine mollusca up to several hundred thousand years old (Wehmiller and

Belknap, 1978). When these kinetic models are better understood, it should be possible to use racemization to derive environmental temperature deviations for samples of known age (e.g., Schroeder and Bada, 1973; McCullough and Smith, 1976).

Geochemical criteria. The concentrations of elements such as fluorine, nitrogen, and uranium in fossilized bone are, within the same mineralizing environment, time-dependent. Consequently, bones of similar ages within a single deposit should have similar concentrations of F, N, and U. Such data are useful primarily to verify whether or not fossils are coeval (e.g., a lag of fossils exposed by erosion). These elements were used to prove that "Piltdown man" was a hoax: The jaw and skull had widely different concentrations, and both differed from the animal bone with which they were supposedly found.

Varves and other rhythmites. Annual rings are produced in a number of inorganic deposits. Glacier-margin lakes in Scandinavia show a seasonal rhythm of rapid sediment influx from melting snow, followed by slower organic deposition during the summer, thus creating seasonal laminations. By various correlation techniques, successive lake basins were originally interlinked to provide a 15,000-year chronology for the Baltic Sea basin whereby it was possible to date the Pleistocene-Holocene boundary at 7912 B.C. This was accomplished a generation before the development of ^{14}C dating. Subsequent research has discounted the reliability of varve counting in shallow lakes, because summer storms can produce multiple laminae in a single year. Varve counting has been unsuccessfully attempted in North American glacial lakes, as well as at lower latitudes, where silts and solubles fluctuate on a periodic basis. Laminate increments can also be identified in ice sheets (Greenland, Antarctica) on the basis of seasonal snow accumulation and melting; such ice cores, studied in terms of $^{18}O/^{16}O$ ratios, have been approximately dated back to 120,000 years by estimating the thickness of the pressure-fused and compacted part of the cores on the basis of various physical laws (see Figure 2-5).

Dendrochronology. Tree-ring dating was developed in the American Southwest, where it now provides accurate calendric dates for countless sites spanning the last 2,000 years; it also provides inestimable paleoclimatic data for several major regions (Fritts, 1976; Hillam, 1979). A special case is the bristlecone pine of southern California, where living trees provide a 4,000-year tree-ring chronology that has been extended to provide calibration for ^{14}C back to 5,400 calendar years B.C. (Damon et al., 1974). Dendrochronological work is currently making good headway in central Europe, where, in conjunction with ^{14}C dating, partly incomplete tree-ring series span 8,700 ^{14}C years and have begun to provide more representative time scales for environmental phenomena (Frenzel, 1977).

Since 1965, chronometric dating has undergone no revolutionary changes. Radiocarbon remains the overwhelmingly dominant technique; potassium-argon dating has been more widely implemented, and its limitations are now better appreciated; large-scale paleomagnetic dating has assumed fundamental importance for early to mid-Pleistocene stratigraphy; dendrochronology has been successfully implemented in Europe. But applications of most of the other techniques remain limited because of lack of suitable materials, limitations in effective dating ranges, and shortages of qualified laboratories and personnel. It appears that the next 15 years will continue to witness incremental improvements but no major breakthroughs in chronometry.

Like prospecting and provenance studies, chronometric dating provides empirical data as well as a theoretical framework for archaeology. Whereas prospecting and provenance studies serve to draw attention to intrasite and intersite spatial systems, chronometry is essential to define the temporal coordinates that allow examination of systemic developments.

CHAPTER 10

Archaeobotany: vegetation and plant utilization

The archaeobotanical[1] record

Identification of plant remains from archaeological contexts has a long and venerable tradition, extending well back into the middle of the nineteenth century. However, specializations with a strong archaeological flavor are more recent developments. Perhaps a third of the archaeobotanists working in North America today had their basic training in anthropology programs (Burgess, 1980), and some of the most effective comparative botanical collections have been developed in the anthropology departments of several museums and universities. This trend can be explained by two principal concerns: (a) that paleobotanical materials, which can be identified only with the aid of extensive reference collections, derive increasingly from archaeological sediments and (b) that archaeobotanical residues require professional interpretation as a central aspect rather than a peripheral aspect of an archaeological research program. Whereas paleobotanical methods and results are concentrated in a half dozen or so major specialized journals, this is not true for archaeobotanical work, which is dispersed in a number of other media.

These archaeological, as opposed to botanical, developments have favored diversification of related research techniques, transcending the traditional concern with analysis of pollen grains. There now is much greater emphasis on macroscopic plant remains such as seeds, fruits, twigs, and leaves, that are commonly found in a carbonized state in archaeological strata. Another area that has profited from this upswing in archaeobotanical interests is the study of the microscopic silica structures of plants, known as plant opals or phytoliths.

However, archaeological study of botanical residues requires more than site sediment extraction and reference collections. There remains a

[1]Unfortunately, there is no term in common use that emphasizes the archaeology part of archaeobotany to the same degree as it is emphasized in the terms geo-archaeology and zoo-archaeology.

great need for ecological field studies that concentrate on modern plant distributions and associations. This expertise is an essential element in archaeobotanical interpretation, no less basic than it is for the interpretation of pollen evidence, in conjunction with modern pollen-rain sampling, in paleobotanical work.

Perhaps the most important aspect of modern archaeobotanical research is that it focuses less on environmental reconstruction than on the interrelationships between people and plants. A large part of human subsistence, from the earliest times, has been derived from plant foods. In fact, a full appreciation of prehistorical subsistence is impossible without successful retrieval, identification, and contextual interpretation of potential plant foods. Plants are, of course, pertinent for far more than food. They provide wood for construction and fuel, fibers for clothing, tools, and other crafts, and ingredients and components for medicine and socioreligious symbols (Ford, 1979). This human dependence of such long standing has always placed demands on plants, large and small. As human groups increased in number and size, these demands accelerated to the point that exploitation patterns had the potential to modify the subtle ecological balance of vegetation communities. In agricultural societies these basic patterns of exploitation have in fact been complemented by deliberate removal of indigenous plant communities to make way for new simplified populations of apparently greater productivity. Then, in modern industrial settings, this human proclivity for transforming the vegetation has been intensified to the point that blatant exploitation and even eradication of biotic resources have profoundly changed or destroyed entire landscapes. A conceptual survey of archaeobotany must therefore draw attention to the fundamental role of plants in human subsistence systems and the impact of people on the vegetation.

Plant resources can be localized in four microhabitats: (a) in the canopies of trees, (b) at ground level, (c) below ground, and (d) in aquatic settings. The tree-canopy habitat was exploited by most of the earliest mid-Tertiary anthropoids, and today it provides a variety of edible leaves, barks, fruits, and seeds for many monkeys and apes. These forest resources, including many nonedible raw materials, remain accessible to ground-dwelling humans and in several world environments still provide a critical microenvironment for exploitation. The plant foods and nonedible fibers that are within arm's reach on the earth's surface, or in the lowest horizon of the vegetation cover, have traditionally been exploited by ground-dwelling monkeys and apes, and they remain a key focus for human activities. Resources below the ground include a wide range of subterranean foods and fibers that continue to be collected even today by some human groups and are actively exploited by a wide range of animals. In fact, cultigens developed by early farmers and planted in the soil served to increase the productivity of edible resources below and above the ground. Finally, a range of special habitats is provided by streams, rivers, marshes, freshwater lakes, and the seashore. There, along banks adjacent to moving or standing water, and in tidal flats and estuaries, and along the open coasts of saltwater seas and oceans, our human ancestors have long found a special selection of biotic resources. Most familiar are, of course, the animal foods, but the wide varieties of shore and aquatic plants have also provided not only sources of nourishment but also prized fibers applied to a great diversity of tasks, ranging from the grasses used for bedding to durable materials essential for various kinds of woven products. A general outline of the resources peculiar to these key microhabitats is given in Table 10-1.

Retrieval of archaeobotanical information

The basic categories of archaeobotanical information have been well outlined by Dimbleby (1978:Chapters 7–10) and Ford (1978) and summarized by Evans (1978:Chapter 2) and Ford (1979).

Palynology. The oldest and still one of the most important quantitative techniques in paleobotany involves the retrieval, identification, and counting of fossilized pollen grains. A high percentage of plants are wind-pollinated and therefore produce a substantial output of mobile and durable pollens. Each plant family, and often each genus, has pollen with a distinctive morphology. Seen under strong magnification, these grains vary in terms of outline and shape, major prominences and openings, and even the details of surface ornamentation. Much of the tedious work in palynology is preparatory, because minute quantities of pollen must be extracted by destruction of the organic or mineral matrix within which they are preserved. Laboratory identification of the grains according to morphological type, family, genus, and even species subsequently hinges on competent microscopic identification. Between 200 and 500 grains of pollen must be identified and counted per sample, with reference to comparative

Table 10-1. A classification of plant and animal resources

	Habitat			
	Canopy	Ground level	Below ground	Aquatic
Edible Resources[a]				
Plant	Leaves, bark, fruits, seeds, etc.	Full range of plants and plant parts, mushrooms	Roots, tubers, fungi, etc.	Selected shore plants, sea grasses, kelp, etc.
Animal	Small to medium-sized mammals, bird eggs, insects, snails, etc.	Small to large vertebrates, insects, snails, etc.	Small vertebrates, insects, snails, etc.	Riverine, lake, and seashore mammals; fish, birds, mollusca, crabs, etc.
Nonedible raw materials				
Plant	Wood, bark, leaves, fiber, etc.	Wood, bark, leaves, resins, fiber, etc.	Fiber, roots, etc.	Fiber, grasses, etc.
Animal	Bones, eggshell, feathers, hides, etc.	Bones, horn, hides, fur, sinews, fat, dung, etc.	Bones, hides, fur, etc.	Shell, bones, etc.
Mineral	—	Stone, mud, sand, etc.	Stone, soil nutrients, ores, fossil fuels, etc.	Sand, stone, etc.

[a]All food categories include wild and domesticated forms, and nonedible raw materials may be derived from domesticated forms.

materials, a process often conditional on sophisticated technology such as scanning electron microscopy.

Palynology is, above all, a comparative technique requiring diversified collections of modern and fossilized pollen, and it is a technique that also requires much experience. Identification to the level of genus or species often is particularly difficult, but it may be essential for useful ecological evaluation. Once the basic identifications have been completed, the pollen fluctuations can be evaluated through time, calibrated where possible by ^{14}C. The evaluation of such a pollen profile in terms of diachronic vegetation change remains a major problem. Modern pollen rain from many different microenvironments in which species abundance is known is one essential ingredient. Another critical problem is selective preservation: To what extent is any individual pollen spectrum truly comparable with a modern pollen rain, even when the quantitative parameters happen to coincide? If satisfactory answers to this question can be provided, then statistical evaluation of the pollen spectra and of their changes through time can proceed. During the last decade or so, such interpretative procedures have gained greatly in sophistication, and the particular issues of archaeological sediments for pollen preservation and interpretation have been increasingly appreciated (Bryant, 1982; Fall et al., 1981). Good comprehensive introductions to palynological research have been provided by Kummel and Raup (1969), Tschudy and Scott (1969), Faegri and Iversen (1975), and Moore and Webb (1978).

Macrofossils. There are wide ranges of macrobotanical remains that can be retrieved from many archaeological and other organic sediments. For example, beginning during the 1950s, several palynological schools increasingly insisted on complementing standard palynological research by identification of plant seeds, fruits, nuts, charcoal, tissues, fibers, and other diagnostic residues (Delcourt et al., 1979) from the sediment matrix that provided the pollen. Such evidence provides a cross-check for the pollen data, as, for example, whether or not the major pollen types are also represented by other forms of evidence, or, conversely, whether or not the macrobotanical remains include species not represented in the pollen record (Grüger, 1972).

Another direction in such macrobotanical research is the retrieval of identifiable organic residues from bulk samples of archaeological sediment. The basic principle is that organic materials have different densities than mineral grains, thus allowing for separation by several flotation techniques (Watson, 1976; Keeley, 1978). Much of the apparatus for flotation is cumbersome, and the process is time-consuming; thus the simple and effective methods are most desirable. One such technique, known as froth flotation, involves the addition of paraffin to pulverized sediment. The wax selectively impregnates organic material, and in a detergent solution the phosphate froth floats the organic residues on the water's surface (Jarman et al., 1972). The segregated organic matter is then skimmed off and eventually dried, sorted, and identified (Van Zeist and Bakker-Heeres, 1979). The potential of such residues for reconstructing paleonutrition and seasonality of occupation requires no emphasis (Wing and Brown, 1980).

Other types of macrobotanical identification involve high magnification of wood or wood structures preserved in charcoal (Schweingruber, 1978; Deacon, 1979). Such research requires regional expertise and appropriate comparative materials. These are available for some parts of North America, Europe, Africa, and Southeast Asia. Charcoal is particularly abundant in archaeological contexts, and we have only begun to exploit its potential for the identification of major fuel and timber sources. Plant impressions are another major resource in archaeobotany; for example, the chaff frequently used as a temper for pottery and mudbrick may be identifiable, as are the casts and even the preserved grains of seeds and the like (Renfrew, 1973). Plant leaves are sometimes recorded in great detail by impressions preserved in consolidated muds, fine volcanic ash, and lime deposits generated by springs or in standing waters.

Coprolites. Fossilized human and animal feces, or coprolites, are particularly useful for determining dietary patterns by providing both abundant pollen and macrobotanical residuals (Bryant, 1974; Thompson et al., 1980). Pollen not corroborated by macrobotanical remains generally reflects background conditions indicative of the environmental setting. The other plants, identified by pollens, seeds, fruits, cuticles, and the like, directly record diet and have the potential to indicate the seasonality of site occupance. In addition, insects and even gastrointestinal parasites may be present, providing information of paleopathological interest (Hall, 1979).

Phytoliths. The study of phytoliths or plant opals has made substantial progress since the early 1960s (Rovner, 1971; Pearsall, 1978). These silica bodies can be identified according to shape and size, but they remain very difficult to attribute to genus, let alone species. Even as comparative materials have continued to accumulate and scanning electron microscopy has come to complement optical microscopy, the problems of identification have not yet been fully solved. However, the widespread interest shown in this research direction suggests that more satisfactory results will be forthcoming with time. This is fortunate, because phytoliths often are concentrated in the ash lenses and hearths of archaeological sediments. Even basic recognition of such morphotypes as monocots, grasses, and sedges can provide valuable dietary and background information, and phytolith silica is amenable to isotope analysis with $^{18}O/^{16}O$ and $^{13}C/^{12}C$.

C_3 *and* C_4 *plants.* Almost all temperate plants and most trees assimilate carbon dioxide in a "normal" three-carbon molecule (phospho-glyceric acid). However, as a result of long-term adaptation to a hot dry climate and periodic fires, most tropical grasses and succulents have developed respiratory systems that favor "anomalous" four-carbon molecules (malic acid). These C_3 and C_4 photosynthetic pathways further result in differential depletion of the heavy carbon isotope ^{13}C. This leads to distinct $^{13}C/^{12}C$ ratios in the related phytoliths, as well as in the bone structures of herbivorous mammals, providing a potential paleoclimatic indicator in subtropical regions (Vogel, 1977; Vogel et al., 1978). In human bone, $^{13}C/^{12}C$ ratios further provide a potent index of the intake of tropical plant foods such as maize, sorghum, millet, and sugar cane (Van Der Merwe and Vogel, 1978; Bender et al., 1981). High levels of C_4 foods among Woodland or Mississippian Indians will reflect primarily cultigens of Mesoamerican origin, not exclusively maize, of course, but also including various beans, grain amaranths, cucurbits, and even gathered indigenous plants such as grain chenopods (Yarnell, 1977).

Paleobotanical interpretation

Interpretation of assemblages of pollen and fossil plant remains is complicated by two fundamental considerations (Evans, 1978:13ff.): (a) the processes whereby the structure and composition of living communities are transformed into fossil assemblages and (b) the ecological interpretation of such assemblages. The various factors that affect the transformation of a living biological community into a fossil assemblage are illustrated in Figure 10-1.

The living community itself is complex, both in terms of its spatial

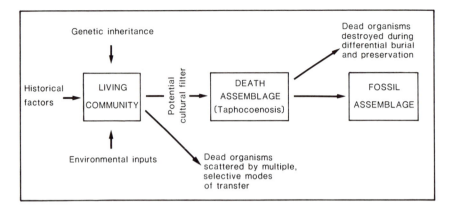

Figure 10-1. Transformation of a living biotic community into a fossil assemblage. Modified from Evans (1978:Figure 1).

patterning and in terms of vertical organization. It reflects various environmental inputs at different scales, as well as its genetic inheritance and historical factors such as plant migrations and geographical controls of the related migration rates. At death, the manifold organisms of this community may be scattered by a wide range of processes, many of which, such as wind and running water, selectively transfer objects of particular shape, size, or mass. Cultural factors may also filter and thereby bias the selection of organisms eventually assembled in a particular death community or taphocoenosis.

A subsequent stage of modification centers around differential preservation, because only a small part of the accumulated organisms will be suitably buried, and only a fraction of these will in fact be preserved. Thus, a fossil assemblage is a highly biased and incomplete reflection of a living community. It has been transformed through transport, differential burial, and selective preservation. There may also be substantial cultural intervention, such as deliberate human collecting or production, or long-term decimation by overexploitation or extraction. Finally, the original living community was in its own terms already difficult to analyze and interpret. It would therefore be presumptive to equate a fossil assemblage with a living community.

Some of the problems of interpreting a fossil assemblage can be illustrated with the example of pollen:

1. Pollen accumulates at different rates on different surfaces. The surface receptivity of a lake or bog is far greater than that of bare stony ground. Similarly, preservation conditions following burial are infinitely better in areas of active sedimentation and in aquatic microenvi-

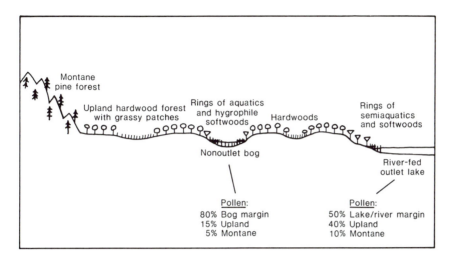

Figure 10-2. Vegetation mosaic of a drainage basin and differential habitat biases for two typical pollen traps: a no-outlet bog and a river-fed lake.

ronments. As a result, short-term accretion and preservation of the pollen rain are subject to considerable variation.

2. Pollen is primarily studied from restricted areas of active sedimentation, such as a water body, a floodplain, or an archaeological site. This means that the sediment catchment must be measured against the pollen catchment. Natural mobilization and sedimentation factors will bring together a selection of the pollen rain received throughout the geomorphic catchment. This means that pollens from several local microenvironments will be mixed. At the same time, aerodynamic factors continue to introduce pollen from a broad catchment related to the boundaries of the sedimentary system. For example, concentric rings of aquatic, semiaquatic, and water-tolerant terrestrial plants will contribute diverse pollens to the accumulating sediment of a bog or lake. This local pollen will be mixed with tree and grass pollens transported from many kilometers away, from surfaces and substrates that are totally different. A percentage of pollen will even be derived from different climatic environments, such as montane forests tens or hundreds of kilometers beyond the local sediment catchment. As a consequence, pollen traps that ultimately provide pollen records suitable for study reflect areally diversified habitats, in both geomorphic terms and biotic terms. Interpretation of local versus regional vegetation mosaics consequently poses a major challenge (Figure 10-2). These problems can be partially compensated for by extensive sampling of modern pollen

rains, as well as by attention to pollen density per unit sediment (Davis et al., 1973; Jacobson and Bradshaw, 1981).

3. Overrepresentation and underrepresentation of pollen constitute a third major problem. Many plants are insect-pollinated, and the majority of such pollens are not dispersed in patterns comparable to those for wind-pollinated plants. Insect-pollinated species consequently suffer, even under the best of circumstances, from primary underrepresentation in the modern pollen rain. Pollen productivity also varies from genus to genus; it is high for pine, birch, and hazel and low for maple. The mass and aerodynamic structures of pollens also vary considerably: Dense spherical grains, often with heavy ornamentation, are dispersed poorly, whereas flat ellipsoidal grains with air sacks (e.g., pine and spruce) readily fly in the upper atmosphere over distances of hundreds of kilometers. For example, Nichols et al. (1978) have been able to reconstruct Holocene upper-air wind patterns in the Arctic from the long-distance influx of alder, pine, and spruce pollens. Other pollen grains are easily decomposed and therefore are poorly represented, if at all (e.g., poplar, maple, ash, chestnut, birch, and juniper).

4. Once pollen is buried in sediment, differential preservation begins to take its toll. Generally, preservation is optimal in permanently water-saturated, acidic, reducing environments. It is intermediate to poor and unpredictable in neutral or slightly alkaline sedimentary environments subject to alternating wetting and drying. Preservation is minimal in highly alkaline environments, particularly in the presence of sodium. These gradients of pollen preservation imply that pollen will be progressively destroyed in a time-dependent fashion in response to varying subsoil conditions (see Figure 7-17). Good preservation during one set of conditions may, centuries or millennia later, be reversed as the soil environment responds to fundamental changes in the regional ecosystem. This means that pollen density varies greatly and that preservation in low-density sediments is bound to be highly selective, with only small fractions of the toughest types of grains surviving. At this point, the significance of the surviving pollens becomes dubious. Most of the grains preserved within a particular preparation may be derived from older bedrock (e.g., Cretaceous spores). Other pollen types may also have been reworked from older beds (e.g., Tertiary or early Pleistocene pollen incorporated into Holocene deposits). To some extent, such mixing of older grains may be detected on the basis of morphology, size, degree of corrosion, and differential glow under fluorescent or ultraviolet light. But selective and total de-

structions of the pollens of many genera once incorporated into a particular sediment can never be compensated for. This calls for great caution in the evaluation of pollen from sediments in dry environments with very low pollen densities per unit sediment.

5. A final caveat is that pollen profiles may not be complete, or they may be affected by differential rates of sedimentation within a single depositional medium. The first of these difficulties is acute in peat bogs, where natural fires and artificial peat cuttings can create discontinuities that may be difficult to detect. The second of these points can be made on the basis of detailed paleomagnetic sampling from lake basins, which reveal remarkable inconsistencies from one profile to another (Thompson, 1973).

In sum, a pollen assemblage reflects primary biotic diversity, differential accumulation, the geomorphic medium of sedimentation, the geochemical environment of preservation, and possible postdepositional disturbance.

Despite these many difficulties, pollen spectra and profiles provide highly potent quantitative tools with which to gauge spatial and temporal variability (Butzer, 1971a:249ff.). For example, pollen spectra can be used to reconstruct regional pollen maps that do not necessarily reflect vegetation, but that, with the assistance of comparative pollen rains, may well provide an approximate delimitation of the broad patterns of dominant biotic elements. The transformed picture may therefore be roughly equivalent to the generalized vegetation maps shown for different continents in standard atlases. With adequate radiometric controls, a group of dated diagrams can also serve to provide such regional pollen maps for successive time slices. At a more detailed level, relating one or more pollen spectra to a variable local biotic environment may also be possible by systematic comparisons with a sufficiently wide range of modern analogues (Webb and Bryson, 1972) interpreted in conjunction with contemporaneous sedimentation and soil-forming patterns. Pollen diagrams can also shed light on the processes and patterns of regional biotic change (e.g., vegetation successions, plant migration rates, and fluctuations in the positions of ecologically sensitive ecotones, such as the treelines in montane, subpolar, and arid regions). Finally, pollen diagrams, at sufficient detail, can be used to identify the impact of human activities, such as brief episodes of forest clearance and cultivation or long-term transformation of a regional biotic landscape (Edwards, 1979).

The fruits, nuts, seeds, and charcoals studied by other paleobotanical techniques may be sufficiently abundant to provide semiquantitative data, particularly as derived from archaeological sediments by flotation (Asch et al. 1972, 1979; Pals and Voorrips, 1979). Apart from seasonality of occupation and the likelihood of carbonization and preservation (Hally, 1981), a specific problem in evaluating such archaeobotanical remains is the cultural filter of human subsistence activities (Table 10-2). For example, desirable plant foods may continue to be collected in similar proportions from an expanding catchment even while such resources are declining in abundance in response to an environmental change; or a shift in emphasis to a certain kind of nut or seed may be nothing more than a response to overexploitation within a collecting catchment of other more desirable plant foods. Other intrasite variations in subsistence activities will be discussed later.

A particular caution applies to other pollen and macrobotanical remains extracted from archaeological sediments. Modern pollen and other organic residues can easily be introduced into samples collected from older strata, either during the sampling process or by contamination of section faces after excavation and prior to sampling. This is borne out by the quantity of modern objects commonly retrieved from flotation samples; uncarbonized materials should always be excluded from such study. However, many of the processes that now transport uncarbonized botanical remains far down into a profile of seemingly undisturbed soil have also operated in the past (Minnis, 1981). These include various forms of bioturbation (see Chapter 7) and mechanical illuviation of pollen grains and even seeds through uncompacted, porous, and naturally fissured sediments by gravity and percolating waters. Small quantities of unusual cultigens from unexpectedly early strata must therefore be evaluated with great care.

Overall macroenvironmental interpretation of paleobotanical records is complicated by further general considerations. These include multiple possibilities for biotic response to environmental changes through adaptation (e.g., dwarf forms), migration (but with local survival in adjacent refugia), and extinction. The net result is that large-scale adjustments of regional vegetation patterns are complex, and this very complexity will make interpretation of the simplified fossil assemblage difficult. Recolonization after a major environmental change will be slow and will be complicated by the distances from various colonizing communities, the differential mobility of different genera, local edaphic succession related to soil-forming trends, and colonizing successions related to light-demanding and shade-tolerant forms slowly tending

Table 10-2. *Archaeobotanical evidence for grain-crop processing*[a]

		Activity	
	Threshing	Cleaning[b]	Parching, storage, Cooking
Product	Many weeds; some domesticated seeds/grains of several species; many spikelet fragments	Mainly cultigens of several species, some weed seeds, spikelets	Overwhelmingly seeds/grains of one cultigen; very few weed seeds
By-product	Husks (chaff) and straw	"Tail corn" winnowed out	
Site context	Refuse (in middens), fodder (in structures), fuels (in ovens)	Cleaning floors	Ovens; storage jars or pits; middens; coprolites

[a]Adapted from Dennell (1976). [b]Cleaning by shaking in baskets or sieving out smaller weed seed.

toward the intricate vertical structure of climax communities. For example, the forest recolonization of Europe during the Holocene is as much a reflection of such interdependent factors as it is a function of gross climatic change (Godwin, 1975; Simmons and Tooley, 1981). However, even successional assemblages provide important information on regional and local environments, particularly when carried out in conjunction with sediment and soil studies.

At the stratigraphic level, vegetation changes through time can have temporal value well beyond the traditional attempts to match biotic discontinuities in adjacent profiles. Turner and West (1968) demonstrated cyclic developments of vegetation during the 10 to 30 or more millennia characteristic of several European interglacials. These evolutionary stages reflect a combination of climatic, edaphic, and other successional factors that cumulatively serve to identify broad temporal stages of true stratigraphic value. Another stratigraphic implication was recognized after systematic study of progressively younger floras within a single area, such as The Netherlands, where the cumulative extermination of exotic semitropical genera was time-dependent during the late Cenozoic (Van der Hammen et al., 1971; Zagwijn, 1975).

Optimal results in generating macroenvironmental information can be achieved by combining pollen data and macrobotanical data obtained from ecotones (King and Graham, 1981). Such sensitive settings, exemplified by tree-grass and tree-tundra contacts, are most prone to change in response to the crossing of low environmental thresholds. The centers of large biomes, on the other hand, tend to be far less sensitive to all but the largest changes, such as those with wavelengths of 5,000 to 25,000 years (see Table 2-3).

Dendroecology and dendroclimatology

Tree-ring studies are not limited only to matters of dating. The annual growth ring is in many ways similar to a varve. At middle latitudes, growth is strong during the spring months, when moisture is abundant and energy and insolation are increased. Then, during the hot and relatively dry summer months, the rate of growth decreases, tapering off even further during the cool autumn. Eventually, growth ceases entirely during the winter months. Consequently, the thickness of the annual growth increment is proportional to the growing-season climate. In warm semiarid areas, the available moisture primarily controls the rate of radial growth. The tree ring of a moist year is wide, whereas

that of a dry year is narrow. In subpolar regions, rainfall is less significant, because late spring snows maintain a high water content in the
soil; instead, midsummer temperatures are most closely correlated with
radial growth. The factors that actually determine radial growth are a
great deal more complex, and they include lag effects of as much as 15
months. A satisfactory evaluation of these interrelationships has been
possible only because of the introduction of multivariate techniques,
primarily as a result of the work of Fritts (1971, 1976).

The interrelationships between tree-ring dating and dendroclimatology have long been recognized. However, earlier work tended to use
simple measurements, employing limited sample numbers and comparing these with one or two climatic variables. Not surprisingly, correlations from one area to another and even between points within a
region were unsatisfactory. Paleoclimatic interpretation became possible only after sufficient numbers of variables were considered and a
stronger sense of regional tree ecology was developed. By understanding the complexities of tree growth according to local edaphic variables
and microclimatic differences, by dealing with larger samples (i.e.,
many trees), and by considering sporadic effects such as fires, disease,
and years of high seed production, it has been found possible to eliminate the background "noise" in tree-ring series. Sophisticated new
techniques have also been applied, such as X-ray measurements of cell
size and cell density, which reflect on productivity and dry-matter
accumulation. Such a sophisticated appreciation of dendroecology has
allowed the emergence of dendroclimatology as a reliable tool. This
technique is most effective in areas of climatic "stress," where tree-ring
growth varies significantly from year to year in response to multivariate climatic inputs.

Fritts (1976) and also LaMarche (1978) have provided invaluable reconstructions of medium-range climatic anomalies for the semiarid
western United States spanning many centuries. Observations of
stream flow and rainfall fluctuations in the meteorological record have
also proved to be closely correlated with regional tree-ring parameters.
The implication is that dendroclimatological data can be converted into
proxy climatological statistics that can be used to extend the observational record for certain world regions by centuries (Fritts et al., 1979).
However, that such proxy data can be extended from the tree-ring
region proper to reconstruct hemispheric circulation anomalies has not
yet been demonstrated satisfactorily (Baker, 1980). During the last decade or so, dendroclimatology has begun to be successfully imple-

mented in several other world areas, such as western Europe (Frenzel, 1977; Hillam, 1979) and temperate South America (LaMarche, 1978).

Dendroclimatology can also be applied in more complex studies, as in combination with shifting mountain tree lines and forest-steppe boundaries. A particularly useful example has been provided by La-Marche (1973) for the White Mountains of California. There the climate was 2°C (3.5°F) warmer from before 5400 to 2200 B.C., then cooler and wetter from 1500 to 500 B.C., followed by cold and dry conditions around A.D. 1100 and 1500. Similar examples of Holocene tree-line fluctuations have been documented for the Alps (Frenzel, 1977).

Altogether, dendroclimatology promises to provide increasingly detailed insights into medium- and short-term climatic variability in many areas of prehistorical settlement. A particularly good example is the year-to-year analysis of climatic anomalies contemporary with Pueblo Indian settlement on the Colorado plateau (Fritts, 1976). In conjunction with palynology and macrobotanical analyses, it should eventually prove possible to provide accurate regional assessments of human impact on the vegetation, as well as possible responses to environmental stress.

Human utilization of plants

The significance of wild plants and vegetable fibers for human food and daily activities long antedates the emergence of sophisticated cultural systems. Even after the domestication of specific cultigens, exploitation of native vegetation intensified rather than decreased. Today, although forest stands at middle latitudes have stabilized in industrial societies that produce synthetic fibers and manage their forest resources, the surviving woodlands of the tropics are being cut down at a rate that promises total destruction within 60 years in the New World and Asia and within 120 years in Africa. The uses of this wood include timber for construction, household objects and furniture, tools and weapons, in addition to the now insatiable demands for fuel.

Similar needs, on a smaller scale, applied in prehistorical times. A winter lodge among the Mistassini Cree in northern Québec requires 200 prime spruce logs, obtained within a radius of as much as 400 meters. Bog moss (*Sphagnum*) is extensively used to cover the roof and close up the chinks. Less elaborate structures among the Mbuti pygmies of the Congo require a frame of branches and a cover of large leaves. Wild plants for food, medicinal purposes, clothing, and dyes are intensively foraged by the surviving hunter-gatherer societies on all the major continents. It would therefore be difficult to overemphasize the active roles of past peoples, even during the Pleistocene, in harvesting, manipulating, and periodically overexploiting specific plant resources (Dimbleby, 1978). Thus, human impact on vegetation is not at issue. The question is rather one of population size and economic demand, with the foraging and sometimes destructive role of African elephants providing a useful idea of the potential role of dispersed bands of mobile hunter-gatherers.

To some degree, berries, fruits, nuts, and underground bulbs and edible roots regenerate effectively and thrive when harvested regularly. But even if not selectively decimated, their distribution may be modified or perhaps extended, judging by the vegetation disturbance associated with black bear foraging in berry patches. In assessing "natural" plant interrelationships and productivity, it should be borne in mind that all herbivores cumulatively affect the plant cover in a discernible way, although such normal systemic interactions may be difficult or impossible to quantify on more than a local level (Gwynne and Bell, 1968). Much as squirrels bury nuts, the actions of human foragers probably favored accidental dispersal or competitive generation of certain economic plants or, through such use, gave an advantage to less desirable plant competitors.

Accidental and deliberate burnings of vegetation are sufficiently common among modern peoples that they must also be assumed in prehistorical settings. Fire facilitates hunting, as well as grazing, by reducing tree growth and favoring grasses and fire-tolerant woody plants. At the same time, fire temporarily removes unpalatable plant growth with a high cellulose content in the cell walls in favor of fresh shoots with high protein concentrations (West, 1973); this attracts game, which is more visible in broken vegetation, and it generally, if temporarily, improves pasturage. The overall effect is to expand the patches of open ground and accentuate vegetation boundaries (grass-bush and grass-tree contacts), although the major world grasslands certainly are not of human origin (Harris, 1980:21ff.). Convincing prehistorical records of local human disturbance are not yet available, although two mid-Pleistocene pollen profiles from Britain and another from Germany verify local forest disappearance and subsequent recolonization by pioneer plants; only one of these levels is associated with artifacts and charcoal powder, and the three may be contemporaneous, suggesting that a climatic explanation is at least equally likely (Turner, 1975). However, several short-term Mesolithic sites in Britain are clearly linked with evidence of fire disturbance (see Chapter 8) (Simmons and Tooley, 1981). In semiarid, subtropical Australia (New South Wales), charcoal particles, evidence of burning, increased dramatically about 125,000 B.P., favoring a proliferation of *Eucalyptus* and associated fire-adapted species that was unparalleled in the previous quarter-million years of the pollen record; in subhumid, tropical Queensland, this same shift began about 35,000 B.P. Singh and associates (1981) strongly suspected human intervention.

Intensive disturbances of vegetation around long-term settlements have been verified at the pre-Neolithic site of Lepenski Vir (see Chapter 8), where local soil erosion was entrained, probably through the combination of firewood gathering, deliberate clearance, trampling, and refuse dumping. Whatever the causes, much bare ground was exposed around this site, evidently removing the climax vegetation and probably leading to a new plant succession, beginning with weeds and grasses (see Figure 8-2) (cf. Baker, 1972; De Wet and Harlan, 1975).

Cultivation adjacent to early agricultural communities certainly involved local deforestation and devegetation by cutting or burning or both (Iversen, 1956) (see Chapter 8). Some prehistorical groups appear to have fed cattle on woodland browse, in some cases deliberately gathered (Troels-Smith, 1960; Simmons and Dimbleby, 1974; Simmons and Tooley, 1981), a practice still known in the Mediterranean world and in the southeastern United States. Over longer periods of time, deforestation or woodland browsing/grazing or both will favor ecosystem simplification, with reduced photosynthetic productivity and periodic consumption of most of the net biotic production by herbivorous macroconsumers, prone to increasing fluctuations in population (Woodwell, 1970). In cool wet environments, such degraded ecosystems (plagioclimax) favor acidification, rising water tables, and the expansion of bracken heaths or sphagnum moors (see Figure 8-4). In drier settings, an open xeric vegetation with reduced habitat diversity will result (Fall et al., 1981).

During the course of the Holocene, small-scale, low-technology dry farming was gradually replaced by intensive irrigated horticulture or floodplain agriculture in dry environments or by plow farming in cooler and wetter lands, where increasingly heavy animal-drawn plows were introduced to work in two- or three-field rotational systems (Sherratt, 1980; Denevan, 1981). The associated dispersal routes and adaptive mutations of cultigens are critical for localization of the original centers of domestication, for an understanding of the processes that led to primary or secondary domestication, and for identification of cultural contacts in both the New World and the Old World (Renfrew, 1973; Ford, 1979). At the same time, the plant data provide their own intrinsic information in regard to nutritional strategies, seasonality, and periodic stress (Cowan, 1978; Wetterstrom, 1981).

The large-scale spread of agriculture well beyond the confines of the native habitats of specific cultigens eventually led to wholesale replacement of native vegetation by new plant communities, dominated by monocultures, often of exotic species (Thomas, 1956). The cultivated plants frequently were concentrated in pure stands, as much as 98%–100% in a single crop (Dennell, 1974) (Figure 10-2). These cultigens were repeatedly selected, consciously or unconsciously, for their adaptability to new environments, their resistance to disease, and their enhanced productivity (Flannery, 1973). Most world landscapes today are characterized by plant communities that are homogeneous on a subcontinental scale. The resulting ecosystems and many of their key components are cultural artifacts: High net productivity and stability are ideally maintained through high inputs of energy, in terms of cultivation, weed control, and exclusion of other macroconsumers, and through addition of fertilizers. This process is documented by persistent weedy competitors specific to particular soils and climates in early Neolithic Germany (Knörzer, 1979), Iron Age Britain (Turner, 1979), and nineteenth-century Michigan (Webb, 1973).

These artificial ecosystems became increasingly fragile, as the prehistorical record of soil erosion demonstrates (see Chapter 8). When the rising costs of maintenance proved uneconomical, lands were abandoned, often in such a deteriorated state that centuries or millennia of regeneration were necessary to restore them to a reasonable level of productivity. Overutilization and excessive artificial stresses on ecosystems are therefore uneconomical over the medium range as well as the long range. That is, short-term maximization generally is incompatible with sustained biotic productivity. Overexploitation by human activities probably has not led to the extinction of any plant species, but unique communities and habitats have been destroyed. Of particular practical significance is that when stress disrupts the biotic ecosystem, the hydrological cycle and soil balance are directly affected (see Chapters 2 and 8). Such changes in the amplitudes, frequencies, and cumulative effects of small-scale and large-scale landscape processes have fundamental significance for the water, soil, and biotic resources so essential to human survival. Even on a global scale, the cumulative impact of millennia of deforestation, desertification, and salinization had increased planetary albedo by some 5% even prior to this century. This probably led to a net cooling of 1.2°C through increased reflection of solar radiation (Sagan et al., 1979). This temperature decrease is at least half the difference between modern global temperatures and those experienced during the warmest phases of the Holocene, some five to eight millennia ago (Butzer, 1980e).

In conclusion, archaeobotany is more than the study of paleoenvironmental indicators or even economic residues that reflect dietary intake and the seasonality of subsistence activities. It also provides a critical record of the reciprocal relationships between people and plants in dynamic ecosystems remarkably sensitive to most forms of human activity (see Table 11-2).

CHAPTER 11

Zoo-archaeology: faunas and animal procurement

Issues in archaeozoology

The study of fossil bones and other animal remains has a long tradition in the geological sciences. The related modern field of paleontology now borrows heavily from biological theory and, depending on its subject matter, also from zoology. A special direction of paleontological work was early associated with prehistorical excavations, and many nineteenth-century archaeologists had paleontological backgrounds. During the first half of this century, paleontologists were rarely involved in excavation; instead, they were relied on to identify selections of the more interesting bones retrieved. Commonly published as appendices to archaeological reports, such limited and often unrepresentative data were widely treated as if they provided a true spectrum of the wild animals living in an environment or the wild and/or domesticated animals eaten by a prehistorical group.

During the 1960s, many archaeologists began to appreciate that animal remains can provide as much economic information as the artifacts recovered from a site. The far-reaching implications of this realization were impressed on Americanist archaeologists by the work of White (1953–4) and subsequently reinforced by the Mexican Tehuacán and Oaxaca projects (Flannery, 1967, 1968; MacNeish, 1967, 1972). In any event, there has been rapid development in zoo-archaeological research facilities and training since the late 1960s (Burgess, 1980). The new generation of zoological archaeologists in North America will now complement similar groups already functioning at the universities of London, Groningen, and Munich.

The primary goal of zoo-archaeology is elucidation of prehistorical subsistence patterns, but the higher aspiration is to study the relationships between people and animals as they interact spatially and as their mutual adaptive patterns change through time. There are important complementary research modes as well:

1. Taphonomic work (Voorhies, 1969) has begun to identify the selective processes of bone accumulation and preservation specific to different types of microdepositional environments as a result of mechanical accretion, natural deaths, carnivore activity, and human subsistence modes (Behrensmeyer and Hill, 1980; Gifford, 1981).

2. Statistical criteria have been applied to deal with the problems of sample bias and the representativeness of archaeofaunas (e.g., the minimum number of individuals) (Casteel, 1976; Klein, 1978; Grayson, 1979, 1981). Such screening procedures have considerable implications for evaluating the nature of archaeological sites as kill sites or habitation loci and distinguishing them from carnivore accumulations; they may further allow evaluations of prehistorical hunting techniques and their efficiency by comparing the zoo-archaeological assemblage with the age and sex structures of wild herds on the hoof (Reher, 1974; Klein, 1979).

3. Prehistorical animal extinctions continue to be the subject of much debate, particularly in regard to the possible role of early hunters in decimating or eradicating certain species or genera at the close of the Pleistocene (Martin and Klein, 1982).

These themes have provided the subjects for a spate of theoretical reports. There also are a number of manuals devoted to bone identification, measurement, and interpretation (Cornwall, 1956; Olsen, 1964; Kurtén, 1968; Chaplin, 1971; Schmid, 1972; Gilbert, 1973; Clason, 1975; Driesch, 1976; Meadow and Zeder, 1978). Nonetheless, few descriptions of properly excavated large faunal assemblages have been published. Zoo-archaeology must therefore be considered a fresh and rapidly expanding field in which research efforts remain to some degree experimental. Many more exacting large-scale excavations of faunal assemblages from a variety of sedimentary and topographic contexts will be required before interassemblage comparisons can provide systematic results or representative insights into human procurement techniques. Consequently, this chapter will focus on the more interesting issues as currently perceived: taphonomy, environmental interpretation, procurement activities, and human impact on faunas.

Taphonomy

The basic problems of evaluating bone assemblages are similar to those encountered in archaeobotany (see Chapter 10 and Figure 10-1). Critical factors include the type of death and the resulting modifications in

bone in different microdepositional environments (see Table 4-1) in regard to weathering, transport, burial, fossilization, and ultimate selective preservation.

Geological accumulations. Not infrequently, animals that are very young, weak, or very old die during times of climatic stress: during the dry season in semiarid tropical environments; during cold wet weather at higher latitudes. Unless these animals are later trampled into the ground, buried by flood or wind deposits, or covered by rising lake waters, the fleshy body parts will be consumed and dismembered by scavengers and microorganisms, and their bones will be desiccated, oxidized, and decomposed. Even when they are buried or submerged, bone mineralization will depend on the long-term level of the water table or lake, the presence of lime, iron, silica, or phosphate mineralizing solutions, and the concentration of destructive sodium salts (see Chapter 7). Preservation under such circumstances is rare, even for isolated bones that are large and durable. The exceptions include aquatic habitats around nonsaline lakes and chance preservations of carcasses and body parts that float down rivers, often into lakes or estuarine settings. Concentrations of fossils in so-called natural bone beds are unusual and generally reflect special microdepositional environments (e.g., springs and lake margins) and exceptional conditions (e.g., peat bogs, oil seeps, and tar pits, where periodically animals become bemired and are rapidly mineralized).

Animal Accumulations. Although the regular attrition visited on young and old herbivores by carnivores is no more likely to favor preservation than natural death, some carnivores concentrate their activities around favorable microdepositional environments (Behrensmeyer and Boaz, 1980). Hyena lairs provide a good example, with these strong-bodied carnivores dragging portions of their prey into fissures and caves, where bone may be preserved as a result of percolating solutions or circulating waters rich in calcium carbonate (e.g., within limestone bedrock or calcareous coastal dunes). Brain (1981) and Klein (1975, n.d.1) have described the Makapansgat bone beds and other South African hyena accumulations. Such accumulations are biased against ver' heavy or bulky items, such as the adult crania of large ungulates, ar also against softer bones, especially juvenile postcranial elemen Long bones lacking epiphyses will be unusually common. Foxes ? jackals may also collect bones in more modest lairs.

Faced with competition from hyenas and lions, leopards often eat their prey in trees, and the bones may accumulate in fissures below, as at Swartkrans (Brain, 1976, 1981); because felids are ill-suited for crunching bone, articulated postcranial pieces are prominent in the accumulations of leopards and Pleistocene cave "lions." Porcupines are vegetarians, but they hoard bones in the deep interiors of caves, not for food, but as a means of keeping their incisors trimmed; such bones generally show extensive gnawing marks (Brain, 1981). Birds of prey, particularly owls, roost in caves and periodically regurgitate the indigestible bones and fur of their prey (rodents, bats, birds, and other small animals) in the form of tightly packed owl pellets. Although surface materials may periodically wash down into caves, fissures, and shafts, some of which have also served as natural pitfalls and death traps, most such accumulations represent carnivore or human refuse.

Hominid kill and habitation sites. Human hunting activities have long favored the accumulation of animal bones in selected microenvironments, many suitable for burial and preservation of bones. The basic characteristics of such accumulations include the presence of artifacts, a high degree of bone fragmentation, and, possibly, evidence of fire (charring, charcoal, or hearths) (Thomas, 1971; Noe-Nygaard, 1977; Frison, 1978; Brain, 1981). Distinctive patterns of abundance and dispersal of skeletal parts distinguish kill sites (considerable bone articulation, axial bones relatively common, species diversity low, limited dispersal and fragmentation) from habitation or terminal processing sites (bones disarticulated, fragmented, and dispersed, appendicular bones relatively common, species diversity relatively high). Butchery and special processing sites have intermediate properties (Sivertsen, 1980) (see Chapter 13). The associated artifacts also are central to such site interpretation, and a total absence of lithics in cave or open-air site strata with fragmented bones strongly suggests carnivore activity or death traps, rather than human occupation (Clark, 1977; McGuire, 1980). Sedimentation in hominid sites is generally accelerated through a host of related activities (see Chapters 6 and 8), but, even so, more often than not it is ineffective to ensure burial and therefore fossilization in open-air situations. Gifford and Behrensmeyer (1977) documented the disturbance of a four-day camp by subsequent scavenging and by repeated floods in an arid environment next to a shallow, sandy stream bed in Kenya.

Investigations of fossil bone accumulations must deal with a host of

agencies and processes, including the following: type of death; transport by geomorphic agents, animals, or people; weathering, burial, and fossilization; nature and history of the microdepositional environment. To one degree or another, this requires analysis by or advice from both geo-archaeological and zoo-archaeological experts in regard to the following factors: sedimentary matrix; orientation, inclination, dispersal, and aggregate patterning of different bone parts of different masses (see Chapter 7); physical condition in regard to weathering, abrasion, gnawing, breakage, cutting, etc.; composition in regard to species, age, sex, and community structure. Parts of this research inventory have been discussed to some extent by Behrensmeyer and Hill (1980) and by Gifford (1981), but as yet there is no generally accepted body of procedures or a representative body of data for taphonomy. Broad agreement is most conspicuously centered around the basic argument that preserved bone is a very incomplete and biased palimpsest for the animals originally present in any biotic community.

Ecological evaluation of fossil assemblages

The evaluation of a preserved bone assemblage in terms of living communities and their inferred environmental preferences is complex and difficult. It should therefore be profitable to identify key problems and directions for study. These include the biases of initial accumulation or collection and of selective preservation, the relationships of small and large mammals and nonmammalian faunas to microenvironments and macroenvironments, the contribution of geochemical studies, the criteria of seasonality, and the stratigraphic implications of faunal assemblages and guide fossils.

Bias in initial accumulation. The hydraulic, gravity, animal, and human agencies that bring bones together into suitable microdepositional environments all select differently for animal and bone size and animal type. Except for long-distance river transport of whole carcasses, generally buoyed by the gases of decomposition, geomorphic processes sort bones according to size in relation to transport energy. This is particularly apparent in lags of river gravels, where preserved bones correspond closely in mass to the modal range of pebbles (e.g., teeth among fine gravel, larger bones among coarse gravel). Similarly, gravity deposits accumulating at the bases of surface fissures and cave shafts tend to favor bones or bone fragments in well-defined categories that most commonly correspond to the heaviest submaximum of rock-particle distribution represented. These relationships have begun to be tested empirically for hydraulic transport (Boaz and Behrensmeyer, 1976; Hanson, 1980), but no broadly valid rules have yet been established. My own qualitative experience from various East African and South African sites is that both water and gravity effects discriminate against (a) small fragile bones other than teeth, (b) articulated bones, and (c) large bones and especially whole crania and pelves, except under special conditions such as buoyant carcass transport. Complex bone preservation for most body parts of different sizes appears to be associated with direct burial rather than with transport of such material or with partial hydraulic sorting and rearrangement (Gifford and Behrensmeyer, 1977). Evaluation of bone dispersal should therefore include testing of the "hydraulic equivalent" of bones of particular shapes and mass in laboratory flumes, as well as systematic orientation studies (see Chapter 7).

Animal predation is equally selective, with carnivores and scavengers taking those herbivores that they can hunt and transport most efficiently in terms of energy expended vis-à-vis potential energy sources ingested. This automatically favors specific types of animals and, indirectly, body parts of restricted size classes. Different carnivore accumulations will therefore favor different sizes: rodents and birds; medium-sized herbivores; and so on. Carnivore bones will also be well represented in carnivore collections (e.g., in a hyena lair), whereas they are rare in hominid sites.

The patterns of human predation are similarly biased according to (a) the risk factor in attacking fierce animals, (b) the suitability of the available hunting techniques to take reasonably large numbers of those accessible herbivores with much meat, and (c) the effort required to transport whole animals or body parts to a habitation site. The result is that archaeological bones are at least as much a reflection of technology, mobility patterns, and subsistence modes as of the biotic community (Frison, 1978; Klein, 1979, n.d.2).

Bias in preservation. Prior to mineralization, bone is highly susceptible to both chemical breakdown and physical abrasion or crushing. Some 20% to 25% of dry fresh bone is nonmineral, overwhelmingly protein collagen. Dehydration and oxidation, as a bone is first exposed on the surface, open the porous internal structure of the calcium phosphate (hydroxyapatite) (Rottländer, 1976) and soon etch out canal systems and weaker growth structures, with the nonmineral compounds shrinking. Such subfossil bone is light and brittle and, unless buried promptly, will crumble no later than a year or two after being exposed on the surface (Ingersoll et al., 1977:Chapter 14). If initially spared from scavengers (Binford and Bertram, 1977), fresh bone will survive transport much better than subfossil bone, but except under special conditions, very small bones and fragile bones will not survive trampling into the soil surface or transport by water or gravity. The major exception is prompt burial by cave soilwash, flood silts, windborne dust, or volcanic ash, without actual removal. If this critical stage is passed successfully, survival will depend on soil-water circulation and composition. Acidic waters, particularly in a subsoil environment that is not permanently anaerobic, will gradually leach the mineral components while the organic compounds are oxidized. Highly alkaline waters, with sodium concentrations, will introduce solutes that expand and contract within the intermineral voids as they absorb water and then dehydrate, thus bursting the bone structures and leading to disintegration. With intermediate pH conditions, and in the presence of mineralizing waters, a number of substances begin to precipitate within the intramineral structures: calcium carbonate, gypsum, barite, iron oxides and sulfides, silica, aluminosilicates, or secondary phosphate compounds (Parker and Toots, 1980). Eventually the voids are filled, the density increases dramatically, and the bone has been lithified. Any subsequent episodes of erosion and transport usually will find such fossil bone durable, unless exposed at the surface for protracted periods of time.

This sequential process of burial and lithification naturally favors large bones and large fragments as well as very hard bones, such as teeth. Such preferential preservation of bones of the largest mammals has been demonstrated quantitatively in the Amboseli game park in East Africa (Behrensmeyer and Boaz, 1980). The Amboseli experiments have further verified that animals that prefer wet habitats tend to be better preserved, presumably because of more favorable burial conditions, suggesting that habitual proximity to good microdepositional environments will also bias fossil faunas. Preservation in carnivore and archaeological matrices is variable: Hyenas commonly crush smaller bones and softer parts, whereas owl pellets are ideal for preservation of microfaunal remains. People tend to fragment long bones to get at the marrow, and many bones are destroyed by in-site trampling, fire, and organic acids resulting from human activity. Eventual fossilization is primarily due to calcification in calcareous soil environments or calcification deriving from calcium released from wood ash.

Microhabitats. Animals have diverse mobility patterns and ecological tolerances. Migratory birds and most gregarious mammals are highly mobile, and they may cross or exploit different microhabitats; they may even occupy different biomes at different seasons or because of unusual adaptability. On the other hand, a wide range of large solitary herbivores, rodents, insects, land snails, marine mollusca, reptiles and amphibians, fish, and foraminifera are tightly linked to specific ecological niches. Their well-defined preferences for certain foods, topographic matrices, and exposures often lend them unusual ecological significance. Not surprisingly, research during the last two decades has increasingly focused on such small, specialized nonmigratory and mainly nonmammalian forms (Brothwell and Higgs, 1970; Evans, 1972, 1978:Chapter 3; Anderson, 1981). Some of these detailed studies deal explicitly with archaeological sites (Lubell et al., 1976), others with ecological reconstruction of more universal habitats (Grindley, 1969; Thunnell, 1979; Preece, 1980).

Macroenvironments. The majority of the medium- and large-sized herbivores that dominate most types of fossil assemblages were migratory, spanning different habitats and displaying great ecological plasticity in response to short- and long-term environmental variability (see Chapter 2). It is, in a sense, unfortunate that most of the faunas that were preserved and have been studied are of this type, because their interpretation is correspondingly difficult – a problem compounded by their compositional bias as well as the presence of extinct species and genera among Pleistocene assemblages. But, even so, sophisticated studies of the structure of modern biotic communities (Klein, 1978, n.d.1; Andrews et al., 1979) as well as anatomical (e.g., dental) adaptations (Kurtén, 1968) have shown that the obstacles are not insuperable. In fact, given large, meticulously studied assemblages and adequate neozoological experience, it is possible to identify faunas not only from particular biomes, but even from mixed habitats, ecotones, and biotic mosaics.

For example, at Nelson Bay cave on the southern coast of South Africa, Klein (1980) has been able to show that a gregarious grassland or savanna fauna with black wildebeest, bastard hartebeest, spring bok, warthog, and zebra was replaced by a different constellation of

solitary bush or woodland forms such as bushbuck, bushpig, and grys-
bok between about 12,000 and 8000 B.P. The sediment record verifies
an initially open vegetation with incomplete ground cover, ultimately
replaced by denser vegetation, stabilization, and soil development
(Butzer and Helgren, 1972). Similarly, at Border Cave, on the Swazi-
land-Natal line, there is an inverse relationship between the frequencies of bushpig, buffalo, tragelaphine antelopes (kudu/nyala), and im-
pala during periods of temperate or warm climate and the frequencies
of warthog, zebra, and alcelaphine antelopes during periods of frost
weathering (Butzer, Beaumont and Vogel, 1978; Klein, 1980).

Geochemical data. Faunal residues provide a variety of potential sources
for environmental and ecological information. For example, the amino
acids of bone collagen appear to record temperature and moisture histories, although the variables remain poorly understood (Hare, 1980).
The records of C_3 and C_4 plants preserved in fossil herbivore bones, as
determined by $^{13}C/^{12}C$ ratios (Vogel, 1978) (see Chapter 10), promise to
shed light on dietary shifts that reflect habitat changes in lower-latitude
grasslands. Similarly, the $^{13}C/^{12}C$ ratios in human bones relate to diet,
and in several New World contexts they appear to document shifts
from hunting and mollusk gathering to wild-plant foraging and agriculture, based on exotic cultigens (Bumsted, 1981). The concentrations of
strontium, a relatively stable mineral component of bone, provide
other insights for animal and human diets (Parker and Toots, 1980);
strontium concentrations are much higher in mollusca than in plant
foods, and they may indicate significant dietary shifts through time in
some archaeological sites (Schoeninger and Peebles, 1981). The protein
molecules of human bone can also be preserved for many millennia,
allowing identification of blood groups and biological relationships in
the archaeological burial record (Lengyel, 1975). Radioimmunoassays
can, in fact, identify residual proteins in fossils dating millions of years,
and they promise to provide revolutionary data on the genetic relationships of fossil hominids and hominoids to each other and to living
forms (Lowenstein, 1980). In regard to the dating of fossil bone, see
Chapter 9.

Seasonality. Most ungulates have well-defined birth seasons in environments in which cold or dry seasons control plant productivity. As a
result, the eruption of specific teeth, the shedding of antlers, and so
forth, can be used to determine the age of an animal at time of death

and thus to approximate the time of the year (Bahn, 1977; Klein, 1978, n.d.1; Spiess, 1979; Monks, 1981). Migratory birds, marine mammals, mollusca, fish with seasonally distinct feeding habitats, and even the seasonal growth forms of insects can be used to infer the time of year (Churcher, 1972; Parkington, 1972; Akazawa, 1980). Daily growth-line counting in the clam *Meretrix lusoria* has documented not only seasonal patterns but also the time spans involved in the accumulation of Japanese shell middens (Koike, 1979). Molluscan seasonality has also been identified by $^{18}O/^{16}O$ analysis, applied to the final growth ring, because such shell increments record seasonal changes in isotope temperatures of the waters and even allow differentiation of marine and estuarine habitats (Shackleton, 1970, 1973; Killingley, 1981). Despite these technical advances, seasonality studies of archaeological bones and shell are still very time-consuming, with few qualified specialists willing to undertake them. Also, they often require very large samples from well-defined temporal units. As a result, there is little systematic information for most areas and time spans.

Faunal stratigraphy. Traditional studies of faunas have emphasized primarily their application as stratigraphic markers or leitfossils. Within the Pleistocene, a number of large forms, such as elephants and rhinos, evolved rapidly and can readily be identified from diagnostic teeth. However, absence of a particular form is inconclusive, and the appearance or disappearance of a specific leitfossil cannot be expected to be truly synchronous in different biomes spread across large landmasses such as Eurasia. These problems can be partly circumvented by assemblage analysis, whereby characteristic associations of large mammals are linked with specific biostratigraphic zones (see Chapter 5) (Kurtén, 1968; Butzer, 1971a:Chapter 17; Kahlke, 1975). Particularly informative in Europe are several mid-Pleistocene (mixed steppe-woodland) faunas and the alternating glacial (mixed tundra-steppe-woodland associations) and interglacial (temperate forest associations) faunas of the later Pleistocene. A similar change has been documented for the close of the Pleistocene in North America, an event frequently attributed to extinction at the hands of prehistorical hunters (Martin and Klein, 1982). More exact dating of Pleistocene-Holocene faunal turnovers in Europe, South Africa, and North America indicates that replacement took up to five millennia in complex biomes. Overall, animal evolutionary rates vary considerably from one family to another, with many small animals evolving quickly, although some of the largest animals, such as elephants, also radiated rapidly. Rodents are believed to have special stratigraphic value because of their evolutionary rates and sensitivities to changes in microhabitats (Jánossy, 1975); however, for this very reason, long-range correlations on microfaunal criteria are suspect.

In early Pleistocene to mid-Pleistocene contexts, faunas have stratigraphic significance for archaeology, particularly in regions where other dating is impossible. In later time ranges, a reverse process is more important, namely, to date faunal replacements by chronometric techniques in order to understand their ecological implications.

Hunters and their prey

The important interrelationships between people and animals were first verified for sites in East Africa dating to 1.8 million years ago, and they have subsequently been documented by the zoo-archaeological components of countless sites. In Olduvai Bed I, the indications are that a wide range of large and small animals, including reptiles, were utilized and, at least in part, hunted along the shores of a seasonally fluctuating lake (Leakey, 1971). Acheulian sites of mid-Pleistocene age suggest that reasonably effective hunters concentrated their procurement activities around waterholes, marshy grounds, rivers, and lakes, although the marked bias in favor of big game may in part reflect differential preservation or excavation procedures; see the discussion of Clason and Prummel (1977) in regard to screening techniques. By early Upper Pleistocene times, marine food resources were being actively exploited, including mollusca, fish, marine mammals, and birds (Osborn, 1977; Volman, 1978; Klein, 1979; Emslie, 1981). But the hunting abilities of prehistorical groups between 130,000 and 35,000 years ago were still limited. In South Africa, dangerous game and flying birds were rarely taken, and for all but the most docile bovids, very young or old animals predominate (Klein, 1979, 1982). Only at the close of the Pleistocene and during the Holocene were efficient hunters, equipped with a wide range of procurement techniques such as bows and arrows, javelins, and a variety of traps and snares, first able to exploit the full range of animal resources or even to specialize on an optimal selection thereof (Noe-Nygaard, 1974; Frison, 1978; Davis and Wilson, 1978; Klein, 1979, 1982; Binford, 1981).

This brief outline touches on the deliberate selection of animals according to species and age, in relation to other factors such as size, ferocity, mobility, preferred habitat, and available technology. Many more detailed site-specific examples will be necessary before patterns begin to emerge and other critical questions can be answered, such as hunting and fishing strategies in regard to abundance and predictability of resources and food preferences (Parkington, 1972; Stark and Voorhies, 1978; Limp and Reidhead, 1979; Smith, 1979*a*).

Animals supplied a wide range of raw materials: hides and furs for clothing, matting, and shelter construction; skins, horns, and organs for containers; sinews for fiber; bones, antlers, teeth, and shell for tools and ornaments; fat and dung as fuel (Cornwall, 1968:Chapter 4) (see Table 10-1). But, first and foremost, prehistorical hunters were dependent on animals as sources of food.

Animal bones provide a useful index of caloric yields, although the minimum numbers of individuals of various species documented for a site level cannot simply be converted into pounds of meat per hoof and, by extension, calories per hunter. Butchery practices, transport factors, and group size significantly affected the proportions of wasted and spoiled food (Lyman, 1980). Another intangible is the ratio of animal foods to plant foods, because these categories are preserved and quantified in different ways, and their relative preservations are rarely equal in any one site. Dietary reconstructions such as those of Flannery (1968) and MacNeish (1967) represent valuable models no more accurate than their underlying assumptions. It probably is not possible to estimate group size without making questionable inferences about caloric yields and intakes.

Seasonal availability of various animal and plant foods can be estimated under favorable conditions of preservation and reasonable models of subsistence patterning. But the available models do not consider year-to-year variability in animal biomass and plant productivity in response to climatic anomalies, disease, and ecological interactions (Reher, 1977; Baker and Brothwell, 1980). Such variables could be simulated mathematically, given ecosystemic data that are not now generally available. Consequently, the critical seasonal and yearly interactions among biomass, productivity, and human demography (births, deaths, group size) can at present be no more than surmised for prehistorical foragers.

Prospects for modeling settlement patterns in relation to diet and animal mobility are more encouraging, because adequate qualitative data can be generated by means of bio-archaeological studies, technological information, and behavioral analogues (MacNeish, 1972; Flannery, 1976).

A final issue in regard to prehistorical hunting is the potential effect of human predation on animal biomass. The Pleistocene archaeological record suggests that over a span of some 2 million years, early hominids were transformed from their status of incidental or minor carnivores to modern humans, assuming the role of dominant world predators. It is therefore not only possible but also probable that the biomass of preferred game was seriously altered in some habitats and biomes and that significant ecosystemic adjustments among other herbivores and their dependent carnivores took place. Several historical extinctions, near extinctions, and local extinctions can be directly attributed to hunters (e.g., the North American bison, the North African elephant, and the quagga zebra and blue antelope of South Africa). But the zoo-archaeological record, however tantalizing, does not directly verify either decimation or extinction as a result of prehistorical hunting (Martin and Klein, 1982).

A wave of animal extinctions marked the terminal Pleistocene on each continent, coincident both with the dispersal of efficient hunters and with environmental shifts from Pleistocene to Holocene equilibrium levels. The extinctions were not simultaneous within any one biome, and they affected several different kinds of animals, including a large range of birds (Grayson, 1977). This suggests complex ecosystemic responses to more than one causal factor. Just as prehistorical predation has not been directly linked to any one extinction, neither have environmental changes (Thompson et al., 1980). Nonetheless, environmental transformations

> can create severe stress without actually eliminating a particular habitat. Deterioration would initiate interspecific competition between animals of similar, yet not identical, ecological roles, resulting in possible eliminations of the less adaptive species of this fauna. Re-establishment of the original environmental conditions at lower or higher altitudes or latitudes would also entail the fragmentation of ranges and a complicated process of ecological shifts and readjustments for both plants and animals. Final re-occupation of the restored habitat would be restricted to the more successful members of the original fauna. Thus, environmental changes can create stresses of many kinds that affect different forms in different ways at different times (Butzer, 1971a:508).

In combination with selective hunting pressures, biome shifts and fragmentation will compound competitive pressures, particularly against animals with long gestation periods, which are prone to reduction in critical herd size, or animals affected by isolation of breeding populations in increasingly patchy environments (Klein, 1982).

Domestication and faunal change

The domestication of herd animals in the Near East during the first few millennia of the Holocene require an entirely new perspective on the interrelationships between people and animals. A number of potentially adaptable species such as sheep, goats, cattle, and pigs were modified by selective breeding through direct or indirect human manipulation. Changed in size, bone morphology, and variability ("breeds") (Zeuner, 1963; Uerpmann, 1973; Bökönyi, 1974; Bender, 1975:39–50), these new gregarious species were tended and favored by people to the extent that they began to displace other native animals from their habitats, often altering those habitats so dramatically that other species could not continue to thrive in them. These and similar domesticates, locally complemented by transport animals and barnyard fowl, spread through Eurasia and parts of Africa and ultimately into the Americas and Australia.

The browsing of cattle and goats in woodlands and the grazing of sheep and cattle in open country reduced the productive capability of increasingly scrubby woodlands, as well as the pasturage value of increasingly close-cropped grasslands. As important as these domesticated animals were to supplement cultivators' diets or to provide herders' livelihoods, they contributed significantly to devegetation, and this removal of the protective ground cover favored accelerated runoff and soil erosion (see Chapter 8). Their habitats ravaged, their niches destroyed or occupied, and under increasing predatory pressures from farmers and herders, the native herbivores were decimated and restricted to marginal, distant, and fragmented portions of their original ranges. Swept up in such fundamental ecosystemic changes, carnivores were also deprived of their food supply and, for the first time in human history, were aggressively hunted because of the threat they presented to domesticated stock. The changing habitats were also reflected among nonmammalian faunas and mollusca, increasingly favoring xeromorphic open-field forms in dry-farming areas (Evans, 1975:Chapter 6) and hydromorphic forms in irrigated and other wet-field agricultural systems (Higham and Kijngam, 1979).

At the same time, the very nature of the archaeological record was changed through a series of potent new cultural transformations, as

Table 11-1. *Zoo-archaeological evidence for domesticated-animal processing*[a]

	Herding	Milking	Shearing	Labor	Ritual/pets	Skinning	Preliminary Butchering	Advanced Butchering	Cooking, Preserving Storage
Product	Coprolites; high-phosphorus soil; fly pupae; fodder residues; pictorial art	Straining equipment, pots, bowls, gourds	Wool, fabrics, thread; weaving or sewing equipment	Yokes, harnesses, saddles, carts, wagons, plows; metal or woodworking artifacts	Unprocessed bone; burials; representations	Hair, fur, leather, and tanning residues; cutting and scraping tools, awls	Semiarticulated or sawed non-fleshy bones (facial, teeth, podials, tail, horns) of mainly male animals under 2 years or old animals of both sexes; cutting, scraping, and bashing tools	Disarticulated, in part split or worked, fleshy or marrow-rich bones (limb, shoulder, pelvic, vertebral, skull); cutting and bashing tools	Burnt or boiled fragmented bone (marrow bones, podials, horns); spits, pots, stone bowls, grinding equipment
Use	Fuel	Milk and milk by-products or derivatives	Clothing and other fibers	Transport, traction	Ceremonial, household	Clothing, containers, structural materials	Tools; containers (e.g., horns); glue; after boiling	Tools, food, fuel	Food
Site Context	Corrals, stalls, barns; animal quarters of compound farmsteads; hearths (dung)	Farm compounds or specialized work areas, recorded by post-molds or complex foundations			Ceremonial structures in or near living areas	Found in specialized work and habitation areas, middens		Found inside structures (hearths, ovens, storage pits, containers) or in the open (hearths, middens)	

[a] Based in part on suggestions by Cornelia Wolf.

described in Table 11-1. These transformations, in conjunction with those accompanying the dispersal of cultivated plants (see Table 10-2), created a range of new products, by-products, and site contexts reflecting the new economic mode and the diverse activities that constituted it.

In final evaluation, the different strands of bio-archaeological research focus preeminently on the small-scale data most intimately related to human activities, in much the same way as does archaeosedimentology (see Chapters 6 and 7). These several subfields consequently contribute results and insights critical for evaluating prehistorical socioeconomic systems. The basic analytical components in archaeobotany and zoo-archaeology are outlined in Table 11-2, which parallels the comparable Table 3-1 for the study components in geo-archaeology.

The methodologies of bio-archaeology and geo-archaeology are, in fact, remarkably similar, because each must deal with a variety of factors (incomplete record, sample bias, multiple causation, ambiguous systemic response) by a comparative approach based heavily on modern experience. The results and conclusions are no more or less foolproof than those of other observations sciences, but they are a vast improvement over deductive technological and economic interpretation of the artifactual record. In conjunction with other empirical investigations, such as lithic-wear analysis (Hayden, 1979; Keeley, 1980) and experimental archaeology (Ingersoll et al., 1977; Gould, 1978, 1980; Coles, 1979; Kramer, 1979; Watson, 1979; Carlton, 1981), they promise to revolutionize the data yield and the interpretative potential of archaeology in the 1980s.

Table 11-2. *Analytical components in bio-archaeology[a]*

Landscape context

1. Site microenvironment, evaluated in terms of transport, accumulation, burial, and mineralization (see Figure 10-1) by means of sediment, geochemical, and pertinent taphonomic studies, including three-dimensional plotting of bones, with orientation and inclination; removal of bone and pollen and flotation samples
2. Site mesoenvironment, as based on plants and animals specific to restricted habitats (aquatic, seashore, subsoil, tree canopy, bush, cave, etc.) in relation to the topographic matrix (see Chapter 4)
3. Site macroenvironment; in particular, identification of the biome or biotic mosaic, as based on different plant and/or animal communities represented and complemented by interpretation of modern aerial photography and satellite imagery

Stratigraphic context

1. Reconstruction of floral and faunal changes through time, as recorded in microstratigraphic units and determined by laboratory analysis; comparison with sediment data and with the archaeological record of changing human activities
2. Evaluation of the local biotic sequence, as representative of changes in the environmental mosaic
3. Comparison of local biostratigraphy and fossil assemblages with external reference profiles and assemblages for biostratigraphic correlation and for chronostratigraphic control

Site formation

1. Identification of the accumulation agency as geological, animal, or human; nature of biases in initial accumulation
2. Detailed interpretation of the accumulation processes and attritional factors in temporal and microspatial terms
3. Evaluation of any lines of evidence relevant to seasonality of occupation and total duration of site utilization by animals and humans
4. Identification of primary plant and animal remains, their secondary products (carbonized or digested plants; coprolites; gnawed, worked, or smashed bone and shell), and their tertiary residues (organic compounds, charcoal, phosphates, etc.)
5. Patterns of human activities as recorded by other archaeological criteria (stratification patterns; hearths, pits, post-molds, and structures; artifacts and other exotic materials, their patterning and dispersal; identification of activity areas, such as food-processing areas, workshops, middens, sleeping areas, etc.)
6. Assessment of collecting, hunting, planting, and herding techniques based on assemblage and internal-sample analyses as well as technological information
7. Assessment of processing and utilization techniques based on activity patterning, technology, and modification of plant and animal remains (e.g., Tables 10-2 and 11-1)

Site modification

1. Evaluation of cultural transforms modifying distributions and concentrations of bio-archaeological residues after their abandonment
2. Evaluation of noncultural biogenic, geomorphic, and geochemical transforms subsequently modifying archaeological context through dispersal or disturbance and fossilization, alteration, or selective destruction

External biotic modification

1. Quantification of selective collecting and hunting activities adjusted for differential preservation; study of group age and sex structures for various animal species
2. Assessment of possible overexploitation, frequently indicated by progressive species impoverishment, decreasing body size, etc.

Table 11.2 (*cont.*)

3. Evaluation of local biotic evidence (pollen, macrobotanicals, snails, rodents, etc.) for open or disturbed vegetation
4. Identification of cultivated plants and domesticated animals, their genetic variability, their similarities to specific wild progenitors, and (in the case of animals) their group age and sex structures
5. Determination of the significance of weeds and other anomalous vegetation patterns for agricultural and pastoral sites; information on soil profiles and their potential fertility and productivity; ratios, as well as kinds, of wild animals to domesticated ones, and their temporal changes
6. Assessment of local and regional vegetation cover and hydrological factors, as recorded in soil profiles and sediments due to accelerated erosion (see Chapter 8)
7. Assessment of the cumulative direct and indirect impacts of human interference, biotic exploitation, and general land use in light of integrated geo-archaeological and socioeconomic data; evaluation of sustained landscape productivity or degradation in regard to wild and domesticated plants and animals used for food, fuel, and other raw materials

ªSee also Tables 3-1 and 3-2.

PART III

Synthesis

CHAPTER 12

Spatial integration I: quantitative models for pattern analysis

Components, subsystems, and human ecosystems

The basic goal of a contextual approach is study of the archaeological record as part of a human ecosystem within which communities once interacted spatially, economically, and socially with the environmental matrix into which they were adaptively networked (See Chapter 1). The methodological inputs of the biological, physical, chemical, and earth sciences outlined in Chapters 3 to 11 served to identify major environmental components. As argued in detail, these components represent dynamic variables that characterize several critical subsystems of ecological interaction between prehistorical peoples and their biophysical environments: settlement loci as special sedimentary subsystems, land use as landscape intervention, the utilization of plants and animals as biotic intervention or even ecosystemic transformation.

Now that the interactive subsystems have been identified, it is appropriate to integrate them by focusing on subsistence-settlement systems in space and time. This complex and difficult array of themes marks the interface between contextual archaeology and social archaeology. It also delineates the fundamental contributions of all modes of archaeological research to an understanding of modern human ecosystems and human culture. Such a task is formidable, and we are unlikely to realize success in the immediate future. But it remains a central objective, and it is incumbent on archaeologists to design and implement research trajectories that will contribute substantially to a comprehensive model of human ecosystems that will incorporate realistic parameters of spatial variability and that, ultimately, will transcend time.

The contextual approach articulated here suggests a sequence of explorations: the use of mechanical or semiquantitative models to examine spatial patterning (Chapter 12), the value of socioecological models in elucidating the dynamics of local and regional systems (Chapter 13), the empirical reconstruction of settlement systems (Chapter 14), and, finally, the nature and maintenance of adaptive systems (Chapter 15). Unlike the preceding empirical section (Chapters 3–11), which outlined ecological components, their methodologies, and related interactive subsystems, this concluding part (Chapters 12–16) emphasizes theoretical viewpoints, examples liable to alternative interpretations, and models that cannot yet be properly tested. This is at once the most exciting and most frustrating of research areas. I do not pretend that the views and themes selected, championed, and challenged are representative of the full range of ideas and efforts marshaled by my colleagues during the last decade. But they are consistent with the contextual goals defined, and they are offered as constructive contributions to a debate and a search that has only just begun.

Spatial archaeology

In order to examine the spatial patterning of past human activities, archaeology has borrowed a number of analytical techniques from geography and adapted them with a certain measure of success. Other archaeological approaches have been developed directly from ecological theory. The result is a substantial body of literature, generated during the 1970s, that merits the designation of spatial archaeology. The elements of this subfield include raw materials, artifacts, features, structures, activity sites of all kinds, routes, resource spaces, and the people who ordered them (Clarke, 1977). Spatial archaeology deals with a set of elements and relationships representing "human activities at every scale, the traces and artifacts left by them, the physical infrastructure which accommodated them, the environments that they inpinged upon and the interaction between all these aspects" (Clarke, 1977:9). Three scales are singled out for study: (a) the microscale, within structures (e.g., shelters, rooms, houses, graves, granaries, and shrines), (b) the semimicroscale, within sites (e.g., domestic settlements, ceremonial centers, cemeteries, and temporary camp locations), and (c) the macroscale, between sites (e.g., large-scale archaeological distributions within integrated site systems or dispersed across landscapes) (Clarke, 1977:11–15).

Intrastructural and intrasite studies are critical to an understanding of human activity patterning, as reflected in site formation (see Chapter 6), in artifactual associations (Isaac, 1971; Whallon, 1973, 1974; Bordes, 1975; Clark, 1979; Sivertsen, 1980), and in structural configurations

(Fletcher, 1977; Raper, 1977). However, our present concern is with the larger-scale systemic interactions represented in site complexes and intersite networks and their related resource spaces.

Spatial analysis provides both tools and perspectives with which to examine prehistorical settlement distributions. But before examining these in any detail, it is important to have a clear understanding of the nature and purpose of spatial analysis in geography. Each of the several different approaches provides deductive models for economic organization, as patterned in response to locational constraints. The key variables are space, economic functions, and political and administrative structures. The basic concerns are (a) the locations and flow patterns of people, goods, services, and information and (b) the vertical organization of the related structures and demographic aggregates. As Lukermann (1972) pointed out, such an approach is limited by two unrealistic assumptions: (a) an undifferentiated environment, without variations in relief, soils, and productivity, and (b) an ahistorical premise, "the immediate genesis of a full-scale operating economy but no relicts or lags in that economy" (Lukermann, 1972:156). These assumptions already pose serious problems in analyzing modern market and industrial economies, and such problems are exacerbated for archaeological interpretation of settlement and exchange networks.

Space is not a homogeneous topological abstraction. Regardless of whether the perspective is economic, social, religious, cognitive, or environmental, not all points in space are of equal value (Butzer, 1978e). In particular, environmental space is complex and heterogeneous, with the factors of climate, topography, soils, hydrology, vegetation, and animal communities not simply superimposed on one another. Their interrelationships are defined within ecosystems and in response to different sets of variables. Each element has a particular organism- or ecosystem-specific relevance on the small, intermediate, or large scale. Mosaic patterning is the rule rather than the exception at all but the largest scales, and the size, frequency, and internal variability of patches within such mosaics differ from one environment to another.

The mosaic nature of landscape context (see Chapter 4) lends importance to the ecological concepts of patchiness and grain. Wiens (1976) defined a *patch* as an area demarcated from its surroundings by environmental discontinuities; the term *grain* refers to the biotic response to an environmental mosaic. Patchiness is a function of the number of patch types and the dimensions and relative distinctions among them. Grain is either fine or coarse, depending on the mobility of an organism and the scale of its significant habitat. Consequently, the number of organism-specific resource units is smaller in an environmental mosaic with patches of widely differing sizes than in one with patches of approximately equal sizes (Wiens, 1976). The significance of patch and grain for mobility patterns associated with hunting and gathering activities has been shown by Winterhalder (1981). The importance of soil and topographic variability for agricultural mosaics and communication lines requires no emphasis.

Spatial distributions are not adequately described in synchronic processual relationships. This applies to both the human patterning and the biophysical distributions that relate to it. Physical and biotic configurations vary with several temporal scales and amplitudes, whereas individual ecosystemic components respond to different degrees and with different periodicities. For example, plant productivity varies from week to week during the seasonal cycle, which, in turn, varies from year to year in terms of its exact timing and amplitude. The movements of animal populations may be even more rapid, and often seemingly erratic, whereas soil properties vary more slowly in response to changes in soil moisture and drainage. Fundamental changes, such as equilibrium shifts resulting from human interference or climatic variation, may take years, centuries, or millennia (see Tables 2-2 and 2-3). Differential time lags between environmental inputs and response are paralleled by other complex lags in socioeconomic adaptation (Winterhalder, 1980). Finally, adaptations are rarely momentary; they tend to be cumulative, reflecting local environments in which a human group has previously learned and in which its predecessors have learned (Wagner, 1974).

Geographers have devised transformation methods, such as the spatial smoothing technique of Tobler (1975) and the algorithm of Rushton (1972), that can reduce the distortions due to environmental variations and lag effects from spatial patterns. Similar transformations have been espoused by several workers in economic anthropology (Smith, 1976a, 1976b). Such transformations are not designed to serve as explanatory (positive) theory, but rather as normative devices that isolate and identify deviations from an ideal ordering model to pose problems of specific interest for examination and explanation (Chisholm, 1975). Archaeologists are not primarily interested in modeling an idealized exchange of goods and services under conditions of uniform demand across an unbounded economic landscape. They are, however, very much concerned with potential spatial deviations reflecting a nonuniform environment or decision making with respect to social, religious, and cognitive criteria, as well as economic and strategic considerations (see Chapter 13). This distinction of normative versus positive approaches should be borne in mind during the subsequent discussion of spatial techniques and theory.

Gravity models

The premise of simple gravity models is that the intensity of interaction between two settlements is directly proportional to the numbers of people living in them and inversely proportional to the intervening distance (Hodder and Orton, 1976:187–95; Hodder, 1978; Crumley, 1979; Morrill and Dormitzer, 1979). The gravity equation is given by

$$I = \frac{P_1 P_2}{R}$$

where I is a measure of interaction, P_1 and P_2 are the populations of the settlements, and R is the distance between them.

Jochim (1976:56–62) has developed a useful gravity model to analyze the interactions between a human population and several preferred resources. Because such interaction is proportional to the dietary importance of a particular resource, then

$$I = kp$$

where k is a constant and p is the dietary proportion of a resource. The density of such resources is expressed by

$$M = wna$$

where M is the mass of a resource cluster, w is the weight of an individual, n is the number of individuals, and a is the area. The gravity model can then be reformulated to include distance between a group and a dietary resource:

$$kp = \frac{Pwna}{R^2}$$

where P is the group population and R is the distance between the group and the resource. Distance can then be determined by rearranging the equation:

$$R^2 = \frac{Pwna}{kp}$$

The constant k and the population P can be ignored in considering relative distance in order to obtain a practicable relationship:

$$R^2 = \frac{wna}{p}$$

This resource gravity model can be implemented to express relative distances to sample resources (Table 12-1). All other conditions being equal, site locations will be closer to less mobile resources, more dense resources, and less clustered resources (Jochim, 1976:60). The model has been applied as a normative device to predict seasonal resource distribution for Mesolithic hunter-gatherers in the upper Danube watershed.

For an urbanized agricultural society, Tobler and Wineburg (1971) applied a common gravity model to an unusually good body of textual and archaeological evidence to obtain a realistic "predicted-location" map for Late Bronze Age trading centers in Anatolia. However, the network so established ignores the fact that many proximal nodes are separated by major topographic barriers. Gravity-related linkages can also be distorted by the presence of large urban centers with the coercive power to attract distant resource flows.

The special problem of linear arrangements of settlements along a river valley or coast has been approached by means of gravity models (Steponaitis, 1978) and by the linear nearest-neighbor technique, which describes clustering or systematic spacing (Dacey, 1960; Washburn, 1974; Stark and Young, 1981). Reynolds (1976) has also tested riverine settlements by means of a double-dependent Markov chain.

von Thünen's model

The 1826 model of von Thünen (1966) posits that an isolated population center in a uniform environment will create distinct land-use rings, forming a set of concentric circles related to distance. Immediately around the center, the first ring is dominated by intensive, cash-crop market gardening and dairy farming; the second ring comprises woodland for fuel, charcoal, and lumber; the next three rings include various combinations of cereal crops, pasture, and fallow; the last ring is devoted to extensive stock raising. In effect, economic activities will be governed by the law of diminishing returns with distance, particularly with the traditional modes of transportation available during the early nineteenth century (Hodder and Orton, 1976:229–36; Smith, 1976a:7–10; Haggett et al., 1977:214–15).

Table 12-1. *Relative distances to sample resources according to Jochim's gravity model*

Characteristics of sample area	Resource type			
	Plant species	Small-game species	Fish species	Large herbivores
Low plant potential	0.04	0.45	0.17	7.00
Large fish run	0.07	0.70	0.42	12.50
Low plant potential and large fish run	0.06	0.61	0.37	11.80
Low plant potential and herd migration	0.04	0.48	0.19	11.00

Source: Adapted from Jochim (1976:Table 12).

Von Thünen's model has basic similarities to the "site-catchment analysis" of Vita-Finzi and Higgs (1970). These authors argued that subsistence activities normally are limited by the distance from a site that can be walked in two hours, so that a two-hour perimeter, equated with a circle 10 km in diameter, is used to define the catchment of a prehistorical hunter-gatherer site, with several circles of smaller diameter applied to farming settlements. The land-use rings can be adjusted to allow for irregular topography and differences in productivity. There are some unsatisfactory aspects of the site-catchment technique in current practice (Higgs, 1972, 1975; Vita-Finzi, 1978): (a) the application of modern land-use categories (e.g., irrigated land, irrigated crops, arable land, rough grazing, or good grazing/potentially arable) to the definition of hunter-gatherer catchments; (b) the assumption that Pleistocene biotic distributions were similar to or identical with modern ones; (c) the assumption that technology is an independent variable that will determine the range of resources to be exploited and thus will affect the location and shape of the catchment – although technology is to some degree responsive to the nature and distribution of resources. For other critiques, see the work of Hodder and Orton (1976:230–6) and Roper (1979). Nonetheless, the more exacting examples of catchment work, particularly those of Dennell and Webley (1975), Flannery (1976:Chapter 4), and Barker (1981) on agricultural communities, are scientifically rigorous and provide valuable insights for intermediate-scale resource variability. Suggestions for comparable maps of potential productivity, biomass, and agricultural yields are made in Chapter 8.

Von Thünen himself (1966:268) recognized the basic weaknesses of the model of land-use rings in that it assumes economic isolation, a single mode of transport, rational economic behavior, and a uniform environment. He therefore suggested alternative models to take account of multiple centers and multiple transport means, as well as soils of variable productivity (von Thünen, 1966:216; Haggett et al., 1977: Figures 6.12 and 6.13). A particularly sophisticated model of this type, devised by Foley (1977) for East Africa, is of great interest for foraging behavior in a differentiated habitat: Plant productivity and animal biomass are quantitatively rated for upland forest, open woodland, bush, riverine forest, floodplain savanna, lake edge, and grassland. Foley (1977) explicitly recognized that human energy expenditure is not solely a function of distance decay but is also dependent on technology, resources, habitat, and topography. A different ring model applicable to urban centers has been proposed by Hammond (1972); it distinguishes ceremonial, residential, and resource spaces within a variable environment.

Central-place theory

Central-place theory (CPT) is a macroscale normative theory designed to quantify the horizontal and vertical organization of settlement systems. Christaller (1966), who formulated the tenets of CPT in 1933, focused preeminently on site hierarchies and their related economic spheres (Smith, 1976a:10–32). Critical to such hierarchies is the range of goods, resources, and services available in a particular settlement. These determine a vertical ordering scale that should be reflected spatially in the distances among sites of different rank order and in their nesting patterns. Three governing principles are recognized (marketing, traffic, and administrative) and are believed to be reflected in the number of next-lower-order settlements typically served by each central place, together providing the k value (Christaller, 1966) (Figure 12-1). These differences will not significantly affect the shape of the polygonal territories, but will govern the pattern of evolving hierarchical nesting. Where the marketing principle is dominant, the supply of goods from central places should be as near as possible to the dependent places, which are best located for access to three central places (k is 3, a number obtained by counting a third of the six border settlements plus the central place). Where the traffic principle dominates, transport costs and distance dictate that major settlements lie on radially intersecting roads; dependent centers lie on the midpoints of roads linking two central places ($k = 4$, with half the six border settlements plus the central place). Finally, where the administrative principle is critical, settlements lie within the hexagonal territory, rather than on its perimeter, because of the direct linkage between the dependencies and a single central place ($k = 7$, with six lower-order settlements all within the hexagon).

Because functional settlement hierarchies and specialized centers are essential ingredients, CPT is relevant only to permanent agrarian communities with a measure of urbanism. Applications to archaeological problems have been attempted, as discussed by Hodder (1972), Marcus (1973), Johnson (1975, 1977), Flannery (1976:Chapter 6), and Hodder and Orton (1976:60–9). Several practical problems rapidly emerge from such considerations: (a) incomplete archaeological survey or incomplete preservation; (b) inadequate temporal controls whether or not

Marketing Principle (k=3)
Dependent places shared by several central places at intersection of hexagons

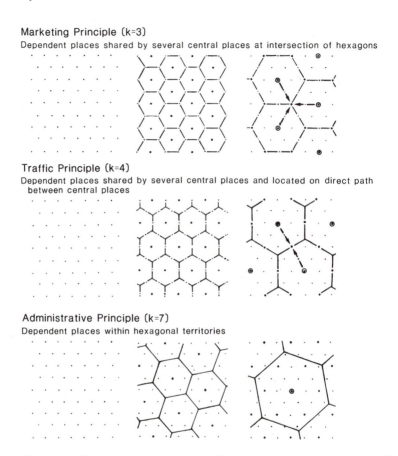

Traffic Principle (k=4)
Dependent places shared by several central places and located on direct path between central places

Administrative Principle (k=7)
Dependent places within hexagonal territories

Figure 12-1. Three-stage hierarchies for Christaller central-place networks with k = 3, k = 4, and k = 7. Modified from Haggett et al. (1977:Figure 57).

sites are strictly contemporaneous, and insufficient information as to site growth and possibly changing rank order; (c) unreliable or incomplete data on site size or population and on economic activities. Unless an unusual wealth of written documents is available, center ranking and overall hierarchical differentiation are prone to error, increasing the probability that incorrect hexagonal patterns will be constructed.

Even if ranking problems can be properly resolved for an unusually good archaeological record, selection of the *k* hierarchy becomes critical. Theoretically, it seems unlikely that the rationalized marketing principle pertains to prehistorical settlement distributions; yet Marcus (1973) and Smith (1979*b*) adopted a *k* = 3 hierarchy for the lowland Maya and the Aztec of the Valley of Mexico. Given the primary importance of religious, symbolic, and political factors in Aztec territorial organization (Licate, 1980), a $k = 7$ hierarchy is more appropriate (Evans, 1980). In fact, Earle (1976) achieved more satisfactory results for the Valley of Mexico by using a nearest-neighbor cluster analysis. Flannery (1976:170–1) acknowledged that a modified hierarchy, with a more nearly continuous sequence of centers, without distinct tiers, might be preferable for the Maya example. In any case, an incorrect k hierarchy will have serious repercussions for functional interpretation and resource space demarcation. Further, the sequences of numbers of centers and dependencies differ markedly: 1-2-6-18-54-162 for $k = 3$, 1-3-12-48-172 for $k = 4$, and 1-6-42-294-2058 for $k = 7$, with corresponding effects on functional interpolation for obscure sites and predictive value for undiscovered sites using CPT hexagons.

Even when all the requirements of CPT have been met, the contribution to spatial archaeology may well be flawed by the simplifying assumptions inherent in the theory itself: a flat, featureless plain and a stepwise hierarchical structure with fixed k values. Lösch (1967) provided an alternative to Christaller's CPT (Haggett et al., 1977:148–53; Bell, 1980), integrating it with geographical reality by assuming that rank orders are fluid rather than rigidly graduated, that k hierarchies are not fixed but variable, and that settlements of similar sizes need not have identical functions. Thus Lösch's spatial model can be adjusted for irregularities in settlement and resource distribution, because it emphasizes market competition rather than hierarchies. It therefore can be used to identify patterned dynamics – given a complete data base. Because the available information is by definition incomplete, it can be argued that spatial geometries have little more than heuristic value in the interpretation of archaeological settlement networks. Any apparent success in the interpretation of site functions or in locating "missing" centers probably is fortuitous. Nonetheless, CPT provides more than a packing theory to arrange population and resources in a landscape, because it assumes that territorially competitive behavior between like centers is as important as hierarchical geometry. There are, then, possibilities to shift the emphasis of the basic theory from hierarchies to resource spaces by means of an appropriate transformation.

Another related technique is to draw perpendicular lines at the midpoints between verified centers to obtain what are called Thiessen polygons (Hodder and Orton, 1976:59–60, 78–80, 187; Bell, 1980). Assuming that the centers are indeed contemporaneous, these polygons give equal weight to centers of different size and consequently underrepresent the service areas and resource spaces of larger towns, unless the hierarchy of settlements is predetermined. The use of rank-size distributions (rank of center versus population) would be potentially useful in such a procedure (Adams and Jones, 1981).

Hunter-gatherer settlements have been examined by Wobst (1976) by means of mating networks bounded by hexagonal territories that lack vertical structure. Whatever the intrinsic merits of a model that emphasizes social context over environmental context in forager catchments, Wobst then proceeds to argue that linear environments create a strong locational dichotomy between centrally and marginally placed groups, with the probability that such arrangements might "overburden the social mechanism available to egalitarian band societies" (Wobst, 1976:56). By implying that linearly arranged populations cannot long remain egalitarian, he confuses settlement hierarchy with social inequality. It therefore seems implausible when Wobst argues that purportedly marginal locations such as coastal islands, peninsulas, oases, mountain valleys, and the upper ends of watersheds "discriminate" against their occupants in terms of mating networks, resulting in underexploitation of such productive areas (Wobst, 1976:57). The concentrations of middens along any coastal sector of northern Spain with ready topographic access to the watermark (Clark, 1971) speak against such a theory.

In concluding this discussion of CPT and related network methods, attention must be drawn to a location-allocation model being developed by Bell and Church (1980) to assess archaeological settlement configurations without attempting to transform physical space or achieve geometrical regularity (Bell, 1980). The method assigns relative weights to strategic criteria, resource constraints, principles of economic efficiency, political control, and transportation interconnection; for example, see the regional heterarchy model of Crumley (1979). The assumption is that an archaeological settlement pattern is not chaotic but rather the result of political, economic, and ecological forces working themselves out on the landscape. The resulting central-place systems are nested but do not require hexagonal packing, while covering all discretely distributed settlements. The elimination of the packing requirement leads to k systems in which fewer centers are needed to provide services but in which consumers also have flexibility in central-place selection. Such a multiple-objective approach, in focusing on the properties of the solution rather than the deduced geometry, promises to provide a more flexible and more general CPT. This technique has been profitably applied to linear settlement along the Ramessid Nile Valley by Kauffman (1981).

Resource-concentration models

CPT and its derivatives serve to describe or analyze spatial relationships between settlements of different size and, implicitly, between settlements and their resource spaces. Such concerns are mainly appropriate to permanent settlements among which there are differences in size and function. Different models and techniques must be applied to deal with location strategies, mobility patterns, and decision-making factors among hunter-gatherers and pastoralists with more flexible patterns of residency and for whom access to resources is far more important than distance to markets. Jochim's gravity model (1976:58–60) illustrates one method to incorporate mobility (predictability), density (productivity), and clustering (dispersal) of resources. Resource-catchment analyses that explicate differential productivity in relation to site proximity provide another example. However, such methods do not deal with subsistence strategies on a sufficiently large scale (Kay, 1979) and consequently fail to provide a general settlement theory for hunter-gatherers and pastoralists.

The spatial problem can initially be simplified by assuming static resources. Three different models may be considered. Many implicit traditional models assume environmental uniformity (Figure 12-2A). Correspondingly, human groups can be expected to spread out into all habitable zones, achieving a quasi-random distribution at a given density that depends on technological skills and social constraints. Other models that recognize the differential plant productivity and animal biomass of different biomes (Butzer, 1971a:Chapter 9; Lieth, 1973) nonetheless assume a relatively uniform distribution of resources within each biome. Such primitive ecological models imply higher group density in preferred biomes, creating stepped population gradients between marginal and optimal environments, with major discontinuities at or near the boundaries (Figure 12-2B). More sophisticated ecological models allow for discrete resource concentrations within biomes with differing overall productivity, as well as within the patchy environments of associated ecotones. In this case, settlement strategies will be geared to both predictable and unpredictable resources of variable productivity across a far more complex ecological gradient (Figure 12-2C).

The importance of choosing from these alternatives can be judged

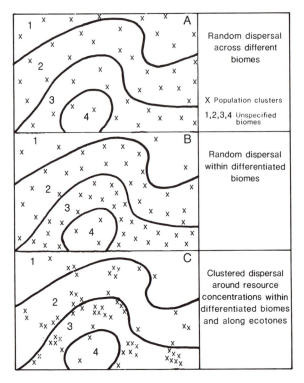

Figure 12-2. Alternative models for large-scale settlement patterns of prehistorical hunter-gatherers.

from two recent interpretations of Acheulian settlement distribution during early and middle Pleistocene times. Isaac (1972:Figure 7) has proposed a modified gravity model to explain the slow rates of directional change in technology and lithic typology during the million years spanned by the African Acheulian: Low-density, uniform dispersal of groups is proposed. Under such minimal gravity conditions information flow is negligible, and there is little directional change; much of the observed variability is explained by stochastic processes (the random-walk hypothesis developed by D.L. Clarke) (Clarke, 1968). For later Pleistocene times, Isaac (1972) has proposed a higher-density distribution of groups, prone to increasing aggregation and thereby favoring regional patterning of rule systems and language that then create intelligibility barriers and partial cultural isolates. Isaac's model does not take resource variability into account, a factor militating against uniform dispersal in most environments. On the other hand, Deacon

(1975:550) accepted the impression that Acheulian "distributions cross-cut the broad ecological zonation excluding apparently only the extremes of dry desert . . . and forest" at face value, having denied significant environmental changes through time. This is not so, because Acheulian sites in Africa, regardless of contemporary ecozonation, were linked with water sources in what then were semiarid or subhumid macroenvironments, and any associated fossil assemblages imply grassland or grass-woodland mosaics (Butzer and Cooke, 1981). Deacon (1975:553) further postulated random clumping of Acheulian population units, implicitly related to inefficient utilization of resources in space.

The basic weakness of these models is that they attribute less efficiency to early hominids than modern ethological observations have demonstrated for the spatial behavior of other primates, carnivores, birds, and ants. Both ethnological and ethological studies have supported three premises articulated by Renfrew (1978): (a) Basic social groups are defined by the habitual association of persons within a territory. (b) Human social organization is segmentary in nature, so that spatial organization is cellular and modular. (c) Basic social groups do not exist in isolation, but affiliate into larger groups that interact periodically. These assumptions can be incorporated into several medium-scale settlement models for prehistorical hunter-gatherers that posit a fundamentally rational utilization of resources (Figure 12-3). The first (Figure 12-3A) represents a mesic environment with a relatively uniform or quasi-random distribution of groups in relation to abundant water and dispersed plant and animal foods of good predictability. The average limits of a particular group's operational environment may intersect with those of another group, but the territorial strategies of ants suggest that discrete spherical territories (Hölldobler and Lunsden, 1980) may provide a better model, even for early hominids. Figure 12-3B shows a diffuse concentration of groups in relation to equally diffuse concentrations of food resources, water, and topographic features relevant to site location. Examples include edaphic conditions within the topographic matrix that affect water availability, productivity, and the frequency of suitable site locations. Figure 12-3C presents a linear arrangement of group networks in relation to a similar alignment of resources along a seashore, a mountain valley, a river, or a spring line dictated by medium-scale topography. Finally, Figure 12-3D illustrates a radial concentration of groups around a circular or elliptical resource set, such as a lake, a marsh, or a spring-fed oasis.

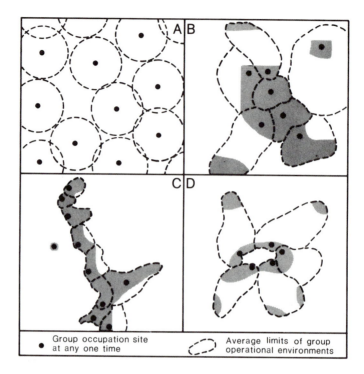

Figure 12-3. Medium-scale settlement patterns for hunter-gatherers, as modified by dispersed and localized resources (shaded areas). Modified from Haggett et al. (1977).

Dynamic perspectives on stable versus mobile resources are introduced in a model derived by Horn (1968) from the spatial behavior of Brewer's blackbird. This suggests different optimal group sizes in relation to stable, evenly dispersed food resources, as opposed to mobile concentrated resources. This notion was subsequently developed by Wilmsen (1973) into a mathematical social-interaction formulation for hunter-gatherers based on the gravity model. The basic interrelationships can be described as follows:

1. Mean procurement effort, as a function of distance traveled, is minimized in the case of stable dispersed resources when groups are dispersed and evenly spaced in resource proximity, whereas a central location is more efficient than dispersal for mobile clustered resources. In practice, this generalization is complicated by the mixed vegetable intake (fixed) and animal foods (both mobile and fixed) of humans, as compared with a simpler bird diet; see the ethnographic contradictions

presented by Dyson-Hudson and Smith (1978). A more complex formulation, developed as an index of diversity, has been given by Harpending and Davis (1977), demonstrating that hunter-gatherer mobility should be high in a poor environment with few resources, particularly when they are seasonally out of phase with each other; on the other hand, mobility should be low when resources show little spatial variation and when they vary in phase.

2. Territory size is a function of resource strategies and technology, as well as resource limitations.

3. The population of any group is dependent on resource dispersal and on the aggregation and distribution of all other groups in a fixed area.

4. Interaction intensity is proportional to proximal group size, so that interactions within a bounded area will be greater than interactions between units across boundaries.

5. The relationships so established apply to only one point in time.

Finally, a different application of Horn's model (1968) has been developed by Winterhalder (1981), incorporating optimal foraging theory (Orians, 1975), which applies to the decisions ideally made by a predator in maximizing potential energy intake per time spent foraging.

1. Winterhalder (1981) argued that hunter-gatherers in an environment with stable, evenly distributed resources will tend toward regular dispersion of the smallest viable social units, whereas unpredictably located and clustered resources will favor aggregation of social units at a central place. Following MacArthur and Pianka (1966), he also considered the interrelationships between the number of resource types contributing to a particular group's diet and the average search costs.

2. Economy will dictate a reasonably broad diet rather than a specialized narrow diet (an important consideration for evaluating the carrying capacity of increasingly omnivorous early hominids).

3. The diet breadth of economically efficient hunter-gatherers will be affected by changes in the abundances of only higher-ranked resource items. The number of patch types exploited in food procurement will affect time costs in terms of searching and collecting, as well as harvest yields (MacArthur and Pianka, 1966). For example, it is economical to decrease the number of patch types included in foraging itinerary when resource density increases. Similarly, hunter-gatherers in a habitat with small-grained patch types will tend toward generalized use of available patch types, whereas a large-grained habitat will encourage specialized use of patch types.

4. Finally, there is a relationship between time spent in a patch and the net energy intake (Charnov, 1976). "Optimal" hunter-gatherers will abandon a patch before its resources are depleted, simply because the increasingly marginal return in that patch becomes equal to the average return from the total set of patch types generally exploited. An increase in resource density reduces the time required for exploitation and therefore accelerates movement among the set of patch types being visited.

These component arguments to Winterhalder's optimal foraging strategy represent the most sophisticated model available for hunter-gatherer resource strategies in environmentally variable space. A corollary to these hypotheses is the argument of Dyson-Hudson and Smith (1978) that territoriality can be expected when critical resources are sufficiently abundant and predictable in space and time, so that the costs of exclusive use and defense of an area are less than the benefits accruing from resource control. On the other hand, when resources are prone to rapid unpredictable changes, a flexible and more mobile adaptive strategy appears to be preferable. In this way, behavioral adaptations, social organization, and environmental space are systematically interrelated.

Resource concentration and predictability can also be applied to the location of agricultural settlements, but continue to be neglected because of the overriding concern with commodity exchange within hierarchical networks. Needless to say, goods and services may be appropriate to market economies, but the related networks do scant justice to subsistence economies. More satisfactory is Johnson's analysis (1978) of spatial variability in determining recent pastoral mobility patterns, as is the model for the origins of pastoralism by Lees and Bates·(1974) that also focuses on spatial and temporal resource patterning.

Common to all of these efforts dealing with resource concentration is point pattern analysis for interaction and distance (Hodder and Orton, 1976:Chapter 3). The different models use a wide range of mathematical (or at least semiquantitative) techniques and procedures, of which various distance measures (nearest-neighbor analysis) for point densities are the most common (Hodder, 1972; Washburn, 1974; Whallon, 1974; Wood, 1978; Adams and Jones, 1981; Stark and Young, 1981). Quadrat methods that compare real frequency patterns against random distributions have also been explored (Thomas, 1972; Whallon, 1973), with gravity statistics sometimes incorporated in the process. Effective tests remain difficult to demonstrate, however, because of the paucity of hard archaeological data.

One of the better examples of its kind is a regional survey of Paleo-indian sites in a part of New Mexico (Judge and Dawson, 1972; Judge, 1973). Five types of sites were identified by Wood (1978) on the basis of lithic artifact variability (multiple activity; multiple activity, armament dominant; multiple activity, processing dominant; limited activity, armament; limited activity, processing). These were then analyzed in terms of location with respect to critical resources (horizontal and vertical distances to nearest water, distance to overview, distance to hunting area, and distance to potential trap area). The distance statistics show a general correspondence and a degree of internal logic for the location of sites in relation to resource strategies, but the sample size (16 sites) is too small to provide conclusive arguments. Like the other models discussed earlier, that of Wood (1978) is primarily of heuristic value rather than operational value. Evidently there remains a need for alternative and complementary mathematical approaches to locational behavior, specifically simulation studies (Zimmerman, 1978).

CHAPTER 13

Spatial integration II: socioecological models for settlement analysis

Scale settlement analysis

An archaeological site can be defined as the tangible record of a locus of past human activity. Such sites vary in scale from the locus of a single processing task to a complex urban settlement. They also range in duration from an ephemeral sojourn to milennia of sequential occupation. The spatial dimension provides a reference plane for human activities. Contextual archaeology is concerned with the location of sites in a contemporaneous landscape, the function of such sites, the subsistence and interactive networks defined by groups of contemporary sites, and the changing configurations of such sites and networks through time. The general spatial perspectives of Chapter 12 can now be applied to a more explicit examination of sites in terms of variable resource spaces and the subtle constraints placed on such interactions by perception, information, and technology.

Two modal classes of settlements can be selected for heuristic purposes: the simple and often rudimentary traces of prehistorical hunter-gatherer sites, on the one hand, and the complex records of agricultural, pastoral, and mixed-farming communities, on the other. The one can be modeled on the typical residues encountered in Paleolithic and Mesolithic sites in the Old World and Paleoindian and Archaic sites in the New World. The other can be modeled on traditional villages surviving into the present but also documented by numerous historical and archaeological studies on different continents. Such classes evidently create a dichotomy that is spanned by many intermediate subsistence forms and their settlement residues; they also do not do proper justice to forager sites that lack stone artifacts, on the one hand, and complex urban communities, on the other. They do, however, provide useful models with which to illustrate scale hierarchies and to point to basic functions and interactive spheres.

Table 13-1 provides one such model for hunter-gatherer settlements

Table 13-1. *Hunter-gatherer settlements and networks formulated for Paleo-lithic and Mesolithic archaeological residues*

Microscale
Intrasite activity patterning in regard to animal, plant, and tool processing; eating, sleeping, and ritual; waste disposal. Inferred from nature, distribution, and association of bone residues, plant remains, artifacts and related lithic debris, and structures.

Semimicroscale
Site aggregation and function as a focus of limited or multiple activities of brief or protracted duration, during course of annual or multiannual group rounds, with repeated episodes of temporary group fragmentation.

Limited activity:
1. Quarry and/or workshop sites: Located near or adjacent to lithic material source, such as a pebbly stream bed or rock outcrop. These are specialized preliminary stone-processing sites occupied for a few hours or days. Characterized by large quantities of concentrated waste flakes/chips produced in artifact preparation; hammer stones; uncompleted artifact roughouts and broken unused pieces; rare finished or use-worn tools; little or no bone refuse; rare hearths.
2. Kill and/or butchery sites: Located near water or topographic trap/obstacle, such as a marsh, pitfall, cliff, defile, or box canyon. These preliminary meat-processing sites, occupied for a few hours or days, typically include incomplete, partly articulated skeletons of one or more animals (few genera and species, mainly large; nonfleshy bones and crania well represented), with limited dispersal. Small numbers of stone tools, predominantly heavy-duty chopping and cutting items, possibly including (projectile) points or (hafted) microliths, but little or no stoneworking debris.

Multiple activity:
1. Short-term camps: Minor sites, recording several days' residence by subgroups of mobile hunters or collectors, near special resources in open air or under rock overhangs. May include remains of small animals, evidence of intermediate processing of large animals, or shell/fish middens. Moderate number and diversity of lithic artifacts, together with isolated hearths and/or temporary structures.
2. Long-term camps: Complex and major sites, representing diversified activities of a total group over several weeks or months. Location selected with respect to water and food resources, suitability for shelter against extreme weather or hazards (wind, sun, rain, flood, fire, other predators) in open air or caves, often providing camouflage or an overview, usually in a complex topographic matrix. Bone refuse abundant, but disarticulated, highly fragmented, and dispersed, representing many species and individuals, with meat or marrow bones most common, often charred or burnt. Moderate to abundant lithic materials and high ratio of stone to bone. Tool kit emphasizes a variety of light-duty cutting and scraping tools, with moderate proportions of stone debris, mainly due to use-retouch, sharpening, or refashioning; maximum variety of artifact types. Special-activity areas, as for hide processing or woodworking, indicated by concentrations of special tools; other special loci marked by carbonized plant remains, hearths, ash, etc.; structures recorded by post-molds, rock arrangements, and the like. Large shell middens provide a special case. Multiple reoccupation of same location may record repeated residence at centrally located base camps or periodic/seasonal exploitation at resource-specific sites near major waterholes or aquatic/marine habitats.

Macroscale
Intersite patterning, including the full network of limited and multiple-activity sites of variable duration used by a group and its temporary subgroups during the course of one to several years. Defines an operational area that comprises a topographic matrix with different degrees of biotic complexity. Depending on predictability and mobility of dispersed and concentrated resources, a variety of circular or oscillatory movements, either seasonal or annual, define the mobility pattern (Figure 13-1). Linkages between the operational areas of several contiguous or adjacent groups favor different polygonal, linear, or circular networks of nonhierarchical interaction (see Figure 12-3).

and their related networks using the internal scale terminology of Clarke (1977) in relation to the external spatial spheres of Butzer (1971*a*:401–2). Examples of such sites and networks in the New World have been published by Frison (1978), Johnson and Holliday (1980), Judge and Dawson (1972), Wood and McMillan (1976), Flannery (1968, 1976), MacNeish (1972), and many others; examples from the Old World have been published by Howell (1966), Freeman (1978), De Lumley (1969, 1975), Klein (1973), Chavaillon et al. (1978), Isaac (1977), Clark (1960, 1975), Deacon (1976), Mellars (1978), and others. A detailed model for related stone and bone has been outlined by Sivertsen (1980), and an alternative ethnoarchaeological record for nonlithic sites in an environment without suitable raw materials for stone-tool making has been described by Yellen (1977). Experimental work in regard to stone-tool making, critical in appreciating the inherent problems of interpreting occupation floors, has been discussed by Ammerman and Feldman (1974). Table 13-1 is based on these sources, as well as on my own interpretations of Acheulian and Mousterian sites in Spain (Butzer, 1971*a*:456–61; 1981*c*) and Middle and Late Stone Age sites in the interior of South Africa (Butzer, 1978*f*; Butzer, Beaumont, and Vogel, 1978; Butzer et al., 1979; Butzer and Vogel, 1979).

The second model, for agricultural and pastoral settlements and their networks, is presented in Table 13-2. Innumerable archaeological examples can be cited from the Near Eastern Pre-Pottery and Pottery Neolithic, from the early Neolithic Linear Pottery of Germany and The Netherlands, from the Mississippian of the eastern United States, the Anasazi, Hohokam, and Mogollon of the American Southwest, and the Formative of Mesoamerica and Peru. More elaborate Bronze Age to Iron Age (Europe), early historical (Near East and East Asia), and Classic (Mesoamerica) villages, towns, and cities can also be cited. Particularly informative, too, are the microscale and semimicroscale ethnoarchaeological studies that have begun to emerge from projects in the Near East and Mesoamerica to complement earlier analyses of rural lifeways in medieval Europe. Information on pastoral communities is still limited (David, 1971; Hole, 1974, 1978*a*; Sterud, 1978; Johnson, 1978). Table 13-2 draws on a selection of these resources, on the settlement geography of Niemeier (1972), and on recent mapping by Elisabeth Butzer and myself of partly abandoned mixed agricultural and pastoral communities in the sierra of eastern Spain. An extra level of differentiation is required in Table 13-2 in order to distinguish intrasite

Table 13-2. *Agricultural and pastoral settlements and networks formulated for the ethnographic present or historical past*

Microscale
Intrastructural activity patterning in regard to animal, plant, and tool manipulation and processing; storage, eating, sleeping, and ritual; waste disposal. Inferred from structures, artifacts, and bone and plant residues.

Semimicroscale
Intrasite components and their functions as a focus for limited or multiple activities during the course of temporary, seasonal, or all-year operations by the community and its diverse social and task-specific subgroups. These comprise living, storage, animal, and other special-purpose structures, as well as the cemeteries, gardens, fields, pastures, and woodlots associated with the site:

Living structures:
1. Permanent houses of differing groundplans and profiles, one or more floors, and various construction materials of different durability. Commonly differentiated internally into community and segregated areas (e.g., processing, eating, sleeping rooms/sectors, sometimes enclosing a nonroofed courtyard or garden). Associated refuse heaps.
2. Temporary structures, including huts and cabins used repeatedly during periods of farmwork in distant fields, as well as tents and other structures used temporarily by pastoralists.

Storage structures:
Sunken grain bins, raised granaries, barns, silos, lofts, storerooms, ice houses, etc., for human food storage; barns, lofts, silos, etc., for animal fodder; sheds and barns for storage of tools and transport devices.

Animal structures:
Covered stalls, stables, chicken coops, pigeon lofts, kennels, etc.; open corrals with permanent walls of wood, mud, or stone; corrals with impermanent fences of wood, thorn, matting, etc.; associated dung heaps, butchery refuse areas, and the like.

Other special-purpose structures:
Wells, exterior ovens, pottery and brick kilns, metalworking furnaces, wood and hide workshops, ceremonial and administrative buildings, fortifications and the like, with their associated waste accumulations.

Open spaces:
Cemeteries, horticultural and ornamental gardens, orchards, threshing floors, cultivated and fallow fields, meadows and unimproved pasturage, transhumance "runs," woodlots, other commonage, as well as associated roadways and trails; fences, earth baulks, rock walls, and hedge plantings; terraces and drainage ditches, irrigation works, and so forth.

Mesoscale
Intrasite aggregation into single-roofed or semiattached farm compounds. Community patterning and socioeconomic segregation, as a core of houses surrounded by storage buildings and animal compounds; dispersal or aggregation of special-purpose structures; separation of farming, pastoral, and craft-specialist families; social segregation according to wealth and prestige. Field layouts reflecting utilization mosaic, rotational patterns, and proprietary arrangements.

Composite settlement types:
1. Isolated settlements, such as a farmstead or pastoral camp.
2. Dispersed settlements, such as clusters or swarms of farm compounds.
3. Linear nucleated settlements, arranged along roads, canals, or valleys.

Table 13-2 (*cont.*)

---

4. Geometric, nonlinear nucleated settlements arranged around a fortress, ceremonial center, town square, village green, or animal compounds, or with respect to bounding walls or earthworks.
5. Irregular nucleated settlements, commonly arranged around multiple intersecting roads or in relation to complex topography.
6. Regular planned settlements, with checkerboard grids or concentric rings cut by radial roads.
7. Composite agglomerated settlements with multiple road networks reflecting temporal accretions or socioeconomic segregation.

Field patterns:
1. Irregular, with curved or polygonal boundaries.
2. Regular, with rectangular, trapezoidal, or square shapes.
3. Regular, with linear plan, arranged in parallel stripes (length/width ratio exceeds 10), often perpendicular to roads, canals, streams, or other topographic features.

Macroscale
Intersite patterning: on the one hand, interlinked with diversified resource spaces; on the other hand, organized around one or more higher-order nodes related to defensive, administrative, ceremonial, or market functions. Settlement location primarily reflects access and distance to water, agricultural and pastoral resources, communications lines, markets, and nonedible raw materials or finished products, in the context of a particular technology. Settlement hierarchy primarily reflects market, ceremonial, administrative, or military functions, in the context of a particular subsistence, redistributive, or market economy. Both location and hierarchy affect population size and are modified by linguistic, religious, judicial, or political boundaries or major topographic barriers. All these variables contribute to the pattern of spatial and vertical interaction in a nested hierarchy within a particular ecozone.

---

structures and components (semimicroscale) from intrasite aggregation patterns (mesoscale).

It is now possible to examine the different intrasite patterning of hunter-gatherers and farmer-herders on the macroscale, distinguishing spatial-temporal parameters from interactive subsistence and demographic variables.

Large-scale mobility models for hunter-gatherers

Implicit models for the spatial behavior of prehistorical hunter-gatherers have long had evolutionary overtones. The basic premise is a progression from unspecialized free-wandering bands to specialized hunter-gatherers with well-defined centrally based movements to agriculturalists with permanent settlements (Braidwood, 1960). This model was explicated by MacNeish (1964, 1967, 1972) to describe the archaeological record from the Tehuacán Valley of central Mexico within a framework of eight temporal phases spanning some six major environmental zones during the last 10,000 years. For example, the first (Ajue-

reado) phase (ca. 12,000–8700 B.P.) includes 13 sites or site components, all small, scattered across several environments without apparent correlation to seasonal activity. These were therefore characterized
as "nomadic microbands – that is, groups of families who hunted game
in all seasons without regard to any well-regulated subsistence scheduling or well-defined territories" (MacNeish, 1972:71). For the second
(El Riego) phase (ca. 9000–7000 B.P.), there are 11 large sites or components (identified with distinct macrobands) and 29 small ones (identified as satellite microband sites) believed to demarcate three or four
contemporaneous community groupings. These were described as seasonal micro-macrobands with territoriality and a subsistence system
devoted to specific ecozones and resources at different times of the
year. By 900 B.C., settlement was organized around some five or six
permanent villages, each with one or more associated hamlets, with
60% of the food being obtained from agricultural products. Finally, by
the twelfth century A.D., the valley comprised five or more city-states
with a vertical hierarchy of small and large associated sites. The archaeological background for this scheme, complemented by excellent
bio-archaeological data and interpreted in the context of distinct ecozones, is unusually good. However, the mobility patterns and social
organization attributed to the hunter-gatherer communities are hypothetical, predicated on a stadial evolutionary model of socioeconomic
patterning (Mortensen, 1972).

An alternative deductive approach is to assume that early hunter-
gatherers shared the capacity of large gregarious herbivores to exploit
concentrated and dispersed resources by different adaptive strategies
and to adjust their seasonal movements according to the waxing and
waning of resource productivity through an annual cycle. The mid-
Pleistocene Acheulian sites at Torralba and Ambrona, central Spain,
suggest such a case (Butzer, 1965, 1971a; Howell, 1966; Freeman, 1978).
These sites are situated along the only low-level and low-gradient
mountain pass cutting the west–east range that divides the high plains
of Old and New Castile. Torralba and Ambrona suggest a focus of
seasonal campsites situated along this animal migration route between
winter pastures (grassland and pine parkland) to the south and summer pastures (steppe grassland) to the north. During spring and autumn, hunters probably preyed systematically on migrating herds
forced to pass through the narrow mountain route with its marshy
tracts and box canyons (Figure 13-1). During winter and summer, these
people may have subdivided into several subgroups, fanning out over

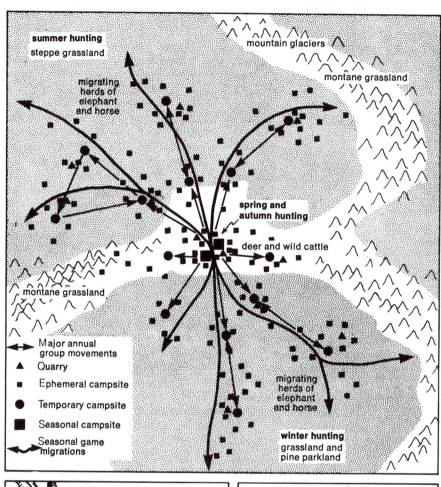

summer hunting
steppe grassland

mountain glaciers

montane grassland

migrating
herds of
elephant
and horse

**spring and
autumn hunting**

deer and wild cattle

montane grassland

**Major annual
group movements**

▲ Quarry

■ Ephemeral campsite

● Temporary campsite

■ Seasonal campsite

Seasonal game
migrations

migrating
herds of
elephant
and horse

winter hunting
grassland and
pine parkland

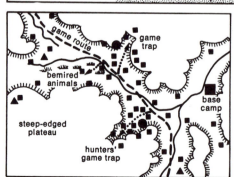

game route

▲ game trap

bemired
animals

base
camp

steep-edged
plateau

hunters'
game trap

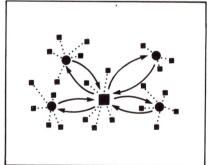

a succession of temporary camps (occupied over several weeks by medium-sized groups) and ephemeral special-activity sites (occupied by special-purpose subgroups) situated with an eye to water sources, the location of animal herds, and the availability of flint and quartzite quarries. Such an interpretation is suggested by the unique concentration of sites and surface artifacts within the Torralba-Ambrona pass and again in the river systems of the Tajo and Duero far to the south and north. It is also supported by other findings: migratory birds found among the fauna; much exotic flint carried in over distances of many tens of kilometers (H. P. Schwarcz, personal communication). A radial oscillatory pattern of seasonal movement seems applicable (Figures 13-1 and 13-2E).

Torralba and Ambrona suggest a special case of the concentrated-resource model of Figure 12-3B. Other hypothetical examples might include an African lowland with sandy soils, high water tables, and relatively predictable water supplies even during the dry season. There long-term camps preferably might be situated in areas of optimal water supply, maximum productivity, and higher biomass. Wet-season hunting and gathering operations could range out in a radial pulsating fashion to take advantage of seasonal resources at some distance (Figure 13-3) (Yellen, 1977; Silberbauer, 1981). Even in high-productivity areas with limited resource concentration, as in the case of the Bambuti-Bambote pygmies of the Zaire woodlands (Terashina, 1980), radial dispersal of hunters to temporary camps is common, although the radius of movement is only 3 to 5 km, as compared with about 15 km in the Kalahari. Another specific case is that of a complex of river valleys and caves in the hill country of southwestern France. There Bordes et al. (1972) used differentiated lithic tool kits and the faunal record to posit a half dozen different models for seasonal multiple-purpose sites and temporary limited-activity sites during the late Pleistocene (David, 1973; Bahn, 1977; Spiess, 1979).

These examples suggest a number of potential mobility patterns related to different exploitative strategies predicated on the concentration

Figure 13-1. A seasonal mobility model for Acheulian hunter-gatherers in mid-Pleistocene Spain, based in part on information from Torralba and Ambrona. During spring and autumn, the hunters preyed systematically on migrating herds forced to pass through the mountain routes (lower left detail map); during winter and summer, the hunters subdivided into smaller groups and fanned out into a succession of temporary sites and ephemeral camps, selected with regard to water supplies, location of animal herds, and availability of flint and quartzite quarries. The mobility model is abstracted at the lower right. From Butzer (1977b:Figure 10) (copyright Sigma Xi, with permission).

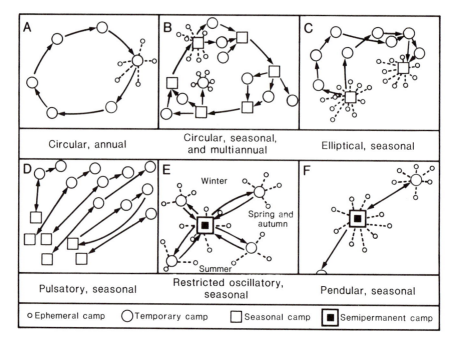

Figure 13-2. Macroscale mobility models for hunter-gatherers.

and seasonality of resources (Figure 13-2). To give primacy to spatial and temporal variables, camps have been distinguished according to their spans of use: ephemeral (several hours to a few days), temporary (several days to several weeks), seasonal (several months), semipermanent (several months, repetitively over several years). Functional and social implications (Table 13-1) are not explicit but can be inferred for specific cases.

Figure 13-2A shows a set of seasonal camps that define a quasi-random annual circular movement. This is the classic free-wandering model that may be applicable to an environment with dispersed, relatively uniform resources. More probable is that seasonal stress will favor alternate use of longer-term seasonal camps, occupied for several months, and several shorter-term temporary camps, used for several weeks each. If dry-season or cold-season stress is sufficiently great, a group might be expected to split into several subgroups, some possibly all males, to optimize the use of scattered and less predictable resources. In this way, the movement will consist of seasonal dispersal and reaggregation, directed to different uses of diffuse and concen-

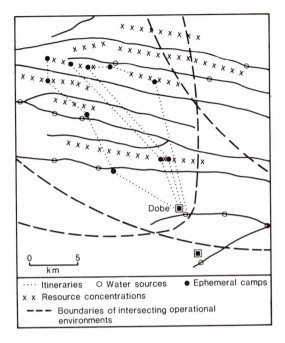

Figure 13-3. Two foraging itineraries of the Dobe group of Kalahari bushmen to key resource concentrations (mongongo nut woodlands); each lasted 18 days, and they took place a month apart. Ephemeral sites on both 50-km trips were occupied an average of three to four days. The Dobe operational area has a mean radius of about 15 km. Adapted from Yellen (1976:map 2.3). Copyright 1976 by the President and Fellows of Harvard College, with permission.

trated resources. Over a period of years, the resulting trajectory will describe a roughly circular form (Figure 13-2B).

Another possible response to seasonal alternations of want and plenty is suggested by the elliptical nomadic pattern of Johnson (1978:Figure 7). Adapting this to a hunter-gatherer procurement strategy, one would envision long-term seasonal camps along a productive ecozone, such as a river valley during the African dry season; then, during the rainy season, mobility might be increased as dispersing subgroups use a string of temporary camps to take advantage of widespread but ephemeral resources, while simultaneously avoiding the recurrent fevers endemic to wetter lowlands at that time of year (Figure 13-2C). The seasonal pulsatory movements of lowland nomads into mountain valleys (Johnson, 1978) also suggest analogues for hunter-gatherers who exploit the complex topography of cooler highlands after winter snows have melted to optimize their use of seasonal plant growth and gain ready access to game. In this way, pressures on the lowland resource base will be reduced, allowing for autumn storage of vegetable foods and winter hunting of regenerated game herds after the return to seasonal campsites there (Figure 13-2D).

Many long-term camps, used seasonally but revisited year after year, are located near strategic waterholes or near topographically constricted migration routes of gregarious herbivores. Such sites, like Torralba-Ambrona (Figure 13-1), serve as semipermanent base camps for many months each year, when game herds are aggregated near a few reliable waterholes or are forced to file through nearby passes. Under such circumstances, a well-defined oscillatory movement could emerge, with strong group aggregation focused on such an area of concentrated resources during one season, followed by radial outward dispersal of subgroups at other times of the year (Figure 13-2E). Parallels can be noted with Johnson's model (1978) of transhumant herders driving their animals across mountain barriers to exploit pastures in two different ecozones, as well as with Kay's reconstruction (1979) of Wisconsin Indian movements to seasonal hunting grounds concentrated along networks of river systems.

Presumably, the seasonally specialized, broad-spectrum subsistence activities of many Terminal Pleistocene hunter-gatherer societies favored semipermanent settlements in areas of high productivity or high biomass. These may also have provided locales suitable for early manipulation of and experimentation with vegetable foods that, in some instances, led to the tending and even deliberate planting of occasional stands of cultigens such as barley and wheat. At those times of the year when wild grains and fresh plants were unavailable, the group may have subdivided to make greater use of more mobile animal herds and of more dispersed vegetable foods (Figure 13-3). The resulting pattern might represent a seasonal pendulum (Figure 13-2F).

Heuristic mobility models of this kind can also be developed for more complex agrarian societies and urbanized societies, although their configurations will need to include vertical as well as horizontal dimensions and allow far greater significance to exchange networks. But intergroup exchange is important even for hunter-gatherers (Earle and Ericson, 1977). Specifically, the California ethnographic-archaeological record (ca. 1780–1830) shows that population level, size of operational area, and the need for short- or long-distance trade were closely related to dependability and productivity of resources (Hornbeck, 1981).

Subsistence-settlement generalizations for hunter-gatherers

The preceding discussions of resource-concentration and mobility models suggest that a number of basic patterns and relationships can be formulated for resource distributions, subsistence strategies, group networks, and demographic aggregations. These generalizations are presented as probabilistic hypotheses (i.e., normative models for spatial behavior):

1. Groups in environments with regionally clustered resources probably will tend to aggregate in macropatterns related to diffuse, linear, and annular concentrations (Figure 12-3B–D) and characterized by relatively large asymmetrical operational areas whose shapes reflect expansion along the path of least resistance and toward the greatest resource availability. In environments with abundant resources and relatively uniform distribution of resources (Figure 12-3A), group dispersal probably will tend to be more random, with smaller circular operational spheres. In other words, the shapes of operational areas (Table 13-1) will depend on resource distribution patterns and mobility patterns, as well as on the topographic matrix.

2. Groups in low-productivity environments with limited numbers of resources, seasonally out of phase, probably will tend to be more mobile than those in environments with little spatial variability and higher productivity (Harpending and Davis, 1977). The radius of the operational environment will be determined more by such resource characteristics than by walking distance and traversibility.

3. Groups in environments with stable, evenly distributed resources probably will tend to be smaller than those in environments in which resources are localized and/or unpredictable (Horn, 1968; Wilmsen, 1973; Winterhalder, 1981). The more homogeneous the environment in space and time, the more likely that population numbers will be relatively stable.

4. Groups probably will opt for a reasonably broad diet when possible, in order to reduce their dependence on the fluctuating productivity of a limited number of highly ranked resource types, as well as to optimize average food search time and harvest time (MacArthur and Pianka, 1966; Winterhalder, 1981).

5. Groups probably will exploit fewer mosaic patches as resource density increases, and vice versa (Winterhalder, 1981).

6. Groups in fine-grained mosaic environments probably will tend

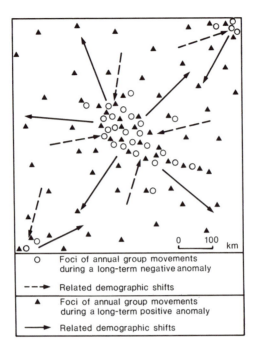

Figure 13-4. Model for the impact of long-term climatic anomalies on hunter-gatherer settlement distribution. Modified from Butzer (1977b: Figure 11).

toward generalized use of available patch types, whereas coarse-grained habitats will be more conducive to specialized patch use (Winterhalder, 1981).

7. Groups probably will tend to exert territorial rights to maintain exclusive use of highly productive and predictable habitats (Dyson-Hudson and Smith, 1978), whereas mobility and intergroup flexibility may be preferable in environments with unpredictable resources prone to great fluctuations in productivity.

8. Groups probably will tend to optimize their use of available resources by alternatiing seasonal aggregation and dispersal. Such dispersal may be in response to extreme stress during the season of minimal productivity, or it may be used to exploit scattered resources in marginal parts of the operational environment during the season of maximum productivity (Figure 13-2C).

9. Groups probably will find it uneconomical to overutilize patchy resources, because diminishing returns will increase harvest time (Charnov, 1976; Winterhalder, 1981).

10. If resources are uniformly distributed, group size probably will tend to be proportional to the radius of a circular operational environment; if the resources decline through time, then either group size will decrease or the operational radius will increase, and vice versa, unless resource preferences are changed (Butzer, 1978c).

11. Long-term trends toward improved resources probably will tend to favor centrifugal dispersal of groups to exploit increasingly productive peripheral areas, leading to reduced pressure on central primary habitats (Butzer, 1977b) (Figure 13-4).

12. Long-term trends toward diminished resources probably will tend to favor centripetal convergence of groups on more predictable and more productive habitats, leading to greater pressure on these resources, intergroup competition, eventual group reduction, and macroscale isolation of group clusters in areas of concentrated resources (Butzer, 1977b) (Figure 13-4).

These probabilistic relationships bring into focus a set of environmental controls for resources that emphasize spatial and temporal variability in relation to the critical resources used by hunter-gatherers. They do not, however, take into account biotic competition and disease, and the equally important sociocultural factors are, at best, implicit. In order to remedy this imbalance, Table 13-3 provides a much broader framework to evaluate resource opportunities and limitations, not only for hunter-gatherers but also for agricultural and pastoral economies. The table can be rearranged as a complex input-output flow diagram.

Spatial determinants for agricultural settlement

The intrasite aggregation and intersite patterning of agricultural-pastoral settlements (Table 13-2) reflect a combination of environmental and sociocultural factors (Flannery, 1972a). This proposition can be discussed with reference to a range of key variables that collectively determine the forms and processes of agricultural settlement at a medium and large scale.

Intrasite resources. The nature and spatiotemporal distribution of economic resources affect the location of a settlement and the disposition of its resource space within the constraints of the socioeconomic subsystem and a complex array of larger-scale regional interactive factors:

1. The topographic matrix contributes to a definition of what lands

Table 13-3. *Resource opportunities and limitations*

Resource type	Spatial variability	Temporal variability	Biotic competition and disease	Cultural and socioeconomic factors
I. Water	I. Parameters:	I. Predictable variation: seasonality of thermal and moisture regimes, as affecting water supply, plant productivity, biomass, and traversibility	I. Ecological competitors:	I. Resource perception
II. Unprocessed or perishable plant foods (gathered or cultivated) and animal foods (wild or domesticated)	1. Absolute distance 2. Effective distance 3. Absolute abundance 4. Relative abundance 5. Relative concentration 6. Spatial predictability		1. Large herbivores and carnivores 2. Small mammals and birds 3. Invertebrates (e.g., beetles, locusts, ants, worms)	II. Cultural biases, attitudes, and ideologies III. Available technology for extraction and manipulation of energy and matter
III. Processed plant and animal foods		II. Unpredictable variation:	II. Dangerous predators	IV. Social organization and economic structures
IV. Raw materials for artifacts (stone, clay, ores), clothing, ornaments, furniture, shelter, transportation, and fuel	II. Controls: 1. Regional climate 2. Topographic matrix 3. Soils and hydrology 4. Biotic patterning	1. Year-to-year fluctuations 2. Short- and long-term trends involving climate (e.g., severity of season of vegetative dormancy), plant productivity (due to climate, disease, or successional factors), animal biomass cycles, epidemic disease	III. Endemic disease (e.g., malaria, other fevers, parasites, bacteria, fungi, etc., affecting people, animals, and plants)	V. Intragroup and intergroup competition VI. Exchange systems for energy, matter, and information
V. Finished nonedible products of all kinds				VII. Ecological imbalance due to selectivity, overuse, or destruction in course of extraction and exploitation

are potentially suitable for cultivation, pasturage, or more extensive use, in relation to smooth surfaces, gentle gradients, soil erodibility and drainage, flood hazards, and water supplies. For example, relatively steep slopes require terracing for productive crop or orchard use, and even moderate slopes are prone to rapid erosion under cultivation or intensive grazing. Wet locales may delay planting in the spring and impede harvesting in the autumn, generally limiting their use to pasturage, plant collecting, fowling, and hunting. During the course of early Neolithic settlement in central Europe, sheep and goats were pastured in dry uplands and cattle in wetlands, with both cattle and sheep allowed to browse and root in wooded, broken terrain (Sielmann, 1972).

2. The soil matrix (i.e., the detailed variability of soils and unconsolidated surficial sediments) is related to the topographic matrix, bedrock variations, and landscape history; in turn, it defines both opportunities and limitations for agriculture and grazing. Critical factors are soil depth, stoniness, rock outcrops, clay and sand contents, organic matter and nutrient concentrations, moisture capacity, presence of toxic salts, and liability to waterlogging or erosion (see Chapter 8). For example, heavy lowland soils may be too difficult to work with a given technology or may be prone to waterlogging and flooding; light upland soils may be too thin and sandy for good yields or may be susceptible to summer drought or excessive erosion.

Early Neolithic farming in central Europe was overwhelmingly concentrated on well-drained loessic soils of intermediate texture (68%–87% of the sites are so located in drier basins, 96%–100% of those in more moist basins) (Sielmann, 1972). Only the introduction of heavy moldboard plows (Sherratt, 1980) in western Europe during Roman times allowed effective cultivation of clay soils, favoring a substantial expansion of agriculture over the next millennium. In Belgium and France, Celto-Roman cultivation had been limited to upland soils of intermediate texture, but subsequent Germanic settlement was able to concentrate on heavier alluvial soils, thanks to the new plow technology. In Britain, on the other hand, late Roman rural depopulation allowed Saxon colonists to select areas of more open vegetation that marked drier substrates, such as loess-mantled terrace gravels or the rims of limestone escarpments (downs).

With a simpler, essentially stone technology that lacked plows, the early seventeenth-century Hurons of Ontario selected low-productivity, sandy soils. Sites were concentrated along topographic breaks that gave access to water, fish, and game below and easily worked but drought-prone soils above. Although villages were shifted every decade or two, the productivity of cultivated maize and gathered foods allowed a density of 25 to 50 people per square kilometer, the highest achieved in pre-European Canada (Heidenreich, 1971). A similar topographic arrangement for early Iron Age agricultural settlement in Zimbabwe has been illustrated by Prendergast (1979). Poorly drained lowlands were used for cattle pasture, vegetable crops, and riverine fishing, whereas the leached, sandy upland soils were left in woodland for fuel, timber, small game, and honey; villages and their surrounding grainfields were concentrated on the clayey free-draining soils of the intermediate slopes.

3. The biotic matrix (i.e., the grain and patch types of vegetation prior to land clearance) will be predicated on the topographic and soil matrix. Complex land-use patterns will eventually eliminate some of the original elements of the biotic mosaic, because they happen to be prime units for cultivation or pasture. The remaining elements of that mosaic, whether managed or not, will continue to define potential resources for food and medicinal plants, fuel and timber, fish and aquatic birds, and small and large game; ecological competitors for field crops, stored food, and grazing, as well as predators for stock, will also reflect on the surviving elements of the biotic mosaic. The roles of wild plant and animal foods in complementing cultivated forms vary considerably from case to case, but they were important in most agricultural landscapes until a few centuries ago; in regard to Europe, see the work of Phillips (1980:Chapters 5–7).

Resource variability in space is critical for site location, and it influences the trajectory of land development as well as the emerging patterns of land use. But these resources do not subsequently become "constants" of the human ecosystem. Instead, resources behave as biophysical processes that continue to interact with the human subsystem, responding in complex ways to manipulation or extraction. Tillage, manure, field rotation, and grazing have short-term and long-term effects on the nutrient and hydrological cycles (see Chapter 8), affecting annual crop yields and soil capacity for sustained agrarian productivity over decades and centuries. Different components of the soilscape also respond differently to wet and dry years and cold and warm years, with continuing repercussions for crops and herds. Altogether, such short-, medium-, and long-term variability, depending on its amplitude, will provide continuing feedback for land-use configurations and socioeconomic strategies. In other words, the interplay between agricultural communities and their resources is as dynamic and indefinite as that for hunter-gatherers.

Intrasite socioeconomic factors. The socioeconomic subsystem of each community comprises an array of internal capacities and constraints critical for sustained or intensified resource exploitation. Several dietary, procurement, and maintenance variables determine the internal structure of settlements and their associated resource spaces:

1. The available technology and subsistence strategies at any point in time are based on a particular association of cultigens, domesticated animals, and wild foods. Some of these resource types may have been introduced or may have been available during the earliest phase of agricultural settlement; others were acquired later through diffusion or during immigration of new settlers. The efficiency of these strategies depends in part on the available land-clearance techniques (fire, tree girdling or felling, etc.), the tools used for cultivation (digging sticks, hoes, various plows), the available draft and transport animals (cattle, camel, horse, donkey, llama), and the available knowledge of fertilization techniques (animal manure, night soil, nitrogen-fixing legumes).

2. Socioeconomic organization complements the extractive and manipulative technology through a matrix of proprietary rights, work obligations, task scheduling, extractive patterning, intragroup reciprocity, and vertical redistribution of energy and matter (Homans, 1941). These social norms and economic structures steer day-to-day lifeways and the seasonal round of activities, and they determine the efficiency of the subsistence technology and resource extraction that are reflected in scheduling strategies and land-use patterns.

3. Socioeconomic organization, subsistence, and settlements are in turn influenced by a wide range of symbolic and aesthetic values, ceremonial needs, and social stimuli. These affect most realms of activity through ideological interpretation, resource perception, environmental attitudes, scheduling flexibility, and receptiveness to new information and technology (Cohen, 1976a). Collectively, such factors place a tangible imprint on microscale, semimicroscale, and mesoscale settlement form and function, including individual structures, settlement layout, and field patterns (Table 13-2).

Intersite interactions The mesoscale and macroscale arrangements and vertical nesting of settlements and their resource spaces reflect a host of environmental, spatial, historical, and socioeconomic variables:

1. The large-scale, regional topographic matrix, comprising valleys, level lands, hill tracts, mountain ranges (see Figures 4-10 to 4-12), influences site location and communications routes and is responsible for much of the observed spatial distortion from a perfectly symmetrical set of nested hexagons (see Figure 12-1). Navigable rivers can serve as communications arteries (e.g., the Nile), whereas other rivers may present major obstacles to traffic as a result of deeply incised valleys (e.g., the Colorado) or extensive fringes of marshy floodplain. The spacing and orientation of valleys, expressed in the random or geometric branching of tributaries and in the density of drainage lines, further condition the patterning of communications, settlement loci, and resource spaces. The same applies to the presence or absence and the extent of flat, rolling, or moderately irregular plains, as well as to roughness and relief of the uplands that constitute watersheds between adjacent drainage basins. Finally, trend-parallel and transverse mountain valleys control land-use patterns and communications lines. At this scale, the topographic matrix modifies gross biotic as well as climatic patterning, frequently with tangible influences on settlement density and interlinkage.

2. Another major component in intersite patterning is the historical trajectory of agricultural land use, including repeated phases of expansion or intensification in response to new settlers or new technology or internal demographic and socioeconomic changes. It is also not unusual that a succession of different ethnic groups and cultures, over the millennia, will have left a complex but nonetheless real imprint on the cumulative expression of the cultural landscape. In Europe this historical factor explains the aggregation of several distinct composite settlement types within regions of modern ethnic uniformity, as a result of cumulative phases of settlement history (Schroeder and Schwarz, 1969).

The process of "filling in" by different settlers or by means of new technologies can be illustrated for medieval Europe (Figure 13-5). Early German settlement in the Leipzig area (ca. A.D. 1025–1125) led to a gradual expansion of older Sorbian villages into composite settlement forms (E. Butzer, n.d.). Later, direct colonization led to large-scale deforestation and creation of new settlements, with differing functional layouts, on previously unused soils of lower quality (ca. A.D. 1125–1200). During the next 150 years, growth was concentrated in the towns, with some infilling of marginal lands; settlers were then derived mainly from local demographic expansion (until the middle of the four-

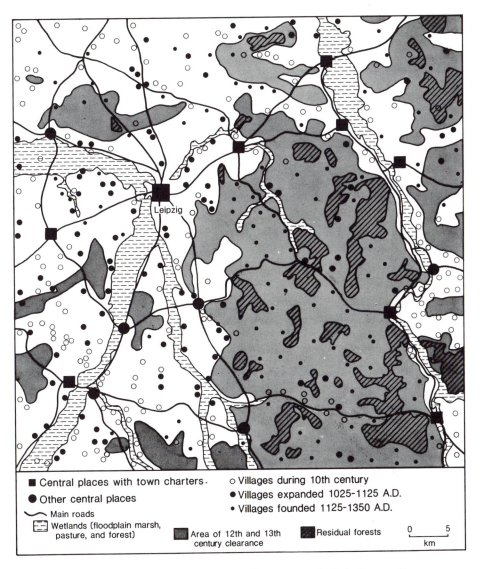

Central places with town charters. ○ Villages during 10th century
● **Other central places** ● Villages expanded 1025-1125 A.D.
〜 Main roads · Villages founded 1125-1350 A.D.
⊟ Wetlands (floodplain marsh,
pasture, and forest) ▓ Area of 12th and 13th ▨ Residual forests   0   5
century clearance   km

Figure 13-5. Medieval agricultural colonization in the Leipzig area, Germany. Between A.D. 1025 and 1350, 122 of the original 306 settlements in this 5,330-km^2 area were considerably expanded (mainly on the fertile loessic soils in the west), and 116 new settlements were added (mainly in originally forested areas with leached sandy soils). Modified from E. Butzer (n.d.).

teenth century). Because of marked differences in productivity, resource spaces in the old fertile settlement areas averaged as low as 5 km^2, as compared with 20 km^2 on the new, less fertile lands. The number of villages (with an average resource space of 12.6 km^2, as compared with 725 km^2 for the Dobe !Kung, Figure 13-3) and the total rural population were essentially unchanged 500 years later, although Leipzig had grown into a major urban center as a result of its trading privileges and ideal central location.

In North America, such multiple overlays can be observed in the field patterns of areas of former French settlement in Québec, the Midwest, and Louisiana and Spanish settlement in the Southwest. Similarly, the traces of Hohokam, Mormon, and modern irrigation works in the Salt River Valley of Arizona often are superimposed, the Indian networks influencing later layouts. At the geo-archaeological level, successive transformations and overlays of an irrigation landscape over six millennia are uniquely documented for Mesopotamia (Adams, 1981).

3. Proximity is critical in the process of "filling out" in an underdeveloped region. The location and spacing of the earliest permanent villages will continue to affect potential occupation of intervening settlement locations (and resource spaces) during the course of centuries and millennia, as new communities compete with old ones for the extensively used arable land and claims on the seemingly unused woodland. Israeli settlement on Palestinian commonage provides a modern example of an ancient problem, paralleled a century earlier by French intrusion in Algeria. The differential growth rates of villages are part of the same issue, as centers of higher order emerge to assume market and other functions that modify subsequent demographic and traffic developments of other communities within their service spheres. Finally, there is the difficult matter of social space (Doxiades, 1970), leading to dispersed settlement in one area during one phase of colonization and heavily nucleated settlement in another. Crowding is perceived differently in different cultures, and the results usually are evident within settlements, as well as in their size and spacing.

4. Security plays an important role in settlement strategies at all scales (Rowlands, 1972), from defensibility of the individual farm compound to fortified villages and erection of castles and forts to control access routes. The creation of medieval border marches in Europe illustrates one such process. Defensive installations may also be maintained around the perimeter of site networks, near sources of critical raw

materials, and around segregated quarters within towns. Other settlements are focused around fortified temples or churches or the castle of a local potentate. Such security considerations affect the degree of settlement nucleation, the shapes of individual settlements, and the location of villages and centers. They may trigger fundamental transformations in settlement networks, such as abandonment of hamlets and small villages in favor of a few large villages, within the span of a generation or two. The impetus may be external, but it may equally well be internal, such as uncontrolled banditry or intersettlement strife.

5. Exchange networks and their associated structures play a basic role in the emergence of central places. Large and populous settlement networks tend to require increasingly complex and diversified modes of economic integration. Periodic markets may serve the needs of simple networks of subsistence-oriented villages, but more complex horizontal and vertical flows of produce, products, and services are required in societies with sophisticated technologies. This, in turn, favors the development of a settlement hierarchy. The resulting exchange network includes reciprocity between equally ranked social units and communities, redistributive exchange between communities of unequal rank, intermediate exchange between central places, and external exchange between different site networks (Renfrew, 1975). The means of exchange, through markets, middlemen, or centralized forces of mobilization, vary greatly from one period, culture, or polity to another. The patterns that emerge reflect initially on environmental and social gradients, but as a vertical settlement hierarchy develops, they tend to be increasingly dominated by technological, demographic, socioreligious, and political forces (Trigger, 1972; Smith, 1976*a*, 1976*b*; Earle and Ericson, 1977; Hirth, 1978; Renfrew, 1978).

6. In most complex societies, site networks are modified or substantially transformed by processes that subordinate economic criteria to overarching religious, political, or military superstructures (Johnson, 1970). Boundaries are set to intersite networks, redefining the nature of intermediate and external exchange, and ranked hierarchies may be revised or superimposed, with low-order settlements being created, transformed, or eliminated.

Given the complexities of environmental, sociocultural, economic, and supraorganic factors that influence or control agricultural settlement at different scales, it is apparent that a typological general settlement theory is less than ideal to interpret any specific case. Instead, the key factors discussed earlier provide the rudiments of a general settle-

Table 13-4. *Analytical matrix for agricultural settlement patterning*[a]

Intrasite resources (site location, land-use development, sustained productivity)

    Topographic matrix (spatial disposition of potential land-use categories)

    Soil matrix (differential short- and long-term potential for agricultural productivity)

    Biotic matrix (fundamental patterning of wild plants, pasture, timber, and wild animals)

Intrasite socioeconomic factors (internal settlement structure, field patterns, capacity for stable or intensified resource exploitation)

    Technology (equipment and subsistence strategy for extraction and manipulation)

    Organization (socioeconomic structures regulating subsistence efficiency)

    Cultural values (attitudes, perception, flexibility, and receptiveness for information)

Intersite interactions (horizontal network and vertical hierarchy of settlements)

    Regional topographic matrix (location, spacing, and patterning of sites and communications routes)

    Historical trajectory (overlays of successive settlement imprints, with lag phenomena)

    Proximity (sequential occupation, differential growth, and social space)

    Defense (nodes or perimeters of fortification, nucleation processes)

    Exchange structures (economic integration, emergence of complex settlement hierarchies)

    Organizational superstructures (development of bounded settlement networks, with imposed economic structures and rank hierarchies)

---

[a]Key variables are listed, with consequent processes and configurations in parentheses.

ment theory that emphasizes interactions as much as configurations (Table 13-4).

Real versus perceived environments

Aztec territorial differentiation resulted from a process of mental and social action. The Aztec perceived space as existential not geometrical, real not abstract, organic not neutral. In addition to man and other earthly creatures, space was inhabited and dominated by supra-human beings, who in a direct way determined the human condition (Licate, 1980:28).

As complexes of symbols and meanings, the territorial forms that the Aztecs erected or adopted reflected and articulated values of how earth space should be organized; as signs and directions, they mirrored and shaped norms of how earth space should be experienced. Beliefs were translated and actualized in the ordering of the phenomena of the cultural landscapes of the empire by the actions of key social institutions (Licate, 1980:43).

These comments clearly express the importance of noneconomic dimensions in evaluating the spatial configuration of settlement systems. Space can, in fact, be regarded from several different perspectives as a set of available resources, as a sphere of political or military control, or in terms of social identification or symbolic value (Cohen, 1976a; Butzer, 1978e). In conceptual terms, even the environment itself can be disjoined into different components by adapting the classification of Sonnenfeld (1972) to the rudimentary example of prehistorical hunter-gatherers:

1. The *geographical environment* is the overarching physical and biological landscape within which the human group and related groups live and interact.

2. The *operational environment* is the resource space spanned by short-term and long-term subsistence activities of one particular group.

3. The *modified environment* is the immediate sustaining area of a habitation site in which frequent or effective activity results in tangible modification or transformation of the environment.

4. The *perceived environment* consists in those parts of the geographical and operational environments, both visible and nonvisible, of which the group is aware and in regard to which decisions are made. These distinct environments can be illustrated by a model of partly overlapping sets (Figure 13-6).

The geographical, operational, and modified environments collectively constitute the real or objective environment. The perceived or behavioral dimension is that part of the real environment that is perceived by human beings, with motives, preferences, modes of thinking, and traditions drawn from their sociocultural context (Kirk, 1963). That part of the real world that is excluded from a society's perceived environment has no relevance to decision making and spatial behavior (Kirk, 1963). For example, coal beds are useless to a society that does not recognize their existence or utility or that lacks the technology to extract them. The incomplete overlap between real and perceived environments has been illustrated by Davidson (1972). He argued that site determinants for preagricultural settlement were a matter of proximity to water and access to hunting and collecting areas, whereas the concerns of agricultural communities were primarily focused on suitable soils and cultivable terrain. In other words, the prehistorical perception

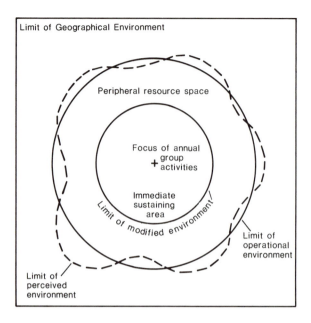

Figure 13-6. A model for environmental space and its perception by hunter-gatherers.

of optimal versus marginal environments, or of suitable site locations, was fundamentally different for hunter-gatherers and village farmers (Figure 13-7A). When compounded by environmental changes, this important divergence should be even greater (Figure 13-7B), with the practical impact that archaeological sites of Paleolithic foragers and Neolithic farmers were concentrated in different parts of the same landscape. Davidson (1972) consequently argued that a cognitive behavioral approach to environmental archaeology can help to avoid static appraisals of resource values in settlement survey or reconstruction, instead providing a fuller appreciation of group adjustment to the environment (Davidson et al., 1976a; Crumley, 1979).

Cognitive mapping is not limited to resource perception; it also includes spatial components: (a) distance, as a function of technology, travel time, and social factors; (b) location, as a function of economic, social, symbolic, and aesthetic factors; (c) accessibility, as a function of the cultural value placed on ease or difficulty of physical and social access. Such spatial perspectives will influence the delimitation and utilization of an operational area by a particular group, as well as the intensity of interaction between neighboring groups. Evidently, the

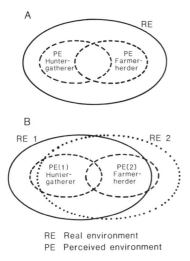

RE Real environment
PE Perceived environment

Figure 13-7. Different perceived environments of hunter-gatherers and farmer-herders, assuming a constant real environment (A) or an environmental shift from Pleistocene to Holocene conditions (B). Modified from Davidson (1972: Figure 1).

identification of environmental components, resource opportunities and their spatial patterning, subsistence goals, measures of performance, and scheduling strategies (Churchman, 1968) are all intimately related to group perception. Ultimately, the relationship between perceived and real environments is critical to adaptation (Gibson, 1970) and is therefore of considerable relevance to contextual archaeology.

An immigrant population probably will assess a new environment with the aid of a given set of imported information and technology to yield an initial perceived environment (Brookfield, 1969). This is then evaluated in terms of resources, and the resulting stock of new and old information of these decisions is further evaluated to modify both the perceived environment (indirectly) and future decisions (directly). If environmental resources, population numbers, and technology remain constant, and if no new information is locally generated or imported, then the perceptual subsystem should achieve a steady state (Brookfield, 1969). Such a situation could well have arisen on many occasions during the Pleistocene, when there was no introduction of new technology or information for millennia at a time. In fact, the perceived environment may be far more responsive to new information than to changes in the real environment. Although resources are a property of the real environment, it is advantageous to view them "as an evalua-tion placed on the perceived environment" (Brookfield, 1969:64). This applies to hunter-gatherers evaluating their resource space in terms of game and plant foods, as well as to more complex societies, where leaders evaluate the environment according to a greater fund of infor-mation and technology. In either case, decisions are made with respect to perceived needs and anticipated future conditions that may or may not coincide with objective reality (Flannery and Marcus, 1976).

> We cannot pretend to understand man on the earth without some knowledge of what is in the mind of man. . . . Decision makers operate within an environment as they perceive it, not as it is. We have to come to terms with this fact. But to do so in conceptual terms is one thing, to find ways of incorporating the environment as per-ceived into our whole evolving empirical method is a problem of quite another order (Brookfield, 1969:75–6).

Table 13-5. *Perception, spatial behavior, and the archaeological record*[a]

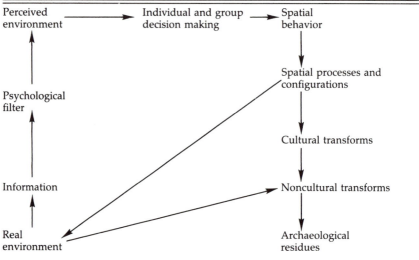

[a]Based in part on suggestions by T. P. Volman.

Brookfield (1969:66) articulated three goals, with "only limited hope of achievement": (a) descriptive simulations of generalized perceived environments; (b) explanation of the perceived environment in terms of its information sources, so as to evaluate its vulnerability to changes and responsiveness to new information inputs; (c) testing the simulation in terms of accuracy, resolution, depth, scope, and continuity.

The very real difficulties of defining the perceived environment of a living culture and of evaluating its emphases and dynamics (Bunting and Guelke, 1979) are infinitely compounded when dealing with an extinct and alien ahistorical society. The archaeological data base is finite. It may be possible to reconstruct the contemporary real environment and to deduce an incomplete range of activities from the residues preserved. But ethnographic analogues have tenuous validity for generalizing prehistorical cognitive values (Leach, 1973). The only way to gauge a potential perceived environment and the apparent decision-making process linking it to cultural activities (Table 13-5) would be with a deductive predictive model (Bell and Church, 1980). Such an approach is stimulating and useful for discussion of issues such as innovation versus diffusion, but testing will be predicated on assumptions in regard to a concept of prehistorical optimality. The primary value of the perceptual perspective in an analysis of spatial integration is that it draws attention to the inherent limitations of a rational interpretative mode.

CHAPTER 14

Spatial integration III: reconstruction of settlement systems

Site location

Spatial behavior is fundamentally rational in economic terms, but it is not necessarily optimal and is never exclusively economic (see Chapter 13). The principle of least effort is not exclusively human: Cattle trails converging on a feedlot and animal tracks to waterholes run straight over as much as several kilometers. However, in more distant areas of reasonable grazing, such pathways are adjusted to surface roughness, and their normal sinuosity suggests a relationship to body momentum as well as a measure of random walk. Traditional roads suggest a similar compromise among minimal distance, topography, and a variety of less tangible factors. Consequently, human spatial behavior seldom truly approximates the optimization principle, that is, a minimum of effort for a maximum of return (McFarland, 1978). Two critical imponderables interpose themselves in the conception and implementation of mobility and subsistence strategies. First, the distribution, predictability, and competitive variables that control resource opportunities and limitations (see Table 13-3) require complex decisions that allow for multiple alternative choices. Second, cultural and socioeconomic variables increase the multiplicity of alternative choices that can be made with respect to perceived rather than real environments (see Table 13-4).

Accordingly, site location is essentially rational, often less than optimal, and always to some degree idiosyncratic. The decisions of hunter-gatherers relate to sites selected for relatively short time spans in relation to large resource spaces, and they involve elements of risk, diversity, and long-term productivity different from those that influence the decision making of farming communities. The perceived merits of a site and its settlement space differ accordingly, but in each case the implicit delineation of spatial parameters approximates a facsimile of the real environment.

The intrinsic difficulty in predicting site location is that subsistence strategies not only are predicated on resource spaces and technology but also include multiple options in terms of scheduling and demographic aggregation. The primary goals of procurement scheduling are to provide a satisfactory supply of food and raw materials while maintaining a reasonable balance between search and pursuit costs and harvest costs, on the one hand, and resource yields, on the other (input–output ratios) (Winterhalder, 1981). Secondary goals of the resource-use schedule include dietary preferences and diversity, prestige functions of foods and their related procurement activities, and sex-role differentiation (Jochim, 1976). Demographic aggregation is interrelated by virtue of the dependence of population grouping on resource distribution, density, and predictability, on the one hand (Jochim, 1976), and the maintenance of cooperative social ties and reproductive viability, on the other (Wobst, 1974). As a result of this functional interdependence, actual site location probably will represent a satisficer rather than optimal adjustment to environmental parameters (Wolpert, 1964).

In other words, subsistence and sociocultural requisites dictate flexible spatial and temporal responses rather than static two dimensional human settlement strategies. Consequently, a probabilistic rather than deterministic approach to site location and patterning is called for.

Archaeological site survey

The definition of an archaeological site as the tangible record of human activity at a specific place (see Chapter 13) is difficult to implement in many field situations. Lithic artifacts and potsherds can be transported and reworked by several geomorphic agents and by later human activities, thereby being moved or dispersed over shorter or greater distances (see Chapter 7). Small sites, particularly those with low artifact densities, pose a particular problem.

Plog et al. (1978) preferred a narrow definition of *site* as a spatially bounded aggregation of cultural materials of sufficient quantity and quality to allow inferences about behavior at that location. This is reasonable for human activities of the last few millennia, and where the majority of vestiges remain visible on the surface of a landscape that has undergone little significant change. In dealing with hunter-gatherer sites of greater antiquity that have been affected by widespread burial or erosion, every occurrence of typologically distinctive artifacts assumes importance. More often than not, features that record specific activities are absent, behavior cannot be inferred with confidence, and extensive dispersal can be excluded only by geo-archaeological study. These disparate concerns can be resolved by describing such nonsites as *occurrences*. Their value for site and settlement patterns will be relative.

Archaeological surveys traditionally have involved a variety of procedures, some rigorous, other opportunistic (Hester et al., 1975: Chapter 3): (a) selective surface collection; (b) complete collection of visible materials, including occurrences; (c) collection along systematic transects; (d) combinations of systematic and random sampling according to a superimposed local or regional grid; (e) collection around specific cultural or landscape features. The value of such surveys depends on the level of recording detail and the nature of the archaeological record under study. The procedural problems are critical to interpretation, as argued by Binford (1964), Mueller (1975), Schiffer et al. (1978), Plog et al. (1978), and Lewarch and O'Brien (1981). Several useful criteria have been identified by Schiffer et al. (1978):

1. *Abundance:* the density of sites or artifact types per unit area.

2. *Clustering:* the degree of spatial aggregation.

3. *Obtrusiveness:* the probability that materials can be detected by a single technique, particularly in regard to subsoil features and geochemical modification.

4. *Visibility:* the degree to which an observer can detect materials at or below a given point as a function of surface exposures, ground and vegetation patterns, geophysical prospecting, and test excavation.

5. *Accessibility:* in regard to climate and biota, terrain and roads, and land-use patterns.

Decisions as to the type of probability sampling, density of control, and appropriate technology should be made accordingly.

A landscape approach to settlement survey

Sampling procedures are only one part of the problem. The systematic geomorphic processes affecting selective site destruction, burial, or surface preservation are equally important. Consequently, a geo-archaeological strategy is called for. The following questions can be raised as an essential preliminary step to survey implementation (Butzer, 1960a: 1617):

1. What are the locational parameters of known prehistorical sites in the study area?

2. What are the relationships between such settings and the sediments, soils, and terrain of the study area? Which situations are likely to have been deliberately selected by prehistorical groups or accidentally preserved from natural obliteration?

3. What regional generalizations can be made about the likelihood of sites? Do discernible archaeological gaps relate to erosion of coeval sediments or surfaces, to more recent sedimentation over broad areas, or to a lack of former habitation, either because of unattractive mesoenvironments or because of location in the interstitial space between operational environments?

4. What proportions of the sites of a particular period are likely to be preserved? Or are the known sites representative of the former density of contemporaneous settlement?

5. What were the geomorphic, hydrological, and biotic conditions characteristic during this particular settlement phase, and how may they have influenced site selection?

Such formulations draw attention to the factors that affected site location as well as subsequent site dispersal, burial, erosion, or preservation. In view of the limited resources generally available for subsurface testing of any kind, there is an urgent need for a geo-archaeological strategy to be incorporated into surveys for all but the most recent archaeological traces.

An example of such a geo-archaeological survey has been provided for the Nile Valley of Middle Egypt (Butzer, 1960a, 1961; Kaiser, 1961). Predynastic sites (ca. 4000–3150 B.C.) originally appeared to be lacking along a 175-km floodplain stretch that had remained an area of low-density settlement until the first millennium B.C. (Butzer, 1976c:79–80, 101). Several factors were responsible for the remaining gaps in site recovery (Figure 14-1). First, this sector of the Nile floodplain is characterized by large basins that were difficult to bring under hydraulic control, thus inhibiting agricultural development. Livestock raising remained the dominant subsistence form until after ca. 1050 B.C., and modern settlement spacing was achieved only during Roman times (Butzer, 1960b). Second, site preservation and exposure were unfavorable. Most Predynastic and early historical sites were originally located along the raised banks of the Nile, where they are now buried under several meters of more recent alluvium or topped by younger settlement mounds. Preserved and exposed sites have been found only along the desert edge of the floodplain, in the form of cemeteries and peripheral settlements possibly related to a limited range of activities. Systematic comparisons with other late prehistorical sites in Upper Egypt showed that desert-edge sites normally are encountered where older alluvial fills form clearly defined stepped terraces at the edge of the modern floodplain. In Middle Egypt, such situations are rare. The eastern valley margin mainly has steep rocky cliffs rising abruptly above a narrow alluvial strip, whereas along the western margins, older sediments slope almost imperceptibly down to and under the modern floodplain edge. These old surfaces have been swept by sheetwash, obscured by dune fields or drifting sands (Butzer, 1959), buried under encroaching Nile muds, destroyed through progressive incorporation of the low desert surface into intensively modified agricultural lands, or camouflaged by superimposition of large Coptic and Islamic cemeteries.

The resulting geo-archaeological map (Figure 14-1) has predictive value for potential discovery of further Predynastic and Dynastic settlements and cemeteries along different valley-margin sectors of Middle Egypt.

Another geo-archaeological strategy, for the location of potential pre-Clovis sites in North America, has been outlined by Drew (1979). Modifying an archaeogeomorphic site classification by Butzer (1971a: 228), Drew discussed the possibilities that alluvial, basin, coastal, underwater, cave, slope, eolian, and volcanic sedimentary contexts of the requisite age would be exposed and whether or not these would provide reasonable media for original location and ultimate preservation of Pleistocene sites. On these grounds he proposed a testing program in terms of general areas, specific basin selection, and local survey and excavation procedures.

Probability sampling of entire areas is logical for a comprehensive survey, particularly if relatively young sites are of primary interest. If only those sites and occurrences of a specific period are of concern, it is economical as well as more effective to take a *landscape approach*, based on a geo-archaeological strategy:

1. Surficial sediments and erosional surfaces (e.g., stream terraces, alluvial fans, platforms, and the like) must be identified and mapped by aerial-photo stereo pairs (Gumerman and Lyons, 1971; Lyons and Avery, 1977; Dickinson and Shutler, 1979), with field verification. Conventional scales of 1:18,000 to 1:55,000 apply to most such photography, with 1:35,000 a convenient scale for on-photo exploratory mapping.

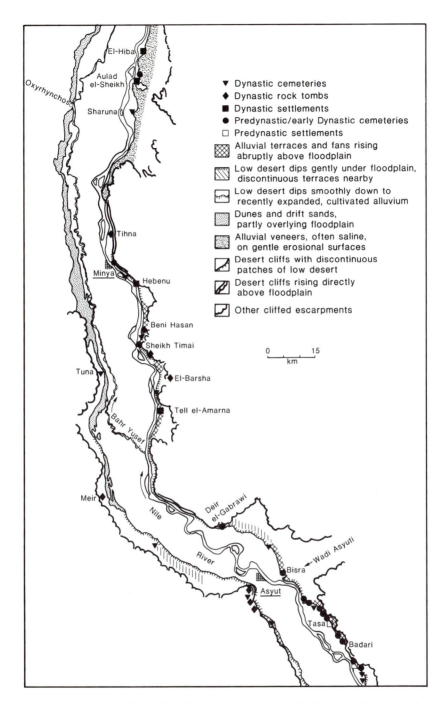

Figure 14-1. Geo-archaeological parameters for Predynastic site survey along the desert margins of Middle Egypt.

2. The sedimentary units identified during the course of mapping are then evaluated in the field to reconstruct a geomorphic history, possibly linked to radiocarbon controls.

3. Known sites of a particular archaeological phase are then related to this spatiotemporal framework to provide guidelines for the formulation of a rational archaeological ground survey of these components.

4. The first stage of the ground survey should focus on those landscape elements, such as an alluvial terrace or fan, most likely to contain concentrations of well-preserved sites. The experience gained will then dictate the grid scale, sampling frequency, and intensity for stage two.

5. The second stage of the ground survey should span all landscape units likely to include intact or reworked archaeological residues of the period in question, using different sampling scales and intensities for central and peripheral units. The results will identify spatial patterns for preferential location or preservation critical to detailed formulation of the strategy for stage three.

6. The third stage of the ground survey will include all forms of subsurface exploration and testing, including (a) examination of all natural exposures in the coeval and next-younger sediment units; (b) augering, core drilling, and test-pit excavation in areas with surface indications of buried sites (Reed et al., 1968; Butzer, 1977a; Stein, 1978; Schwartz and Tziavos, 1979), and (c) magnetic and geochemical prospecting of promising sites (see Chapter 9), with trenching as warranted. Detailed aerial photography and infrared sensing may be available to facilitate such identification (Gumerman and Neely, 1972; Dunnell, 1980b).

7. Following completion of the site survey, the site location should be evaluated in terms of resource patterning and the physical hazards of original occupation and subsequent preservation. Several procedures are called for, including laboratory analysis of sediment samples from appropriate horizontal transects and vertical profiles, application of any available detailed soil maps, and interpretation of false-color satellite imagery (at a scale of 1:250,000 or better).

On completion of such an archaeological landscape survey, site patterning can be evaluated in terms of preservation, spatial lacunae, concentration in specific landscape units, and relation to potential biotic resources, which can be simulated from soil data and substrate conditions reflected in the satellite imagery. The groundwork has now been laid for a more comprehensive settlement analysis and systemic interpretation (Davidson et al., 1976a). Detailed excavations at one or more

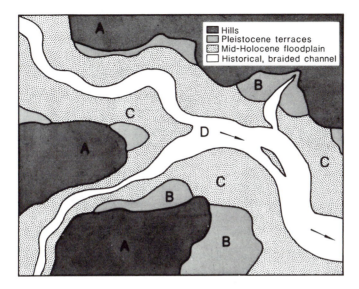

Figure 14-2. A model for Iberian and Roman site location in eastern Spain. (A) Marginally productive montane environment with low-intensity, discontinuous Roman settlement. (B) Gravelly, low-nutrient soils marginal for agriculture. Roman sites concentrated near lower edges. (C) Medium-textured soils of valley floor, coeval with Roman settlement; major site concentrations in part buried under alluvium along lower margins. (D) Ephemeral gravel bars and overspills due to recent soil erosion upstream; Roman sites destroyed.

sites, coupled with a bio-archaeological research program, become appropriate at this stage. A simplified model for such a landscape approach to site location is shown in Figure 14-2.

As a note of caution, it must be emphasized that no matter how thorough any survey is, the verified record is bound to be incomplete. Surface indicators, such as potsherds, are progressively destroyed or reburied with time, so that the common empirical impression of an exponential increase in the numbers of sites in successively younger archaeological phases may be the result of progressive loss of information about older sites (Kirkby and Kirkby, 1976). Furthermore, site recovery rates from different settlement periods are interdependent and are influenced by overall settlement density. As Kirkby and Kirkby (1976) were able to demonstrate, ratios of sites from different periods cannot simply be interpreted in terms of changes in populations and their distributions through time. Errors will be greatest for phases with low population densities. In combination with progressive obliteration through time, this implies that "[interpretations] of cultural patterns for the earliest periods in any area are not only the most suspect, but may be missed altogether" (Kirkby and Kirkby, 1976:252).

Reconstruction of settlement patterns: hunter-gatherers

At various points in time, selected parts of the Old World and New World continents were periodically or permanently inhabited by human groups. The sum of the operational environments at any one time defines the settled world, the *oikoumene*. Practical, if temporary, limitations to unbounded expansion were imposed seasonally or permanently by a variety of factors: severe cold, high elevation, aridity, almost inpenetrable forests and swamps. Nonetheless, sooner or later, tranformations in technology, organization, and sociocultural limiting factors would allow further extension of the *oikoumene*. Yet even within these macroconstraints, real or perceived, settlement in many parts of the world was discontinuous until a century or two ago. This reflects, to some degree, resource aggregation, productivity and predictability, the available technological and social organization, and a host of culture-specific attitudes and perceptions. Consequently, settlement patterns cannot simply be predicted with respect to the sum total of potentially suitable site locations.

Given the empirical and theoretical limitations to inductive settlement mapping and deductive reconstruction, is it indeed possible to study prehistorical settlement patterns? In a literal sense, this is indeed possible only for fairly recent time ranges, for sedentary communities, and where preservation has been exceptional. A sense of these practical limitations as well as the possibilities of a generalized settlement reconstruction can be gained by examining a number of examples representative of the problems encountered with specific types of archaeological records in different time ranges.

As a first example, we can consider a Pleistocene case study from the Middle Stone Age ("Middle Paleolithic") of southern Africa. During 1974–7 I attempted a rough approximation of the associated settlement record in the Kimberley area, where most of the Middle Stone Age probably can be attributed to a single variant, the Alexandersfontein facies (Butzer, 1976d). Based on study of the extant museum collections, test excavations, and Goodwin's (1929, 1936) original definitions, this facies is characterized by abundant blades (i.e., flakes at least twice as long as wide), some Levallois blades and points (i.e., ones struck from prepared cores), and relatively few pieces with secondary trim-

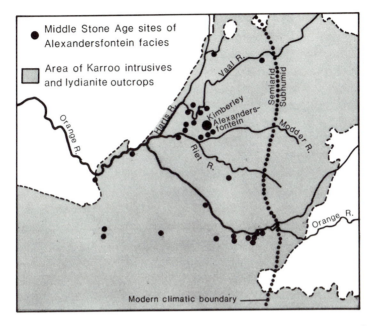

Figure 14-3. Distribution of Middle Stone Age sites of Alexandersfontein facies in the Orange-Vaal Basin of southern Africa.

ming or retouch, mainly some triangular points with convergent edges. (It is uncertain whether or not there are two distinct subfacies, characterized by differences in blade length and the presence or absence of Levallois or discoid cores.) Raw material was exclusively selected from a metamorphosed shale or lydianite, found along many contacts between Permian and Triassic shales and later Mesozoic (Karroo) intrusive volcanics (dolerite or diabase). No bone or primary sites are preserved, but sites and occurrences are widespread and distinctive within a circumscribed environment, bounded by available lydianite outcrops and the modern semiarid/subhumid climatic boundary (Figure 14-3). Without implying a correlation with contemporary climate, the Alexandersfontein facies appears to have been linked to specific raw materials and ecological conditions. Stratigraphically, the facies is associated with Riverton Formation, Member III, a widespread lithostratigraphic unit substantially older than 40,000 radiocarbon years and probably of early Upper Pleistocene age (Butzer et al., 1979).

Opportunistic surveying, limited by minimal funding and personnel, was carried out around the type site (Figure 14-4A) by means of radial

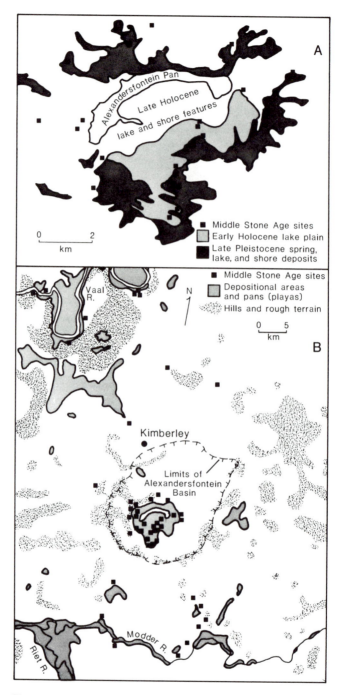

Figure 14-4. Sites of Alexandersfontein facies as surveyed by the author around the type site (A) and as currently known for the Kimberley region, between the Vaal and Modder rivers (B).

transects, extended laterally along any transverse topographic features. Some 28 occurrences, labeled sites as a matter of convenience, and with a minimum of 150 artifacts and a concentration of 2 to 75 artifacts per square meter, were identified in an area of 110 km^2. Three other sites were located by exploration within the limits of the 330-km^2 internal basin draining to the Alexandersfontein pan (playa). Twenty further sites were located between the adjacent Vaal Valley (Humphreys, 1973) and Modder floodplain (Figure 14-4B) and 20 others in the wider region (Figure 14-3), several of these on the basis of information provided by museum records or through the courtesy of G. J. Fock, others from Sampson's Orange River survey (MSA 1 and 5) (Sampson, 1972). In general, sites are located where calcified spring beds are being eroded, in wash deposits at or below former lake shorelines, and in piedmont areas around dolerite outcrops, presumably near lydianite veins, which unfortunately are very difficult to locate in the field. However, most of the sites are not only secondary but also badly dispersed because of repeated geomorphic impact. Only one of the excavated sites can be considered as semiprimary (type CE' of Chapter 7). Although it provides little information as to subsistence activities, this Alexandersfontein record does suggest a model for settlement distribution near water and raw-material sources that were locally concentrated in an erosional landscape, cut by several rivers and dotted by numerous pans and associated small depositional basins.

The predictable but dispersed resource space of the modern Dobe San, who are heavily dependent on mongongo nuts, covers some 725 km^2 in the semiarid northwest Kalahari (Yellen, 1977:Chapter 4). However, there is much flexibility in group composition, and the adult members are derived from an area of more than 12,000 km^2 (Yellen, 1977:Figure 1-2). Similar patterns are evident in the central Kalahari, where the Gwi exploit less productive but equally predictable resources, particularly the wild tsama melon (Silberbauer, 1981:Figure 16). With plant floods somewhat comparable to those available to the Botswana Gwi, the Alexandersfontein operational area must have exceeded the basin limits (330 km^2) and probably spanned a large tract of country between the Vaal and Modder rivers, perhaps approximated by the 6,000 km^2 shown in Figure 14-4B. Thus the 80,000-km^2 triangular sector of the Orange-Vaal Basin with Alexandersfontein-type sites (Figure 14-3) may once have supported a dozen or so Middle Stone Age groups.

Taking another approach, there are at least 28 sites (i.e., 0.25 per km^2) in the immediate survey area (Figure 14-4A). Allowing for de-struction of a good 50% of the original sites during some 100,000 years, the original density may have been 0.5 site/km^2 in this area of concen-trated resources. The original site density in the overall pan basin was at least four times that indicated by the recovered number of sites, considering the lack of systematic survey and the extensive destruction (i.e., 0.35 site/km^2). The higher-density figure can be used to extrapo-late an original tally of at least 3,250 sites along 1,300 km of (now) permanent river frontage averaging 5 km in width (6,500 km^2) (Figure 14-3). The lower-density figure would further suggest 25,725 sites in the intervening spaces, giving a total of about 30,000 sites, of which only 71 or 0.24% have been recovered. These figures are conservative, but they illustrate the degree to which average search efforts, given average preservation, can hope to locate Pleistocene sites.

Accepting the hypothesis of a dozen or so groups, and positing that they will have created 15 major artifactual concentrations per year, all 30,000 sites can be accounted for by 2,000 years of continuous occupa-tion in the area shown in Figure 14-3. If the Alexandersfontein facies indeed spans the entire duration of Riverton Member III, this estimate is again too low, because Member III deposits are far more substantial than those of Member V, dated 4500 to 1300 B.P. (Butzer et al., 1979).

The distribution of Alexandersfontein facies happens to be largely coincident with the region of late Holocene rock engravings and similar to the modal area used by the speakers of distinct San languages in this region during the early nineteenth century (Butzer et al., 1979:Figures 2 and 8) (Figure 14-5). The majority of the 10,500 rock engravings here record occupation during the last four millennia, with marked stylistic and technical changes accompanying a shift to riverine base camps after the onset of drier conditions around 1300 B.P. In other words, the model suggested for the Alexandersfontein facies is consonant with utilization of the same area by groups of a single identity-conscious unit circa 4000 to 1300 B.P., a time of more abundant water and vegeta-tion. This suggests that spatiotemporal models based on the final phases of Later Stone Age settlement are indeed useful in explaining Middle Stone Age residues in the same environment. Significantly, the same area was unoccupied for at least 50,000 years prior to 15,000 B.P. and again from 5500 to 4000 B.P. In sum, Pleistocene settlement in the South African interior was spatially delimited and temporally discrete, with periods of total regional abandonment that spanned many tens of millennia.

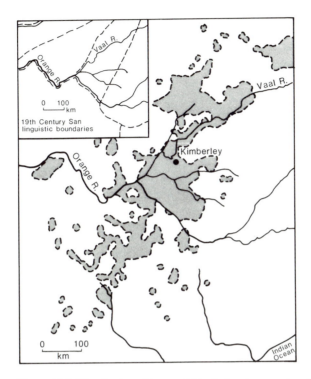

Figure 14-5. Distribution of late prehistorical rock-engraving sites (ca. 4000 B.P. to nineteenth century) in the interior of southern Africa. Compare with Figure 14-3. Modified from Butzer et al. (1979).

The Alexandersfontein settlement model is compatible with other regional surveys of prehistorical hunter-gatherers in terms of localization of site concentrations, delimitation of occurrence, and relatively finite time spans. For example, sites with a localized chocolate-colored flint of the Tanged Point technocomplex are concentrated along floodplains in a 50,000-km^2 sector of central Poland and date circa 11,600 to 9800 B.P. (Schild, 1976). Patterns of site locations for Paleoindian settlements in New Mexico circa 10,000 to 7000 B.P. have been illustrated by Judge and Dawson (1972); those for Mesolithic settlements in Czechoslovakia circa 10,000 to 6500 B.P. have been illustrated by Vencl (1971). Notable differences in the priorities of water supplies, overviews, and raw materials are apparent for different activity sites. A geo-archaeological survey of Mesolithic and younger site locations adjacent to the lower Rhine has shown that Mesolithic surface sites are limited to the upland plains and smaller tributary valleys, because in the floodplain

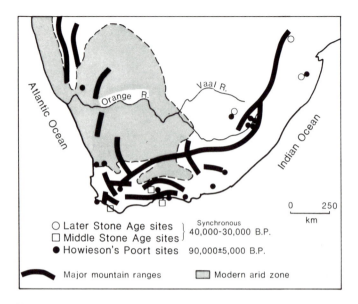

Figure 14-6. Howieson's Poort sites, dating to the cool isotope stage 5b, are limited to the montane and coastal parts of southern Africa. The earliest Later Stone Age sites (40,000–30,000 B.P.) were coeval with the Middle Stone Age in different parts of the same area.

proper they are buried in or under an alluvial body dated 9000 to 6000 B.P. (Brunnacker, 1978b).

Although the turnover rate of distinctive lithic assemblages accelerated toward the close of the Pleistocene (Isaac, 1972; Butzer, 1981c), these later hunter-gatherer settlement patterns support the impressions of the Alexandersfontein study that the Pleistocene *oikoumene* was discontinuous and that many, perhaps marginal, environments were settled only for a few millennia at a time. For example, an area such as the Sahara may have been occupied for a cumulative span of perhaps 1% of the million years or more represented by the Acheulian in northern Africa. During the late Pleistocene, one can detect distinct and disjunctive technocomplexes in what are today different macroenvironments. About 90,000 B.P. (± 5,000 years) (Butzer, Beaumont, and Vogel, 1978; Butzer, 1978f), during a cool climate phase (isotope stage 5b), a unique Middle Stone Age industry with abundant microliths, including geometric forms and suggestive of composite hafted tools (the Howieson's Poort) (Volman, 1981), was localized in the montane and coastal sectors of southern Africa (Figure 14-6). At that time, macrolithic Middle Stone

Age traditions apparently persisted in parts of the interior, and these once again replaced the Howieson's Poort after several millennia. Later, shortly before 40,000 B.P., a few sites of another technocomplex (Early Later Stone Age) with microliths, few formal tools, rare blades, and occasional bone tools and eggshell beads, appear in the mesic montane zone of central and southeastern Africa (Van Noten, 1977; Butzer, Beaumont, and Vogel, 1978; Butzer and Vogel, 1979). However, the traditional Middle Stone Age technocomplex persisted in a very small number of sites of the Cape region for another 10 millennia (Deacon, 1979; Volman, 1981) (Figure 14-6). Even then, more numerous Later Stone Age groups did not occupy the now-semiarid interior until after 15,000 B.P.

It is possible that Middle Stone Age groups, very few in number, were seasonally restricted to the winter rainfall zone of the southernmost Cape, whereas the earliest Later Stone Age groups sporadically exploited the montane zone of the Transvaal and Natal during warmer and wetter times of the year from better defined operational areas in the lake region of east-central Africa. In this way, much of southern Africa could have remained essentially uninhabited for many millennia, with little likelihood of encounters between groups of different identities. Although not proven beyond reasonable doubt, these arguments speak for distinct "partial cultural isolates," with delimited territories and some form of specific ecological adaptation, since about 100,000 B.P. This interpretative model, if substantiated by future work, is potentially of great significance for the Paleolithic record.

The picture of spatial heterogeneity of hunter-gatherer settlement networks that begins to emerge for the African Middle Stone Age becomes increasingly complex in the Nile Valley after 18,000 B.P. From that time until the establishment of agricultural economies some 12 millennia later, there were at least three and often five concurrent industries in Egypt (Figure 14-7) (Butzer and Hansen, 1968; Phillips and Butzer, 1973; Smith, 1976c; Wendorf and Schild, 1976, 1980; Bar-Yosef and Phillips, 1977; Butzer, 1979). These industries represented no mere tool-kit or facies differences and frequently were distinct in terms of fundamental technology as well as raw materials used. Their quasi-contemporaneous sites may occur as little as a few kilometers apart, and in some cases distinct industries alternate with each other at the same site; others tend to cluster in different areas. However, site networks cannot be reconstructed, because very exact temporal controls would be necessary for what are probably not more than seasonal sites.

Intergroup warfare is indicated by cemeteries with a high proportion of skeletons with projectile wounds. The 13 preagricultural nilotic industries have a mean duration of 2,800 years (σ 2,200), not unlike those of historical and late prehistorical linguistic families (e.g., Celtic, Germanic). The appearances and disappearances of these industries commonly coincide with environmental changes (Figure 14-7), suggesting repeated ecological readjustments.

The available faunas associated with Nile Valley sites are dominated by wild cattle and hartebeest, with some gazelle, wild ass, hippopotamus, warthog, and an extinct buffalo. The faunal samples are too small to indicate whether or not there were differences in hunting preferences among the groups responsible for these industries, but some sites have abundant fish bones as well as some turtle and crocodile. The tool types suggest that fishing was particularly important in several of these adaptations.

Of particular interest are the grinding stones associated with some, but not all, sites of several industries (Kubbaniyan, Afian, Qadan, Isnan, Figure 14-7) that may also include microliths with sickle sheen. This argues for plant processing, a claim supported by large pollen of Gramineae type in one Isnan locale and carbonized barley grains in a Kubbaniyan site. Several centuries of unusually high floods, associated with a "wild" Nile that repeatedly flooded to 8 or 9 m above its active floodplain circa 12,000 to 11,500 B.P., appear to have terminated this specialized grain-collecting adaptation. Later populations in the Nile Valley were few and small and were mainly concentrated on aquatic exploitation, until the influx of Neolithic colonists from the western deserts (Butzer, 1976c:Chapter 2).

Terminal Pleistocene sites in Israel show more technological uniformity, but different tool kits, in areas that are now arid and humid (Bar-Yosef, 1975). The many cave occupations produced remarkably thick strata as compared with the shallow but far more extensive nilotic sites, suggesting repeated and prolonged residence. Site sizes increase from a range of 150 to 400 m^2 for the Kebaran (ca. 18,000 B.P.) to 500 to 7,000 m^2 for the Natufian (ca. 10,500 B.P.). The Natufian settlement layouts, size, and faunas indicate diversified local adaptations reflected in four typical settlement patterns (Bar-Yosef, 1975).

These trends parallel those in Egypt but demonstrate that the rapid, end-Pleistocene transformations of subsistence and settlement patterns were unique within each ecological mosaic. There were, then, few large interstitial voids. But the spatial behaviors of the "intensive"

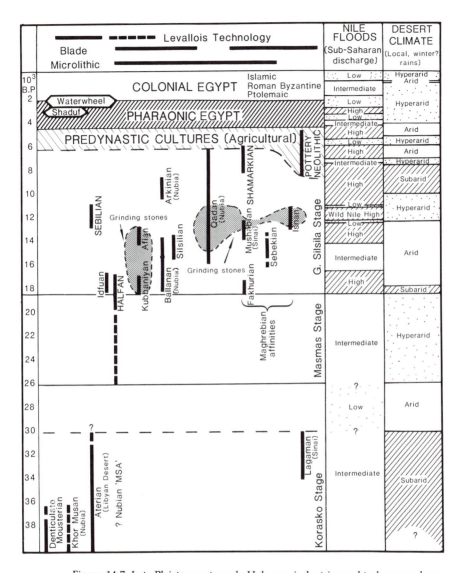

Figure 14-7. Late Pleistocene to early Holocene industries and technocomplexes in the Nile Valley and Sinai. Industries found in both Nubia and Upper Egypt are shown in full capitals; others are localized. The presence of three to five concurrent industries (often distinct at the technological level) after 18,000 B.P. is remarkable. Note: Khor Musan includes "Buhen"; Halfan includes Khor el-Sil; Afian includes "Late Sebilian"; Isnan includes Menchian; Sebekian includes "E" and (?) "Dabarosan"; Qadan includes "Wadi"; Fakhurian includes "D"; Shamarkian includes Elkabian and "Qarunian"; Pottery Neolithic includes Khartum Neolithic, "Abkan," Fayum "A," and Merimde.

broad-spectrum foragers in Egypt and Israel, on the one hand, and the "extensive" hunter-gathers in Poland and New Mexico, on the other, were substantially different in terms of density and complexity. Subsequent early Holocene adaptations maintained this dichotomy in relation to resource concentration, predictability, and mobility. For example, the Archaic of eastern North America and the Mesolithic of Europe were focused on abundant riverine resources and suggest limited mobility, whereas the American "desert traditions" and the Smithfield of the dry South African interior were reflected in spatial patterns more reminiscent of those characteristic before 20,000 B.P. The same dichotomy persisted among extant hunter-gatherers into recent times (e.g., between the Mbuti pygmies of the Congo rainforest and the Shoshone of the Great Basin).

Reconstruction of settlement patterns: agricultural communities

The archaeological trace of sedentary occupation is far more tangible in the landscape than that of mobile hunter-gatherers, in part because structural features were intended to have some permanence, in part because of the cumulative imprint of repeated long-term use. When, in addition, durable materials were employed in construction and fields were delineated by embankments or deep plow traces, the settlement record frequently continues to provide detailed information many millennia later. Not all agricultural settlements were permanent (i.e., occupied over a generation or two), and not all hunter-gatherer sites were impermanent. But, on the whole, the possibilities for archaeological reconstruction of the settlements and resource spaces of prehistorical agricultural communities are an order of magnitude greater than those for reconstruction of hunter-gatherer site complexes. Furthermore, in the case of large permanent villages and towns, the spatial record of community behavior is relatively intelligible (Table 13-2). It can be studied intensively at the microscale, the semimicroscale, and the mesoscale to generate detailed and reliable socioeconomic information that is next to impossible to obtain from the hunter-gatherer record. This, then, is the subject matter for the primarily inductive settlement archaeology called for by Willey (1953:1), Chang (1968), Trigger (1968), Parsons (1972), and Tringham (1972). Equally so, this is the type of archaeological record amenable to the kind of deductive sociocultural interpretation called for by other recent programmatic statements (Hill, 1972).

This brief review is limited to a characterization of the types of spatial configurations that can be discerned from the archaeological record of prehistorical agricultural communities and their ecological context. Such an exploration can best make use of a selection of examples.

The nature of settlement and land-use patterns in nonirrigated mesic landscapes from Neolithic to historical times is particularly well documented for Britain in works compiled by Evans and Limbrey (1975) and Limbrey and Evans (1978); they are supplemented by a series of detailed maps for the pre-Roman, Roman, Dark Age, and Norman periods published by the British Ordnance Survey that include gazetteers of all sites, ranging from pottery and tile kilns to forts, temples, and shrines. This is the type of data base employed in the exemplary spatial analyses of Hodder (1972, 1977). Good illustrations of the types of settlement layouts and field criteria (see Chapter 8) can be seen in the work of Evans (1975:Chapters 6–7), and the various field marks have been discussed by Bradley (1978). The full potential of this vast body of information for the functional and ecological interpretation of changing settlement networks through seven millennia has only begun to be exploited.

Similar bodies of information have been generated in The Netherlands and in parts of Germany and Scandinavia, but they remain to be collated and evaluated in a more accessible and comprehensive form. Smaller surveys are less suitable for macroscale spatial analysis, but they commonly provide greater depth of understanding of settlement processes through time. An example is the South Etruria survey of Potter (1979), which serves as a model for settlement continuity and change in the dry-farming landscapes of the Mediterranean Basin.

Comparable to the macroscale data for Britain are the monumental surveys of settlement and irrigation networks in Mesopotamia documented and interpreted by Adams (1965, 1981) and Adams and Nissen (1972). A stimulating spatial analysis of part of these data has been attempted by Johnson (1975). One persistent problem here is the absence of geo-archaeological fieldwork, with the result that the potential role of major changes in river courses and discharge (De Meyer, 1978:1–56) cannot yet be separated from the artificial regulation and reallocation of water supplies within or between canal networks. The merits of detailed mapping can be appreciated from the mesoscale survey of fourth millennium B.C. field systems on an alluvial fan in southeastern Iran by Pricket (1979).

In the New World, the survey of the Basin of Mexico by Sanders et al. (1979) provides a similar landmark at the macroscale level, with 25 maps covering some 3,500 km^2 in terms of settlement and land-use criteria. Preliminary spatial analyses have been attempted by Earle (1976) and Smith (1979b) (cf. Evans, 1980), and a more comprehensive study has been begun by T. L. Bell. The Basin of Mexico study complements other regional analyses in Mesoamerica by Flannery (1976) and Harrison and Turner (1978), as well as several specifically urban studies.

These examples, which can be complemented by further, smaller-scale surveys from several other regions, demonstrate the substantial nature of the documentation for some prehistorical agricultural settlement networks. The data base is not perfect, and geo-archaeological and chronometric refinements are commonly needed. But reasonable frameworks for systematic regional analysis exist, and they call for the development and testing of spatial models tailored to the nature of the available information. These models should seek to elucidate the patterns of site location, the utilization and modification of resource spaces, and the interactions within and between site networks. Such comprehensive explanatory models of the human landscape should transcend the classic goal of abstract spatial behavior by identifying resource patterns as well as those interactions between societies and their environments that are reflected in cultural configurations and other imprints on the biophysical landscape. This will require new multidimensional criteria that can be applied to the component data that can be generated by an explicitly contextual approach. It is therefore vital that new archaeological projects incorporate strategies that will allow more comprehensive analysis of such human landscapes.

CHAPTER 15

Diachronic systems I: cultural adaptation

Temporal integration

In the preceding chapters we have considered models and empirical data that seek to describe and explain the spatial processes and configurations of human ecosystems. Two modal categories, mobile hunter-gathers and sedentary farmers, were considered in order to emphasize the variability in spatial behavior. But discussion was necessarily synchronic in order to emphasize the geographical expression of phenomena that archaeologists traditionally view in temporal perspective. A time axis is essential, however, in order to examine the dynamics of individual human ecosystems as well as the record of continuity and change in human history. These diachronic objectives differ in scale rather than in substance, because the trajectory of continuity and change represents the longer-term interactions and transformations of multiple human ecosystems.

Seen in the perspective of thousands or millions of years of prehistory, the archaeological record demonstrates significant changes in human form as well as in cultural behavior: (a) tangible "modernization" of the genus *Homo* from our Tertiary apelike ancestors toward the living peoples of today, (b) an overall increase in intellectual capacity, and (c) a substantial increase in cultural complexity. These biological and cultural changes represent a fundamental evolution in which the two variables were inextricably interwoven. Beyond these basic premises, there is little agreement at the level of semantics, conceptualization, or processual interpretation.

The paradigms favored for the investigation of human origins are unsuitable to examine phenomena of the last 5 or 10 millennia. What may be true at the megascale of Pleistocene prehistory may be incorrect, inapplicable, or inappropriate for the short time spans and complex detail of the historical era. In part, the problem is one of scale, macroevolution versus microevolution, a distinction that poses no problems in biological terms but that is difficult to apply to cultural phenomena, raising the question whether or not biological and cultural changes can indeed be objectively interrelated except in the most general of terms. In part, too, the problem centers around the cultural paradigm itself, whether culture is seen as a set of hierarchical phenomena interesting sui generis or whether culture is additionally perceived as a structured but flexible means to ensure group success and, ultimately, species survival. The drawing of simplistic dichotomies (e.g., structural and functional; ideological and materialist) obscures the complexity and integrity of human culture as an integrative process that at once serves psychological, social, and material needs.

The primary concerns of the cultural anthropologist and the archaeologist are less a reflection of fundamentally different concepts of culture than of paradigms suitable for study of the different phenomena that are tangible to the two disciplines. There also are fundamental differences in immediate research goals for a synchronic approach, such as that pervasive in anthropology, and the diachronic preoccupation of most archaeologists.

The underlying assumption is that prehistorical research and historical research are justified not as esoteric reconstructions but as direct contributions to an understanding of the nature of human culture. Directly or indirectly, such efforts provide a diachronic dimension essential to elucidate the dynamics of cultural systems. The term *dynamics* here implies more than rate, amplitude, and direction of change; it also encompasses the intrinsic nature of the interactive processes interpreted in the past and present and anticipated in the future.

The often perplexing patterns of individual and group behavior in situations of chronic or sudden stress exemplify one such facet. Beyond the more general problem of social relationships within and between groups, the interactions between human populations and the nonhuman components of their ecosystems are equally pertinent. Diachronic experience is critical to the formulation and testing of behavioral models in regard to aggression, altruism, sexuality, and, above all, resource utilization and ecology. To what degree has culture emerged as an extrasomatic means to regulate such behavioral modes and so to ensure an acceptable measure of subsistence success and overall population survival? To what degree are such regulatory responses genetically programmed? The related sociobiological controversy is but one aspect of the larger unresolved problem of exactly how biological evolution and cultural adaptation are interrelated (Durham, 1978).

In any field of research, the problems posed prefigure the potential methods of investigation. Once identified, these methods require an explicit conceptual framework to facilitate analysis and to avoid confusion. The paradigm so defined represents a finite universe, deliberately restricted in order to allow exploration of those specific problems. In this sense, anthropological and archaeological paradigms are logically different, despite a common interest in human culture. Similarly, within archaeology, the contextual and social paradigms are also structured differently, despite a shared diachronic concern for human culture. In selecting the adaptive paradigm that follows, I do so in the interest of an effective approach to the interactive human and nonhuman components of the human ecosystem.

Cultural adaptation

David Clarke originally characterized the basic attributes of cultural systems as "activities, artifacts, and beliefs, not in their own guise but as 'information' controlling and regulating these three derivative expressions of cultural tradition" (Clarke, 1968:85). In developing the cybernetics analogy, he compared culture to "an information system, wherein the messages are accumulated survival information plus miscellaneous and random noise peculiar to each system and its past trajectory" (Clarke, 1968:85) (Flannery and Marcus, 1976). Such cultural systems are subject to equilibrium oscillations in response to variations within the containing environment: (a) phase oscillations, whereby the coupled systems adjust almost simultaneously; (b) lag phenomena, in which new information is incorporated into the cultural system measurably later than the environmental transformation; (c) lead phenomena, in which actual or potential transformations are consciously or unconsciously anticipated, leading to adjustments in the cultural system (Clarke, 1968:Figure 11).

Constant interaction is not limited to the interrelationships between cultural systems and their environments and the resulting spatial-temporal readjustments. There also are fundamental interactions within the system and between its multiple subsystems. The resulting oscillations, adjustments, and transformations commonly represent responses to new information, including both external elements that may be accepted and integrated or modified (diffusion) and internal elements generated by recombinations of existing components to produce notably different results (innovation) (Clarke, 1968).

Much innovation appears to be the result of the multiplication of oscillating and "searching" trajectories permitted within a cultural system, allowing multiple stochastic development that "may chance upon an arrangement with emergent and latent potentialities" (Clarke, 1968:93). Whatever its origin, the new information (a) may be compatible with existing information, confirming that information or leading to a net gain, (b) may present an alternative variety to the set of information in hand, signaling alternative choices and trajectories, or (c) may be contradictory, in part or in total, leading to uncertainty or favoring destruction of part of the original body of information (Clarke, 1968).

This culture-as-information approach is complemented by the approach of cultural adaptation. This is another borrowed concept, in this case taken from the biological sciences, and it, too, has both merits and disadvantages. In its original form, biological adaptation can be internal (physiological) (i.e., system-regulating, as in the maintenance of constant body temperature) or external (evolutionary) (i.e., the adaptation of a system with its external environment to promote evolutionary change) (Alland, 1975). Cultural adaptation derives from the latter variant and implies long-term nongenetic adjustments of cultures to their environments (Alland, 1975). The advantages of a dynamic paradigm that focuses on continuity and change, rather than on static evolutionary stages or sets of accumulated traits, are obvious. However, there is an immediate problem: How does one measure adaptation or distinguish adaptive traits from maladaptive traits?

Two basic criteria have been offered: One is essentially biological, namely, that adaptation implies long-term demographic "success" (Alland, 1975; Durham, 1978). The other is economic, namely, that adaptation can be inversely related to total energy expended per individual per unit time (Alland, 1975; Kirch, 1980a). These diagnostic measures are to some degree incompatible, because demographic viability may be possible only with drastic socioeconomic readjustment and curtailment.

The paradoxes involved in determining just what is adaptive are particularly apparent in the range of modern examples of recent group stress analyzed in a volume assembled by Laughlin and Brady (1978): Whether or not the particular groups discussed are well adapted cannot be determined objectively, because the requisite time depth is missing, a major failing of the ahistorical neo-ecological approach. Even a century or so of data accumulation, as for the Dassanetch in the constantly changing deltaic environment of the Omo River in southwestern Ethiopia (Butzer 1971*b*:131–44, 175; Almagor, 1972; Carr, 1977) allows identification of adaptive mechanisms, but no measures for adaptive success, because recent demographic expansion among the Dassanetch has led to intensive environmental degradation, with strong resultant pressures for significant cultural transformation. Returning to the original definition, adaptation refers to long-term success, not short-term success. In fact, Slobodkin and Rapoport (1974) insisted that adaptive success must be measured with respect to a particular time depth. Any shortcomings in its application to contemporary situations does not justify dismissal of adaptation as a useful archaeological concept, because in archaeological research the time depth is adequate.

Adaptation nonetheless remains a theoretical concept, with population "crashes" or extinctions providing the only unequivocal measures of maladaptation (Rappaport, 1978). There is, of course, no fundamental problem in analyzing the adaptation of groups and cultural systems that have not survived. However, in evaluating groups and societies that do survive, it may be more practicable to concentrate on adaptive mechanisms, rather than measures, as is implicit in Buckley's concept of "complex adaptive systems."

Buckley (1968) combined the cybernetics and biological analogues to define such an adaptive system as (a) one that is in constant interchange with the environment, (b) one that provides a potential pool of adaptive variability with which to identify new and more detailed varieties and constraints within that environment, and (c) one that incorporates this information into a structure for preserving and propagating the more successful system variables. As a corollary, adaptive strategies can be defined as sets of behaviors, either simultaneous or sequential, that reflect cognitive mapping of the environment and by which the system adjusts to both external and internal changes. One of the advantages of Buckley's systemic concept is that it represents an open-system model that emphasizes the interactions between the sociocultural and environmental subsystems within a larger system (Wood and Matson, 1975). Another is that it emphasizes variability, thereby allowing for cultural selection (Kirch, 1980*c*), a true evolutionary mechanism (Dunnell, 1980*a*). Lastly, Buckley's adaptive concept emphasizes cognition and decision making and therefore implicitly allows for alternative adaptive solutions to transcend the deterministic tendency of technoenvironmental models (see Bettinger, 1980:237–40).

Adaptive strategy is a critical variable in culture–environment interactions because it can be related to the ecological niche (i.e., the functional role and externally imposed constraints of the population) (Odum, 1971:234). In a space defined by habitat, resources, and time, adaptive strategy determines the shape of the niche (Kirch, 1980a). For example, a broad niche is an optimal strategy in an environment that is highly variable, coarse-grained, or of low productivity. When confronted with deteriorating circumstances, a population must experiment with new combinations of plant and animal foods, the broader niche providing substitutes for increasingly precarious resources, and possibly ensuring the viability of a familiar subsistence-settlement system. Optimizing strategies are not adaptively optimal in marginal environments or even in productive but moderate-risk environments. One alternative is the "most-prudent" or minimax strategy, which minimizes the maximum risk, ensuring the best of the nonoptimal outcomes in any one situation (Clarke, 1968:95; Bettinger, 1980). An example of a minimax strategy is the blending of different staple crops that prefer different weather conditions to ensure maximum returns in any sequence of good and bad years (Clarke, 1968:119). These points, touched on briefly here, are complemented by the discussion of optimal foraging strategy in Chapter 12 (Winterhalder, 1980, 1981) and by the explicit models for hunter-gatherer and agricultural subsistence presented by Bettinger (1980) and Green (1980a).

Changes in adaptive strategy can be usefully linked to the process of cultural selection, which operates in response to environmental constraints that channel or direct the potential range of behaviors, as well as through cognitive processes that reflect intelligence, perceived needs, cultural values, anticipation of future needs, and behavioral assessment (Rappaport, 1971b; Kirch, 1980a; Orlove, 1980). Three kinds of selection have been identified by Kirch (1980a:122–3):

1. Stabilizing selection. In a situation of a high degree of adaptiveness to a stable environment, selection will tend to eliminate variant peripheral behaviors, thus keeping the total range of variation to a minimum.

2. Directional selection. In a situation of stress, such as a rapid environmental perturbation or the colonization of a new environment, certain formerly peripheral behaviors may be selected in the course of experimentation and change to achieve a new adaptive system.

3. Diversifying selection. In a patchy heterogeneous environment, two or more adaptive norms may develop and coexist within a single cultural population.

Thus, selection pressures will tend to be stabilizing, directional, or diversifying depending on whether the environment is stable, changing, or complex, respectively.

Whereas adaptation basically is a strategy for survival, adaptability is the capacity of the system to adjust. Adaptability depends on the ability of the system to incorporate new information. The more behavioral variability that is tolerated, the more probable it is that new ideas will be harmonized with existing values and thus will be found to be acceptable.

> The more options are accepted the more probable it becomes that, by chance or intent, a change of adaptive value will occur. Therefore, toleration of high variability in a group's behavior should be a factor of high adaptive value. . . . Communities will adopt new attributes not necessarily because they correctly discern their adaptive value, but because the new behavior has consistency with the group's formal and functional patterns and only produces a slight shift in their form (Fletcher, 1977:142–3).

> Many human groups must be expected to be unable to adopt new spatial arrangements simply because they are irreconcilable with a community's internally coherent spatial model (Fletcher, 1977:146).

There is more to the behavioral equation than tolerance for variability. Adaptability is enhanced when a system incorporates a sufficient variety of activity modes and material attributes, whether in complex systems or in unspecialized rudimentary systems in which a diversity of resources reduces system vulnerability. On the other hand, a specialized and highly institutionalized system probably will become more conservative in proportion to its success; less receptive to new ideas, it may prove nonadaptive outside of a specifically defined environment or may be unable to cope with external variation (Clarke, 1968:98; Sahlins, 1977).

In concluding this examination of cultural adaptation and its inherent processes, the definition of adaptive system can be modified to explicitly identify the key variables and their material manifestations in a form applicable to past societies. This definition, illustrated by Figure 15-1, can be formulated as follows: The three-dimensional intersection defined by social behavior, technology, and resource opportunities and limitations represents an *adaptive system* that is reflected in subsistence strategies and settlement patterns and that responds and adjusts in relation to internal processes as well as changes in the human and nonhuman environment.

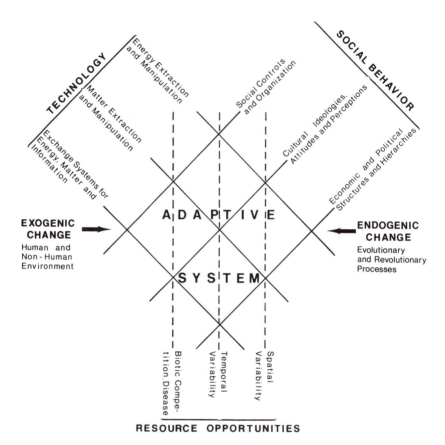

Figure 15-1. A three-dimensional model for the interactive variables of an adaptive system.

Dynamic modes of adaptive systems

In order to develop an effective methodology to examine adaptive systems and their temporal dynamics in Chapter 16, it is first necessary to agree on an appropriate concept of scale analysis. Such a concept can be developed from biology, along the following lines.

Modern ecosystems are perceived by biologists as interactive communities defined by various parameters and adjusting to internal and external changes by multiple positive and negative feedbacks. The emphasis is processual and synchronic. On the other hand, the character of temporal trajectories can be evaluated only by an evolutionary perspective based on the paleontological record. Through the course of the

Cenozoic, and particularly during the Pleistocene, three types of biotic changes are apparent:

1. There are evolutionary transformations during which new communities of plants and animals emerge, this process often being accelerated in response to stress or as new environments are colonized. Extinctions and appearances of new genera tend to be more frequent during such transformations, although individual lineages evolve in temporal patterns that frequently do not coincide with complex biotic changes. In other words, the evolution of new biotic communities involves new associations of both new and old forms that collectively represent a new level of adaptive success.

2. Community evolution is distinct from *individual replacement*, whether phyletic (i.e., linear evolution of differently adapted forms) or ecological (i.e., lateral displacement by more competitive species and genera).

3. The third type of change is *biotic succession,* in which a catastrophic event such as a fire, hurricane, or extreme climatic trend temporarily destroys a biotic association, which then progressively reconstitutes itself via an ephemeral sequence of recolonizing communities (see Figure 8-2).

Several major evolutionary transformations can be identified during the 65 million years of the Cenozoic. One of these is the emergence of true grasslands, coupled with adaptive radiation of cursorial ungulates between 15 and 10 million years ago during Miocene times. Another case is the progressive displacement of semitropical woodland communities from middle latitudes during the 2 million years of the Pleistocene. These changes were favored by sixth-order environmental trends (see Table 2-2) accelerated by fifth-order climatic oscillations, and, through positive feedback, they themselves induced secondary environmental transformations. But the inherent evolutionary momentum of increasingly complex terrestrial ecosystems was as significant as the external steering mechanisms that accelerated and directed the trajectory of evolutionary change.

A different order of biotic change is represented by the frequent and relatively rapid shifts of continental biomes during the course of individual Pleistocene glacial-interglacial cycles (fifth-order changes; see Table 2-2). These large-scale oscillations promoted individual replacement (e.g., among large herbivores) without real evolutionary transformation; instead, each equilibrium shift led to community displacement, accompanied by regional biotic successions that took several millennia.

More subtle biotic readjustments can be identified in response to fourth- and third-order changes (see Table 2-4); such adaptations were seldom of more than local significance.

These ecosystemic features provide analogues with important implications for human adaptive systems, as can readily be seen in the overview presented in Table 15-1:

1. Fundamental evolutionary transformations, involving the development of radically new adaptive modes, are relatively uncommon and tend to have continental or global repercussions. Examples of such morphogenesis in the prehistorical and historical record include hominization, the appearance of diversified cultural systems toward the close of the Pleistocene, agricultural origins, colonization of new environments, urbanization, industrialization, and, most recently, attempts to "modernize" the Third World. Each of these *adaptive transformations* was accompanied by changes along all three axes shown in Figure 15-1: social behavior, technology, and resource utilization.

2. Regional adaptive systems are repeatedly marked by discontinuities in equilibrium levels or long-term directional trends (i.e., metastable or dynamic equilibrium conditions) (see Figure 2-3). These changes generally center around resources or production, as a result of better or maladaptive information (Rappaport, 1978) or environmental variation; in response, substantial technological or behavioral accommodations are facilitated or required. Certain culture traits may be adopted or discarded. Such important accommodations, and the resulting directional selection within persistent adaptive systems, can be described as *adaptive modifications* – less fundamental than transformations but transcending the regular adjustments to recurrent perturbations that are a standard part of equilibrium maintenance. Perhaps the best measure of whether such adaptive modifications are positive or negative is given by long-term demographic trends (Figure 15-2). Repeated positive and negative deviations of this kind commonly define the large-scale population cycles linked to sociopolitical periodicities (e.g., in various early civilizations and, more recently, in India under the Moghuls and the British raj). These are the trends labeled ascendance, climax, and retrogression in the historical developmental scheme of Willey and Phillips (1958) and in the formative, coherent (classic), and postcoherent stages in Clarke's (1968) model of "culture system ontogeny." However, ecosystemic modification provides a better model, because it does not presume a sequential interplay of predictable processes (Butzer, 1980c). In fact, adaptive systems normally

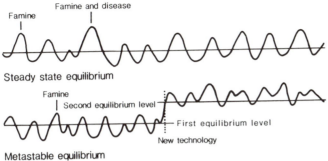

Figure 15-2. Demographic curves approximate the quality of human adaptation. One common type of equilibrium is the steady state (top), in which recurrent famine and epidemic disease lead to repeated population fluctuations without long-term directional change. In more complex societies, new adaptive strategies may allow one or more jumps in equilibrium levels (metastable equilibrium, below), and subsequent demographic oscillations may be of smaller amplitude; negative social and environmental inputs can also have a reversed impact. Modified from Butzer (1980c:Figure 1).

survive repeated modifications of this kind with or without changes in cultural identity.

3. Adaptive systems are also marked by short- and medium-term oscillations that involve no equilibrium shifts or long-term trends. The positive- and negative-feedback processes balance out to maintain a steady state (Figure 15-2). Economic and social crises are resolved by minor or short-term readjustments within either the behavioral spectrum or the technological spectrum of the adaptive system. Examples include perturbations such as epidemics, famines, destructive wars, and dynastic changes. Such *adaptive adjustments* constitute an integral part of equilibrium maintenance.

The three scale classes of adaptive transformation, modification, and adjustment provide a useful model to examine the prehistorical record in systemic terms. The relevant criteria are systematically formulated in Table 15-1.

Two primary stimuli for change are identified in Figure 15-1, exogenic and endogenic:

1. The external stimuli include the following: the frequency and severity of geological hazards (Sheets and Grayson, 1979), direct climatic events (Apeldoorn, 1978; Hinchey, 1979; Torry, 1979), and indirect climatic repercussions (Butzer, 1980c, 1981b); directional trends in the productivity of the biophysical environment due to climatic change (see Table 2-4) or ecosystemic disbalance (see Chapter 8) (Gibson, 1974;

Table 15-1. *Dynamic modes of adaptive systems*

Adaptive transformation

Cases of cultural morphogenesis, with development of radically new adaptive modes, involving cultural selection in terms of social behavior, technology, and resource utilization.

Transformations eventually have continental or global repercussions for subsistence, settlement, and demography.

Transformations may or may not be interlinked with biological evolution (macro or micro).

Examples: Pliocene-Pleistocene hominization; cultural and adaptive diversification toward the close of the Pleistocene; early Holocene agricultural and pastoral origins; middle and late Holocene agricultural expansion into new environments and related ecosystemic transformations; urbanization; the Industrial Revolution.

Adaptive modification

Cases of substantial revision of adaptive strategies within the context of a viable and persistent adaptive system, involving technological and behavioral accommodations to external and internal inputs and processes and adoption or loss of cultural traits.

Such modifications eventually have regional repercussions for subsistence, settlement, and demography and may or may not result in changes in cultural (e.g., ethnic or linguistic) identity.

Examples: elaborations of late prehistoric and historical adaptive systems through agricultural intensification, demographic expansion, and state growth; periodicities in Mesoamerican, Egyptian, and Mesopotamian civilizations; cycles of growth, florescence, and decline within other regional adaptive systems.

Adaptive adjustment

Cases of minor and short-term readjustments within the existing behavioral and technological spectrum of the adaptive system to resolve economic and social crises and thus maintain the systemic steady state.

Such adjustments interlink with local and regional demographic oscillations.

Examples: geophysical disasters, epidemics, famines, destructive wars, and dynastic changes.

Kirch, 1980*b*; Butzer, 1981*a*); colonization of new environments (Kirch, 1980*b*; Green, 1980*b*); intergroup competition such as migration and warfare (Carneiro, 1970; Vayda, 1974); the diffusion of new information generated outside of the ecosystem, as, for example, through the process of trade (Renfrew, 1975; Earle and Ericson, 1977).

2. The internal stimuli include innovation, demographic processes (Cohen, 1976*b*; Turner et al., 1977; Hassan, 1980, 1981; Kirch, 1980*b*), hierarchical elaborations (Flannery, 1972*a*; Redman, 1978), cybernetics difficulties (Flannery, 1972*a*; Rappaport, 1978), and excessive demands on agricultural producers (Wittfogel, 1957; Butzer, 1980*c*) (Figure 15-3). A more complete but not exhaustive group of variables (Wenke, 1981) is outlined in Table 15-2. It should be noted that the biophysical and

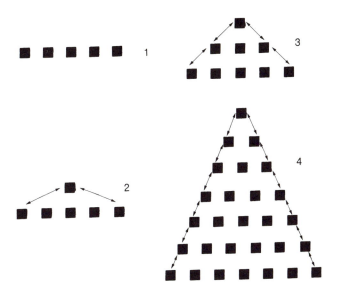

Figure 15-3. Sociopolitical hierarchies, whether simple or complex, can be compared to the organization of trophic levels in a food chain. These schematic models illustrate different modes of energy and information flow for increasingly complex sociopolitical hierarchies in preindustrial societies. The first model shows no vertical structure, with horizontal but no vertical information flow, and slow change. The second indicates limited vertical structure, with some vertical information flow, and increased dynamism. The third depicts elaborate vertical structure, characterized by efficient energy and information flow, with each level as well as the whole system in steady-state or dynamic equilibrium. The fourth represents a top-heavy vertical structure, with impeded information flow, increased energy expenditure for system maintenance, excessive demands on the productive substrate, and a metastable equilibrium. Modified from Butzer(1980c:Figure 2).

sociocultural components of the environment are integral parts of the adaptive system: It is their inherent dynamism that lies largely outside of the control of the system's human participants. A change in any one of the exogenic or endogenic variables will require readjustments in one or more of the others, because the parts of the human ecosystem are interdependent. These feedback loops commonly will span two or more of the columns in Table 15-2, as, for example, the complex processes of acculturation.

It is apparent that both external and internal stimuli or processes are integral to any interpretation of adaptive change. This point must be emphasized, because one school of archaeological thinking, reflected in a conference volume edited by Hill (1977), attributes prehistorical

Table 15-2A. *Exogenic stimuli and processes of adaptive change*

Biophysical components	Sociocultural components
1. Seasonal, predictable hazards, such as quality and timing of season of primary productivity, in relation to water supply as well as abundance of plant and animal foods.	1. Interregional contact via exchange networks, involving direct trade, market exchange, middlemen, and specialized trading centers
2. Aperiodic, unpredictable hazards, related to geology (earthquakes, landslides, volcanic eruptions, destructive floods), climate (hurricanes, tornadoes, catastrophic anomalies in quality/timing of growing season), and epidemic disease, and their recurrence intervals	2. Diffusion, as verbal, visual, and abstract information; tangible products, technology, and behavior; tangible and intangible associations with such products, technology, and behavior
3. Medium- to long-range trends in resource productivity involving directional changes (dynamic-equilibrium shifts) lasting 10–1,000 years, related to climatic or local tectonic changes as well as ecological disbalance (ecosystem simplification, soil depletion or destruction, hydrological or topographic change); frequent secondary links with endemic disease	3. Migration, in the form of infiltration of immigrants (with or without the formation of enclaves), colonization of interstitial spaces, competitive exclusion, and circumscription through surrounding of the settlement network by other peoples
4. Environmental discontinuities, associated with major equilibrium shifts lasting 1,000–25,000 years or with colonization of new, ecologically divergent environments	4. Warfare, with direct demographic and economic costs; impaired external or internal security; internal adjustments to mobilize manpower and resources; external adjustments such as gain or loss of land, special resources, and access to exchange networks; domination, decimation, enslavement, and colonization.

Table 15-2B. *Endogenic stimuli and processes of adaptive change*

Positive-feedback mechanisms	Negative-feedback mechanisms
1. Innovation in technology, subsistence strategies, social organization, the arts, and the ideational realm.	1. Population pressures confronting limited resources and technological constraints eventually force demographic curtailment and stable or declining productivity, possibly linked with ecological disbalance.
2. Rapid population growth, made possible through innovations, diffusion of technology, and positive environmental changes, generates a secondary demand for intensification or expansion of agriculture, thus favoring further innovations.	2. Vertical overelaboration of the administrative and social components eventually leads to hierarchical instability (metastable equilibrium), as the top-heavy sociopolitical structure becomes increasingly prone to delayed, inadequate, or incorrect information flow between the system elements, while the increased energy expenditure for system maintenance places excessive demands on the productive substrate.
3. Socioeconomic and sociopolitical processes, made possible by successive innovations and increased productivity, favor one or more positive feedbacks such as the emergence of settlement hierarchies, economic specialization, redistributive networks, social stratification, and an administrative elite.	

change preeminently, if not exclusively, to extrasystemic triggering mechanisms. The point is equally relevant in regard to causality models of adaptive change that mechanically couple polarized cultural and environmental subsystems (Wood and Matson, 1975).

An adaptive system with its bounding environment provides a matrix of resources and constraints for the potential range of behavioral variability (Figure 15-1). In exploiting these opportunities and in confronting the fluctuating boundary conditions, the individuals within a cultural system have the choice of an infinity of potential subsistence-settlement options that can be either adopted or rejected. In this sense, adaptive response, however environmentally conditioned and spatially rationalized, is explicitly the result of human perception and decision making. This position can be argued as follows:

1. The constraining role is highly generalized, and both technology and social organization repeatedly bend the constraints.

2. Decisions are made with respect to a perceived environment rather than a real environment; there is an almost unlimited number of perceptions of the environment, and many of these may be adaptively equivalent.

3. Cultural systems are more sensitive than biological systems, making them more receptive to "noise," thus possibly explaining some of the remarkable variety among human cultures in similar environments. In fact, much of the apparent noise may represent patterned responses to perceived environments.

4. The potential numbers of possible adaptations to the full range of environmental variability consequently are even greater than the vast variety documented in the ethnographic record of living peoples.

5. Actions are conceived and taken by individuals, however many or anonymous they may be. But they must be examined and approved by the community in the context of accepted information before decisions can be translated into responses. In this sense it is the community rather than the individual that is the arbiter of adaptive change.

6. Regardless of whether or not external and internal stimuli are real, cognitive perception generates a positive or negative feedback that, over the long term, represents cultural adaptation – irrespective of whether or not that adaptation is ultimately successful.

7. The fact that choices among a wide range of potential options are made with respect to available and acceptable information is critical, because decisions may be suboptimal, and in the medium- or long-range view they may even be maladaptive. Whether or not we can

identify the cognitive dimension in an actual case study, explicit consideration of this variable serves to remind us that there can be no causality between environmental parameters and adaptive patterning and that adaptive response to an exogenic change cannot be uniquely predicted.

CHAPTER 16

Diachronic systems II: continuity and change

The preceding methodological discussion of adaptation and adaptive systems provides a conceptual framework capable of dealing effectively with the interrelationships between people and their environment. This paradigm allows systemic integration of the many environmental variables and, above all, the interactive processes that have been the subject of this book. This paradigm is ideally suited for diachronic analysis, and it subsumes the spatial dimension. In this concluding chapter, the adaptive-system paradigm will be applied to briefly examine two key adaptive transformations in human history and then to evaluate the adaptive modifications that permitted the remarkable persistence of hydraulic systems over some five millennia in Egypt and Mesopotamia. This presentation will take the form of an interpretative synopsis, lightly documented, that is intended to illustrate the roles of multiple variables in cultural change or continuity.

Adaptive transformation in the Pleistocene record: hominization

In considering cultural adaptations in a diachronic perspective, the fundamental differences between early prehistorical and historical adaptive systems must be emphasized. In the case of the Lower and Middle Paleolithic, prior to about 35,000 B.P., we are dealing with rudimentary adaptive structures characterized by few components and interlinkages, initially perhaps not substantially more complex than those of modern chimpanzees. In the case of the Upper Paleolithic and more recent adaptive systems there is evidence for intricate multicomponent structures analogous to the systems common to modern humanity and prone to an almost unlimited range of partly idiosyncratic variation. The material residues of Lower Paleolithic adaptive systems show minimal directional variation over hundreds of thousands of years, whereas material culture has been notable for exponential rates of change in more recent millennia, when ethnic discontinuities have appeared every few thousand years as nations and empires have waxed and waned.

Whatever phylogenetic lineages are recognized, early hominid radiation was rapid between about 5 and 1 million years ago. There was progressive divergence, or at least character displacement, whether behavioral, ecological, or morphological (Brown and Wilson, 1956). The location of all early hominid sites in mosaic environments along ecotones of the seasonally dry African savanna argues for a sympatric range, with exploitation of multiple interfingering ecological opportunities (Butzer, 1977b, 1978g).

Presumably the cultural innovations reflected in early stone tool making and animal butchery at sites such as Olduvai and Koobi Fora laid the foundations (Zihlman and Tanner, 1978) for unprecedented species success, greatly accelerating character displacement (Butzer, 1977b). At such a point, perhaps about 2 million B.P., a polymorphic group of more evolved hominids began to diverge rapidly from other hominids of the time. By a million years ago, at the latest, these protohumans had increased in numbers and had completely displaced their closest relatives, the remaining lineage(s) of australopithecines. Whether this disappearance was due to direct or indirect competition for resources, or even to outright aggression or predation, is at present unknown.

The fact that geographical distributions and even site locales overlapped makes microenvironmental differentiation of the earliest hominids particularly difficult. Also, most nonarchaeological early hominid sites represent places of natural burial, or of death and burial. Dental wear, such as abrasion and chipping, differs considerably from one specimen to another and suggests that early hominids used a considerable variety of food types, differing according to seasonal and regional opportunities. This is, of course, exactly what some early archaeological sites such as those in Olduvai Bed I (Leakey, 1971) demonstrate. The very versatility of early hominid diets makes the interpretation of dental wear difficult and may well obscure significant differences in overall dietary preferences, food-procurement activities, and foraging and hunting abilities.

The most widespread and durable of mid-Pleistocene cultural manifestations was the Acheulian (Butzer, 1971a:Chapter 26; Butzer and

Isaac, 1975). This Lower Paleolithic stone-tool complex dates between 1.5 million and 200,000 B.P. and is characterized by large bifacially worked tools, especially hand axes and cleavers. Those Acheulian sites that preserve animal bone indicate a heavy emphasis on large game, but logic and chance preservation of plant remains argue that vegetable foods also were important. The overall range of bone remains argues that hunting was still opportunistic rather than specialized, but in contrast to the record of earlier sites such as Olduvai Bed I, there is evidence that larger, often adult, animals were hunted, that hunters favored the most readily bagged forms of big game in any one area, and that dietary preferences focused attention on a generally smaller range of food sources.

It is therefore apparent that the Acheulians, who initially were biological representatives of *Homo erectus*, were culturally distinct from the earlier australopithecines and the earliest bearers of human culture. They dispersed over a much larger geographical range, and the repetitiveness of their archaeological residues suggests a strongly patterned, if rudimentary, human way of life. It is probable that the subsistence strategy required larger territories, and thus far fewer Acheulians could be supported in any one area than had been the case for the australopithecines. Mobility and the periodicity of seasonal activities may also have been significantly greater.

The adaptive system(s) of the Acheulians were remarkably stable in both time and space. A notable feature of Acheulian material culture is that stone-tool assemblages show no steady, unilinear progression to more varied, sophisticated, and artistic forms through time (Isaac, 1972, 1977). This argues for a long-term steady state, with little directional change. But it also implies a very low level of manipulative, cognitive, and organizational skills, presumably related to biological and intellectual limitations, as well as to the very small store of cumulative experience on which early humans had to build.

Change was more often random than cumulative, and the transition to *Homo sapiens* and ultimately to Upper Paleolithic adaptive systems was painfully circuitous and slow. The price in human suffering of such an inefficient evolutionary trajectory must have been high: In the course of almost 1.5 million years it is probable that many thousands of Acheulian isolates disappeared without issue in marginal environments or in the face of natural events beyond their adaptive capacity.

By 500,000 B.P. the Acheulians inhabited much of the three Old World continents, but their environmental adaptations cannot be dis-

cerned from the surviving material culture, which exhibits little geographical variation of a functional rather than a stylistic nature. Instead, the known sites from Africa, Europe, and Asia suggest an underlying preference for open grassy environments, with large herds of
gregarious herbivores. The modern environments of such sites include
deserts and forests, but their geo-archaeological context indicates that
semiarid or subhumid macroenvironments prevailed at the time of occupancy (Butzer and Cooke, 1981). Such sites range from what were
tropical savannas in equatorial East Africa to what were montane grasslands in glacial-age Spain. Temperature conditions were less important
than was a rich and relatively dependable supply of game. In fact, the
cold glacials opened up large areas of light woodland or parkland in
middle-latitude Europe, greatly increasing the biomass of large herbivores that were attractive to Acheulian hunter-gatherers, who sought
out a familiar niche. The warmer interglacials, on the other hand, saw
a return of closed forests and a low biomass, reducing the human
carrying capacity. At low latitudes, desert and rainforest were unfavorable. The Acheulian perspective of an optimal environment was predicated on open habitats with high animal biomass.

Within the wide macroenvironmental range of such open grassland
or savanna vegetation, it appears that sites were preferentially located
with respect to water resources (stream channels, springs, karstic
caves, lakeshores, and coasts) and suitable stone for working. In some
habitats, Acheulian groups appear to have circulated through a number of temporary or seasonal camps in the course of their annual
rounds, whereas in others they favored a cycle based on an advantageous base camp, used repeatedly at a specific time of year (see Figures
13-1 and 13-2).

The picture given here of small bands of technologically simple
hunter-gatherers, scattered at intervals across the open landscapes of
Africa and Eurasia, is compatible with the osteological evidence for
considerable biological variability (especially cranial polymorphism) of
Homo erectus in time and space. If sufficiently numerous populations
were isolated in a peripheral continental area or by surrounding unattractive biomes, spurts of biological evolution or cultural innovation or
both would have become increasingly likely.

Such progressive regional centers with accelerated directional selection become evident for the period between 500,000 and 200,000 B.P., in
the form of increasingly polytypic biological populations (representing
early forms of *Homo sapiens*, according to many authors), and as a multi-

tude of transitional material cultures ultimately superseded by regional variants of the Middle Paleolithic (Middle Stone Age in sub-Saharan Africa, Mousterian in Eurasia). As larger and more differentiated populations now dispersed from one or more centers, major biological and cultural discontinuities appeared in the archaeological record of surrounding areas, where population numbers were very low, and in the records of central areas of Acheulian activity, where stabilizing selection and steady-state equilibrium had long inhibited change.

Given the simple technology and organization of the Acheulians, it is probable that aperiodic fluctuations in the food resource base caused recurrent hardship. Would repeated environmental stress or long-term ecological changes have had a net positive or negative impact on human evolution? Overall, stress should have favored survival of the better-adapted groups. In areas with diffuse concentrations of Acheulian groups, alternating sets of good and bad years may, in fact, have accelerated evolution (Clark, 1960; Hiernaux, 1963).

During decades in which resource productivity was high, groups would tend to multiply and disperse, at least initially favoring isolation of breeding populations, with random loss of genes (genetic drift). During decades of declining productivity, groups would abandon marginal areas, and a centripetal movement focused on the most reliable sources of food and water would set in. At such times the remnants of temporarily isolated breeding populations would be drawn into larger regional aggregates, favoring gene flow. On a sufficiently large scale, environmental fluctuations could stimulate biological evolution through a feedback mechanism involving continued selection for ability to manipulate culture, on the one hand, and alternating genetic drift and gene flow, on the other (Butzer, 1977b).

It is therefore probable that environmental factors played a basic role in the biological evolution and cultural adaptation that led to the emergence of *Homo sapiens*. In my view, one prerequisite to such evolution was an unequal distribution of resources at the subcontinental scale, so that subcontinental regions included several areas of intermediate size with sufficient density and productivity of resource opportunities to support sizable clusters of population groups, while large intervening areas were incompletely occupied. The second prerequisite was long-term cyclic variation in resource productivity that created sufficient ecological stress to promote natural selection and also set into motion alternating centrifugal and centripetal movements of dispersed breeding populations (see Figure 13-4), to favor genetic drift and gene flow, on the one hand, and directional selection for new adaptive traits, on the other. Such circumstances would provide potentials for rapid local change in peripheral or marginal settings, with subsequent transformation of the biological and cultural populations in the central or optimal settings, an example of punctuated equilibrium in the sense of Eldredge and Gould (1972) (Butzer, 1977b).

The traditional picture of the advent of anatomically modern *Homo sapiens sapiens* involves a European scenario in which the Neandertalers and their Mousterian material culture were replaced circa 37,000 B.P. by large populations of essentially modern Cro-Magnon type coming in from the east; these new Upper Paleolithic peoples were superior in their technological and organizational skills, and they developed the first cave art.

However, modern-looking *Homo sapiens sapiens* at Border Cave in South Africa (Rightmire, 1979) is linked with the Howieson's Poort industry and can be dated (by extrapolation of radiocarbon-dated sedimentation rates and correlation of cold-climate roof-spall horizons) to the cold isotope stage 5b, circa 90,000 B.P. (Butzer, Beaumont, and Vogel, 1978). Another modern physical type is represented in the Mousterian levels of Jebel Qafzeh Cave in Israel, where it may have appeared as early as 65,000 B.P. (Farrand, 1979). These fossils imply that rapid biological evolution was going on in Africa, and perhaps also in Asia, at a time when traditional Middle Paleolithic industries continued to dominate the Old World.

In Europe, the Mousterian–Upper Paleolithic interface appears to date earlier in the east than in the west: earlier than 44,000 B.P. in parts of the Balkans (Klein, 1973), as compared with about 35,000 B.P. in northern Spain (Butzer, 1981c). This implies that replacement of the Neandertalers in Europe was by no means sudden. It may even be possible, as more precise information becomes available, to confirm a degree of cultural continuity in parts of France and northern Spain.

In overviewing the process of hominization that was essentially completed between about 90,000 and 20,000 B.P., there are vague configurations implying interregional gradients in biological evolution and in the complexity of material culture. The repeated temporal discontinuities also apparent in the record suggest that trends were not identical from place to place and were not uninterrupted in any one region, let alone subject to linear or exponential directional change. The Acheulian dispersal into new extratropical environments clearly involved a major adaptive response. The question whether adaptational changes permitted this expansion of the *oikoumene* or whether the expansion dictated readaptation is not resolvable and to some degree is redundant. Particularly interesting is the pattern of new biomes occupied and the traditional niche selected.

An important distinction should be drawn between material culture, on the one hand, and intangible adaptive strategies, on the other: It appears that tool kits were far less important for human adaptation in a changeable environment than were organizational devices. Yet standard archaeological procedures are almost exclusively focused on the artifactual residues and their patterning. Consequently, although the biophysical evidence leaves no doubt as to repeated environmental changes of different amplitudes and wavelengths, there is no archaeological case for causally related technological or behavioral readjustments. The argument that both culture and environment served as catalysts for human evolution (Butzer, 1977c) is consonant with the evidence, but it must be made on theoretical grounds.

Early Pleistocene to middle Pleistocene lifeways were necessarily adjusted to survival in environments variable in space and often unpredictable in time. With limited technology and minimal information, protohuman groups had little material and social facility to mitigate the impact of environmental perturbations. Their key strategy appears to have been one of high flexibility and risk minimization, based on multiple-resource options perceived in a large and heterogeneous economic space. Holling (1973:21) described such a system as resilient and capable of absorbing and accommodating future events "in whatever unexpected form they may take." Such a high degree of flexibility would favor a steady-state equilibrium. In the event of a directional trajectory, during the later mid-Pleistocene, perturbations probably favored dynamic readjustments within the existing adaptive system, rather than abrupt changes that would be perceptible as discontinuities in the archaeological record. It is therefore probable that the observed discontinuities represent reoccupations of long-abandoned areas and that directional selection was limited to peripheral areas that were demonstrably precocious in their biological or cultural evolution.

Holocene adaptive transformations: taming the environment

During the last 10 millennia of the Pleistocene, cultural evolution became accelerated and diversified to the degree that it totally overshadowed biological evolution. Microevolution continued, of course, including reductions in facial size and cranial musculature in response to better food processing, as well as complex physiological adaptations resulting from selection for individuals less susceptible to the epidemic and chronic diseases arising from greater settlement densities, dietary shifts, and the utilization of new biomes and habitats. But primary interest focuses on the dramatic cultural transformations that preceded, accompanied, and resulted from the invention of food-producing subsistence modes.

The achievement of intellectual capacities and cultural systems similar to those of modern humans was first demonstrated by the Upper Paleolithic peoples of Eurasia, who aggregated in large groups, utilized good site locales repeatedly over longer periods, effectively hunted selected big game in subarctic environments, and colonized the New World. The rapid dispersal of Paleoindians across North America and down the mountainous spine of the Americas to Tierra del Fuego that began about 12,500 B.P. took less than four millennia. The rapidity and apparent success of the Paleoindian movements, across almost the full range of available world environments, constituted perhaps the most impressive feat of Pleistocene man. It argues not only for viable subsistence modes but also for organizational talents, initiative, and flexibility in no way inferior to those displayed by the western European nations after A.D. 1492. The repeated stone-tool innovations of the Upper Paleolithic suggest stylistic and technological sophistication, and the Magdalenian cave art (ca. 17,000–11,000 B.P.) speaks for artistic competence and aesthetic values comparable to our own. These specialized big-game hunters represented only one adaptive response generated by modern humans endowed with complex cultural capacities. The way of life evolved by these hunters was successful, surviving in the adaptations of the modern Eskimo, but in the long run it was less successful than the broad-spectrum foraging modes developing in the complex ecosystems of warmer environments.

The late Paleolithic of the Nile Valley and Israel, as discussed in Chapter 14, represented a new concentration of subsistence efforts on highly productive and reliable plant foods that required new harvesting and processing techniques (e.g., hafted sickles and grinding equipment). In other regions, hunting methods were developed that ensured high food returns from systematic exploitation of small mammals, whereas aquatic habitats favored large-scale fishing and other seafood-gathering activities. In each case, attention was turned to a variety of small plant foods or small-bodied animals that could be regularly harvested in quantity with relatively little risk, provided that sophisticated traps, baskets, nets, and weirs were available. This shift to small, short-lived, highly productive "*r*-selected" species represents a global trend between 18,000 and 8000 B.P., allowing larger and more sedentary populations in habitats rich in such species (Hayden, 1981). Such broad-spectrum foragers managed their resources with expert information and refined subsistence strategies designed to tap a variety of resources in the course of the seasonal cycle (Harris, 1977). Not surprisingly, most surviving hunter-gatherers in the ethnographic record were adapted to one form or other of broad-spectrum foraging.

The impetus toward end-Pleistocene adaptive transformation may have been an increase in population pressure as technologically competent populations began to expand and occupy previously under-utilized resource spaces. Cohen (1976*b*) argued that as the potential for territorial expansion was exhausted, population growth stimulated dietary readjustments. A shift from desirable but scarce large game to more plentiful but less palatable secondary resources (*r*-selected species) would increase the supply and reliability of edible calories. There is little doubt that demographic changes accompanied and followed changes in technology or subsistence patterning or both. But we have yet to identify an instance in which demographic pressures actually preceded shifts in prehistorical technology and settlement. Cohen's 14 archaeological criteria of demographic change (Cohen, 1976*b*:78–83) are based on observed (i.e., ongoing or completed) socioeconomic changes, so that he cannot hope to prove prior demographic stress on archaeological criteria. Better-documented case studies in more recent millennia (Butzer, 1976*c*; Kirch, 1980*b*) have suggested that demographic changes were more likely to accompany adaptive transformations, although they evidently helped trigger or force subsequent adaptive modifications.

A more probable stimulus for end-Pleistocene adaptive transformations was the combination of dynamic, innovative cultural systems against a background of regionally distinct resource patterns. Environments with abundant large game (*K*-selected species) (Hayden, 1981) saw the development of specialized hunting economies, whereas diversified habitats with a wide range of suitable *r*-selected species favored the development of intensive and complex harvesting strategies. This trend to diversification, experimentation, and innovation probably was accelerated by end-Pleistocene biome shifts as well as human expansion into new environments, examples of which have been docu-

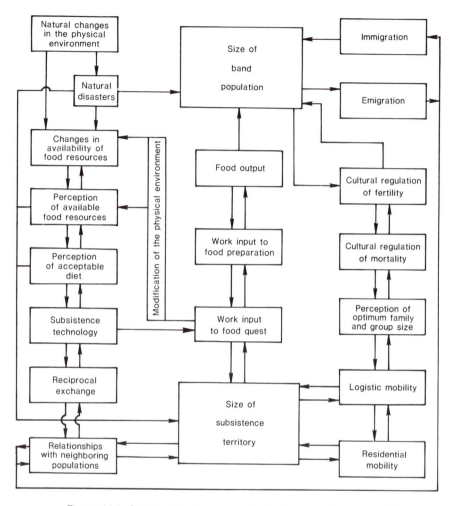

Figure 16-1. Systematic interactions affecting hunter-gatherer population levels. From Harris (1978:Figure 1). Copyright © 1978 Gerald Duckworth and Co. Ltd., with permission of University of Pittsburgh Press and Gerald Duckworth and Co.

mented for the European Mesolithic (Phillips, 1980:Chapter 4), the South African Wilton (Deacon, 1976), and the Archaic of the east-central United States (McMillan and Klippel, 1981). Harris (1977, 1978) has articulated several stress models that incorporate environmental change, degree of sedentism, harvesting-efficiency, and population pressure. The change from Pleistocene steady-state interactions to end-Pleistocene dynamic equilibrium, with positive-feedback loops, is illustrated in Figures 16-1 and 16-2.

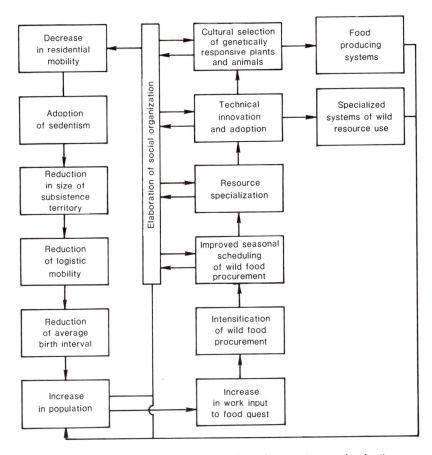

Figure 16-2. Positive-feedback interactions favoring increased sedentism, more efficient exploitation of wild foods, and/or food production. From Harris (1978:Figure 2). Copyright © 1978 Gerald Duckworth and Co. Ltd., with permission of University of Pittsburgh Press and Gerald Duckworth and Co.

Even before the close of the Pleistocene, the increased diversity of subsistence strategies between and within different environments had created a mosaic of diverging adaptive systems in the Near East (see Chapter 14). The resulting spatial gradient in information favored periodic diffusion of technology, followed by local reprocessing of new information according to multiple permutations. These repeated recombinations favored further innovations, to increase diversification as well as the regional dynamism of adaptive change, in terms of subsistence strategies, resource scheduling, and settlement patterning. In a context of controlled resource exploitation, combined with such a diversified bank of information, it is highly probable that deliberate manipulations of suitable plants and animals eventually included planting and breeding and conscious or unconscious selection. In this sense, early domestication was an integral part of a broader adaptive transformation that included many other viable and even competitive options. Whether or not domestication could take place depended on the presence of suitable domesticates. Whether or not domestication did take place depended both on the available domesticates and on the comparative resource productivities of wild and cultivated foods.

Nowhere did early domestication immediately assume a dominant subsistence role. Instead, the archaeological record typically shows two millennia or more of mixed economies, including large permanent settlements sustained almost exclusively by wild plant and animal foods (e.g., Jericho and Tell Bouqras) and complex local mosaics of either dominantly foraging or dominantly farming communities. In southwestern Asia, this transitional period of protofarming (Figure 16-3), with multiple subsistence and settlement options within each adaptive system, dates approximately 10,500 to 8000 B.P. Even thereafter, different adaptive systems, predicated primarily on domesticated crops and livestock, preferred different sets of domesticates, used different tool kits, and adopted different settlement styles; for a partly dated review of the literature, see the work of Bender (1975). Only about 6800 B.P. (calibrated to 5500 B.C.) did a standard model of dry-farming agriculture with a full range of cereals and herd animals emerge in the summer-dry Mediterranean environments between Iran and the Aegean Basin. But by the same time, other adaptive variants on this farming model were already widely dispersed in temperate Europe and the arid Sahara. The picture in Mesoamerica is similar, with the agricultural transition beginning as early as 9000 B.P. and terminating after 3000 B.P. (MacNeish, 1964, 1972; Flannery, 1968), a time when agricultural traits were already established in Peru and were penetrating the American Southwest as well as the Mississippi Basin.

The protoagricultural transition remains poorly understood, because the artifactual record is ambiguous, the bio-archaeological data base is incomplete, and interpretative models are biased by the sharp conceptual dichotomy between wild and domesticated resources. The imperfect record suggests remarkably diverse adaptive modes, much intraregional variability, and temporal shifts in economic emphases or equilibria. The process was not irreversible, because groups could revert to full-time foraging during years of unusual stress, and domesticated plants and animals could also become feral (i.e., revert to the wild state).

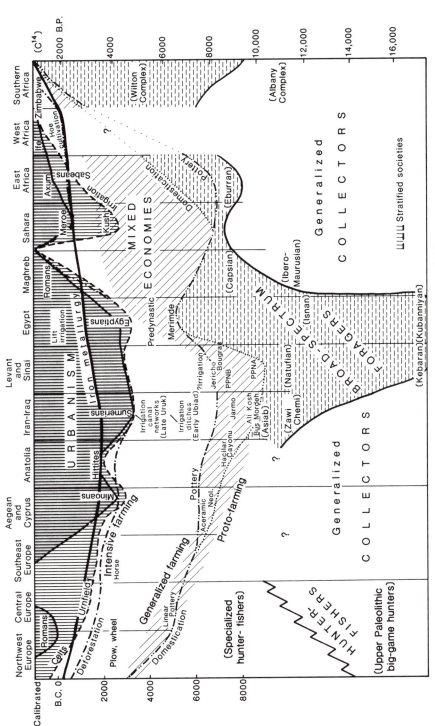

Figure 16-3. Human adaptations in later prehistory: Near East, Europe, and Africa.

The process of agricultural transformation did not follow a predictable linear trajectory, but was spatially and temporally discontinuous because of episodes of accelerated growth and regression that were not necessarily synchronous or general.

Even when once established, agricultural subsistence was a dynamic adaptation. Agriculture did not necessarily provide more and better food at less cost. Agriculture is labor-intensive and demands population. Furthermore, the high-starch and poor-quality-protein diet was not ideal and often was unreliable, and nucleation promoted crowding, poor sanitation, and disease, thus reducing fertility and increasing mortality. Generalized farming, complemented by wild foods, provided a better diet and greater flexibility, but it could support only a smaller population, and it required large resource spaces. Specialized farming (e.g., irrigation) could support larger populations on specialized, less nutritious diets, but it was susceptible to severe fluctuations in production and was carried out in restricted areas favorable to the periodic ravages of epidemic disease as well as decimation by endemic parasites. Socioeconomic processes included trends toward property defense, kinship reciprocity, rigid sexual division of labor, craft specialization, stratification, and territoriality. Thus the agricultural transformation was characterized by systemic interplay that increased its complexity through time.

Paradoxically, this transformation sought to increase resource productivity and reliability, but the resulting pressures for greater intensification led to ecosystem simplification and reduced diversity. This eventually increased the risks of short-term environmental perturbations and long-term degradation, possibly requiring demographic curtailment or greater energy expenditures or both (Sanders and Webster, 1978).

Agricultural colonization of new habitats within a region of developing protoagriculture was an integral part of the adaptive transformation. In fact, Flannery (1973) argued that cultivation and stock raising became competitive subsistence options only when wild plants and animals could not be harvested in sufficient quantity, after groups had moved from productive and complex montane environments into drier and less productive lowlands of the Near East. At that point, familiar potential domesticates assumed critical importance.

The colonization of new biomes, such as the woodlands of temperate Europe and the better-watered highlands and oases of the Sahara, represented a new adaptive transformation. This can be outlined in several stages in a model that is supported by archaeological data from the Neolithic of southeastern and central Europe, as well as data from arid environments such as the Sahara and lowland Mesopotamia:

1. It is probable that the initial dispersal was made possible by a small number of enabling innovations that facilitated the segregation of reproductively viable groups equipped to move into potentially suitable unoccupied lands such as those beyond the Aegean Basin or the Saharan borderlands. Emigration followed, with the creation of new settlements (e.g., in Yugoslavia and Bulgaria and in desert floodplains and oases).

2. Within a generation or two, numerous adaptive innovations were necessary in response to local conditions. New soil types had to be evaluated with respect to more familiar ones. Land-clearance techniques had to be adapted to different vegetation communities, such as deeply rooted grass swards in grass-forest mosaics in Europe, and to different edaphic conditions on floodplains and in the channels of intermittent or spring-fed streams in the Sahara and lowland Mesopotamia. Shifts and changes in the planting season in response to winter cold, summer heat, and drought were experimented with. If summers were both hot and wet, as in Bulgaria, crops could be planted in the spring instead of autumn. Traditional strategies of site location, settlement organization, and building construction probably required reevaluation in regard to drainage, access to better soils, climate, important raw materials, and new demographic trends.

3. Interactions with resident hunter-gatherers, such as those apparent in Yugoslavia, favored further reevaluation of foraging techniques to make use of special foods and medicinal plants and to improve hunting and fishing strategies. Outbreeding of domesticated cattle and pigs with their wild prototypes, as verified in Hungary, provided better-adapted livestock. At the same time, a selection of technological and organizational traits may have been adopted by the indigenous foragers, including tool types and incidental or permanent keeping of some domesticated animals, perhaps initially acquired by theft.

4. The stage was then set for further expansion and adaptation as groups of settlers leapfrogged to more distant habitats that approximated familiar ecological requisites (e.g., the loess basins of central Europe and the more mesic highlands of the Sahara). More fundamental adaptation followed in these new settlement centers, including conscious or unconscious selection of new plant mutations for greater productivity under different conditions of climate and competition.

New crops, some initially representing "weeds," emerged in the fields and orchards of temperate Europe. Stock raising selected against sheep and goats in the wet floodplains of Hungary and the upland forests of Germany, but in favor of cattle and pigs.

5. Spatially concentrated in the disjunct basins of central Europe and the isolated highlands of the Sahara, and open to increased contact with indigenous foragers, the discontinuous population clusters of agricultural settlers began to develop regional identities, favoring cultural and biological divergence and the emergence of new adaptive systems. In their turn, local hunter-gatherers were increasingly assimilated or absorbed, but in unusual cases they were driven off or eliminated.

6. Eventually the new regional agricultural system was ready for further modification to allow another sequence of successful expansion, either into new biomes, such as the north European glacial plain and the Maghreb, or by way of filling in unoccupied interstitial spaces, as in southeastern and central Europe.

This basic colonization model can be applied to examine a range of similar processes, from the Neolithic expansion into temperate Europe to the Anglo-American settlement of the United States, with minor adjustments. Central to such transformations are two antithetical trends, namely, a diversifying and directional selection for the most successful traits of the adaptive system coupled with a fundamental modification and increasing simplification of the ecosystem. New long-term hazards to sustained productivity began to emerge in the form of soil depletion and destruction and hydrological change, often associated with floodplain salinization. In their efforts to control the environment in the interest of reducing risk and increasing productivity, people unwittingly imposed a Near Eastern subsistence landscape on new and frequently unsuitable environments. At first, habitats were altered, then frequently eliminated, until the original biome had been transformed almost beyond recognition. Eventually, agricultural success became equated with an imposed cultural landscape that was perceived as a taming of nature. But, although seemingly tamed, these simplified ecosystems were increasingly fragile, unpredictable, and liable to irreparable deterioration (see Chapter 8).

The final stage in ecosystemic transformation was the intensification of agricultural systems that accompanied the evolution of complex societies. In the Near East and East Asia, intensification was intimately linked with hydraulic manipulations, in particular, artificial irrigation involving canalization, water control, and lifting devices. On the floodplains of the Tigris-Euphrates, Nile, Indus, and Huangho, such artificial irrigation began to supplement dry farming and natural irrigation. High-productivity agriculture, in turn, allowed increasing population densities and, in the growing urban centers, specialized craftsmen such as potters, metalsmiths, woodworkers, and shipbuilders. Industrial products were exchanged over great distances by the new merchant class. In the resulting urban societies, multitiered economies and complex social stratification became the rule, not the exception. These, in turn, supported the increasingly large political superstructures that dominated ancient history.

The positive-feedback mechanisms favoring increased productivity, population increases, social inequality, and the emergence of the state have been incorporated in a comprehensive model by Redman (1978) (Figure 16-4). The organizational structures provided by the state sought to protect both the population and agricultural productivity from environmental perturbations by spatial averaging (through effective exchange networks and annexation of adjacent adaptive subsystems with different resources) as well as temporal averaging (storage of surplus production for redistribution during times of shortage) (Isbell, 1978).

A similar ecological role in dry-farming areas was played by the introduction of plow agriculture, supplemented by repeated technological innovations in plow types, animal traction, field rotation, and fertilization. Here, too, socioeconomic stratification ensued, together with the development of settlement hierarchies and increasing degrees of urbanization (Figure 16-3). Urban centers, based on intensively utilized rural hinterlands, served to define a new reciprocal relationship between culture and environment that was as different from extensive subsistence farming as Neolithic adaptations had been from Pleistocene foraging lifeways.

In sum, the train of end-Pleistocene to late prehistorical adaptive transformations exemplified in the Near East, Europe, Asia, Mesoamerica, and Andean South America comprised an apparently inexorable series of strong positive-feedback loops, generally involving greater human control over the environment. Each feedback sequence involved socioeconomic, demographic, and ecological changes of a fundamental kind, equilibrium thresholds that required redefinition of the interrelationships between the key variables.

Although end-Pleistocene environmental shifts may have given impetus to the contemporaneous diversification of foraging modes, subse-

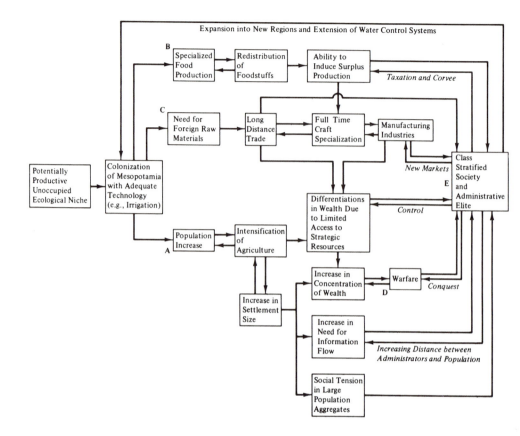

Figure 16-4. Positive-feedback interactions favoring the emergence of a stratified urban society in Mesopotamia. From Redman (1978:Figure 14.2) (copyright
Academic Press Inc., with permission).

quent transformations such as agricultural origins, expansion, and intensification, as well as urbanization and industrialization, show no
significant linkage to environmental flux. The environmental potential
had a far greater impact in the sense that the most durable domesticates were originally native to restricted areas of the Near East, Southeast Asia, and Mesoamerica. The first steps in their domestication necessarily took place in these same areas. But from that point onward,
agricultural adaptive systems attempted to accommodate these exotic
domesticates to new environmental circumstances. As a result, the

world's major agricultural systems were compromises between historical trajectory and regional environmental opportunities and constraints. This suggests that the major adaptive transformations of the
archaeological record were to a large degree idiosyncratic or even stochastic, rather than deterministic. People have traditionally sought to
impose adaptive solutions developed elsewhere and under different
circumstances in new situations or environments. This inherent bias is,
of course, central to the concept of culture. It also points to the implicit
purpose of adaptive systems, to provide a *modus vivendi* with the biophysical environment that is consonant with the predilections of the
cultural heritage.

Modifications of regional adaptive systems:
historical periodicities

The great adaptive transformations that resulted in intensive agricultural systems, urbanized societies, and centralized states also made possible the high civilizations that have so long been major foci for archaeological and historical research in Mesoamerica, the Near East, and East
Asia. The repeated rise and fall of the associated kingdoms and empires
have generally been interpreted in ontogenetic terms. But, as pointed
out earlier, these sociopolitical structures can also be examined as regional adaptive systems subject to external and internal inputs and requiring periodic accommodations in technology or behavior.

Complex societies frequently responded to novel inputs by relatively
sudden equilibrium shifts, leading to more fundamental sociopolitical
transformations, with or without a change in adaptive strategy. It appears that the time trajectories of high civilizations, in particular, have
tended to resemble a metastable-equilibrium pattern, marked by
thresholds at which positive and negative shifts in the equilibrium level
have taken place (see Figure 15-2). Whereas the established developmental model for civilizations generally assumes a succession of ever-
higher homeostatic plateaus, followed by abrupt collapse, the systemic
model can do justice to both the steady-state and metastable-equilibrium concepts, while also allowing for long-term, nondisjunctive directional trends (dynamic equilibrium) (Butzer, 1980c).

It is therefore possible to view civilizations as ecosystems that
emerge in response to sets of ecological opportunities, that is, eco-
niches to be exploited. Over a span of time, a variety of internal (social)

and external (environmental) adjustments will inevitably take place; some of these will be "successful," leading to demographic expansion, and others will be "retrograde," requiring demographic curtailment. These demographic trends commonly are associated with and are parallel to the ups and downs of political power, although this is not always the case. However, political structures generally are less durable than either cultural identity or ethnic consciousness, and these, in turn, are less persistent than the basic adaptive system on which they are predicated. This is consistent with the ecosystem analogy, because the structural components of a population are devices to ensure adaptive success (not vice versa).

The processes integral to ascendancy and retrogression are reconcilable with a systemic model. Ascendancy can be identified as a sociopolitical transformation in which structural organization favors an optimal flow of energy within the system. A useful ecological concept is that of trophic levels among biotic communities, in which organisms with similar feeding habits define successive tiers interlinked in a vertical food chain. An efficient social hierarchy comprises several "trophic" levels arranged in a low-angle pyramid, supported by a broad base of agricultural producers and linked to the central administrative apex by a reasonable number of middle-echelon bureaucratic agencies (see Figure 15-3). The vertical structures serve to channel food and information, and an efficient energy flow implies conditions allowing each trophic level to flourish in a steady state or even a dynamic equilibrium.

A flatter pyramid with little or no vertical structure will provide less information flow and thus will limit the potential productivity of the substrate. This version of the model allows for growth, with new technological or organizational devices of external or internal origin favoring expanded energy generation at lower trophic levels. On the other hand, a steeper pyramid, with a top-heavy bureaucracy, will place excessive demands on the producers and thus will jeopardize the food chain (see Table 15-2). The steep-pyramid model represents a system prone to metastable equilibrium, with external and internal inputs liable to undermine the productive substrate and thus to destroy the nonproductive superstructure; the probable result will be a much-simplified pyramid.

This ecosystemic view of civilizations can be illustrated with reference to ancient Egypt (Butzer, 1976c, 1980c, 1981b).

The political history of Egypt has traditionally been organized into several cycles: the Old Kingdom (ca. 2760–2225 B.C.), the Middle Kingdom (2035–1668 B.C.), and the New Kingdom (1570–1070 B.C.). Each reached its apex during an episode of strong central government, followed by a long period of stagnation and eventual decline. The First Dynasty (ca. 3170–2970) represents another such culmination of a less clearly delineated protohistorical development. Each phase of political devolution was accompanied by economic deterioration and temporary or substantial demographic decline. The greatest population density, prior to the radical technological improvements of the last 100 years, was achieved during early Roman times.

Episodes of growth in Egypt were made possible by such innovations as improved irrigation organization, devices for controlled water distribution during bad flood years, lift mechanisms to allow cultivation of marginal areas or several crops per year, and new cultigens better suited for poorer or drier soils and for summer cultivation (in an agricultural system originally geared only to postflood winter crops). The basic impact of such improved organizational efficiency, new technology, and expansion and intensification of agriculture was to increase both the labor force and national productivity. In response, it is probable that the population of Egypt increased from less than a million under the First Dynasty to about 5 million in the second century B.C.

It has commonly been assumed that floodplain irrigation provided an ecosystem that is uniquely productive and predictable, one in which environmental inputs do not generate significant change. In fact, however, this is a gross oversimplification.

Predynastic, Old Kingdom, and Middle Kingdom agriculture was based on no more than rudimentary flood-basin irrigation that lacked the lift technology essential to (a) cultivate the entire floodplain, (b) guarantee a reasonable minimum of food during poor flood years, and (c) allow more than a single crop per plot per year, except in gardens watered by hand. Pharaonic agriculture was extensive, rather than intensive, with perhaps half the agricultural lands used for grazing or left fallow in 2000 B.C., and large parts of the potentially fertile floodplain were still underdeveloped in the eleventh century B.C.

Irrigation was organized not centrally but locally. Food-storage facilities were limited to private domains until the New Kingdom, and even then public redistribution in times of need was ineffective. A substantial body of data shows that flood levels declined drastically during the Second Dynasty (ca. 2970–2760 B.C.), that catastrophic Nile failures recurred at least several times at the end of the Old Kingdom (ca. 2250–2000 B.C.), that equally catastrophic aberrantly high floods marked the second half of the Middle Kingdom (1840–1770 B.C.), and that major negative readjustments in Nile hydrology took place over several generations shortly after 1200 B.C., when the Nubian floodplain was no longer inundated by the Nile and had to be abandoned.

These facts provide a different perspective for evaluation of the long intervals of economic stagnation, demographic decline, and political discontinuity in pharaonic Egypt. The common denominators in each case were rural depopulation and decreasing economic productivity. The responsible processes were complex and involved at least two of three major factors: excessive demands on the productive population; a high incidence of poor or destructively high Nile floods; insecurity due to political instability, foreign rule, or invasion. Each retrograde phase coincided with negative social developments within the society, as well as negative environmental or social interventions from without.

In the cases of the Old and New Kingdom, internal social evolution was unfavorable for at least three centuries prior to political breakdown, suggesting that external inputs may have triggered drastic readjustment of a sociopolitical system already in a state of metastable equilibrium. However, for the First and Second Dynasties and the Middle Kingdom there is no tangible evidence of overtaxation; instead, breakdown took place within a century of the first hints of political weakness, arguing for severe and unpredictable stress exerted on an otherwise functional system. Strong oscillations in productivity since the eighth century B.C. were less coherent, as a result of recurrent foreign intervention.

Several key variables can be identified in this analysis of the periods of growth and decline. First, a potent but not universal factor was a progressive social pathology, linked to our model of a top-heavy and metastable sociopolitical pyramid. Wittfogel (1957) described this as progressive overexploitation of the masses by a growing unproductive elite, with resulting social disequilibrium and eventual politicoeconomic collapse. This process can be discerned in the cases of the Old and New Kingdoms, as well as during the late Roman and Byzantine periods. It is not verifiable during the Second Dynasty nor during the decline of the Middle Kingdom.

The importance of leadership, then as now, is equally apparent as a second key variable. Foreign intervention is a third. Until the Hyksos invasion of 1668 B.C., Egyptian society had been remarkably self-sufficient and had functioned to some degree as an approximation to a closed system; after the Hyksos interlude the New Kingdom Empire resembled an open system, and with the Assyrian incursion in 664 B.C., Egypt became a subsystem of a much larger socioeconomic network that embraced the Near East and ultimately the whole Mediterranean world.

A fourth critical variable was ecological stress, as a result of Nile behavior. The co-agency of Nile failure in the New Kingdom collapse is beyond question, and it is plausible in the disintegration of the Old Kingdom. In Second Dynasty and late Middle Kingdom times, aberrant Nile behavior was not only the single external variable in evidence but also the most prominent agent overall. This does not attribute the role of a determinant to Nile behavior. Instead, at a given level of technology, the Nile ecosystem provided a set of opportunities and constraints to agricultural productivity, varying from season to season, as well as from year to year.

The key variables singled out in this Egyptian example are more or less specific to Egypt. A fuller roster of potential variables affecting regional adaptive systems was given in Figure 15-1 and Table 15-2.

In terms of general evaluation, it can be argued that complex societies are buffered from external variables by multiple layers of technology, social organization, and exchange networks. The instability threshold for such a system is increasingly high in proportion to the number of negative-feedback mechanisms that can absorb or counteract the impacts of external variables, particularly on a short-term basis. But over the longer term, complex, "steep-sloped" systems are not stable; for similar views based on different arguments, see the work of May (1977) and Rappaport (1978). The very multiplicity of systemic components increased the probability of a chance concatenation of negative inputs. For example, the unexpected coincidence of poor leadership, social pathology, external political stress, and environmental perturbation can trigger a catastrophic train of mutually reinforcing events (Figure 16-5) that the system is unable to absorb.

A systemic model has a substantial advantage over the ontogenetic approach because it is nondeterministic and allows for chance. In fact, given the plethora of interlinked variables, modifications of a system that is highly structured, vertical, and metastable tend to be stochastic rather than teleological. It is a matter of probability, not organic inevitability, that cultural systems, like all human institutions, will eventually collapse, given a sufficiently long span of time.

A systemic model can be applied to more than functional or syn-

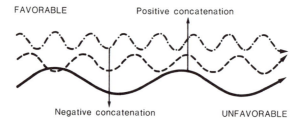

FAVORABLE   Positive concatenation

Negative concatenation   UNFAVORABLE

Figure 16-5. Several processes with varying periodicities may occasionally coincide, reinforcing one another and creating an overall tendency that is strongly unfavorable (low point of trends) or favorable (high point) to the system. Modified from Butzer (1980c:Figure 7).

chronic interpretation. The model proposed here includes synchronic components (see Figure 15-3) as well as temporal or diachronic dimensions (see Figures 15-2 and 16-5). It can therefore accommodate cyclic alternations between centuries when population and productivity increase and other intervals of demographic decline and political devolution. These periodicities are interpreted not as organic cycles of growth and senescence but as readjustments among the processual variables that maintain the adaptive system.

A civilization is indeed a type of adaptive system that can be studied objectively, as Adams (1978) has done in evaluating the impact of short-term agricultural maximization during periods of hierarchical control versus long-term mixed agrarian and pastoral economies during times of political fragmentation to identify two distinct modes of sustained adaptive equilibrium in Mesopotamia. Here, too, the discontinuities simulated by systemic collapse can be examined without recourse to traditional subjective and often moralistic interpretations such as "decadence."

The long course of Egyptian history exemplifies the dynamism of an adaptive system characterized by flexible but persistent social adjustments that were intimately linked to its floodplain environment. Major crises, external and internal, were successively overcome by reorganization of the political and economic superstructure, permitting new leases on national power or at least on economic productivity. Through all of this, the essential components of the sociocultural and environmental adaptations survived more or less intact until the nineteenth century A.D., even though the political identity (and, ultimately, also the ethnic identity) was transformed. In other words, Egyptian civilization did not die during times of political discontinuity. It survived as a flexible adaptive system, and the success of that adaptation is demonstrated in the fundamental continuities that link ancient and modern Egypt. Much the same can be said for ancient Mesopotamia and modern Iraq.

The adaptive system is of a far more basic character than the artistic and political achievements of a civilization. In this sense, it is at the level of the adaptive system that processual studies probably can be implemented with the greatest profit to evaluate cause-and-effect relationships of the kinds implied by adaptive modification and adjustment (see Table 15-1). In conclusion, it is apparent that civilizations behave as adaptive systems, becoming unstable when the energy demands of increasingly complex socioeconomic structures become excessive. Breakdowns result from chance concatenations of mutually reinforcing processes, not from senility or decadence.

Overview and prospect

Perhaps the most eloquent testimony of Pleistocene cultural capacities was the ability of a tropical organism to expand into almost all world environments with minimal physiological adaptation. Again and again, adjustments and embellishments of a flexible repertoire of subsistence modes appear to have allowed successful adaptation to new environments. Regionally, these also seem at times to have permitted higher population densities. However, the steady state was the rule rather than the exception in Pleistocene demographic development, possibly with the same relatively low birth and death rates characteristic of most hunter-gatherers of the ethnographic present. Population levels probably were adjusted to the minimal available resources (at a particular subsistence technology) during unusually poor years.

For the close of the Pleistocene, and even more so during the early Holocene, dynamic population trends can be inferred within at least several regional adaptive systems, presumably in response to changes in environmental resources, harvesting efficiency, settlement organization, and population pressure. These served to establish spatial gradients, also involving information and technology, and thus favored repeated diffusion at rates exceeding those typical of Pleistocene prehistory by several orders of magnitude. Repeated recombinations of information further guaranteed a continuing chain of innovations.

The subsequent prehistorical and historical records, in the wake of agricultural and pastoral origins, are marked by increasingly controlled (and simplified) ecosystems. Equally noteworthy is a new demographic strategy aimed at supporting high population levels, even at the risk of costly involuntary curtailment during recurrent intervals of environmental stress. High birth (and death) rates ensured the labor needed for subsistence strategies that involved low caloric output for heavy work input. Although the cause-and-effect relationships are not clear, increasingly labor-intensive agricultural modes and long-term population growth were repeatedly linked in several regional ecosystems. Dynamic equilibrium in demographic terms became typical of economic growth phases, ultimately to be followed by catastrophic readjustments to a new steady state with substantially lower equilibrium levels as socioeconomic systems became too costly to sustain in regard to energy demands and information flows.

Comparative studies have suggested that all high civilizations that incorporated intensification strategies were metastable and that their growth trajectories can be interpreted as those of accelerating energy extraction, to the point that both the ecosystem and the socioeconomic structures were stretched to capacity, with steady or declining absolute caloric productivity and input-output ratios. This is a materialistic interpretation of civilizations that obviously does little to illuminate their creative vitality. But it does draw attention to the limiting conditions imposed by regional ecosystems, given a particular socioeconomic milieu.

The Industrial Revolution, initially made possible by a colonial redistributive economy and then sustained in its growth and diffusion by a worldwide communications revolution, has created a global megasystem now rapidly approaching its limiting conditions. The phenomenal interregional disparities in population growth, economic productivity, and energy consumption suggest a socioeconomic network with severe cybernetics difficulties, one that is increasingly prone to catastrophic simplification. Contextual interpretation of the archaeological and historical records can provide invaluable monitoring experience for the kinds of socioecological processes that must be built into probabilistic neo-ecological models. The past is essential not only to understand the present but even more important to evaluate the potential outcomes of modern trends. It is here that the contextual approach to the past forms a stimulating and provocative interface with the contemporary problems of regional development, resource management, sustained productivity, and ecological harmony that are becoming central concerns of human geography. As the past continues to unfold, it becomes more and more evident that former generations, "dead" civilizations, and ecological history can tell us as much about the viability of future strategies as can contemporary research.

References

Achenbach, H. 1976. "Probleme antiker und heutiger Wasserwirtschaft im ostalgerischen Trockengrenzbereich in vergleichender Interpretation." *Göttinger Geographische Abhandlungen* 66:169–78.

Adams, R. E. W., 1975. "Stratigraphy." In: *Field Methods in Archaeology,* edited by T. R. Hester, R. F. Heizer, and J. A. Graham, pp. 147–62. Palo Alto: Mayfield.

Adams, R. E. W. and Jones, R. C. 1981. "Spatial Patterns and Regional Growth among Classic Maya Cities." *American Antiquity* 46:301–22.

Adams, R. E. W., Brown, W. E., and Culbert, T. P. 1981. "Radar mapping, Archeology, and Ancient Maya Land Use." *Science* 213:1457–63.

Adams, R. M. 1965. *Land behind Bagdad: A History of Settlement on the Diyala Plains.* Chicago: University of Chicago Press.

——— 1978. "Strategies of Maximization, Stability and Resilience in Mesopotamian Society, Settlement, and Agriculture." *Proceedings of the American Philosophical Society* 122:329–35.

——— 1981. *Heartland of Cities: Surveys of Ancient Settlement and Land Use on the Central Floodplain of the Euphrates.* Chicago: University of Chicago Press.

Adams, R. M., and Nissen, H. J. 1972. *The Uruk Countryside: The Natural Setting of Urban Societies.* Chicago: University of Chicago Press.

Adovasio, J. M., et al., 1977. "Meadowcroft Rockshelter." In: *Early Man in America,* edited by A. L. Bryan, pp. 140–80. Edmonton: Archaeological Researches International.

Agenbroad, L. D. 1978. *The Hudson-Meng Site: An Alberta Bison Kill in the Nebraska High Plains.* Washington, D.C.: University of America Press.

Aitken, M. J. 1976. "Thermoluminescence in Archaeology." In: *Datations absolues et analyses isotopiques en préhistoire,* edited by J. Labeyre and C. Lalou, pp. 1–20. Paris: Union Internationale des Sciences Préhistoriques et Protohistoriques. Centre National de la Recherche Scientifique.

Akazawa, T. 1980. "Fishing Adaptation of Prehistoric Hunter-Gatherers at the Nittano Site, Japan." *Journal of Archaeological Science* 7:325–44.

Albanese, J. P. 1978. "Archeogeology of the Northwestern Plains." In: *Prehistoric Hunters of the High Plains,* edited by G. C. Frison, pp. 375–90. New York: Academic Press.

Alland, A. 1975. "Adaptation." *Annual Review of Anthropology* 4:49–73.

Almagor, U. 1972. "Tribal Sections, Territory and Myth: Dassanetch Responses to Variable Ecological Conditions." *Asian and African Studies* 8:185–206.

Ammerman, A. J., and Feldman, M. W. 1974. "On the 'Making' of an Assemblage of Stone Tools." *American Antiquity* 39:610–16.

Anderson, A. J. 1981. "A Model of Prehistoric Collecting on the Rocky Shore." *Journal of Archaeological Science.* 8:109–20.

Andrews, P., Lord, J. M., and Nesbit Evans, E. M. 1979. "Patterns of Ecological Diversity in Fossil and Modern Mammalian Faunas." *Biological Journal of the Linnean Society* 11:177–205.

Apeldoorn, J. G. van, editor. 1978. *The Aftermath of the 1972-1974 Drought in Nigeria.* Ibadan, Nigeria: Federal Department of Water Resources.

Asch, D. L., Asch, N. B., and Farnsworth, K. B. 1979. "Woodland Subsistence and Settlement in West Central Illinois." In: *Hopewell Archaeology*, edited by D. S. Brose and N. Greber, pp. 80–6. Kent, Ohio: Kent State University Press.

Asch, N., Ford, R. I., and Asch, D. L. 1972. "Paleoethnobotany of the Koster Site: The Archaic Horizons." *Illinois State Museum Reports of Investigations* 24.

Bahn, P. G. 1977. "Seasonal Migration in Southwest France during the Late Glacial Period." *Journal of Archaeological Science* 4:245–57.

Baker, D. G. 1980. "Botanical and Chemical Evidence of Climatic Change: A Comment." *Journal of Interdisciplinary History* 10:813–19.

Baker, H. G. 1972. "Human Influences on Plant Evolution." *Economic Botany* 26:32–43.

Baker, J., and Brothwell, D. 1980. *Animal Diseases in Archaeology.* London: Academic Press.

Barker, G. 1981. *Landscape and Society: Prehistoric Central Italy.* New York: Academic Press.

Bar-Yosef, O. 1975. "The Epipaleolithic in Palestine and Sinai." In: *Problems in Prehistory: North Africa and the Levant*, edited by F. Wendorf and A. E. Marks, pp. 363–75. Dallas: Southern Methodist University Press.

Bar-Yosef, O., and Phillips, J. L. 1977. *Prehistoric Investigations in Gebel Maghara, Northern Sinai.* Monograph 7. Jerusalem: Institute of Archaeology, Hebrew University.

Beck, C. W., editor. 1974. *Archaeological Chemistry. Advances in Chemistry, Vol. 138.* Washington: American Chemical Society.

    1980. "Archaeometric Clearinghouse." *Journal of Field Archaeology* 7:461–5.

Becker, B., and Frenzel, B. 1977. "Paläoökologische Befunde zur Geschichte postglazialer Flussauen im südlichen Mitteleuropa." In: *Dendrochronologie und postglaziale Klimaschwankungen in Europa*, edited by B. Frenzel, pp. 43–61. Wiesbaden: F. Steiner.

Behrensmeyer, A. K., and Boaz, D. E. D. 1980. "The Recent Bones of Amboseli National Park, Kenya, in Relation to East African Paleoecology." In: *Fossils in the Making: Vertebrate Taphonomy and Paleoecology*, edited by A. K. Behrensmeyer and A. P. Hill, pp. 72–93. Chicago: University of Chicago Press.

Behrensmeyer, A. K., and Hill, A. P., editors. 1980. *Fossils in the Making: Vertebrate Taphonomy and Paleoecology.* Chicago: University of Chicago Press.

Bell, T. L. 1980. "Central Place Theory." In: *Interpreting the City*, edited by T. A. Hartshorn, pp. 105–31. New York: John Wiley & Sons.

Bell, T. L., and Church, R. L. 1980. "A Central Place Theoretic Covering Model." In: *Abstracts,* Association of American Geographers Louisville meeting, p. 156.

Bender, B. 1975. *Farming in Prehistory: From Hunter-Gatherer to Food-producer.* New York: St. Martin's Press.

Bender, M. M., Baerreis, D. A., and Steventon, R. L. 1981. "Further Light on Carbon Isotopes and Hopewell Agriculture." *American Antiquity* 46:346–53.

Benedict, J. B., and Olson, B. L. 1978. "The Mount Albion Complex: A Study of Prehistoric Man and the Altithermal." Research Report 1, Center for Mountain Archaeology, Ward, Colo.

Bennett, J. W. 1976. *The Ecological Transition: Cultural Anthropology and Human Adaptation.* New York: Pergamon.

Berger, R. 1979. "Radiocarbon Dating with Accelerators." *Journal of Archaeological Science* 6:101–4.

Berggren, W. A. 1980. "Towards a Quaternary Time Scale." *Quaternary Research* 13:277–302.

Bettinger, R. L. 1980. "Explanatory/Predictive Models of Hunter-Gatherer Adaptation." *Advances in Archaeological Method and Theory* 3:189–255.

Biek, L. 1970. "Soil Silhouettes." In: *Science in Archaeology,* edited by D. Brothwell and E. S. Higgs, pp. 118–23. London: Thames and Hudson.

Binford, L. R. 1964. "A Consideration of Archaeological Research Design." *American Antiquity* 29:425–41.

1972. "Hatchery West: Site Definition–Surface Distribution of Cultural Items." In: *An Archaeological Perspective,* edited by L. R. Binford, pp. 163–81. New York: Academic Press.

1981. *Bones: Ancient Men and Modern Myths.* New York: Academic Press.

Binford, L. R., and Bertram, J. B. 1977. "Bone Frequencies and Attritional Processes." In: *For Theory Building in Archaeology,* edited by L. R. Binford, pp. 77–153. New York: Academic Press.

Bishop, W. W. and Clark, J. D. editors. 1967. *Background to Evolution in Africa,* pp. 397–407. Chicago: University of Chicago Press.

Boaz, N. T., and Behrensmeyer, A. K. 1976. "Hominid Taphonomy: Transport of Human Skeletal Parts in an Artifical Fluviatile Environment." *American Journal of Physical Anthropology* 45:53–60.

Bocquet, A. 1979. "Lake-Bottom Archaeology." *Scientific American* 240(2):56–64.

Bökönyi, S. 1974. *History of Domestic Animals in Central and Eastern Europe.* Budapest: Akademiai Kiado.

Bordes, F. 1975. "Sur la notion de sol d'habitat en préhistoire paléolithique." *Bulletin, Société préhistorique française* 72:139–43.

Bordes, F., Rigaud, J. P., and de Sonneville-Bordes, D. 1972. "Des buts, problèmes et limites de l'archéologie paléolithique." *Quaternaria* 16:15–34.

Bosch, P. W. 1979. "A Neolithic Flint Mine." *Scientific American* 240(6):126–32.

Bowen, H. C. 1961. *Ancient Fields.* London: British Association for the Advancement of Science.

Bradley, R. 1978. "Prehistoric Field Systems in Britain and North-west Europe–A Review of Some Recent Work." *World Archaeology* 9:265–80.

Braidwood, R. J. 1960. "Levels in Prehistory: A Model for the Consideration of Evidence." In: *Evolution after Darwin, Vol. 2,* edited by S. Tax, pp. 143–51. Chicago: University of Chicago Press.

Brain, C. K. 1976. "A Re-interpretation of the Swartkrans Site and Its Remains." *South African Journal of Science* 72:141–6.

Brain, C. K. 1981. *The Hunters or the Hunted? An Introduction to African Cave Taphonomy.* Chicago: University of Chicago Press.

Bramwell, M., editor. 1973. *Atlas of World Wildlife.* New York: Rand McNally.

Brill, R. H., editor. 1971. *Science and Archaeology.* Cambridge: MIT Press.

Brink, R. A., Densmore, J. W., and Hill, G. A. 1977. "Soil Deterioration and the Growing World Demand for Food." *Science* 197:625–30.

Brookfield, H. C. 1969. "On the Environment as Perceived." *Progress in Geography* 1:51–80.

Brothwell, D., and Higgs, E. 1970. *Science in Archaeology.* London: Thames and Hudson.

Browman, D. L. 1981. "Isotopic Discrimination and Correction Factors in Radiocarbon Dating." *Advances in Archaeological Method and Theory* 4:241–95.

Brown, W. L., and Wilson, E. O. 1956. "Character displacement." *Systematic Zoology* 5:49–64.

Brunnacker, K. 1971. "Geologisch-pedologische Untersuchungen in Lepenski Vir am Eisernen Tor." In: *Die Anfänge des Neolithikums vom Orient bis Nordeuropa (Fundamenta A/3:II)*, edited by H. Schwabedissen, pp. 20–32. Cologne: Böhlau.

1978b. "Der Niederrhein im Holozän." *Fortschritte, Geologie des Rheinlandes und Westfalen* 28:399–440.

editor. 1978a. *Geowissenschaftliche Untersuchungen in Gönnersdorf.* Wiesbaden: F. Steiner.

Brunsden, D. 1979. "Weathering." In: *Process in Geomorphology,* edited by C. Embleton and J. Thornes, pp. 73–129. London: E. Arnold.

Bryant, V. M. 1974. "The Role of Coprolite Analysis in Archeology." *Bulletin of the Texas Archeological Society* 45:1–28.

1982. "The Role of Palynology in Archaeology." *Advances in Archaeological Method and Theory* 6: in press.

Buckley, W. 1968. "Society as a Complex Adaptive System." In: *Modern Systems Research for the Behavioral Sciences,* edited by W. Buckley, pp. 490–513. Chicago: Aldine.

Bullard, R. G. 1976. "The Archaeological Geology of the Khirbet Shema Area." *Annals, American Schools of Oriental Research* 4:15–32.

Bumsted, M. P. 1981. "The Potential of Stable Carbon Isotopes in Bioarchaeological Anthropology." Department of Anthropology Research Reports, University of Massachusetts.

Bunting, B. T. 1965. *The Geography of Soil.* London: Hutchinson University Library.

Bunting, T. E., and Guelke, L. 1979. "Behavioral and Perception Geography: A Critical Appraisal." *Annals, Association of American Geographers* 69:448–74.

Burgess, R. L. 1978. "Some Results of a Geo-archaeological Survey." *Newsletter, Society for Archaeological Sciences* 1(3):1–2.

1980. "Some Results of Two Surveys on the Archaeological Sciences." *Newsletter, Society for Archaeological Sciences* 3(4):1–3.

Burton, I., Kates, R. W., and White, G. F. 1978. *The Environment as Hazard.* New York: Oxford University Press.

Butzer, E. n.d. "Spatial Organization of Settlement in the Leipziger Bucht in the Early Medieval Period (ca. 800–1250 A.D.)." Unpublished manuscript.

Butzer, K. W. 1959. "Some Recent Geological Deposits of the Egyptian Nile Valley." *Geographical Journal* 125:75–9.

1960a. "Archeology and Geology in Ancient Egypt." *Science* 132:1617–24.

1960b. "Remarks on the Geography of Settlement in the Nile Valley during Hellenistic Times." *Bulletin, Société de Géographie d'Egypte* 33:5–36.

1961. "Archäologische Fundstellen Ober- und Mittelägyptens in ihrer geologischen Landschaft." *Mitteilungen, Deutsches Archäologisches Institut, Abteilung Kairo* 17:54–68.

1964. *Environment and Archeology: An Introduction to Pleistocene Geography.* Chicago: Aldine.

1965. "Acheulian Occupation Sites at Torralba and Ambrona, Spain: Their Geology." *Science* 150:1718–22.

1967. "Geomorphology and Stratigraphy of the Paleolithic Site of Budinho." *Eiszeitalter und Gegenwart* 18:82–103.

1971a. *Environment and Archeology: An Ecological Approach to Prehistory.* Chicago: Aldine.

1971b. "Recent History of an Ethiopian Delta." Department of Geography. University of Chicago Research paper 136:1–184.

1973a. "Spring Sediments from the Acheulian Site of Amanzi (Uitenhage District, South Africa)." *Quaternaria* 17:299–319.

1973b. "Geology of Nelson Bay Cave, Robberg, South Africa." *South African Archaeological Bulletin* 28:97–110.

1974a. "Geo-archaeological Interpretation of Two Acheulian Calcpan Sites: Doornlagte and Rooidam (Kimberley, South Africa)." *Journal of Archeological Science* 1:1–25.

1974b. "Geological and Ecological Perspectives on the Middle Pleistocene." *Quaternary Research* 4:136–48.

1974c. "Modern Egyptian Pottery Clays and Predynastic Buff Ware." *Journal of Near Eastern Studies* 33:377–82.

1975a. "The 'Ecological' Approach to Prehistory: Are We Really Trying?" *American Antiquity* 40:106–11.

1975b. "Pleistocene Littoral-Sedimentary Cycles of the Mediterranean: A Mallorquin View." In: *After the Australopithecines,* edited by K. W. Butzer and G. L. Isaac, pp. 25–71. Chicago: Aldine.

1975c. "Paleo-ecology of South African Australopithecines: Taung Revisited." *Current Anthropology* 15:367–82, 420–6.

1976a. *Geomorphology from the Earth.* New York: Harper & Row.

1976b. "Lithostratigraphy of the Swartkrans Formation." *South African Journal of Science* 72:136–41.

1976c. *Early Hydraulic Civilization in Egypt.* Chicago: University of Chicago Press.

1976d. "Alexandersfontein Basin." *Nyame Akuma (Newsletter of African Archaeology)* 8:46–7.

1977a. *Geomorphology of the Lower Illinois Valley as a Spatial-Temporal Context for the Koster Archaic Site.* Reports on Investigations 34, Illinois State Museum.

1977b. "Environment, Culture and Human Evolution." *American Scientist* 65:572–84.

1977c. "Geo-archaeology in Practice." *Reviews of Anthropology* 4:125–31.

1978a. "Toward an Integrated, Contextual Approach in Archaeology." *Journal of Archaeological Science* 5:191–3.

1978*b*. "Climate Patterns in an Unglaciated Continent." *Geographical Magazine* 51:201–8.

1978*c*. "Changing Holocene Environments at the Koster Site: A Geo-archaeological Perspective." *American Antiquity* 43:408–13.

1978*d*. "Comments on the Infillings of Various Old Babylonian and Kassite Structures at Nippun." *Oriental Institute Communications* 23:188–90.

1978*e*. "Cultural Perspectives on Geographical Space." In: *Dimensions of Human Geography,* edited by K. W. Butzer, pp. 1–14. Research paper 186, Department of Geography, University of Chicago.

1978*f*. "Sediment Stratigraphy of the Middle Stone Age Sequence at Klasies River Mouth, Tsitsikama Coast, South Africa." *South African Archaeological Bulletin* 33:141–51.

1978*g*. "Geoecological Perspectives on Early Hominid Evolution." In: *Early Hominids of Africa,* edited by C. Jolly, pp. 191–217. London: Duckworth.

1979. "Pleistocene History of the Nile Valley in Egypt and Lower Nubia." In: *The Sahara and the Nile,* edited by M. A. J. Williams and H. Faure, pp. 248–76. Rotterdam: A. Balkema.

1980*a*. "Holocene Alluvial Sequences: Problems of Dating and Correlation." In: *Time-scales in Geomorphology,* edited by J. Lewin, D. Davidson, and R. Cullingford, pp. 131–41. New York: John Wiley & Sons.

1980*b*. "The Holocene Lake Plain of North Rudolf, East Africa." *Physical Geography* 1:44–58.

1980*c*. "Civilizations: Organisms or Systems?" *American Scientist* 68:517–23.

1980*d*. "Investigación preliminar sobre la geologia de la Cueva del Pendo." In *El Yacimiento de El Pendo,* edited by J. M. González Echegarray, 17:199–213. Madrid: Biblioteca Prehistoria Hispana.

1980*e*. "Adaptation to Global Environmental Change." *Professional Geographer* 32:269–78.

1980*f*. "Context in Archaeology: an Alternative Perspective." *Journal of Field Archaeology* 7:417–22.

1981*a*. "Rise and Fall of Axum, Ethiopia: A Geo-archaeological Interpretation." *American Antiquity* 46:471–95.

1981*b*. "Long-Term Nile Flood Variation and Political Discontinuities in Pharaonic Egypt." In: *The Causes and Consequences of Food Production in Africa,* edited by J. D. Clark and S. Brandt. Berkeley: University of California Press. (*in press*).

1981*c*. "Cave Sediments, Upper Pleistocene Stratigraphy, and Mousterian Facies in Cantabrian Spain." *Journal of Archaeological Science* 8:133–83.

Butzer, K. W., Beaumont, P. B., and Vogel, J. C. 1978. "Lithostratigraphy of Border Cave, Kwa Zulu, South Africa." *Journal of Archaeological Science* 5:317–41.

Butzer, K. W., and Cooke, H. B. S. 1981. "Palaeoecology of the African continent." In: *Cambridge History of Africa, Vol. 1,* edited by J. D. Clark (*in press*).

Butzer, K. W., Fock, G. J., Scott, L., and Stuckenrath, R. 1979. "Dating and Context of Rock Engravings in Southern Africa." *Science* 203:1201–14.

Butzer, K. W., and Hansen, C. L. 1968. *Desert and River in Nubia.* Madison: University of Wisconsin Press.

Butzer, K. W., and Helgren, D. M. 1972. "Late Cenozoic Evolution of the Cape Coast between Knysna and Cape St. Francis, South Africa." *Quaternary Research* 2:143–69.

Butzer, K. W., and Isaac, G. L., editors. 1975. *After the Australopithecines: Stratigraphy, Ecology, and Culture Change in the Middle Pleistocene.* Chicago: Aldine.

Butzer, K. W., Stuckenrath, R., Bruzewicz, A. J. and Helgren, D. M. 1978. "Late Cenozoic Paleoclimates of the Gaap Escarpment, Kalahari Margin, South Africa." *Quaternary Research.* 10:310–39.

Butzer, K. W., and Vogel, J. C. 1979. "Archaeosedimentological Sequence from the Sub-montane Interior of South Africa: Rose Cottage Cave, Heuningneskrans, and Bushman Rock Shelter." Presented before the South African Archaeological Association, Upper Pleistocene Symposium, Stellenbosch.

Cahen, D., Keeley, L. H., and Van Noten, F. L. 1979. "Stone Tools, Tool Kits, and Human Behavior in Prehistory." *Current Anthropology* 20:661–83.

Cahen, D., and Moeyersons, J. 1977. "Subsurface Movements of Stone Artefacts and Their Implications for the Prehistory of Central Africa." *Nature* 266:812–15.

Carlton, T. H. 1981. "Archaeology, Ethnohistory and Ethnology: Interpretive Interfaces." *Advances in Archaeological Method and Theory* 4:129–76.

Carneiro, R. L. 1970. "A Theory of the Origin of the State." *Science* 169:733–8.

Carr, C. J. 1977. "Pastoralism in Crisis: The Dassanetch and Their Ethiopian Lands." Department of Geography, University of Chicago. Research paper 180:1–319.

Carter, G., editor. 1978. *Archaeological Chemistry II. Advances in Chemistry, Vol. 171.* Washington: American Chemical Society.

Carter, G. F. 1975. *Man and the Land: A Cultural Geography.* New York: Holt, Rinehart and Winston.

Carter, T. H., and Pagliero, R. 1966. "Notes on Mud-brick Preservation." *Sumer* 22:65–76.

Casteel, R. W. 1976. *Fish Remains in Archaeology and Palaeo-environmental Studies.* New York: Academic Press.

Chang, K. C. 1968. "Toward a Science of Prehistoric Society." In: *Settlement Archaeology,* edited by K. C. Chang, pp. 1–9. Palo Alto: National Press.

Chaplin, R. E. 1971. *The Study of Animal Bones from Archaeological Sites.* London: Seminar Press.

Charnov, E. L. 1976. "Optimal Foraging: The Marginal Value Theorem." *Theoretical Population Biology* 9:129–36.

Chavaillon, J., Chavaillon, N., Hours, F., and Piperno, M. 1978. "Le début et la fin de l'acheuléen à Melka-Kunturé: Méthodologie pour l'étude des changements de civilisation." *Bulletin, Société préhistorique française* 75:105–15.

Chisholm, M. 1975. *Human Geography: Evolution or Revolution?* Harmondsworth: Penguin.

Chorley, R. J. 1962. "Geomorphology and General Systems Theory." U.S. Geological Survey professional paper 500-B.

editor. 1969. *Water, Earth and Man.* London: Methuen.

Chorley, R. J., and ؟ennedy, B. A. 1971. *Physical Geography: A Systems Approach.* Englewood Cliffs, N.J.: Prentice-Hall.

Christaller, W. 1966. *Central Places in Southern Germany* (translated from 1933 original by C. W. Baskin). Englewood Cliffs, N.J.: Prentice-Hall.

Christenson, A. L. 1980. "Change in the Human Niche in Response to Population Growth." In *Modeling Change in Prehistoric Subsistence Economies,* edited by T. K. Earle and A. L. Christenson, pp. 31–72. New York: Academic Press.

Churcher, C. S. 1972. "Late Pleistocene Vertebrates from Archaeological Sites in the Plain of Kom Ombo, Upper Egypt." *Life sciences contribution, Royal Ontario Museum*, 82:1–172.

Churchman, C. W. 1968. *The Systems Approach.* New York: Dell.

Clark, G. A. 1971. "The Asturian of Cantabria: Subsistence Base and the Evidence for Post-Pleistocene Climatic Shifts." *American Anthropologist* 73: 1245–57.

 1979. "Spatial Association at Liencres, an Early Holocene Open Site on the Santander Coast, North-Central Spain." *Arizona State University Anthropological Research Papers* 15:121–43.

Clark, J. D. 1960. "Human Ecology during the Pleistocene and Later Times in Africa South of the Sahara." *Current Anthropology* 1:307–24.

 1975. "A Comparison of the Late Acheulian Industries of Africa and the Middle East." In: *After the Australopithecines*, edited by K. W. Butzer and G. L. Isaac, pp. 605–59. Chicago: Aldine.

 1977. "Bone Tools of the Earlier Pleistocene." In: *Moshe Stekelis Memorial Volume*, edited by B. Arensburg and O. Bar-Yosef, pp. 23–37. Jerusalem: Israel Exploration Society.

 1979. *The Kalambo Falls Prehistoric Site, Vol. 1.* Cambridge University Press.

Clarke, D. L. 1968. *Analytical Archaeology.* London: Methuen (second edition with B. Chapman, 1978).

 1972. "Models and Paradigms in Contemporary Archaeology." In: *Models in Archaeology*, edited by D. L. Clarke, pp. 1–60. London: Methuen.

 editor. 1977. *Spatial Archaeology.* New York: Academic Press.

Clarke, W. C. 1976. "Maintenance of Agriculture and Human Habitats within the Tropical Forest Ecosystem." *Human Ecology* 4:247–59.

Clason, A. T., editor. 1975. *Archaeozoological Studies.* Amsterdam: North Holland.

Clason, A. T., and Prummel, W. 1977. "Collecting, Sieving and Archaeozoological Research." *Journal of Archaeological Science* 4:171–5.

Coates, D. R., editor. 1974. *Environmental Geomorphology and Landscape Conservation. II: Urban areas.* New York: John Wiley & Sons.

 editor. 1976. "Urban Geomorphology." Special paper 174, Geological Society of America.

Cohen, E. 1976a. "Environmental Orientations: A Multidimensional Approach to Social Ecology." *Current Anthropology* 17:49–70.

Cohen, M. N. 1976b. *The Food Crisis in Prehistory: Overpopulation and the Origins of Agriculture.* New Haven: Yale University Press.

Coles, J. 1979. *Experimental Archaeology.* London: Academic Press.

Colwell, R. K. 1974. "Predictability, Constancy, and Contingency of Periodic Phenomena." *Ecology* 55:1148–53.

Cook, S. F. 1963. "Erosion Morphology and Occupation History in Western Mexico." *University of California Anthropological Records* 17:281–334.

Cook, S. F., and Heizer, R. F. 1965. "Studies on the Chemical Analysis of Archaeological Sites." *University of California Publications in Anthropology* 2:1–102.

Cook, S. F., and Treganza, A. E. 1950. "The Quantitative Investigation of

Indian Mounds." *University of California Publication of American Archaeological Ethnology* 40:223–61.

Cornwall, I. W. 1956. *Bones for the Archaeologist*. London: Phoenix House.

1958. *Soils for the Archaeologist*. London: Phoenix House.

1968. *Prehistoric Animals and Their Hunters*. New York: Praeger.

Cowan, C. W. 1978. "Seasonal Nutritional Stress in a Late Woodland Population." *Tennessee Anthropologist* 3:117–28.

Creer, K. M., and Kopper, J. S. 1976. "Secular Oscillations of the Geomagnetic Field Recorded by Sediments Deposited in Caves of the Mediterranean Region." *Geophysical Journal, Royal Astronomical Society* 45:35–58.

Crowe, P. R. 1979. *Concepts in Climatology*. New York: St. Martin's Press.

Crowell, J. C., and Frakes, L. A. 1970. "Phanerozoic Glaciation and the Causes of Ice Ages." *American Journal of Science* 268:193–224.

Crumley, C. L. 1979. "Three Locational Models: An Epistemological Assessment for Anthropology and Archaeology." *Advances in Archaeological Method and Theory* 2:143–74.

Curtis, G. H. 1975. "Improvements in Potassium-Argon Dating 1962–1975." *World Archaeology* 7:198–209.

Dacey, M. F. 1960. "The Spacing of River Towns." *Annals, Association of American Geographers* 50:59–61.

Damon, P. E., Ferguson, C. W., Long, A., and Wallick, E. J. 1974. "Dendrochronologic Calibration of the Radiocarbon Time Scale." *American Antiquity* 39:350–66.

David, N. 1971. "The Fulani Compound and the Archaeologist." *World Archaeology* 3:111–31.

1973. "On Upper Palaeolithic Society, Ecology and Technological Change: The Noaillian Case." In: *The Explanation of Culture Change*, edited by C. Renfrew, pp. 277–303. London: Duckworth.

Davidson, D. A. 1972. "Terrain Adjustment and Prehistoric Communities." In: *Man, Settlement and Urbanism*, edited by P. J. Ucko, R. Tringham, and G. W. Dimbleby, pp. 17–22. London: Duckworth.

1973. "Particle Size and Phosphate Analysis – evidence for the Evolution of a Tell." *Archaeometry* 15:143–52.

1976. "Processes of Tell Formation and Erosion." In: *Geo-archaeology*, edited by D. A. Davidson and M. L. Shackley, pp. 255–66. London: Duckworth.

1978. "Soils on Santorini at ca. 1500 B.C." *Nature* 272:243–4.

1980*a*. *Soils and Land Use Planning*. London: Longman.

1980*b*. "Erosion in Greece during the First and Second Millennia B.C." In: *Timescales in Geomorphology*, edited by R. A. Cullingford, D. A. Davidson, and J. Lewin, pp. 143–58. New York: John Wiley & Sons.

n.d. "Geomorphology and Archaeology." In: *Archaeological Geology*, edited by G. Rapp, Jr., and J. Gifford.

Davidson, D. A., Jones, R. L., and Renfrew, C. 1976*a*. "Palaeoenvironmental Reconstruction and Evaluation: A Case Study from Orkney." *Transactions, Institute of British Geographers* (N.S.) 1:346–61.

Davidson, D. A., Renfrew, C., and Tasker, C. 1976*b*. "Erosion and Prehistory in Melos." *Journal of Archaeological Science* 3:219–27.

Davidson, D. A., and Shackley, M. L., editors. 1976. *Geo-archaeology: Earth Science and the Past*. London: Duckworth.

Davis, L., and Wilson, M. editors. 1978. *Bison Procurement and Utilization: A Symposium. Plains Anthropologist* memoir 14.

Davis, M. B., Brubaker, L. B., and Webb, T. 1973. "Calibration of Absolute Pollen Influx." In: *Quaternary Plant Ecology,* edited by H. J. B. Birks and R. G. West, pp. 9–25. Oxford: Blackwell.

Deacon, H. J. 1975. "Demography, Subsistence, and Culture during the Acheulian in Southern Africa." In: *After the Australopithecines,* edited by K. W. Butzer and G. L. Isaac, pp. 543–69. Chicago: Aldine.

1976. *Where Hunters Gathered: A Study of Holocene Stone Age People in the Eastern Cape.* South African Archaeological Society Monograph Series, No. 1.

1979. "Excavations at Boomplaas Cave: A Sequence through the Upper Pleistocene and Holocene in South Africa." *World Archaeology* 10:241–57.

Deevey, E. S., Rice, D. S., Rice, P. M., Vaughan, H. H., Brenner, M., and Flannery, M. S. 1979. "Maya Urbanism: Impact on a Tropical Karst Environment." *Science* 206:298–306.

De Laet, S. J. 1972. "Das ältere und mittlere Neolithikum in Belgien." In: *Die Anfänge des Neolithikums vom Orient bis Nordeuropa, Vol. 5a,* edited by H. Schwabedissen, pp. 185–230. Cologne: Bohlau.

Delano Smith, C. 1978. "Coastal Sedimentation, Lagoons and Ports in Italy." In: *Papers in Italian Archaeology I,* edited by H. M. Blake, T. W. Potter, and D. B. Whitehouse, pp. 25–33. Oxford: British Archaeological Reports, Supplementary Series 4I(i).

Delcourt, P. A., Davis, O. K., and Bright, R. C. 1979. *Bibliography of Taxonomic Literature for the Identification of Fruits, Seeds, and Vegetative Plant Fragments.* Publication 1328, Environmental Sciences Division, Oak Ridge National Laboratory.

De Lumley, H., editor. 1969. "Une cabane acheulienne dans la Grotte de Lazaret." *Memoirs, Société préhistorique française* 7:1–235.

1975. "Cultural Evolution in France in Its Paleoecological Setting During the Middle Pleistocene." In: *After the Australopithecines,* edited by K. W. Butzer and G. L. Isaac, pp. 745–808. Chicago: Aldine.

De Meyer, L. editor. 1978. *Tell ed-Der II (Progress Reports).* Leeuven: Peeters.

Denevan, W. M. 1978. "The Causes and Consequences of Shifting Cultivation in Relation to Tropical Forest Survival." In: *The Role of Geographical Research in Latin America,* edited by W. M. Denevan. Conference of Latin American Geographers, publication 7. Muncie, Indiana.

1981. "Hydraulic Agriculture in the American Tropics: Forms, Measures, and Recent Research." In: *Maya Subsistence,* edited by K. V. Flannery. New York: Academic Press.

Denevan, W. M. and Turner, B. L. 1974. "Forms, Functions, and Associations of Raised Fields in the Old World Tropics." *Journal of Tropical Geography* 39:24–33.

Dennell, R. W. 1974. "Botanical Evidence for Prehistoric Crop Processing Activities." *Journal of Archaeological Science* 1:275–84.

1976. "The Economic Importance of Plant Resources Represented on Archaeological Sites." *Journal of Archaeological Science* 3:229–47.

Dennell, R. W., and Webley, D. 1975. "Prehistoric Settlement and Land Use in Southern Bulgaria." In: *Palaeoeconomy,* edited by E. S. Higgs, pp. 97–110. Cambridge University Press.

De Wet, J. M. J., and Harlan, J. R. 1975. "Weeds, and Domesticates: Evolution in the Man-made Habitat." *Economic Botany* 29:99–119.

Dickinson, W. R. and Shutler, R. 1979. "Petrography of Sand Tempers in Pacific Islands Potsherds." *Bulletin, Geological Society of America* (Part II) 90:1644–1701.

Dimbleby, G. W. 1976. "Climate, Soil and Man." *Philosophical Transactions of the Royal Society of London, Biological Sciences* 275:197–208.

1978. *Plants and Archaeology*, second edition. London: John Baker.

Dimbleby, G. W. and Bradley, R. J. 1975. "Evidence of Pedogenesis from a Neolithic Site at Rackham, Sussex." *Journal of Archaeological Science* 2:179–86.

Dimbleby, G. W., and Speight, M. C. D. 1969. "Buried Soils." *Advancement of Science* 26:203–205.

Donkin, R. A. 1979. *Agricultural Terracing in the Aboriginal New World*. Viking Fund Publications in Anthropology, No. 56. Tucson: University of Arizona Press.

Doxiades, C. A. 1970. "Ekistics, the Science of Human Settlements." *Science* 170:393–404.

Drew, D. L. 1979. "Early Man in North America and Where to Look for Him: Geomorphic Contexts." *Plains Anthropologist* 24:269–81.

Driesch, A. von den, 1976. *A Guide to the Measurement of Animal Bones from Archaeological Sites*. Peabody Museum Bulletin 1, Harvard University.

Dunnell, R. C. 1980a. "Evolutionary Theory and Archaeology." *Advances in Archaeological Method and Theory* 3:38–99.

1980b. "Remote Sensing in Archaeological Sampling Designs." *Transportation Engineering Journal* TE3(15428):349–63.

Durham, W. H. 1978. "The Coevolution of Human Biology and Culture." In: *Human Behavior and Adaptation*, edited by N. Jones and V. Reynolds, pp. 11–31. London: Taylor and Francis.

Dyson-Hudson, R., and Smith, E. A. 1978. "Human Territoriality: An Ecological Reassessment." *American Anthropologist* 80:21–41.

Earle, T. K. 1976. "A Nearest-Neighbor Analysis of Two Formative Settlement Systems." In: *The Early Mesoamerican Village*, edited by K. V. Flannery, pp. 196–223. New York: Academic Press.

Earle, T. K., and Ericson, J. E., editors. 1977. *Exchange Systems in Prehistory*. New York: Academic Press.

Edwards, K. J. 1979. "Palynological and Temporal Inference in the Context of Prehistory, with Special Reference to the Evidence from Lake and Peaty Deposits." *Journal of Archaeological Science* 6:255–70.

Eidt, R. C. 1973. "A Rapid Chemical Test for Archaeological Site Surveying." *American Antiquity* 38:206–10.

1977. "Detection and Examination of Anthrosols by Phosphate Analysis." *Science* 197:1327–33.

Eighmy, J. L., Sternberg, R. S., and Butler, R. F. 1980. "Archaeomagnetic dating in the American Southwest." *American Antiquity* 45:507–17.

Eisma, D. 1962. "Beach Ridges near Selçuk, Turkey." *Tijdschrift K. nederlandsche aardrijkskundige Genootschaap* 79:234–46.

Eldredge, N., and Gould, S. J. 1972. "Punctuated Equilibria: An Alternative to Phyletic Gradualism." In: *Models in Paleobiology*, edited by T. R. Schopf, pp. 82–115. New York: Freeman, Cooper.

Emslie, S. D. 1981. "Prehistoric Agricultural Ecosystems: Avifauna from Pottery Mound, New Mexico." *American Antiquity* 46:853–61.

Ericson, J. E. 1975. New results in obsidian hydration dating. *World Archaeology* 7:151–9.

Espenshade, E. B. 1975. *Goode's World Atlas.* New York: Rand McNally.

Evans, J. G. 1972. *Land snails in archaeology.* New York: Academic Press.
  1975. *The Environment of Early Man in the British Isles.* Berkeley: University of California Press.
  1978. *An Introduction to Environmental Archaeology.* Ithaca, N.Y.: Cornell University Press.

Evans, J. G., and Limbrey, S. editors. 1975. *The Effect of Man on the Landscape: The Highland Zone.* London: Council for British Archaeology.

Evans, J. G., and Valentine, K. W. G. 1974. "Ecological Changes Induced by Prehistoric Man at Pitstone, Buckinghamshire." *Journal of Archaeological Science* 1:343–51.

Evans, S. T. 1980. "Spatial Analysis of Basin of Mexico Settlement: Problems with the Use of the Central Place Model." *American Antiquity* 45:866–75.

Faegri, K., and Iversen, J. 1975. *Textbook of Pollen Analysis* (3rd ed.). New York: Hafner.

Fairbridge, R. W. 1976. "Shellfish-eating Preceramic Indians in coastal Brazil." *Science* 191:353–9.

Fall, P. L., Kelso, G., and Markgraf, V. 1981. "Palaeoenvironmental Reconstruction at Canyon del Muerto, Arizona, Based on Principal Component Analysis." *Journal of Archaeological Science* 8:297–307.

Farquhar, R. M., and Fletcher, I. R. 1980. "Lead Isotope Identification of Sources of Galena from Some Prehistoric Indian Sites in Ontario, Canada." *Science* 207:640–3.

Farrand, W. R. 1975a. "Sediment Analysis of a Prehistoric Rock Shelter: the Abri Pataud." *Quaternary Research* 5:1–26.
  1975b. "Analysis of the Abri Pataud Sediments." In: *Excavation of the Abri Pataud, Les Eyzies (Dordogne)*, edited by H. L. Movius, pp. 27–68. Cambridge, Mass.: Peabody Museum of Archaeology and Ethnology, Harvard University.
  1979. "Chronology and Palaeoenvironment of Levantine Prehistoric Sites as Seen from Sediment Studies." *Journal of Archaeological Science* 6:369–92.

Farrington, I. S., and Park, C. C. 1978. "Hydraulic Engineering and Irrigation Agriculture in the Moche Valley, Peru: c. A.D. 1250–1532." *Journal of Archaeological Science* 5:255–68.

Faugères, L. 1979. "Evolution des climats et transformations des paysages." *Courrier* (Centre Nationale de la Recherche Scientifique, Paris), LA 141 (November, 1979).

Fedele, F. G. 1976. "Sediments as Palaeoland Segments: The Excavation Side of Study." In: *Geo-archaeology*, edited by D.A. Davidson and M. L. Shackley, pp. 23–48. London: Duckworth.

Fladmark, K. R. 1982. "Microdebitage Analysis: Initial Considerations." *Journal of Archaeological Science* 9:(in press).

Flannery, K. V. 1967. "Vertebrate Fauna and Hunting Patterns." In: *The Prehistory of the Tehuacán Valley, Vol I*, edited by D. S. Byers, pp. 132–75. Austin: University of Texas Press.

1968. "Archeological Systems Theory and Early Mesoamerica." In: *Anthropological Archeology in the Americas,* edited by B. J. Meggers, pp. 67–87. Washington, D.C.: Anthropological Society of Washington.

1972a. "The Cultural Evolution of Civilizations." *Annual Review of Ecology and Systematics* 3:399–426.

1972b. "The Origins of the Village as a Settlement Type in Mesoamerica and the Near East." In: *Man, Settlement and Urbanism,* edited by P. J. Ucko, R. Tringham, and G. W. Dimbleby, pp. 3–53. London: Butterworth.

1973. "The Origins of Agriculture." *Annual Review of Anthropology* 2:271–310.

editor. 1976. *The Early Mesoamerican Village.* New York: Academic Press.

Flannery, K. V., and Marcus, J. 1976. "Formative Oaxaca and the Zapotec Cosmos." *American Scientist* 64:374–383.

Fleming, S. 1976. *Dating in Archaeology: A Guide to Scientific Techniques.* New York: St. Martin's Press.

1980. *Thermoluminescence: Techniques in Archaeology.* New York: Oxford University Press.

Fletcher, R. 1977. "Settlement Studies." In: *Spatial Archaeology,* edited by D. L. Clarke, pp. 47–162. London: Academic Press.

Flohn, H. 1979. "On Time Scales and Causes of Abrupt Paleoclimatic Events." *Quaternary Research* 12:135–49.

Florschütz, F., Menéndez-Amor, J., Wijmstra, T. A. 1971. "Palynology of a Thick Quaternary Succession in Southern Spain." *Palaeogeography, Palaeoclimatology, Palaeoecology* 10:233–64.

Foley, R. 1977. "Space and Energy." In: *Spatial Archaeology,* edited by D. L. Clarke, pp. 163–88. London: Academic Press.

Folk, R. L. 1975. "Geologic Urban Hindplanning: An Example From a Hellenistic-Byzantine City, Stobi, Jugoslavian Macedonia." *Environmental Geology* 1:5–22.

Ford, R. I., editor. 1978. "The Nature and Status of Ethnobotany." University of Michigan Museum of Anthropology, Anthropological Paper 67.

Ford, R. I. 1979. "Paleoethnobotany in American Archaeology." *Advances in Archaeological Method and Theory* 2:285–326.

Fowler, P. L., and Evans, J. G. 1967. "Ploughmarks, Lynchets and Early Fields." *Antiquity* 41:289–301.

Freeman, L. G. 1978. "The Analysis of Some Occupation Floor Distributions from Earlier and Middle Pleistocene Sites in Spain." In: *Views of the Past,* edited by L. G. Freeman, pp. 57–116. The Hague: Mouton.

Frenzel, B. 1968. *Grundzüge der Pleistozänen Vegetationsgeschichte Nordeurasiens.* Wiesbaden: F. Steiner.

editor. 1977. *Dendrochronologie und postglaziale Klimaschwankungen in Europa.* Erdwissenschaftliche Forschung 13. Wiesbaden: F. Steiner.

Friedman, I., and Obradovich, J. 1981. "Obsidian Hydration Dating of Volcanic Events." *Quaternary Research* 16:37–47.

Frison, G. C. 1978. *Prehistoric Hunters of the High Plains.* New York: Academic Press.

Fritts, H. C. 1971. "Dendroclimatology and Dendroecology." *Quaternary Research* 1:419–49.

1976. *Tree Rings and Climate.* New York: Academic Press.

Fritts, H. C., Lofgren, G. R., and Gordon, G. A. 1979. "Variations in Climate since 1602 as Reconstructed from Tree Rings." *Quaternary Research* 12:18–46.

Frye, J. C. 1973. "Pleistocene Succession of Central Interior United States." *Quaternary Research* 3:275–83.

Gabriel, B. 1979. "Ur- und Frühgeschichte als Hilfswissenschaft der Geomorphologie im ariden Nordafrika." *Stuttgarter Geographische Studien* 93:135–48.

Gagliano, S. M. 1963. "A survey of Preceramic Occupations in Portions of South Louisiana and South Mississippi." *Florida Anthropologist* 16:105–32.

Geertz, C. 1963. *Agricultural Involution: The Process of Ecological Change in Indonesia.* Berkeley: University of California Press.

Gentry, A. H., and Lopez-Parodi, J. 1980. "Deforestation and Increased Flooding of the Upper Amazon." *Science* 210:1354–6.

Gibson, E. J. 1970. "The Development of Perception as an Adaptive Process." *American Scientist* 58:98–107.

Gibson, M. 1974. "Violation of Fallow and Engineered Disaster in Mesopotamian Civilization." In: *Irrigation's Impact on Society,* edited by T. E. Downing and M. Gibson, pp. 7–20. Anthropological Papers 25. Tucson: University of Arizona.

Giddings, J. L. 1966. "Cross-Dating the Archaeology of Northwestern Alaska." *Science* 153:127–35.

Gifford, D. P., 1981. "Taphonomy and Paleoecology: A Critical Review of Archaeology's Sister Discipline." *Advances in Archaeological Method and Theory* 4:365–438.

Gifford, D. P., and Behrensmeyer, A. K. 1977. "Observed Formation and Burial of a Recent Human Occupation Site in Kenya." *Quaternary Research* 8:245–66.

Gilbert, B. M. 1973. *Mammalian Osteo-archaeology: North America.* Columbia: Missouri Archaeological Society, University of Missouri.

Gilmore, G. R., and Ottaway, B. S. 1980. "Micromethods for the Determination of Trace Elements in Copper-based Metal Artifacts." *Journal of Archaeological Science* 7:241–54.

Gladfelter, B. 1977. "Geoarchaeology: The Geomorphologist and Archaeology." *American Antiquity* 42:519–38.

Gladfelter, B. G. 1981. "Developments and Directions in Geoarchaeology." *Advances in Archaeological Method and Theory* 4:343–64.

n.d. "Paleogeomorphic Settings and Prehistoric Settlement in the American Bottom (Middle Mississippi River)." Presented before the annual meeting of the Geological Society of America, Atlanta, November 17–20, 1980.

Godwin, H. 1975. *The History of the British Flora,* second edition. Cambridge University Press.

Goldberg, 1979a. "Micromorphology of Sediments from Hayonim Cave, Israel." *Catena* 6:167–81.

1979b. "Micromophology of Pech-de-l'Azé II Sediments." *Journal of Archaeological Science* 6:17–47.

1979c. Geology of Late Bronze Age Mudbrick from Tell Lachish." *Journal of the Tel Aviv University Insitute of Archaeology* 6:60–7.

Goldberg, P. S., and Nathan, Y. 1975. "The Phosphate Mineralogy of et-Tabun Cave, Mount Carmel, Israel." *Mineralogical Magazine* 40:253–8.

Goodwin, A. J. H. 1929. "The Middle Stone Age." *Annals, South African Museum* 27:95–145.

1936. "Vosburg: Its Petroglyphs." *Annals, South African Museum* 24:163–209.

Gould, R. A., editor. 1978. *Explorations in Ethno-archaeology.* Albuquerque: University of New Mexico Press.

1980. *Living Archaeology.* Cambridge University Press.

Graham, I. 1976. "The Investigation of the Magnetic Properties of Archaeological Sediments." In: *Geo-archaeology,* edited by D. A. Davidson and M. L. Shackley, pp. 49–63. London: Duckworth.

Gray, D. H. 1972. "Soil and the City." In: *The Physical Geography of the City,* edited by J. R. Detwyler and M. G. Marcus, pp. 135–68. Belmont, Calif.: Duxbury.

Grayson, D. K. 1977. "Pleistocene Avifaunas and the Overkill Hypothesis." *Science* 195:691–3.

1979. "On the Quantification of Vertebrate Archaeofaunas." *Advances in Archaeological Method and Theory* 2:199–237.

1981. "The Effects of Sample Size on Some Derived Measures in Vertebrate Faunal Analysis." *Journal of Archaeological Science* 8:77–88.

Green, S. W. 1980a. "Towards a General Model of Agricultural Systems." *Advances in Archaeological Method and Theory* 3:311–55.

1980b. "Broadening Least-Cost Models for Expanding Agricultural Systems." In: *Modeling Change in Prehistoric Subsistence Economies,* edited by T. K. Earle and A. L. Christenson, pp. 209–41. New York: Academic Press.

Greenland, D. J., and Nye, P. H. 1959. "Increases in the Carbon and Nitrogen Contents of Tropical Soils under Natural Fallows." *Journal of Soil Science* 9:284–99.

Greig, J. R. H., and Turner, J. 1974. "Some Pollen Diagrams from Greece and Their Archaeological Significance." *Journal of Archaeological Science* 1:177–94.

Grindley, J. R. 1969. "Quaternary Marine Palaeoecology in South Africa." *South African Archaeological Bulletin* 24:151–7.

Groenman-van Waateringe, W. 1978. "The impact of Neolithic Man on the Landscape in The Netherlands." *Council for British Archaeology Research Report* 21:135–46.

Grootes, P. M. 1978. "Carbon-14 Time Scale Extended: Comparison of Chronologies." *Science* 200:11–15.

Grove, J. M. 1979. "The Glacial History of the Holocene." *Progress in Physical Geography* 3:1–54.

Grüger, E. 1972. "Pollen and Seed Studies of Wisconsinan Vegetation in Illinois, U.S.A." *Bulletin, Geological Society of America* 83:2715–34.

Gullini, G., editor. 1969. "Contribution to the Study of the Preservation of Mud-brick Structures." *Mesopotamia* 443–73.

Gumerman, G. J., and Lyons, T. R. 1971. "Archaeological Methodology and Remote Sensing." *Science* 172:126–32.

Gumerman, G. J., and Neely, J. A. 1972. "An Archaeological Survey of the Tehuacán Valley, Mexico: A Test of Color Infrared Photography." *American Antiquity* 37:520–7.

Gumerman, G. J., and Phillips, D. A. 1978. "Archaeology beyond Anthropology." *American Antiquity* 43:184–91.

Gunnerson, C. G. 1973. "Debris Accumulation in Ancient and Modern Cities." *Journal of the Environmental Engineering Division* (American Society of Civil Engineers) 99(No. EE3):229–43.

Gwynne, M. D., and Bell, R. H. V. 1968. "Selection of Vegetation Components by Grazing Ungulates in the Serengeti National Park." *Nature* 220:390–3.

Hafsten, U. 1977. "Palaeo-ecological Studies in South-eastern Norway." In: *Dendrochronologie und postglaziale Klimaschwankungen in Europa*, edited by B. Frenzel, 282–96. Wiesbaden: F. Steiner.

Haggett, P., Cliff, A. D., and Frey, A. E. 1977. *Locational Analysis in Human Geography*. London: E. Arnold.

Hall, A. R., and Kenward, H. K. 1980. "An Interpretation of Biological Remains from Highgate, Beverley." *Journal of Archaeological Science* 7:33–52.

Hall, H. J. 1979. "Antelope House: A Paleoscatological Perspective." Ph.D. dissertation, University of Chicago. Ann Arbor, Mich.: University Microfilms.

Hally, D. J. 1981. "Plant Preservation and the Content of Paleobotanical Samples: A Case Study." *American Antiquity* 46:723–42.

Hammond, E. H. 1964. "Classes of Land-surface Form." *Annals, Association of American Geographers* 54:11–18.

Hammond, N. 1972. "Locational models and the Site of Lubaantun: A Classic Maya Centre." In: *Models in Archaeology*, edited by D. L. Clarke, pp. 757–800. London: Methuen.

Hansen, C. L., and Keller, C. M. 1971. "Environment and Activity Patterning at Isimila Korongo, Iringa District, Tanzania." *American Anthropologist* 73:1201–11.

Hanson, C. B. 1980. "Fluvial Taphonomic Processes: Models and Experiments." In: *Fossils in the Making*, edited by A. K. Behrensmeyer and A. P. Hill, pp. 156–81. Chicago: University of Chicago Press.

Hardan, A. 1971. "Archaeological Methods for Dating of Soil Salinity in the Mesopotamian Plain." In: *Paleopedology*, edited by D. H. Yaalon, pp. 181–7. Jerusalem: Israel Universities Press.

Hardesty, D. L. 1977. *Ecological Anthropology*. New York: John Wiley & Sons.

Hare, P. E. 1980. "Organic Geochemistry of Bone and Its Relations to the Survival of Bone in the Natural Environment." In: *Fossils in the Making*, edited by A. K. Behrensmeyer and A. P. Hill, pp. 208–19. Chicago: University of Chicago Press.

Harmon, R. S., Thompson, P., Schwarcz, H. P., and Ford, D. C. 1975. "Uranium-Series Dating of Speleothems." *National Speleological Society Bulletin* 37:21–33.

1978. "Late Pleistocene Paleoclimates of North America as Inferred from Stable Isotope Studies of Speleothems." *Quaternary Research* 9:54–70.

Harpending, H., and Davis, H. 1977. "Some Implications for Hunter-Gatherer Ecology Derived from the Spatial Structure of Resources." *World Archaeology* 8:275–86.

Harris, D. R. 1977. "Alternative Pathways towards Agriculture." In: *Origins of Agriculture*, edited by C. A. Reed, pp. 179–243. The Hague: Mouton.

1978. "Settling Down: An Evolutionary Model for the Transformation of Mobile Bands into Sedentary Communities." In: *The Evolution of Social Systems*, edited by J. Friedman and M. J. Rowlands, pp. 401–17. Pittsburgh: University of Pittsburgh Press.

editor. 1980. *Human Ecology in Savanna Environments.* New York: Academic Press.

Harris, E. C. 1979. *Principles of Archaeological Stratigraphy.* London: Academic Press.

Harrison, P. D., and Turner B. L., II, editors. 1978. *Pre-Hispanic Maya Agriculture.* Albuquerque: University of New Mexico Press.

Hassan, F. A. 1978. "Sediments in Archaeology: Methods and Implications for Palaeoenvironmental and Cultural Analysis." *Journal of Field Archaeology* 5:197–213.

1979. "Geoarchaeology: The Geologist and Archaeology." *American Antiquity* 44:267–70.

1980. "The Growth and Regulation of Human Population in Prehistoric Times." In: *Biosocial Mechanisms of Population Regulation,* edited by M. N. Cohen, R. S. Malpass, and H. G. Klein, pp. 305–19. New Haven: Yale University Press.

1981. *Demographic Archaeology.* New York: Academic Press.

Hassan, F. A., and Lubell, D. 1975. "The Prehistoric Cultural Ecology of Capsian Escargotières." *Libyca* 23:92–8.

Hay, R. L. 1976. *Geology of the Olduvai Gorge.* Berkeley: University of California Press.

Hayden, B. editor. 1979. *Lithic Use-Wear Analysis.* New York: Academic Press.

1981. "Research and development in the Stone Age: Technological Transitions among Hunter-Gatherers." *Current Anthropology* 22:519–48.

Haynes, C. V., and Agogino, G. A. 1966. "Prehistoric Springs and Geochronology of the Clovis Site, New Mexico." *American Antiquity* 31:812–21.

Hays, J. D., Imbrie, J., and Shackleton, N. J. 1976. "Variations in the Earth's Orbit: Pacemaker of the Ice Ages." *Science* 194:1121–32.

Hedberg, H. D., editor. 1976. *International Stratigraphic Guide.* New York: John Wiley & Sons.

Heidenreich, C. E. 1971. *Huronia: A History and Geography of the Huron Indians 1600–1650.* Toronto: McClelland and Stewart.

Helgren, D. M. 1978. "Acheulian Settlement along the Lower Vaal River, South Africa." *Journal of Archaeological Science* 5:39–60.

Helm, J. 1962. "The Ecological Approach to Anthropology." *American Journal of Sociology* 67:630–9.

Hester, T. R., Heizer, R. F., and Graham, J. A. 1975. *Field Methods in Archaeology.* Palo Alto: Mayfield.

Hiernaux, J. 1963. "Some Ecological Factors Affecting Human Populations in Sub-Saharan Africa." *Viking Fund Publications in Anthropology* 36:534–46.

Higgs, E. S., editor. 1972. *Papers in Economic Prehistory.* Cambridge University Press.

editor. 1975. *Palaeoeconomy.* Cambridge University Press.

Higgs, E. S., and Vita-Finzi, C. 1972. "Prehistoric Economies: A Territorial Approach." In: *Papers in Economic Prehistory,* edited by E. S. Higgs, pp. 27–36. Cambridge University Press.

Higham, C., and Kijngam, A. 1979. "Ban Chiang and Northeast Thailand: The Paleoenvironment and Economy." *Journal of Archaeological Science* 6:211–33.

Hill, J. N. 1972, "The Methodological Debate in Contemporary Archaeology: A Model." In: *Models in Archaeology,* edited by D. L. Clarke, pp. 61–106. London: Methuen.

editor. 1977. *Explanation of Prehistoric Change.* Albuquerque: University of New Mexico Press.

Hillam, J. 1979. "Tree-rings and Archaeology: Some Problems Explained." *Journal of Archaeological Science* 6:271–8.

Hinchey, M. T., editor. 1979. *Proceedings of the Symposium on Drought in Botswana.* Hanover, N. H.: University Press of New England.

Hirth, K. 1978. "Interregional Trade and the Formation of Prehistoric Gateway Communities." *American Antiquity* 43:35–45.

Hodder, I. R. 1972. "Locational Analysis and the Study of Romano-British Settlement." In: *Models in Archaeology,* edited by D. L. Clarke, pp. 887–909. London: Methuen.

Hodder, I. 1977. "Some New Directions in the Spatial Analysis of Archaeological Data at the Regional Scale." In: *Spatial Archaeology,* edited by D. L. Clarke, pp. 223–351. London: Academic Press.

1978. "Some effects of Distance on Human Interaction." In: *The Spatial Organization of Culture,* edited by I. Hodder, pp. 155–78. Pittsburgh: University of Pittsburgh Press.

Hodder, I., and Orton, C. 1976. *Spatial Analysis in Archaeology.* Cambridge University Press.

Hole, F. 1974. "Tepe Tula'i, an Early Campsite in Khuzistan, Iran." *Paléorient* 2:219–42.

1978a. "Pastoral Nomadism in Western Iran." In: *Explorations in Ethno-archaeology,* edited by R. A. Gould, pp. 127–68. Albuquerque: University of New Mexico Press.

Hole, F., and Heizer, R. F. 1973. *An Introduction to Prehistoric Archeology.* New York: Holt, Rinehart and Winston.

Hole, F. D. 1978. "An Approach to Landscape Analysis with Emphasis on Soils." *Geoderma* 21:1–23.

Hölldobler, B., and Lunsden, C. J. 1980. "Territorial Strategies in Ants." *Science* 210:732–9.

Holling, C. S. 1973. "Resilience and Stability of Ecological Systems." *Annual Reviews of Ecology and Systematics* 4:1–23.

Homans, G. C. 1941. *English Villagers of the Thirteenth Century.* Cambridge, Mass.: Harvard University Press.

Horn, H. 1968. "The Adaptive Significance of Colonial Nesting in the Brewer's Blackbird." *Ecology* 49:682–94.

Hornbeck, D. 1981. "The California Indians before European Contact." Presented before the International Conference for Historical Geographers (CUKANZUS), University of Toronto.

Howell, F. C. 1966. "Observations on the Earlier Phases of the European Lower Paleolithic." *American Anthropologist* 68:88–201.

Hudson, K. 1979. *World Industrial Archaeology.* Cambridge University Press.

Hugget, R. J. 1975. "Soil Landscape Systems: A Model of Soil Genesis." *Geoderma* 13:1–22.

Humphreys, A. J. B. 1973. "Report on Some Collections of Middle Stone Age Artefacts from Riverton, Kimberley District, South Africa." *Annals, Cape Provincial Museums,* 9:177–85.

Ingersoll, D., Yellen, J. E., and Macdonald, W., editors. 1977. *Experimental Archeology.* New York: Columbia University Press.

Isaac, G. L. 1971. "The Diet of Early Man." *World Archaeology* 2:278–98.
1972. "Chronology and the Tempo of Cultural Change during the Pleistocene." In: *Calibration of Hominoid Evolution*, edited by W. W. Bishop and J. A. Miller, pp. 381–430. Edinburgh: Scottish Academic Press.
1977. *Olorgesailie*. Chicago: University of Chicago Press.
Isbell, W. H. 1978. "Environmental Perturbations and the Origin of the Andean State." In: *Social Archeology*, edited by C. L. Redman et al., pp. 303–13. New York: Academic Press.
Iversen, J. 1956. "Forest Clearance in the Stone Age." *Scientific American* 194:36–41.
Jacobsen, T., and Adams, R. M. 1958. "Salt and Silt in Ancient Mesopotamian Agriculture." *Science* 128:1251–8.
Jacobson, G. L., and Bradshaw, R. H. 1981. "The Selection of Sites for Paleovegetational Studies." *Quaternary Research* 16:80–96.
Jäkel, D. 1979. "Runoff and Fluvial Formation Processes in the Tibesti Mountains." *Palaeoecology of Africa* 11:13–44.
Jankuhn, H. 1977. *Einführung in die Siedlungsarchäologie*. Berlin: W. de Gruyter.
Jánossy, D. 1975. "Mid-Pleistocene Micro-faunas of Continental Europe and Adjoining Areas." In: *After the Australopithecines*, edited by K. W. Butzer and G. L. Isaac, pp. 375–98. Chicago: Aldine.
Jarman, H. N., Legge, A. J., and Charles, J. A. 1972. "Retrieval of Plant Remains from Archaeological Sites by Froth Flotation." In: *Papers in Economic Prehistory*, edited by E. S. Higgs, pp. 39–48. Cambridge University Press.
Jochim, M. A. 1976. *Hunter-Gatherer Subsistence and Settlement: A Predictive Model*. New York: Academic Press.
Johansson, C. E. 1976. "Structural Studies of Frictional Sediments." *Geografiska Annaler* 1-58:201–301.
Johnsen, S. J., Dansgaard, W., Clausen, H. B., and Langway, C. C. 1972. "Oxygen Isotope Profiles through the Antarctic and Greenland Ice Sheets." *Nature* 235:429–34.
Johnson, D. L. 1978. "Nomadic Organization of Space: Reflections on Pattern and Process." In: *Dimensions of Human Geography*, edited by K. W. Butzer, pp. 25–47. University of Chicago Department of Geography, Research paper 186.
Johnson, E., and Holliday, V. T. 1980. "A Plainview Kill/butchering Locale on the Llano Estacado – the Lubbock Lake Site." *Plains Anthropologist* 25:89–111.
Johnson, E. A. J. 1970. *The Organization of Space in Developing Countries*. Cambridge, Mass.: Harvard University Press.
Johnson, G. A. 1975. "Locational Analysis and the Investigation of Uruk Locational Exchange Systems." In: *Ancient Civilization and Trade* edited by J. A. Sabloff and C. C. Lamberg-Karlovsky, pp. 285–339. Albuquerque: University of New Mexico Press.
1977. "Aspects of Regional Analysis in Archaeology." *Annual Reviews in Anthropology* 6:479–508.
Judge, W. J. 1973. *Paleoindian Occupation of the Central Rio Grande Valley in New Mexico*. Albuquerque: University of New Mexico Press.
Judge, W. J., and Dawson, J. 1972. "Paleo-Indian Settlement Technology in New Mexico." *Science* 176:1210–16.

Judson, S. 1963. "Erosion and Deposition in Italian Stream Valleys during Historic Time." *Science* 140:898–9.

Kahlke, H. D. 1975. "The Macro-faunas of Continental Europe during the Middle Pleistocene: Stratigraphic Sequence and Problems of Intercorrelation." In: *After the Australopithecines*, edited by K. W. Butzer and G. L. Isaac, pp. 309–74. Chicago: Aldine.

Kaiser, W. 1961. "Bericht über eine archäologisch-geologische Felduntersuchung in Ober- und Mittelägypten." *Mitteilungen, Deutsches Archäologisches Institut, Abteilung Kairo* 17:1–53.

Kauffman, B. E. 1980. *"The Maximal Covering Location Problem as a Simulation of Decision Making in Ramessid Egypt."* Unpublished M. A. thesis, Department of Anthropology, University of Chicago.

Kay, J. 1979. "Wisconsin Indian Hunting Patterns." *Annals, Association of American Geographers* 69:402–18.

Kay, M. 1978. "Phillips Spring, Missouri: Report of the 1978 Investigations." Illinois State Museum Society for U.S. Army Corps of Engineers (contract No. DACW 41–76–C–0011).

Kay, P. A., and Johnson, D. L. 1981. "Estimation of Tigris-Euphrates Streamflow from Regional Paleoenvironmental Proxy Data." *Climatic Change* 3:251–63.

Keeley, H. C. M. 1978. "The Cost-effectiveness of Certain Methods of Recovering Macroscopic Organic Remains from Archaeological Deposits." *Journal of Archaeological Science* 5:179–83.

Keeley, L. H. 1980. *Experimental Determination of Stone Tool Uses: A Microwear Analysis*. Chicago: University of Chicago Press.

Keepax, C. 1977. "Contamination of Archaeological Deposits by Seeds of Modern Origin with Particular Reference to the Use of Flotation Machines." *Journal of Archaeological Science* 4:221–9.

Killingley, J. S. 1981. "Seasonality of Mollusk Collecting Determined from 0–18 Profiles of Midden Shells." *American Antiquity* 46:152–8.

King, F. B., and Graham, R. W. 1981. "Effects of Ecological and Paleoecological Patterns on Subsistence and Paleoenvironmental Reconstructions." *American Antiquity* 46:128–42.

King, J. E. 1982. "Palaeoecology of the Early Archaic in Illinois." *Journal of Archaeological Science* 9:(in press).

Kirch, P. V. 1978. "Indigenous Agriculture on Uvea (Western Polynesia)." *Economic Botany* 32:157–81.

1980a. "The Archaeological Study of Adaptation: Theoretical and Methodological Issues." *Advances in Archaeological Method and Theory* 3:101–56.

1980b. "Polynesian Prehistory: Cultural Adaptation in Island Ecosystems." *American Scientist* 68:39–48.

Kirk, W. 1963. "Problems of Geography." *Geography* 48:357–71.

Kirkby, A. V. T. 1973. "The Use of Land and Water Resources in the Past and Present Valley of Oaxaca." University of Michigan, Museum of Anthropology, Memoirs 5:1–174.

Kirkby, A., and Kirkby, M. J. 1976. "Geomorphic Processes and the Surface Survey of Archaeological Sites in Semi-arid Areas." In: *Geo-archaeology*, edited by D. A. Davidson and M. L. Shackley, pp. 229–53. London: Duckworth.

Klasner, J. S., and Calengas, P. 1981. "Electrical Resistivity and Soil Studies at

Orendorf Archaeological Site, Illinois: A Case of Study." *Journal of Field Archaeology* 8:167–74.

Klein, R. G. 1973. *Ice Age Hunters of the Ukraine*. Chicago: University of Chicago Press.

——— 1975. "Paleoanthropological Implications of the Non-archaeological Bone Assemblage from Swartklip I, Southwestern Cape Province, South Africa." *Quaternary Research* 5:275–88.

——— 1978. "Stone Age Predation on Large African Bovids." *Journal of Archaeological Science* 5:195–217.

——— 1979. "Stone Age Exploitation of Animals in Southern Africa." *American Scientist* 677:151–60.

——— 1980. "Environmental and Ecological Implications of Large Mammals from Upper Pleistocene and Holocene Sites in Southern Africa." *Annals, South African Museum* 81:223–83.

——— 1982. "Mammalian Extinctions and Stone Age People in Africa." In: *Pleistocene Extinctions*, edited by P. S. Martin and R. G. Klein. Tucson: University of Arizona Press. (*in press*).

——— n.d.1. "The mammalian Fauna from *Equus* Cave: Carnivore and Ungulate Ecology in the Southern Kalahari during the Last Interglacial." Unpublished manuscript.

——— n.d.2. "Stone Age Predation on Small African Bovids." Unpublished manuscript.

Knörzer, K. H. 1979. "Ueber den Wandel der angebauten Körnerfrüchte und ihrer Unkrautvegetation auf einer niederrheinischen Lössfläche seit dem Frühneolithikum." *Archaeo-Physika* 8:147–64.

Koike, H. 1979. "Seasonal Dating and the Valve-pairing Technique in Shell-Midden Analysis." *Journal of Archaeological Science* 6:63–74.

Konrad, V. A., Bonnichsen, R., and Clay, V. 1981. "Soil Chemical Identification of 10,000 Years of Prehistoric Human Activity Areas at the Munsungan Lake Thoroughfare, Maine." Presented before the International Conference for Historical Geographers (CUKANZUS), University of Toronto.

Kozlowski, J. K. "The Origin of Lithic Raw Materials Used in the Paleolithic of the Carpathian Countries." *Acta Archaeologicae Carpathianae* 13:5–19.

Kraft, J. C., Aschenbrenner, S. E., and Rapp, G. 1977. "Paleo-geographic Reconstructions of Coastal Aegean Archaeological Sites." *Science* 195:941–7.

Kraft, J. C., Rapp, G., and Aschenbrenner, S. E. 1980a. "Late Holocene Paleogeomorphic Reconstructions in the Area of the Bay of Navarino: Sandy Pylos." *Journal of Archaeological Science* 7:187–211.

Kraft, J. C., Kayan, I., and Erol, O. 1980b. "Geomorphic Reconstructions in the Environs of Troy." *Science* 209:776–82.

Kramer, C., editor. 1979. *Ethnoarchaeology: Implications of Ethnography for Archaeology*. New York: Columbia University Press.

Kroeber, A. L. 1939. *Cultural and Natural Areas of Native North America*. Berkeley: University of California Press.

Kromer, K. 1978. "Siedlungsfunde aus dem frühen Alten Reich in Giseh. *Denkschriften, Oesterreichische Akademie der Wissenschaften, Philosophisch-historische Klasse* 136:1–130.

Kukla, G. J. 1975. "Loess Stratigraphy of Central Europe." In: *After the Aus-*

tralopithecines, edited by K. W. Butzer and G. L. Isaac, pp. 99–188. Chicago: Aldine.

Kummel, B., and Raup, D. editors. 1969. *Handbook on Palynological Techniques*. San Francisco: W. H. Freeman.

Kurtén, B. 1968. *Pleistocene Mammals of Europe*. Chicago: Aldine.

Ladurie, E. Le Roy. 1971. *Times of Feast, Times of Famine: A History of Climate Since the Year 1000*. Garden City, N.Y.: Doubleday.

LaMarche, V. C. 1973. "Holocene Climatic Variations Inferred from Treeline Fluctuations in the White Mountains, California." *Quaternary Research* 3:621–31.

——— 1978. "Tree-Ring Evidence of Past Climatic Variability." *Nature* 276:334–8.

Lamb, H. H. 1977. *Climate. Vol. 2: Climatic History and the Future*. London: Methuen.

Larsen, C. E., and Evans, G. 1978. "The Holocene Geological History of the Tigris-Euphrates-Karun Delta." In: *The Environmental History of the Near and Middle East*, edited by W. C. Brice, pp. 227–44. London: Academic Press.

Laughlin, C. D., and Brady, I. A., editors. 1978. *Extinction and Survival in Human Populations*. New York: Columbia University Press.

Laville, H. 1976. "Deposits in Calcareous Rock Shelters: Analytical Methods and Climatic Interpretation." In: *Geo-archaeology*, edited by D. A. Davidson and M. L. Shackley, pp. 137–155. London: Duckworth.

Laville, H., Rigaud, J. P., and Sackett, J. 1980. *Rock Shelters of the Perigord: Geological Stratigraphy and Archaeological Succession*. New York: Academic Press.

Lawton, H. W., and Wilke, P. J. 1979. "Ancient Agricultural Systems in Dry Regions." In: *Agriculture in Semi-Arid Environments*, edited by A. E. Hall, G. H. Cannell, and H. W. Lawton, pp. 1–44. Berlin: Springer (Ecological Studies 34).

Leach, E. 1973. "Concluding Address." In: *The Explanation of Culture Change*, edited by C. Renfrew, pp. 761–71. London: Duckworth.

Leakey, M. D. 1971. *Olduvai Gorge. Vol 3: Excavations in Bed I and II, 1960–1963*. Cambridge University Press.

Leakey, R. E. F., Butzer, K. W., and Day, M. H. 1969. "Early *Homo sapiens* Remains from the Omo River Region of South-west Ethiopia." *Nature* 222:1132–8.

Lechtman, H. and Merrill, R., editors. 1977. *Material Culture: Styles, Organization and Dynamics of Technology*. St. Paul, Minn.: West Publishing Co.

Lees, S. H., and Bates, D. G. 1974. "The Origins of Specialized Nomadic Pastoralism: A Systemic Model." *American Antiquity* 39:187–93.

Legget, R. F. 1973. *Cities and Geology*. New York: McGraw-Hill.

Lengyel, I. A. 1975. *Palaeoserology*. Budapest: Akademiai Kiado.

Le Tensorer, J. M. 1977. "L'analyse chimique des remplissages des grottes et abris: principes et limites." *Bulletin, Association Française pour l'Etude du Quaternaire* (Supplément 47):23–7.

Leveson, D. 1981. *Geology and the Urban Environment*. New York: Oxford University Press.

Lewarch, D. E., and O'Brien, M. J. 1981. "The Expanding Role of Surface Assemblages in Archaeological Research." *Advances in Archaeological Method and Theory* 4:297–342.

Licate, J. A. 1980. "The Forms of Aztec Territorial Organization." *Geoscience and Man* 21:27–45.

Liebowitz, H., and Folk, R. L. 1980. "Archaeological Geology of Tel yin'am, Galilee, Israel." *Journal of Field Archaeology* 7:23–42.

Lieth, H. 1973. "Primary Productivity: Terrestrial Ecosystems." *Human Ecology* 1:303–32.

Likens, G. E., editor. 1970. "Effects of Forest Cutting and Herbicide Treatment on Nutrient Budgets in the Hubbard Brook Watershed-Ecosystem." *Ecological Monographs* 40:23–47.

Limbrey, S. 1975. *Soil Science and Archaeology*. New York: Academic Press.

Limbrey, S. and Evans, J. G., editors. 1978. *The Effect of Man on the Landscape: The Lowland Zone*. London: Council for British Archaeology.

Limp, W. F., and Reidhead, V. A. 1979. "An Economic Evaluation of the Potential of Fish Utilization in Riverine Environments." *American Antiquity* 44:70–8.

Lisitsina, G. N. 1976. "Arid Soils – the Source of Archaeological Information." *Journal of Archaeological Science* 3:55–60.

Llagostera Martínez, A. 1979. "9700 Years of Marine Subsistence in the Pacific: An Analysis of Bioindicators in the North of Chile." *American Antiquity* 44:309–24.

Lloyd, S. 1963. *Mounds of the Near East*. Edinburgh: Edinburgh University Press.

Lösch, A. 1967. *The Economics of Location* (translated from the 1943 original by W.H. Woglom and W. F. Stolper). New York: John Wiley & Sons.

Lowenstein, J. M. 1980. "Species-specific proteins in Fossils." *Naturwissenschaften* 67:343–6.

Ložek, V. 1975. "Zur Problematik der landschaftsgeschichtlichen Entwicklung in verschiedenen Höhenstufen der Westkarpaten während des Holozäns." *Biuletyn Geologiczny* 19:79–92.

1976. "Zur Geschichte der Bodenerosion in den mitteleuropäischen Löss-landschaften während des Holozäns." *Stratigraphic Newsletters* 5:44–54.

Lubell, D., Hassan, F. A., Gautier, A., and Ballais, J. L. 1976. "The Capsian Escargotières: An Interdisciplinary Study Elucidates Holocene Ecology and Subsistence in North Africa." *Science* 191:910–20.

Lucas, A., and Harris, J. R. 1962. *Ancient Egyptian Materials and Industries*. London: Arnold.

Luedtke, B. E. 1979. "The Identification of Sources of Chert Artifacts." *American Antiquity* 44:744–57.

Lukermann, F. E. 1972. "Settlement and Circulation: Pattern and Systems." In: *The Minnesota Messina Expedition*, edited by W. A. McDonald and G. R. Rapp, pp. 148–70. Minneapolis: University of Minnesota Press.

Lyman, R. L. 1979. "Available Meat from Faunal Remains: A Consideration of Techniques." *American Antiquity* 44:536–46.

Lyons, T. R., and Avery, T. E. 1977. *Remote Sensing: A Handbook for Archaeologists and Cultural Resource Managers*. National Park Service, U.S. Department of the Interior.

MacArthur, R. H., and Pianka, E. R. 1966. "On Optimal Use of a Patchy Environment." *American Naturalist* 100:603–9.

Machann, R., and Semmel, A. 1970. "Historische Bodenerosion auf Wüstungs-fluren deutscher Mittelgebirge." *Geographische Zeitschrift* 58:250–60.

Mackay, J. R., Mathews, W. H., and MacNeish, R. S. 1961. "Geology of the Engigstciak Archaeological Site, Yukon Territory." *Arctic* 14:25–52.

Mackereth, F. J. H. 1965. "Chemical Investigation of Lake Sediments and Their Interpretation." *Proceedings of the Royal Society of London, Biological Sciences* 161:295–309.

MacNeish, R. S. 1964. "Ancient Mesoamerican Civilization." *Science* 143:531–7.

1967. "A Summary of the Subsistence." In: *The Prehistory of the Tehuacan Valley, Vol. I*, edited by D.S. Byers, pp. 290–309. Austin: University of Texas Press.

1972. "The Evolution of Community Patterns in the Tehuacan Valley of Mexico and Speculations about the Cultural Processes." In: *Man, Settlement and Urbanism*, edited by P.J. Ucko, R. Tringham, and G.W. Dimbleby, pp. 67–93. London: Duckworth.

Maley, J. 1977. "Palaeoclimates of the Central Sahara during the Holocene." *Nature* 269:573–7.

Mankinen, E. A., and Dalrymple, G. B. 1979. "Revised Geomagnetic Polarity Time Scale for the Interval 0–5 m.y. B.P." *Journal of Geophysical Research* 84:615–26.

Marcus, J. 1973. "Territorial Organization of the Lowland Classic Maya." *Science* 180:911–16.

Marsh, W. M. 1978. *Environmental Analysis for Land Use and Site Planning.* New York: McGraw-Hill.

Martin, P. S., and Klein, R. G., editors. 1982. *Pleistocene Extinctions.* Tucson: University of Arizona Press.

Masters, P. M., and Bada, J. L. 1978. "Amino Acid Racemization Dating of Bone and Shell." In: *Archaeological Chemistry II. Advances in Chemistry Vol. 171*, edited by G. F. Carter, pp. 117–38. Washington: American Chemical Society.

Matson, F. R. 1960. "The Quantitative Study of Ceramic Materials." *Viking Fund Publications in Anthropology* 28:34–59.

May, R. M. 1977. "Thresholds and Breakpoints in Ecosystems with a Multiplicity of Stable States." *Nature* 269:471–7.

McCullough, E. A., and Smith, G. G. 1976. "Correction in the Glacial-Postglacial Temperature Difference Computed from Amino-Acid Racemization." *Science* 191:182–3.

McDonald, W. A., and Rapp, G. R., editors. 1972. *The Minnesota Messina Expedition: Reconstructing a Bronze Age Regional Environment*, pp. 234–9. Minneapolis: University of Minnesota Press.

McFarland, D. J. 1978. "Optimality Considerations in Animal Behavior." In: *Human Behavior and Adaptation*, edited by N. B. Jones and V. Reynolds, pp. 53–76. London: Taylor and Francis.

McGuire, K. R. 1980. "Cave Sites, Faunal Analysis, and Big-Game Hunters of the Great Basin: A Caution." *Quaternary Research* 14:263–8.

McIntosh, R. J. 1977. "The Excavation of Mud Structures: An Experiment from West Africa." *World Archaeology* 9:185–99.

McMillan, R. B., and Klippel, W. E. 1981. "Post-glacial Environmental Change and Hunting-Gathering Societies in the Southern Prairie Peninsula." *Journal of Archaeological Science* 8:215–45.

Meadow, R. A., and Zeder, M. A. 1978. "Approaches to Faunal Analysis in the Middle East." *Peabody Museum Bulletin* 2:1–186.

Mellars, P. A., editor. 1978. *The Early Post-Glacial Settlement of Northern Europe: An Ecological Perspective*. London: Duckworth.

Merrill, R. S. 1968. "The Study of Technology." In: *International Encyclopedia of the Social Sciences*, edited by D. L. Sills, 15:576–89. New York: Macmillan.

Michels, J. W. 1973. *Dating Methods in Archaeology*. New York: Academic Press.

Minnis, P. E. 1981. "Seeds in Archaeological Sites: Sources and Some Interpretive Problems." *American Antiquity* 46:143–52.

Monks, G. G. 1981. "Seasonality Studies." *Advances in Archaeological Method and Theory* 4:177–240.

Moore, P. D. 1975. "Origin of Blanket Mires." *Nature* 256:267–9.

Moore, P. D., and Webb, J. A. 1978. *An Illustrated Guide to Pollen Analysis*. London: Hodder and Stoughton.

Moran, E.F. 1979. *Human Adaptability: an Introduction to Ecological Anthropology*. North Scituate, MA: Duxbury.

Morgan, R. P. C. 1979. *Soil Erosion*. London: Longman.

Morrill, R. L., and Dormitzer, J. M. 1979. *The Spatial Order: An Introduction to Modern Geography*. Belmont, Calif.: Wadsworth.

Mortensen, P. 1972. "Seasonal Camps and Early Villages in the Zagros." In: *Man, Settlement and Urbanism*, edited by P.J. Ucko, R. Tringham, and G.W. Dimbleby, pp. 293–7. London: Duckworth.

Moss, A. J., and Walker, P. H. 1978. "Particle Transport by Continental Water Flows in Relation to Erosion, Deposition, Soils and Human Activities." *Sedimentary Geology* 20:81–139.

Mueller, J. W., editor. 1975. *Sampling in Archaeology*. Tucson: University of Arizona Press.

Nichols, H., Kelly, P. M., and Andrews, J. T. 1978. "Holocene Palaeo-wind Evidence from Palynology in Baffin Island." *Nature* 273:140–2.

Niemeier, G. 1972. *Siedlungsgeographie*. Braunschweig: Westermann.

Nietschmann, B. Q. 1972. "Hunting and Fishing Focus among the Miskito Indians, E. Nicaragua." *Human Ecology* 1:41–67.

Nissen, H. J. 1968. "Survey of an Abandoned Modern Village in Southern Iraq." *Sumer* 24:107–17.

Noe-Nygaard, N. 1974. "Mesolithic Hunting in Denmark Illustrated by Bone Injuries Caused by Human Weapons." *Journal of Archaeological Science* 1:217–48.

1977. "Butchering and Marrow Fracturing as a Taphonomic Factor in Archaeological Deposits." *Paleobiology* 3:218–37.

Odum, E. P. 1971. *Fundamentals of Ecology*. Philadelphia: W.B. Saunders.

Olive, P. 1972. "La région du Lac Léman depuis 15,000 ans: données paléoclimatiques et préhistoriques." *Revue de Géographie physique et Géologie dynamique* 14:253–64.

Olsen, S. J. 1964. "Mammal Remains from Archaeological Site." *Peabody Museum Papers* 56:1–162.

Orians, G. H. 1975. "Diversity, Stability and Maturity in Natural Ecosystems." In: *Unifying Concepts in Ecology*, edited by W. H. Van Dobben and R. H. Lowe-McConnel, pp. 139–50. The Hague: W. Junk.

Orlove, B. S. 1980. "Ecological Anthropology." *Annual Review of Anthropology* 9:235–73.

Osborn, A. J. 1977. "Strandloopers, Mermaids and Other Fairy Tales: Ecological Determinants of Marine Resource Utilization – the Peruvian Case." In: *For Theory Building in Archaeology*, edited by L.R. Binford, pp. 157–205. New York: Academic Press.

Pals, J. P., and Voorrips, A. 1979. "Seeds, Fruits and Charcoals from Two Prehistoric Sites in Northern Italy." *Archaeo-Physika* 8:217–35.

Parker, R. B., and Toots, H. 1980. "Trace Elements in Bones as Palaeobiological Indicators." In: *Fossils in the Making*, edited by A. K. Behrensmeyer and A. P. Hill, pp. 197–207. Chicago: University of Chicago Press.

Parkington, J. E. 1972. "Seasonal Mobility in the Late Stone Age." *African Studies* 31:223–44.

Parsons, J. R. 1972. "Archaeological Settlement Patterns." *Annual Review of Anthropology* 1:127–50.

Partridge, T. C. 1978. "Re-appraisal of Lithostratigraphy of Sterkfontein Hominid Site." *Nature* 275:282–7.

Peacock, D. P. S., editor. 1977. *Pottery and Early Commerce*. London: Academic Press.

Pearsall, D. M. 1978. "Phytolith Analysis of Archeological Soils: Evidence for Maize Cultivation in Formative Ecuador." *Science* 199:177–8.

Peng, T. H., Goddard, J. G., and Broecker, W. S. 1978. "A Direct Comparison of ^{14}C and ^{230}Th Ages at Searles Lake, California." *Quaternary Research* 9:319–29.

Pennington, W. 1970. "Vegetation History in the Northwest of England." In: *Studies in the Vegetational History of the British Isles*, edited by D. Walker and R.G. West, pp. 41–79. Cambridge University Press.

Peterson, G. M., editor. 1979. "The Continental Record of Environmental Conditions at 18,000 B.P.: An Initial Evaluation." *Quaternary Research* 12:47–82.

Phillips, J. L., and Butzer, K. W. 1973. "A 'Silsilian' Occupation Site (GS-2B-II) of the Kom Ombo Plain, Upper Egypt: Geology, Archeology and Paleoecology." *Quaternaria* 17:343–85.

Phillips, P. 1980. *The Prehistory of Europe*. Bloomington: Indiana University Press.

Phillips, R. E., editor. 1980. "No-Tillage Agriculture." *Science* 208:1108–13.

Pimentel, D., editor. 1976. "Land degradation: Effects on Food and Energy Resources." *Science* 194:149–55.

Pitty, A. E. 1979. *Geography and Soil Properties*. London: Methuen.

Plog, S., Plog, F., and Wait, W. 1978. "Decision Making in Modern Surveys." *Advances in Archaeological Method and Theory* 1:383–421.

Potter, T. W. 1979. *The Changing Landscape of South Etruria*. New York: St. Martin's Press.

Preece, R. C. 1980. "The Biostratigraphy and Dating of the Tufa Deposit at the Mesolithic Site at Blashenwell, Dorset, England." *Journal of Archaeological Science* 7:345–62.

Prendergast, M. D. 1979. "Iron Age Settlement and Economy in Part of the Southern Zambezian Highland." *South African Archaeological Bulletin* 34:111–19.

Pricket, M. E. 1979. "Settlement and the Development of Agriculture in the

Rud-i-Gushk Drainage, Southern Iran." *Archäologische Mitteilungen aus Iran, Ergänzungsband* 6:47–56.

Proudfoot, B. 1970. "Man's Occupance of the Soil." In: *Man and His Habitat,* edited by R.H. Buchanan, E. Jones, and D. McCourt, pp. 8–33. London: Routledge & Kegan Paul.

1976. "The Analysis and Interpretation of Soil Phosphorous in Archaeological Contexts." In: *Geo-archaeology,* edited by D. A. Davidson and M. L. Shackley, pp. 93–113. London: Duckworth.

Rankine, W. F., and Dimbleby, G. W. 1960. "Further Investigations at a Mesolithic Site at Oakhanger, Selbourne, Hants." *Proceedings, Prehistoric Society* 26:246–62.

Raper, R. A. 1977. "The Analysis of the Urban Structure of Pompeii: A Sociological Examination of Land Use." In: *Spatial Archaeology,* edited by D.L. Clarke, pp. 189–222. London: Academic Press.

Rapp, G. 1975. "The Archaeological Field Staff: The Geologist." *Journal of Field Archaeology* 2:229–37.

Rapp, G., Bullard, R., and Albritton, C. 1974. "Geoarchaeology?" *The Geologist* 9:1.

Rapp, G., Hendrickson, E., Miller, M., and Aschenbrenner, S. 1980. "Trace-Element Fingerprinting as a Guide to the Geographic Sources of Native Copper." *Journal of Metals* 32:35–45.

Rappaport, R. A. 1971a. "The Flow of Energy in an Agricultural Society." *Scientific American* 224(3):116–32.

1971b. "The Sacred in Human Evolution." *Annual Reviews of Ecology Systematics* 2:23–43.

1978. "Maladaption in Social Systems." In: *The Evolution of Social Systems,* edited by J. Friedman and M. J. Rowlands, pp. 49–71, 79–87. Pittsburgh: University of Pittsburgh Press.

Redman, C. L. 1978. "Mesopotamian Urban Ecology: The Systemic Context of the Emergence of Urbanism." In: *Social Archaeology,* edited by C. L. Redman et al., pp. 329–48. New York: Academic Press.

Redman, C. L., and Watson, P. J. 1970. "Systematic, Intensive Surface Collection." *American Antiquity* 35:279–91.

Reed, N. A., Bennett, J. W., and Porter, J. W. 1968. "Solid Core-drilling of Monk's Mound: Technique and Findings." *American Antiquity* 33:137–48.

Reher, C. A. 1974. "Population Study of the Casper Site Bison." In: *The Casper Site: A Hell-Gap Bison Kill on the High Plains,* edited by G.C. Frison, pp. 113–24. New York: Academic Press.

1977. "Adaptive Processes on the Shortgrass Plains." In: *For Theory Building in Archaeology,* edited by L.R. Binford, pp. 13–40. New York: Academic Press.

Renfrew, C. 1975. "Trade as Action at a Distance." In: *Ancient Civilization and Trade,* edited by J.A. Sabloff and C.C. Lamberg-Karlovsky, pp. 3–59. Albuquerque: University of New Mexico Press.

1976. "Archaeology and the Earth Sciences." In: *Geo-archaeology,* edited by D.A. Davidson and M.L. Shackley, pp. 1–5. London: Duckworth.

1978. "Space, Time and Polity." In: *The Evolution of Social Systems,* edited by J. Friedman and M.J. Rowlands, pp. 89–112. Pittsburgh: University of Pittsburgh Press.

Renfrew, C., and Dixon, J. R. 1976. "Obsidian in Western Asia: A Review." In: *Problems in Economic and Social Archaeology*, edited by G. Sieveking, I. Longworth, and K. Wilson, pp. 137–49. London: Duckworth.

Renfrew, J. M. 1973. *Palaeoethnobotany: The Prehistoric Food Plants of the Near East and Europe*. London: Methuen.

Reynolds, R. G. D. 1976. "Linear Settlement Systems of the Upper Grijalva River: The Application of a Markovian Model." In: *The Early Mesoamerican Village*, edited by K.V. Flannery, pp. 180–93. New York: Academic Press.

Rice, P. M., editor. 1982. *Pots and Potters: Current Approaches to Ceramic Archaeology*. State College: Pennsylvania State University Press.

Rick, J. W. 1976. "Downslope Movement and Archaeological Intra-site Spatial Analysis." *American Antiquity* 41:133–44.

Richter, G. 1980. "On the Soil Erosion Problem in the Temperate Humid Area of Central Europe." *GeoJournal* 4:279–87.

Rightmire, G. P. 1979. "Implications of Border Cave Skeletal Remains for Later Pleistocene Human Evolution." *Current Anthropology* 20:23–35.

Rognon, P. 1980. "Pluvial and Arid Phases in the Sahara: The Role of Nonclimatic Factors." *Palaeoecology of Africa* 12:45–62.

Roper, D. C. 1979. "The Method and Theory of Site Catchment Analysis: A Review." *Advances in Archaeological Method and Theory* 2:119–40.

Rottländer, R. C. A. 1976. "Variation in the Chemical Composition of Bone as an Indicator of Climatic Change." *Journal of Archaeological Science* 3:83–8.

Rovner, I. 1971. "Potential of Opal Phytoliths for Use in Paleoecological Reconstruction." *Quaternary Research* 1:343–59.

Rowlands, M. J. 1972. "Defence: A Factor in the Organization of Settlements." In: *Man, Settlement and Urbanism*, edited by P.J. Ucko, R. Tringham, and G.W. Dimbleby, pp. 447–62. London: Duckworth.

Ruddiman, W. F., and McIntyre, A. 1976. "Northeast Atlantic Paleoclimatic Changes over the Past 600,000 years." *Memoir, Geological Society of America* 145:111–46.

Ruhe, R. V., Clark, D. W., and Epstein, M. L. 1980. "Urban Hydrology in Karst and Water-Quality – Inorganic and Organic Systems." Indiana University Water Resources Research Center, Report of Investigation 9:1–139.

Rushton, G. 1972. "Map Transformations of Point Patterns: Central Place Patterns in Areas of Variable Population Density." *Regional Science Association Papers and Proceedings* 28:111–29.

Rust, A. 1962. *Vor 20,000 Jahren*. Neumünster, Holstein: K. Wachholtz.

Sagan, C., Toon, O. B., and Pollack, J. B. 1979. "Anthropogenic Albedo Changes and the Earth's Climate." *Science* 206:1363–8.

Sahlins, M. D. 1977. "Culture and Environment." In: *Horizons of Anthropology*, edited by S. Tax and L. G. Freeman, pp. 215–31. Chicago: Aldine.

Salvador, A., and Opdyke, N. D. 1979. "Magnetostratigraphic Polarity Units: A Supplementary Chapter for the ISSC International Stratigraphic Guide." *Geology* 7:578–85.

Sampson, C. G. 1972. *The Stone Age Industries of the Orange River Scheme and South Africa*. National Museum Bloemfontein, Memoir 6.

Sanders, W. T., and Webster, D. 1978. "Unilinealism, and the Evolution of Complex Societies." In *Social Archaeology*, edited by C.L. Redman et al., pp. 249–302. New York: Academic Press.

Sanders, W. T., Parsons, J. R., and Santley, R. S. 1979. *The Basin of Mexico: Ecological Processes in the Evolution of a Civilization.* New York: Academic Press.

Schalke, H. J. W. 1973. "The Upper Quaternary of the Cape Flats Area (Cape Province, South Africa)." *Scripta Geologica Leiden Rijksmuseum* 15:1–57.

Schiffer, M. B. 1972. "Archaeological Context and Systemic Context." *American Antiquity* 37:156–65.

1975. "Archaeology as Behavioral Science." *American Anthropologist* 77:836–48.

1976. *Behavioral Archaeology.* London: Academic Press.

Schiffer, M. B., Sullivan, A. P., and Klinger T. C. 1978. "The Design of Archaeological Surveys." *World Archaeology* 10:1–28.

Schild, R. 1976. "The Final Paleolithic Settlements of the European Plain." *Scientific American* 234(2):88–99.

Schmid, E. 1972. *Atlas of Animal Bones for Prehistorians, Archaeologists and Quaternary Geologists.* Amsterdam: Elsevier.

Schmidthüsen, J. 1968. *Allgemeine Vegetationsgeographie.* Berlin: W. de Gruyter.

Schoeninger, M. J., and Peebles, C. S. 1981. "Effect of Mollusc Eating on Human Bone Strontium Levels." *Journal of Archaeological Science* 8:391–7.

Schoenwetter, J. A. 1981. "Prologue to a Contextual Archaeology." *Journal of Archaeological Science* 8:367–79.

Schroeder, K. H., and Schwarz, G. 1969. "Die ländlichen Siedlunsformen in Mitteleuropa: Grundzüge und Probleme ihrer Entwicklung." *Forschung zur Deutschen Landeskunde* 175:1–106.

Schroeder, R. A., and Bada, J. L. 1973. "Glacial-Postglacial Temperature Difference Deduced from Aspartic Acid Racemization in Fossil Bones." *Science* 182:479–82.

Schroedl, G. F. 1978. "Excavations of the Leuty and McDonald Site Mounds." Tennessee Valley Authority Publication in Anthropology No. 15:1–231.

Schwarcz, H. P. 1980. "Absolute Age Determination of Archaeological Sites by Uranium Series Dating of Travertines." *Archaeometry* 22:3–24.

Schwarcz, H. P., Goldberg, P. D., and Blackwell, B. 1980. "Uranium Series Dating of Archaeological Sites in Israel." *Israel Journal of Earth-Sciences* 29:157–65.

Schwartz, M. L., and Tziavos, C. 1979. "Geology in the Search for Ancient Helice." *Journal of Field Archaeology* 6:243–52.

Schweingruber, F. H. 1978. *Microscopic Wood Anatomy: Structural Variability of Stems and Twigs in Recent and Subfossil Woods from Central Europe.* Birmensdorf: Swiss Federal Institute of Forestry Research.

Servant, M. 1973. "Séquences continentales et variations climatiques: évolution du Bassin du Tchad au Cénozoique supérieur." Thesis, University of Paris VI.

Shackleton, N. J. 1970. "Stable Isotopic Study of the Palaeoenvironments of the Neolithic Site of Nea Nikomedeia, Greece." *Nature* 227:943–4.

1973. "Oxygen Isotope Analysis as a Means of Determining Season of Occupation of Prehistoric Midden Sites." *Archaeometry* 15:133–43.

Shackleton, N. J., and Opdyke, N. D. 1976. "Oxygen-Isotope and Paleomagnetic Stratigraphy of Pacific Core V28-239, Late Pliocene to Latest Pleistocene." *Memoirs, Geological Society of America* 145:449–64.

Shackley, M. L. 1975. *Archaeological Sediments: A Survey of Analytical Methods.* New York: Halsted.

Sheets, P. D., and Grayson, D. K., editors. 1979. *Volcanic Activity and Human Ecology.* New York: Academic Press.

Shepard, A. O. 1965. "Rio Grande Glaze-Paint Pottery: A Test of Petrographic Analysis." *Viking Fund Publications in Anthropology* 41:62–87.

Shepherd, R. 1980. *Prehistoric Mining and Allied Industries.* London: Academic Press.

Sherratt, A. G. 1976. "Resources, Technology and Trade: An Essay in Early European Metallurgy." In: *Problems in Economic and Social Archaeology,* edited by G. Sieveking, I. Longworth, and K. Wilson, pp. 557–82. London: Duckworth.

—— 1980. "Water, Soil and Seasonality in Early Cereal Cultivation." *World Archaeology* 11:313–29.

Shotton, F. W., and Hendry, G. L. 1979. "The Developing Field of Petrology in Archaeology." *Journal of Archaeological Science* 6:75–84.

Shutler, R., Jr., editor. 1967. "Pleistocene Studies in Southern Nevada." *Nevada State Museum, Anthropological Papers* 13:1–411.

Sielmann, B. 1972. "Die frühneolithische Besiedlung Mitteleuropas." In: *Die Anfänge des Neolithikums vom Orient bis Nordeuropa, Vol. 5a.* Cologne: Böhlau.

Sieveking, G., Bush, P., Ferguson, J., Craddock, P., Hughes, M., and Cowell, M. 1972. "Prehistoric Flint Mines and Their Identification as Sources of Raw Material." *Archaeometry* 14:151–76.

Silberbauer, G. B. 1981. *Hunter and Habitat in the Central Kalahari Desert.* Cambridge University Press.

Simmons, I. G. 1969. "Evidence for Vegetation Changes Associated with Mesolithic Man in Britain." In: *The Domestication and Exploitation of Plants and Animals,* edited by P.J. Ucko and G.W. Dimbleby, pp. 110–19. London: Duckworth.

Simmons, I. G., and Dimbleby, G. W. 1974. "The Possible Role of Ivy in the Mesolithic Economy of Western Europe." *Journal of Archaeological Science* 1:291–6.

Simmons, I. G., and Proudfoot, V. B. 1969. "Environment and Early Man on Dartmoor, Devon, England." *Proceedings of the Prehistoric Society* 35:203–19.

Simmons, I. G., and Tooley, M. J., editors. 1981. *The Environment in British Prehistory.* Ithaca: Cornell University Press.

Singer, C. A., and Ericson, J. E. 1977. "Quarry Analysis at Bodie Hills, Mono County, California." In: *Exchange Systems in Prehistory,* edited by T.K. Earle and J.E. Ericson, pp. 171–88. New York: Academic Press.

Singh, G., Kershaw, A. P., and Clark, R. 1981. "Quaternary Vegetation and Fire History in Australia." In: *Fire and Australian Biota,* edited by A. M. Gill, R. A. Groves, and I. R. Noble, pp. 23–54. Canberra: Australian Academy of Science.

Sivertsen, B. J. 1980. "A Site Activity Model for Kill and Butchering Activity at Hunter-Gatherer Sites." *Journal of Field Archaeology* 7:423–41.

Sjöberg, A. 1976. "Phosphate Analysis of Anthropic Soils." *Journal of Field Archaeology* 3:447–54.

—— 1982. "Archaeometric Theory of Non-artifactual Spatial Patterns of Human Behavior in Archaeological Sites." *Advances in Archaeological Method and Theory* 5:(in press).

Slager, S., and Van Wetering, H. T. J. 1977. "Soil Formation in Archaeological Pits and Adjacent Loess Soils in Southern Germany." *Journal of Archaeological Science* 4:259–67.

Slicher van Bath, B. H. 1963. *The Agrarian History of Western Europe, A.D. 500–1850* (translated by O. Ordish). London: Arnold.

Slobodkin, L. B., and Rapoport, A. 1974. "An Optimal Strategy of Evolution." *Quarterly Review of Biology* 49:181–200.

Smith, A. G. 1970. "The Influence of Mesolithic and Neolithic Man on British Vegetation." In: *Studies in the Vegetational History of the British Isles*, edited by D. Walker and R.G. West, pp. 81–96. Cambridge University Press.

Smith, B. D. 1979a. "Measuring the Selective Utilization of Animal Species by Prehistoric Human Populations." *American Antiquity* 44:155–60.

Smith, C. A. 1976a. *Regional Analysis. I: Economic Systems.* New York: Academic Press.

1976b. *Regional Analysis. II: Social Systems.* New York: Academic Press.

Smith, M. E. 1979b. "The Aztec Marketing System and Settlement Pattern in the Valley of Mexico: A Central Place Analysis." *American Antiquity* 44:110–25.

Smith, P.E.L. 1976c. "Stone Age Man on the Nile." *Scientific American* 235(2): 30–8.

Smolíkova, L., and Ložek, V. 1973. "Der Bodenkomplex von Velky Hubenov als Beispiel einer retrograden Bodenentwicklung im Laufe der Nacheiszeit." *Casopis pro mineralogii a geologii* 18:365–77.

1978. "Die nacheiszeitlichen Bodenabfolgen von Poplze und Šteti als Beleg der Boden- und Landschaftsentwicklung im bömischen Tschernozemgebiet." In: *Beiträge zur Quartär- und Landschaftsforschung, Festschrift Julius Fink*, pp. 531–49. Vienna.

Sonnenfeld, J. 1972. "Geography, Perception and the Behavioral Environment." In: *Man, Space and Environment*, edited by P.W. English and R.C. Mayfield, pp. 244–51. New York: Oxford University Press.

Spencer, J. E., and Hale, G. A. 1961. "The Origin, Nature and Distribution of Agricultural Terracing." *Pacific Viewpoint* 2:1–40.

Spiess, A. 1979. *Reindeer and Caribou Hunters.* New York: Academic Press.

Stafford, T., Jr., 1981. "Alluvial Geology and Archeological Potential of the Texas Southern High Plains." *American Antiquity* 46:548–65.

Stark, B. L., and Voorhies, B., editors. 1978. *Prehistoric Coastal Adaptations: The Economy and Ecology of Maritime Middle America.* New York: Academic Press.

Stark, B.L., and Young, D.L. 1981. "Linear Nearest Neighbor Analysis." *American Antiquity* 46:284–300.

Stearns, C. E. 1967. "Pleistocene Geology of Cape Ashakar and Vicinity." *Bulletin of the American School of Prehistorical Research* 22:6–35.

Stein, J. 1978. "Augering Archaeological Sites." *Southeastern Archaeological Newsletter* 20:11–17.

Steponaitis, V. P. 1978. "Location Theory and Complex Chiefdoms: A Mississippian Example." In: *Mississippian Settlement Patterns*, edited by B.D. Smith, pp. 417–53. New York: Academic Press.

Stern, W. L., and Tippo, D. 1977. *Humanistic Botany.* New York: W. W. Norton.

Sterud, E. L. 1978. "Prehistoric Populations of the Dinaric Alps: An Investigation of Interregional Interaction." In: *Social Archaeology*, edited by C.L. Redman et al., pp. 341–408. New York: Academic Press.

Stockton, E. D. 1973. "Shaw's Creek Shelter: Human Displacement of Artefacts and Its Significance." *Mankind* 9:112–17.

Stross, F. H., and O'Donnell, A. E. 1972. "Laboratory Analysis of Organic Materials." *Addison-Wesley Module in Anthropology*, 22:1–24.

Stuckenrath, R. 1977. "Radiocarbon: Some Notes from Merlin's Diary." *Annals, New York Academy of Sciences* 288:181–8.

Swain, A. M. 1973. "A History of Fire and Vegetation in Northeastern Minnesota as Recorded in Lake Sediments." *Quaternary Research* 3:383–96.

Sweeting, M. M. 1972. *Karst Landforms*. New York: Columbia University Press.

Tarling, D. H. 1975. "Archaeomagnetism: The Dating of Archaeological Materials by Their Magnetic Properties." *World Archaeology* 7:185–97.

Taylor, T. P. 1979. "Soil Mark Studies near Winchester, Hampshire." *Journal of Archaeological Science* 6:93–100.

Taylor, W. W. 1948. *Study of Archeology*. Menasha, Wisc.: American Anthropological Association Memoir 69.

    1972: "Old Wine and New Skins: A Contemporary Parable." In: *Contemporary Archaeology*, edited by M.P. Leone, pp. 28–33. Carbondale, Ill.: Southern Illinois University Press.

Terashina, H. 1980. "Hunting Life of the Bambote: An Anthropological Study of Hunter-Gatherers in a Wooded Savanna." *Senri Ethnological Studies* 6:223–68.

Thomas, D. H. 1971. "On Distinguishing Natural from Cultural Bone in Archaeological Sites." *American Antiquity* 36:366–71.

    1972. "A Computer Simulation of Great Basin Shoshonean Subsistence and Settlement Patterns." In: *Models in Archaeology*, edited by D.L. Clarke, pp. 671–704. London: Methuen.

Thomas, W. D., editor. 1956. *Man's Role in Changing the Face of the Earth*. Chicago: University of Chicago Press.

Thompson, R. 1973. "Palaeolimnology and Palaeomagnetism." *Nature* 242:182–4.

Thompson, R., Aitken, M. J., Gibbard, P., and Wymer, J. J. 1974. "Palaeomagnetic Study of Hoxnian Lacustrine Sediments." *Archaeometry* 16:233–7.

Thompson, R., and Berglund, B. 1976. "Late Weichselian Geomagnetic Reversal as a Possible Example of the Reinforcement Syndrome." *Nature* 263:490–1.

Thompson, R. S., Van Devender, T. R., Martin, P. S., Foppe, T., and Long, A. 1980. "Shasta Ground Sloth at Shelter Cave, New Mexico: Environment, Diet and Extinction." *Quaternary Research* 14:360–76.

Thorson, R. M., and Hamilton, T. D. 1977. "Geology of the Dry Creek Site: A Stratified Early Man Site in Interior Alaska." *Quaternary Research* 7:149–76.

Thunnell, R. C. 1979. "Eastern Mediterranean Sea during the Last Glacial Maximum: An 18,000-Years B.P. Reconstruction." *Quaternary Research* 11:353–72.

Tite, M. S. 1972. *Methods of Physical Examination in Archaeology*. London: Academic Press.

Tobler, W. 1975. "The Geometry of Mental Maps." In: *Spatial Choice and Behav-*

ior, edited by R. G. Golledge and G. Rushton, pp. 275–80. Columbus: Ohio State University Press.

Tobler, W. R., and Wineburg, S. 1971. "A Cappadocian speculation." *Nature* 231:40–1.

Torry, W. I. 1979. "Anthropological Studies in Hazardous Environments: Past Trends and New Horizons." *Current Anthropology* 20:517–40.

Trigger, B. G. 1968. "The Determinants of Settlement Patterns." In: *Settlement Archaeology,* edited by K.C. Chang, pp. 53–78. Palo Alto: National Press.

1972. "Determinants of Urban Growth in Pre-industrial Societies." In: *Man, Settlement and Urbanism,* edited by P.J. Ucko, R. Tringham, and G.W. Dimbleby, pp. 575–99. London: Duckworth.

Trimble, S. W. 1974. "Man-induced Soil Erosion on the Southern Piedmont, 1700–1970." Ankeny, Iowa: Soil Conservation Society of America.

Tringham, R. 1972. "Introduction: Settlement Patterns and Urbanization." In: *Man, Settlement and Urbanism,* edited by P.J. Ucko, R. Tringham, and G.W. Dimbleby, pp. xix–xxviii. London: Duckworth.

Troels-Smith, J. 1960. "Ivy, Mistletoe and Elm: Climate Indicators – Fodder Plants." *Danmarks Geologiska Undersoegelse* 4:4–32.

Tschudy, R. H., and Scott, R. A., editors. 1969. *Aspects of Palynology: An Introduction to Plant Microfossils in Time.* New York: John Wiley & Sons.

Turnbaugh, W. A. 1978. "Floods and Archaeology." *American Antiquity* 43:593–607.

Turner, B. L., Hanham, R. Q., and Portarero, A. V. 1977. "Population Pressure and Agricultural Intensity." *Annals of the Association of American Geographers* 67:384–96.

Turner, B.L., and Harrison, P.D. 1981. "Prehistoric Raised-Field Agriculture in the Maya Lowlands." *Science* 213:399–406.

Turner, C. 1975. "The Correlation and Duration of Middle Pleistocene Interglacial Periods in Northwest Europe." In: *After the Australopithecines,* edited by K.W. Butzer and G.L. Isaac, pp. 259–308. Chicago: Aldine.

Turner, C., and West, R. G. 1968. "The Subdivision and Zonation of Interglacial Periods." *Eiszeitalter und Gegenwart* 19:93–101.

Turner, J. 1979. "The Environment of Northeast England during Roman Times as Shown by Pollen Analysis." *Journal of Archaeological Science* 6:285–90.

Uerpmann, H. P. 1973. "Animal Bones and Economic Archaeology." *World Archeology* 4:307–22.

Van Andel, T., Jacobsen, T. W., Jolly, J. B., and Lianos, N. 1980. "Late Quaternary History of the Coastal Zone near Franchthi Cave, Southern Argolid, Greece." *Journal of Field Archaeology* 7:389–402.

Van der Hammen, T., Wijmstra, T. A., and Zagwijn, W. H. 1971. "The Floral Record of the Late Cenozoic in Europe." In: *The Late Cenozoic Glacial Ages,* edited by K.K. Turekian, pp. 391–424. New Haven: Yale University Press.

Van Der Merwe, N. J., and Vogel, J. C. 1978. "^{13}C Content of Human Collagen as a Measure of Prehistoric Diet in Woodland North America." *Nature* 276:815–16.

Van Noten, F. 1977. "Excavations at Matupi Cave." *Antiquity* 51:35–40.

Van Zeist, W., and Bakker-Meeres, J. A. H. 1979. "Some Economic and Ecological Aspects of the Plant Husbandry of Tell Aswad." *Paléorient* 5:161–9.

Van Zuidam, R. A. 1975. "Geomorphology and Archaeology: Evidences of Interrelation at Historical Sites in the Zaragoza Region, Spain." *Zeitschrift für Geomorphologic* 19:319–28.

Vayda, A. P. 1974. "Warfare in Ecological perspective." *Annual Review of Ecology and Systematics* 5:183–94.

Vencl, S. 1971. "Topografická poloha mesolitických sidlist v Cechách." (The Topography of Mesolithic Sites in Bohemia). *Archeologické Rozhledy* 18:169–87.

Vermeersch, P. M., and Walter, R. 1978. "Die Palisadengräben des Michelsberger Fundplatzes in Thiensies (Belgien)." *Archäologisches Korrespondenzblatt* 8:169–76.

Verron, G., editor. 1976. "Livret-guide de l'excursion A 10: Nord-ouest de la France (Bassin de la Seine, Bassin de la Somme et Nord)." Union Internationale des Sciences Prehistoriques, Nice.

Vita-Finzi, C. 1969. *The Mediterranean Valleys: Geological Changes in Historical Times.* Cambridge University Press.

1978. *Archaeological Sites in Their Setting.* London: Thames and Hudson.

Vita-Finzi, C., and Higgs, E. S. 1970. "Prehistoric Economy in the Mount Carmel Area of Palestine." *Proceedings of the Prehistoric Society* 36:1–37.

Vogel, J. C. 1977. "Isotopic Assessment of the Dietary Habits of Ungulates." *South African Journal of Science* 74:298–301.

Vogel, J. C., Fuls, A., and Ellis, R. P. 1978. "The Geographical Distribution of Kranz Grasses in South Africa." *South African Journal of Science* 74:209–15.

Vogel, J. C., and Kronfeld, J. 1981. "A New Method for Dating Peat." *South African Journal of Science* 77:557–8.

Volman, T. P. 1978. "Early Archaeological Evidence for Shellfish Collecting." *Science* 201:911–13.

1981. "The Middle Stone Age in the Southern Cape." Ph.D. dissertation, University of Chicago.

Von Thünen, J. H. 1966. *Von Thünen's Isolated State* (translated and edited from 1842 original by C. M. Wartenberg and P. Hall). London: Pergamon.

Voorhies, M. 1969. "Taphonomy and Population Dynamics of an Early Pliocene Vertebrate Fauna, Knox County, Nebraska." University of Wyoming, Contributions to Geology, Special Paper 1.

Wagner, P. L. 1974. "Cultural Landscapes and Regions: Aspects of Communication." *Geoscience and Man* 10:133–42.

Walker, D., and West, R. G., editors. 1970. *Studies in the Vegetational History of the British Isles.* Cambridge University Press.

Washburn, D. 1974. "Nearest Neighbor Analysis of Pueblo I-III Settlement Patterns along the Rio Puerco of the East, New Mexico." *American Antiquity* 39:315–35.

Watson, P. J. 1976. "In Pursuit of Prehistoric Subsistence: A Comparative Account of Some Contemporary Flotation Techniques." *Midcontinental Journal of Archaeology* 1:77–100.

1979. *Archaeological Ethnography in Western Iran.* Tucson: University of Arizona Press (Viking Fund Publications in Anthropology 57).

Watts, D. 1971. *Principles of Biogeography.* New York: McGraw-Hill.

Webb, T., III. 1973. "A Comparison of Modern and Presettlement Pollen from Southern Michigan (U.S.A.)." *Review of Paleobotany and Palynology* 16:137–56.

Webb, T., III, and Bryson, R. A. 1972. "Late and Post-glacial Climatic Changes in the Northern Midwest, USA: Quantitative Estimates Derived from Fossil Pollen Spectra by Multivariate Statistical Analysis." *Quaternary Research* 2:70–115.

Wehmiller, J. F., and Belknap, D. F. 1978. "Alternative Kinetic Models for the Interpretation of Amino Acid Enantiomeric Ratios in Pleistocene Mollusks." *Quaternary Research* 9:330–48.

Wendorf, F. and Schild, R. 1976. *Prehistory of the Nile Valley*. New York: Academic Press.

1980. *Loaves and Fishes: The Prehistory of Wadi Kubbaniya*. Dallas: Department of Anthropology, Southern Methodist University.

Wenke, R. J. 1981. "Explaining the Evolution of Cultural Complexity: A Review." *Advances in Archaeological Method and Theory* 4:79–127.

West, O., editor. 1973. "Grassland Session." In: *Proceedings, Annual Tall Timbers Fire Ecology Conference*, edited by E. V. Komarek, 12:5–240. Tallahassee, Florida: Tall Timbers Research Station.

Wetterstrom, W. E. 1981. *Food, Nutrition, and Population in a Prehistoric Pueblo*. Santa Fe, N.M.: School of American Research.

Whallon, R. 1973. "Spatial Analysis of Occupation Floors: The Application of Dimensional Analysis of Variance." In: *The Explanation of Cultural Change*, edited by C. Renfrew, pp. 115–30. London: Duckworth.

1974. "Spatial Occupation of Occupation Floors. II: The Application of Nearest Neighbor Analysis." *American Antiquity* 39:16–34.

Wheatley, P. W. 1965. "Agricultural Terracing." *Pacific Viewpoint* 6:123–44.

White, G. F. 1973. *Environmental Effects of Arid Land Irrigation in Developing Countries*. Paris: UNESCO.

White, T. E. 1953–1954. "Observations on the Butchering Techniques of Some Aboriginal Peoples." *American Antiquity* 19:160–4, 254–64.

Whittaker, R. H., and Lieth, H. 1975. *Primary Productivity of the Biosphere*. New York: Springer.

Wiens, J. A. 1976. "Population Responses to Patchy Environments." *Annual Reviews of Ecology and Systematics* 7:81–120.

Wilk, R., and Schiffer, M. B. 1979. "The Archaeology of Vacant Lots in Tucson, Arizona." *American Antiquity* 44:530–36.

Wilkinson, T. J. 1976. "Soil and Sediment Structures as an Aid to Archaeological Interpretation: Sediments at Dibsi Faraj, Syria." In: *Geo-archaeology*, edited by D. A. Davidson and M. L. Shackley, pp. 275–87. London: Duckworth.

Willey, G. R. 1953. "Prehistoric Settlement Patterns in the Viru Valley." Washington: Bureau of American Ethnology, Bulletin 155.

Willey, G. R., and Phillips, P. 1958. *Method and Theory in American Archaeology*. Chicago: University of Chicago Press.

Wilmsen, E. N. 1973. "Interaction, Spacing, Behavior, and the Organization of Hunting Bands." *Journal of Anthropological Research* 29:1–31.

Wilson, A. L. 1978. "Elemental Analysis of Pottery in the Study of Its Provenance: A Review." *Journal of Archaeological Science* 5:219–36.

Wing, E., and Brown, A. B. 1980. *Paleonutrition*. New York: Academic Press.

Winterhalder, B. 1980. "Environmental Analysis in Human Evolution and Adaptation Research." *Human Ecology* 8:135–70.

1981. "Optimal Foraging Strategies and Hunter-Gatherer Research in Anthropology: Theory and Models." In: *Hunter-Gatherer Foraging Strategies,* edited by B. Winterhalder and E. A. Smith, Chicago: University of Chicago Press, pp. 13–35.

Wintle, A. G. 1980. "Thermoluminescence Dating: A Review of Recent Applications to Non-pottery Materials." *Archaeometry* 22:113–22.

Wintle, A. G., and Huntley, D. J. 1980. "Thermoluminescence Dating of Ocean Sediments." *Canadian Journal of Earth Science* 17:348–60.

Wiseman, J. R. 1980. "Archaeology in the Future: An Evolving Discipline." *American Journal of Archaeology* 84:279–85.

Wittfogel, K. A. 1957. *Oriental Despotism: A Comparative Study of Total Power.* New Haven: Yale University Press.

Wobst, H. M. 1974. "Boundary Conditions for Paleolithic Social Systems: A Simulation Approach." *American Antiquity* 39:147–78.

1976. "Locational Relationship in Paleolithic Society." *Journal of Human Evolution* 5:49–58.

Woillard, G. M. 1978. "Grande Pile Peat Bog: A Continuous Pollen Record for the Last 140,000 Years." *Quaternary Research* 9:1–21.

Wolfe, J. A. 1978. "A Paleobotanical Interpretation of Tertiary Climates in the Northern Hemisphere." *American Scientist* 66:694–703.

Wolman, M. G. 1967. "A Cycle of Sedimentation and Erosion in Urban River Channels." *Geografiska Annaler* 49A:385–95.

Wolpert, J. 1964. "The Decision Process in Spatial Context." *Annals, Association of American Geographers* 54:537–58.

Wood, J. J. 1978. "Optimal Location in Settlement Space: A Model for Describing Location Strategies." *American Antiquity* 43:258–70.

Wood, J. J., and Matson, R. G. 1975. "Two Models of Sociocultural Systems and Their Implications for the Archaeological Study of Change." In: *The Explanation of Culture Change,* edited by C. Renfrew, pp. 673–83. London: Duckworth.

Wood, W. R., and Johnson, D. L. 1978. "A Survey of Disturbance Process in Archaeological Site Formation." *Advances in Archaeological Method Theory* 1:315–81.

Wood, W. R., and McMillan, R. B. 1976. *Prehistoric Man and His Environments: A Case Study in the Ozark Highland.* New York: Academic Press.

Woodwell, G. M. 1970. "The Energy Cycle of the Biosphere." *Scientific American* 223(3):64–74.

Woosley, A. I. 1978. "Pollen Extraction for Arid-Land Sediments." *Journal of Field Archaeology* 4:349–55.

Worthington, E. B., editor. 1978. *Arid Land Irrigation in Developing Countries: Environmental Problems and Effects.* Oxford: Pergamon Press.

Wymer, J. J. 1968. *Lower Palaeolithic Archaeology in Britain: As Represented by the Thames Valley.* London: J. Baker.

Yarnell, R. A. 1977. "Native Plant Husbandry North of Mexico." In: *Origins of Agriculture,* edited by C. A. Reed, pp. 861–875. The Hague: Mouton.

Yellen, J. E. 1976. "Settlement Patterns of the !Kung: An Archaeological Perspective." In: *Kalahari Hunter-Gatherers,* edited by R. B. Lee and I. De Vore, pp. 47–72. Cambridge, Mass.: Harvard University Press.

1977. *Archaeological Approaches to the Present.* New York: Academic Press.

Zagwijn, W. H. 1975. "Variations in Climate as Shown by Pollen Analysis, Especially in the Lower Pleistocene of Europe." In: *Ice Ages: Ancient and Modern*, edited by A. E. Wright and F. Moseley, pp. 137–52. Liverpool: Seel House Press.

Zawacki, A. A., and Hausfater, G. 1969. "Early Vegetation of the Lower Illinois Valley." *Illinois State Museum Reports of Investigations* 17:1–66.

Zeuner, F. E. 1963. *A History of Domesticated Animals.* London: Hutchinson.

Ziegler, A. C. 1973. "Inference from Prehistoric Faunal Remains." Addison-Wesley Module in Anthropology 43.

Zihlman, A. L., and Tanner, N. 1978. "Gathering and the Hominid Adaptation." In: *Female Hierarchies*, edited by L. Tiger and H. Fowler, pp. 163–94. Chicago: Aldine.

Zimmerman, L. J. 1978. "Simulating Prehistoric Locational Behaviour." In: *Simulation Studies in Archaeology*, edited by I. Hodder, pp. 27–37. Cambridge University Press.

Index